T0299056

Agricultural historians have collected and published a remarkable amount of material in recent years, partly as a result of the ongoing series *The Agrarian History of England and Wales.* Missing from the *Agrarian History* volumes covering 1640 to 1850 has been any sustained analysis of agricultural rent, a perhaps surprising omission in view of the enormous sums of money which passed between landlords and tenants annually, and given the importance of the subject in terms of our understanding of the general course of change in agriculture and the economy more generally. In recent years the availability of estate accounts in public archive repositories has made available a range of data for the period *c.* 1690 to the First World War, after which the material is voluminous and well known.

In this book, based on research in archives across the country, the authors have produced a new rent series which will become the basis on which all future researchers in the field will rely.

Agricultural rent in England, 1690–1914

Agricultural rent in England, 1690–1914

M. E. TURNER, *University of Hull*

J. V. BECKETT, *University of Nottingham*

and B. AFTON, *University of Hull*

CAMBRIDGE
UNIVERSITY PRESS

PUBLISHED BY THE PRESS SYNDICATE OF THE UNIVERSITY OF CAMBRIDGE
The Pitt Building, Trumpington Street, Cambridge, United Kingdom

CAMBRIDGE UNIVERSITY PRESS
The Edinburgh Building, Cambridge CB2 2RU, UK
40 West 20th Street, New York NY 10011–4211, USA
477 Williamstown Road, Port Melbourne, VIC 3207, Australia
Ruiz de Alarcón 13, 28014 Madrid, Spain
Dock House, The Waterfront, Cape Town 8001, South Africa

http://www.cambridge.org

First published 1997
First paperback edition 2002

A catalogue record for this book is available from the British Library

Library of Congress Cataloguing in Publication data
Turner, Michael Edward.
Agricultural rent in England, 1690–1914 / M.E. Turner,
J. V. Beckett, and B. Afton.
        p.   cm.
Includes bibliographical references and index.
ISBN 0 521 45053 5 (hbk.)
1. Farm rents – England – History.   2. Farm income – England –
History.   3. Agriculture – Taxation – England – History.   4. Landlord
and tenant – England – History.   5. Agricultural wages – England –
History.   6. Agricultural – Economic aspects – England – History.
I. Beckett, J. V.   II. Afton, B.   III. Title.
HD1930.E5T87   1997
333.33′55′0942–dc20   96-24195   CIP

ISBN 0 521 45053 5 hardback
ISBN 0 521 89358 5 paperback

Contents

List of figures	*page* ix	
List of tables	xi	
Preface	xiii	
Note on the text	xv	
List of abbreviations	xvi	
Two examples of contemporary rent books	xviii	
	Introduction	1
1	Agricultural rent in England	6
2	Contemporary views of rent in eighteenth and nineteenth-century England	37
3	The current state of knowledge	50
4	The determining parameters of a rent index	70
5	Constructing the rent index I: estate records	85
6	Constructing the rent index II: government inquiries	107
7	Constructing the rent index III: other studies	138
8	An English agricultural rent index, 1690–1914	148
9	Rent arrears and regional variations	176
10	The rent index and agricultural history I: the long term	199
11	The rent index and agricultural history II: the short term	225
	Conclusion	253
	Appendix 1 Sources of the rent index	258
	I Estate records	260
	II The Royal Commission on Agriculture 1894–6	279

viii   Contents

III	Printed sources	293
IV	Acreage	302
Appendix 2	Statistical summary	308

| *Bibliography* | 324 |
| *Index* | 340 |

Figures

Examples of contemporary rent books:

1   Rentals of the Mavers Estate at Beighton in Derbyshire.
    Reproduced with permission of Nottingham Manuscripts
    Department, M.4571 Thoresby Rental, 1750   *page* xviii
2   A rental for the Hildyard family estate at Flintham Hall,
    Nottinghamshire. Reproduced with permission of the
    Flintham Collection, Screveton Rent Book   xix

2.1   Rent per acre, 1810–11   *page* 46
2.2   Rent per acre, 1850–1   47
3.1   The Chambers and Mingay rent index, 1700–1880.   51
      Reproduced from J. D. Chambers and G. E. Mingay, *The
      Agricultural Revolution, 1750–1880* (London, 1966)
3.2   A Midland counties rent index, 1650–1850   54
3.3   Unit rents and farm sizes in Northamptonshire, 1727   55
3.4   Unit rents and farm sizes in (a) Oxfordshire,
      (b) Northamptonshire, 1844   56
3.5   Arable and pasture rents in the Midlands, 1650–1850   57
3.6   A nineteenth-century rent index   59
3.7   The county distribution of the Land Tax in 1707   63
5.1   English agricultural rents: details of estates surveyed   86
5.2   Types of estate from which rental details extracted   91
5.3   The effect of industrial land use on the size of rent:
      Holker estate, Lancashire   93
5.4   The value of assessed rents for the Bolton Abbey estate   103
6.1   Rent per acre and size of farm, 1894   117
6.2   Farm size and rent in North Devon, 1894   118

6.3   Rent per acre and size of farm, 1894   120
6.4   Rent per acre and size of farm, 1894   121
6.5   Rent per acre on the Duke of Bedford's estates, 1785–1910   133
8.1   Index of agricultural rent assessed in England,1690–1914   149
8.2   Index of agricultural rent received in England, 1690–1914   150
8.3   The surviving archives over time: (a) Rent due (b) Rent
      received   153
8.4   The chronological history of rent received, 1690–1914:
      (a) Rents (b) Acreages   155
8.5   Castle Howard: rent received per acre, 1690–1914   156
8.6   Density and distribution of rents received, c, 1750, c. 1800,
      and c. 1850   160
8.7   Density and distribution of rents received in the 1880s   161
8.8   A comparison with R. J. Thompson's rent index   166
8.9   A comparison with Schedule A Income Tax returns   167
8.10 A comparison with Bellerby's gross farm rent index for
      the UK   168
8.11 A comparison with the Norton, Trist, and Gilbert rent
      index   169
8.12 The average price of land and the movement of rent,
      1780–1914   173
9.1   Rents due and rents received: (a) Number of archives
      (b) Extent of common acreage   177
9.2   Rent indexes: rent due and rent received from common
      acres   178
9.3   Feast and famine: rent arrears as a proportion of agreed
      rents   180
9.4   Putative rent arrears: as percentage of rent agreed   181
9.5   The variation in land use and land values in
      Northumberland, c. 1847. Reproduced from T. L.
      Colbeck, 'On the agriculture of Northumberland', *JRASE*,
      (1847)   190
9.6   Corn and pasture rents compared: based on Caird's
      agricultural regions   192
9.7   Pasture rents as a percentage of arable rents: based on
      Caird's agricultural regions   193
9.8   Rent per acre for arable, intermediate and pasture
      regions: based on Thirsk's farming regions   195
9.9   Relative rent movements by region: (a) Pasture: arable
      (b) Intermediate: arable (c) Intermediate: pasture. Based
      on Thirsk's farming regions   196

10.1 (a) and (b) The trend of agricultural prices and unit acre
      rents   210
10.2 Regional trends in agricultural labourers' wages,
      1850–1902   212
10.3 Comparison between the course of rents and unit labour
      earnings   214
10.4 Yields on land and consols, based on 10-year averages   218
10.5 Realised rates of return on land and Consols, based on
      10-year averages   221

Tables

1.1 Landlords' expenditure as a percentage of rent
received, 1842–92   *page* 23

1.2 Distribution of St John's College rentals, 1870–1920   28

3.1 A nineteenth-century rent index   58

3.2 Income from agriculture, 1688, 1759, and 1801/3   60

3.3 Income from Schedule A Property and Income Tax for
England and Wales, 1806/7–1848/9   67

5.1 Changes in parish size and variations in annual rent on
the Bolton Abbey Estate, 1790–1870   103

6.1 Rents due and received for major English estates, 1842–92   115

6.2 Summary of rents received from up to 69 tenant farms in
England, 1875–1894   123

6.3 A composite rent index for the nineteenth century, based
on R. J. Thompson   126

7.1 Two nineteenth-century rent indexes compared   145

8.1 Average estate sizes in the rent index   157

8.2 The trend in agricultural rent: a comparison   165

10.1 Agricultural output and rents, 1700–1900   207

11.1 Price indices of crops and animal products, 1640–1749
(1640–1749 = 100)   228

11.2 English wheat yields *c.* 1750–1850/9   237

11.3 Animal product price movements, 1845/9–1905/9   249

Preface

This book began life in research undertaken for the forthcoming *Cambridge Agrarian History of England and Wales, vol. VII, 1850–1914*, which revealed a substantial gap in the record relating to agricultural rent. Time and resources did not permit the original research to progress very far, but it was clear that the archival material existed from which to draw up a far more accurate picture of agricultural rent than has generally been available to agricultural and economic historians. In part this has simply been a question of opportunity. Try as they might, contemporary experts and commentators could find out little about rents because farmers were reluctant to discuss the financial arrangements into which they had entered with their landlords. Increasingly landed families have deposited their papers in public repositories, and the resulting accessibility of those records has fundamentally altered the position. It is not going too far to suggest that this book reveals more about agricultural rents for the period 1690–1914 than contemporaries could have dreamt of.

Our work was made possible by a grant from the Economic and Social Research Council. We have also benefited enormously from the advice and help of many people as we have progressed. We are particularly grateful for the opportunity to develop some of our ideas to audiences at the British Agricultural History Society Conference at Nottingham (Easter 1992) and at the Centre of East Anglian Studies at the University of East Anglia (January 1992). We are grateful to the following for granting us permission to use their archives: the Marquess of Salisbury at Hatfield House, the Duke of Norfolk at Arundel Castle, the Duke of Northumberland at Alnwick, the Duke of Devonshire at Chatsworth, the Duke of Beaufort at Badminton, the Marquess of Bath at Longleat House, Lord Egremont at Petworth House, the Howard family at Castle Howard, M. C. Fetherston-Dilke at Maxstoke Castle, and R. B. Hasell-McCosh at Dalemain House. In addition, we are grateful to Anthony Smith at the Royal Commission on Historical

Manuscripts for advice at an early stage of the project, and to the many archivists and their staff up and down the country who patiently answered our queries and made material available to us.

Our work has also benefited greatly from discussion with colleagues who have worked in related areas, and we should particularly like to thank R. C. Allen, Rod Ambler, Joe Bettey, Paul Brassley, Dan Byford, Christopher Clay, E. J. T. Collins, Barbara English, David Grigg, David Howell, Tim Lloyd, Gordon Mingay, the late Paul Nunn, Patrick O'Brien, Mark Overton, Richard Perren, A. D. M. Phillips, Tony Rayner, Roy Sturgess, F. M. L. Thompson, Sarah Wilmot, Richard Wilson, Donald Woodward, and J. R. Wordie. We are also grateful to various anonymous referees who have commented on our proposals and our conclusions from time to time. Any faults are, of course, our own.

Note on the text

Whereas all of the rents were originally collected in historic prices (i.e. in £ s d), subsequently in the collation of the data into tables and graphs they were all converted to shillings rounded to the first decimal place. Where other prices have been compared with these rents, unless otherwise stated, they have all been converted to £s or shillings as appropriate, and rounded to the first decimal place. In addition, unless otherwise stated, all acreages have been collated to the nearest acre.

Abbreviations

AgHR	*Agricultural History Review*
AO	Archives Office
Allen, *Yeoman*	R. C. Allen, *Enclosure and the Yeoman: The Agricultural Development of the South Midlands 1450–1850* (Oxford, 1992)
BPP	*British Parliamentary Papers*
Bedford, *Story*	The Duke of Bedford, *The Story of a Great Agricultural Estate* (London, 1897)
Caird	J. Caird, *English Agriculture 1850–1* (London, 1852)
Chambers and Mingay	J. D. Chambers and G. E. Mingay, *The Agricultural Revolution, 1750–1880* (London, 1966)
EcHR	*Economic History Review*
Hughes, 'Northumberland'	W. M. Hughes, 'Lead, land and coal as sources of landlords' income in Northumberland between 1700–1850' (University of Newcastle, PhD thesis, 1963)
JRASE	*Journal of the Royal Agricultural Society of England*
JRSS	*Journal of the Royal Statistical Society*
Marshall, *Landed*	W. Marshall, *On the Landed Property of England* (London, 1804)
Marshall, *Review*	W. Marshall, *Review and Abstract of the County Reports to the Board of Agriculture* (5 vols., York, 1818)
Mingay, *AgHist*	G. E. Mingay (ed.), *The Cambridge Agrarian History of England and Wales*, VI, *1750–1850* (Cambridge, 1989)

Parker, *Coke*

RO
Thirsk, *AgHist* (1984/5)

Thompson, 'An inquiry'

Wade Martins, *Holkham*

R. A. C. Parker, *Coke of Norfolk: A Financial and Agricultural Study 1702–1842* (Oxford, 1975)
Record Office
J. Thirsk (ed.), *The Cambridge Agrarian History of England and Wales*, V, *1640–1750*, I, *Regional Farming Systems* (Cambridge, 1984), II, *Agrarian Change* (Cambridge, 1985)
R. J. Thompson, 'An inquiry into the rent of agricultural land in England and Wales during the nineteenth century', *JRSS*, 70 (1907), 587–625, and reprinted in W. E. Minchinton (ed.), *Essays in Agrarian History*, II (Newton Abbot, 1968), 56–88
S. Wade Martins, *A Great Estate at Work: The Holkham Estate and its Inhabitants in the Nineteenth Century* (Cambridge, 1980)

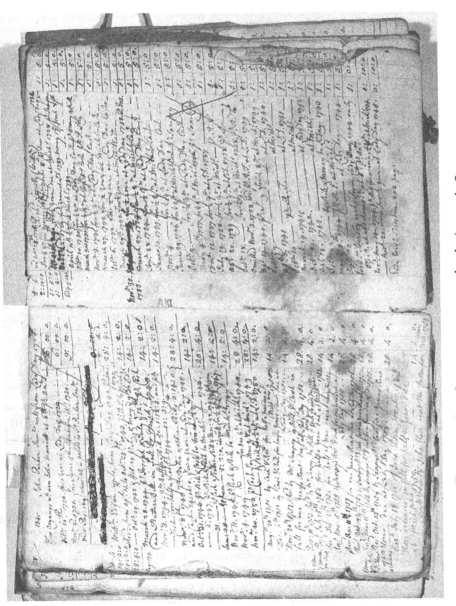

Two examples of contemporary rent books (*see overleaf*)

Examples of contemporary rent books. (1) Neatly rendered rentals of the Manvers Estate at Beighton in Derbyshire, for 1750. This professional-looking rental records assessed rents, but was of limited use in a project on agricultural rent because it contains no information about rent arrears or the rents actually received in relation to unavoidable outgoings such as national taxes or local rates, whether paid by the owner or the tenant. Nor are any acreage figures given. Consequently a complete rental history of the estate cannot be constructed simply from these accounts.

(2) A rental for the Hildyard family estate at Flintham Hall, Nottinghamshire. The assessed rent due from individual tenants is indicated in the margin, and each rent payment was recorded as it was received. However, because the rental is organised by holdings rather than by year, it was almost impossible to use in this volume. The numerous methodological problems which were encountered in constructing a rent index are discussed in chapters 4–7.

Sources: Thoresby Estate Rental, 1750, Nottingham University Manuscripts Department M.4571, reproduced with permission of Thoresby Estates Management; Screveton Rent Book, from Nottingham University Manuscripts Department Accession 1325, reproduced from Flintham Estate Papers.

Introduction

Rent is integral to our way of life in the twentieth century. Almost everyone over the age of eighteen must have had some experience of paying rent, either for a house, an apartment, or for some other form of property; and the principles behind paying rent are not so far removed from the principles behind mortgage repayments. In other words a sum of money is required to pass from the tenant (or mortgage holder) to the landlord (or mortgage lender) at regular intervals. Failure to fulfil the terms of the contract (by non-payment or inadequate payment) may lead, within strictly defined legal limits, to dispossession. In this case the landlord will evict the tenant, or the mortgage lender will foreclose and claim the property. So much is clear, and most of us are well aware of the terms under which such contracts normally operate. In the past the position was different, but not so materially different as we might expect. Some of the terminology has disappeared: we no longer have lifeleaseholds, three-life leases, customary tenancies, or copyholds, but the basic relationship of a money rent paid regularly to a landlord, under conditions agreeable to both parties, goes back many centuries.

Despite this long history, surprisingly little is known about long-run trends in agricultural rent. For hundreds of years farmers and landlords have agreed rents, and money has changed hands. On individual farms and estates a good deal is known about these contractual arrangements, but the total picture to which they contributed is far less clear. We know all too little about long-run movements in rents in England over long periods. This is, to say the least, surprising. Considerable effort has been devoted over the past thirty years or so to collecting an array of statistics on wages, prices, weights and measures, and a host of other agrarian subjects.[1] By contrast, the figures for rent are meagre, and almost entirely lack any systematic form. Volumes

[1] J. Thirsk (ed.), *The Cambridge Agrarian History of England and Wales, IV, 1500–1640* (Cambridge, 1967), pp. 814–70; Thirsk, *Ag Hist* (1984/5), II, pp. 815–902. Mingay *Ag Hist*, pp. 972–1155.

V and VI of the *Cambridge Agrarian History of England and Wales*, covering the period 1640–1850, and widely recognised as the definitive studies of the subject for those two hundred years, contain only passing references to rent. Nor have any other studies attempted to fill the gap. Yet our understanding of rent is likely to affect our understanding of the whole basis of economic and social relationships in the countryside, and of economic relationships more generally.

Rent, we may conclude, has been the large missing number for long-run quantified agrarian history. Long-run price series have been available for many years, and indexes have been constructed from them.[2] Similarly we have had long-run wage series and indexes and, in recent years, indications of the course of capital development.[3] These various series and indexes include separate schedules for agriculture, yet the income from one factor of production – the income from land itself – continues to elude us. We hope in this book to fill the missing gap, at least for the period 1690–1914. This does not mean that we present a radical revision of all that economic historians have ever believed about agricultural rent. That was never likely, and was never anticipated. What we have tried to do is to give substantive backing to what is already known about the general trend in agricultural rent, to give it in graphic and numeric form, and thereby to provide the large missing number. Having provided, we then attempt to assess critically the implications for an understanding of agricultural change and for change in the economy more generally.

In pursuit of our theme, we begin in chapter 1 with a discussion of rent, what it was, how it was assessed, and how it was collected. We have a few illusions to shatter. The stereotypical picture of large farms, rack rents, and bucolic dinners, needs to be tempered to a reality in which small farms and beneficial leasing arrangements persisted almost into the twentieth century in some parts of the country. Above all, we highlight some of the practical reasons that make the collection and analysis of 'rents' rather more complex than might ostensibly seem to be the case. We also emphasise the extent to which rent was a matter of negotiation, on an individual basis, between tenant and landlord (or agent). Whatever Adam Smith and the classical economists may have argued, bargains were struck according to perceived

[2] See for example the many price indexes included in B. R. Mitchell and P. Deane (eds.), *Abstract of British Historical Statistics* (Cambridge, 1962), pp. 471–7, 484–9, 494–8. See also P. K. O'Brien, 'Agriculture and the home market for English industry, 1660–1820', *English Historical Review*, C, no. 397 (1985), 773–800.

[3] On wages at a very rudimentary level see Mitchell and Deane, *Abstract*, pp. 348–52. For capital see B. A. Holderness, 'Agriculture, 1770–1860', and C. H. Feinstein, 'Agriculture', in C. H. Feinstein and S. Pollard (eds.), *Studies in Capital Formation in the United Kingdom 1750–1920* (Cambridge, 1988), pp. 9–34, 267–80, 429–30, 433–4, 437–8, 444–5, 448–9, 452–3.

economic conditions and almost in defiance of any clear notions of accountancy.

In chapter 2 we ask what contemporaries knew about rent. Our survey of material produced by contemporary reporters such as Arthur Young, by the Board of Agriculture, and by essayists writing in the *Journal of the Royal Agricultural Society of England*, suggests that contemporary understanding of rent levels was, at best, vague until well into the nineteenth century. Reporters had considerable difficulty in persuading farmers to tell them anything about their rents; indeed, in the 1990s we probably know more about eighteenth-century rents collectively than was the case in the 1790s, purely because estate documents have been deposited in record offices and opened to the public in the second half of the twentieth century. Lack of information did not stop contemporaries from attempting to gather data, or from trying to produce workable estimates of rent, but this was never on anything like a systematic basis prior to the 1890s.

The lack of hard data has continued to cause problems for historians in the course of the twentieth century, as we argue in chapter 3. Even though various attempts have been made in recent years to interpret trends in rents, either on a long-term national or regional level, or by examining a number of estates over large areas. None has been particularly successful, and we can have relatively little confidence in them. An alternative way of approaching rents is to seek proxies for them from other sources. As we show, however, on the basis of a discussion of the social surveys of contemporary commentators such as Gregory King, and in relation to the eighteenth-century Land Tax and the post-1798 Income Tax, there really are no adequate substitutes. It is for this reason that we believe a rent index can be constructed only by intensive use of contemporary source materials.

The source materials are now widely available, but chapter 4 looks at what should be the determining parameters of a rent index. This immediately propels us into the complex problems of utilising what is, for our purposes, usually incomplete data. We set out to gather material reflecting every area of the country in terms of broad agricultural practice, land use, soil types, and so on, but expectation and reality rapidly came into conflict. We had not appreciated just how widespread beneficial leasing continued to be well into the nineteenth century, and since it was not possible to find a suitable multiplier to convert the customary rents from these contracts into rack-rent equivalents we had to omit large areas of the country. Rack rents were our obvious source of information, but we still had to decide the most appropriate unit of measure: the farm, the field, or the estate. In the end it proved relatively easy to lay down the parameters into which a rent index should fit, but what could actually be collected represented a compromise some distance from the ideal.

Chapters 5 to 7 cover the production of the database from which the rent index has been derived. The data are drawn (in far from equal proportions) from three main sets of material: estate archives across the country; rental series constructed for and in conjunction with the 1890s Royal Commission on Agriculture; and results produced by other historians working on related topics which include agricultural rent. Our work on estate records is set out in chapter 5, which details the selection and sampling process and looks at why we did, or did not, use material from particular archives. It also looks at how we recorded the information, and the problems we met in relation to establishing the acreages on which rents were assessed and collected. In chapter 6 we look at rental material made available as a result of government inquiries into agriculture conducted at various points in the nineteenth century. The inquiries of the 1830s provide little usable information – although some rather general material – but the Royal Commission of the 1890s turns out to be far more helpful, partly because of the much more systematic way in which material was collected over a far longer period of time than just the 1890s. In addition, the agricultural conditions of the period inspired a number of other commentators to prepare their own 'rental histories'. In this context the work of R. J. Thompson, the ninth Duke of Bedford, J. C. Steele, and L. L. Price all provided additional evidence. Critically, however, we point out that since the inquiries were concerned with the agricultural depression, they concentrated attention on the most depressed areas, with a possible bias towards the eastern part of the country. We try to allow for the likely inflection in the index that this may cause, without abandoning the data thrown up by the inquiries. In chapter 7 we examine the written biographies of estates to see what information contained within them we can use in the rent index. Our general conclusion is that, although many of the studies appear to provide useful data, for one reason or another – and usually because of a shortage of acreage figures – the material they contain does not fit the parameters we set. Even so, we have added material to the index wherever possible.

Chapter 8 contains our main findings, presented in a series of graphs, designed first to indicate the trends we have found, and then to test them against the conclusions drawn by commentators from Arthur Young in the eighteenth century to R. C. Allen in the late twentieth century. We also compare them with the findings of various other commentators, to try to establish the magnitude of accuracy and error. We are satisfied that they represent the best possible indication of the pattern of agricultural rents in England between 1690 and 1914. In chapter 9 we refine the findings by looking particularly at how the information enables us to examine times of plenty and times of dearth, as well as to examine regional variations in long-term trends.

Finally, in chapters 10 and 11 we set the conclusions to be drawn from the rent index into the broader picture of agricultural history and the national economy over the period 1690–1914. In chapter 10 we look at the reasons why rents were likely to move in particular directions at particular times, especially in relation to other demands on the farmer including labourers' wages. We then discuss the way in which the index moves in line with, or deviates from, price and wage indicators and the long-term rate of interest. In chapter 11 we move from the longer to the shorter term and disaggregate the whole period into sub-periods in which we test the findings against the broad picture of agriculture in times of boom and times of gloom.

This is a study which almost certainly could not have been done in the past with the kind of magnitude, precision, and detail that we have achieved. Much of our evidence is derived from the papers of landed families, papers which were, until recent times, private property maintained in private hands. As landed families have deposited their archives in public repositories during the second half of the twentieth century an enormous bank of data has become available which still has many secrets to yield up. Similarly important has been technology. The speed and precision with which our data was extracted from the archives and then analysed is a remarkable tribute to the power of modern computer technology. Undertaking this study without such a facility would have been prohibitively expensive. Bringing the data and the technology together in the way that we have done here also opens up new perspectives, some of which are hinted at in the closing chapters, and which we have begun to explore elsewhere.[4] English agriculture still has many secrets to reveal, but the archives and the technology exist to ensure that they remain secrets no longer.

[4] M.E. Turner, J. V. Beckett, and B. Afton, 'Taking stock: farmers, farm records, and agricultural output in England 1700–1850', *AgHR*, 44, 1 (1996), 21–34.

CHAPTER I

Agricultural rent in England

The payment of rent, usually due on Lady Day (25 March) and Michaelmas (29 September) but sometimes also on the other quarter days (25 December and 24 June), was one of the high, or low lights, of every farmer's life. If he had the cash to pay, he could sit back and enjoy the rent dinner and accompanying festivities with peace of mind. If, by contrast, he had to approach the landlord or his agent with the sad news that he could not pay, or at least could not pay now, or could not pay the whole rent, he must have viewed rent day with apprehension. Yet one way and another, year in and year out, millions of pounds changed hands in agricultural rents of one sort or another. It was perhaps the most substantial transfer of resources from one social group – the tenant farmers – to another – the landlords – before the advent of industry and banking in the course of the industrial revolution; and it must have been one of the most discussed and debated issues in rural society: who could afford to pay; who was not paying; who seemed likely to quit their farm at rent day because they could not pay. These and many similar thoughts dominated conversation in village pubs throughout the length and breadth of the land, just as the problems behind them dominate the correspondence between landowners and their agents or stewards.

The business of paying the rent was a matter for landlord, agent, and tenant, but the importance of rent as a guide to the financial health of the community and the nation is undeniable. Yet our collective knowledge of rent and rental payments is remarkably thin, especially in view of the veritable cornucopia of agricultural statistics published in recent volumes of the *Cambridge Agrarian History of England and Wales*.[1] Rent was a matter of private agreement between landlord and tenant. No returns were required by the tax man. As a result, in a collective sense we know all too little about how rents were assessed, the process of agreement between tenant and

[1] Thirsk, *AgHist* (1984/5); Mingay, *AgHist.*

agent, the methods of payment and accounting, and the techniques employed for agreeing abatements, remissions and, occasionally, evictions when farmers could not or would not pay.[2] We look at some of these questions in this chapter, partly to provide the context for the chapters which follow, and partly to flag up some of the problems with which we were faced when constructing a rent index.

The nature of tenure

The rack rent

Informed contemporary opinion revolved around the idea that agricultural rent should be viewed as the produce of the land, part of which was payable by the tenant to the landlord. R.J. Thompson, in a remarkable essay to which we shall return many times in this book, defined agricultural rent in nineteenth-century England and Wales as 'The share of the produce taken by the landlord for the use of the soil and for the equipment of the farm, which we call rent.'[3] As we attempt to explain below, this is a rather more expansive definition of rent than the concept of 'pure' rent as theoretically developed by Ricardo and the classical economists. Thompson, an Assistant Secretary at the Ministry of Agriculture, was a man who, in his daily civil service capacity, would at times have needed to be either suitably precise or suitably vague to meet particular circumstances. This definition carries characteristics of both. It gives us the basic idea of rent, or a monetary transaction, without telling us anything about how rent was constituted, how it was calculated, and what it consisted of. We shall have cause to try to refine the ideas behind his definition as we proceed.

We may begin with the views of Sir William Petty, and of the classical economists. Petty argued in 1662 that rent was a remainder, what was left from the output of corn, for example, after a man had dug, ploughed,

---

[2] Studies of stewards and agents are perhaps the most useful way of analysing the way in which countryside relationships operated. For a summary of the literature see J. V. Beckett, 'Estate management in eighteenth-century England: the Lowther–Spedding relationship in Cumberland', in J. Chartres and D. Hey (eds.), *English Rural Society 1500–1800* (Cambridge, 1990), pp. 55–72; see also D. R. Hainsworth, *Stewards, Lords and People: The Estate Steward and His World in Later Stuart England* (Cambridge, 1992). See also E. Hughes, 'The eighteenth-century estate agent', in H. A. Cronne, T. W. Moody, and D. B. Quinn (eds.), *Essays in British and Irish History in Honour of James Eddie Todd* (London, 1949), chapter 10, pp. 185–99; G. E. Mingay, 'The eighteenth-century land steward', in E. L. Jones and G. E. Mingay (eds.), *Land, Labour and Population in the Industrial Revolution* (London, 1967), pp. 3–27; E. Richards, 'The land agent', in G. E. Mingay (ed.), *The Victorian Countryside* (London, 1981), II, pp. 439–56; B. English, 'Patterns of estate management in East Yorkshire c. 1840–c. 1880', *AgHR*, 32 (1984), 29–48. Historians still rely heavily on manuals written by contemporaries, for example, E. Laurence, *The Duty of a Steward to his Lord* (London, 1727), but there are many others.   [3] Thompson, 'An inquiry', 57.

harrowed, and reaped the soil, carried home, threshed, and winnowed the corn, deducted an amount to carry forward for his seed, deducted his own food and, finally, deducted for the food he had to exchange for clothes and other necessaries of life.[4] In other words it was a remainder after the application of inputs, mainly labour but including some variable capital (seed), and after an allowance for the necessities of life (food and clothing). It was the net product of agriculture which in modern terms we might usually equate with profit. In the course of the eighteenth century the greater variety and complexity of the inputs, both of labour and capital, was recognised, as were the property rights in those inputs, including the property right over the God-given input, the land itself. It was no longer God's, and had not been for a long time, but instead was vested in individual ownership and sometimes collective or common ownership.

The Physiocrats in France involved the concept of class and the laws of natural order to control the mechanism of producing the gross product and then of distributing the net product. The productive class of cultivators 'rented' the land from the proprietary class whose 'rent' was that net product.[5] At no time would the tenant farmers receive net profits, because the net profit from cultivation was the rent. The Physiocrats also believed that rent should bear the burden of taxation which the state deemed it necessary to raise. To tax the cultivators might simply result in their passing on the burden or hiding the burden in the gross product and thereby reducing the size of the net product. A more efficient system was simply to tax rents directly. Arguably, as was suggested by some later economists, the state could assume a co-proprietorial interest in the soil and through taxing the rent it was simply receiving its proper share of the net product.[6] In the reality of eighteenth and nineteenth-century England, when taxes were exacted, who was obliged to pay them? This is one of the many mysteries of English rent negotiating and collecting behaviour because in practice it is not clear if the rent was net or gross of taxes. Nor, indeed, was it necessarily clear to contemporaries, who argued long and hard over what should and should not be included in or excluded from rent. In addition, the separation of investment into the tenants' and the landlords' obligations, which was clear in the eyes of the classical economists, was by no means as clear in reality. Whether or not local rates and taxes and certain items of expenditure such as repairs formed or did not

---

[4] J. M. Currie, *The Economic Theory of Agricultural Land Tenure* (Cambridge, 1981), p. 4, quoting it third hand.
[5] Based on Currie, *Economic Theory*, pp. 5–7. Two other classes were recognised, the 'sterile' class of manufacturers, and an underclass who only earned subsistence and were generally ignored.
[6] *Ibid.*, p. 9.

form part of the money which passed between tenants and their landlords is also not always clear.

Adam Smith was influenced by the thoughts of the Physiocrats but the context of a largely peasant-based France was at odds with an increasingly capitalist eighteenth-century England. Necessarily therefore, as a minimum, Smith had to take into account a third class distinction, one that was envisaged by the Physiocrats – the *menu peuple* – but which was not common in France, namely hired or wage labour. This class was neither cultivator nor proprietor, nor the sterile class of manufacturers. For England therefore, Smith, along with later economists, had to view rent within a more complex system of class differentiation and inter-relationships. Essentially it was a system which became known as, and is certainly more familiar as, income distribution. Physiocracy was not a system of income distribution, and though he was a follower of the Physiocrats in this sense at least Smith had moved the theoretical discussion on considerably. The classical economic system was thus founded on a three-way division of landowners, tenant farmers, and landless labourers. From Smith onwards, therefore, economists viewed rent in fairly hard-nosed business terms as one element of income distribution shares. Wages, profits, and rents were the income shares or returns to labour, capital, and land. Under certain conditions, as in the case of a smallholder, all three income shares accrued to the same person: a hidden wage for his own labour; a hidden profit for his capital employed; and a hidden rent return on the land he owned. All three were confused in the gross product. This led Smith to the conclusion that rent ought to represent about one-third of the gross product.[7] This concept of the land providing three rents prevailed in the late eighteenth century, but in time investment in the land increased and led to a more complicated analysis of the income shares and returns.

In the practical realities of the times in which he lived Smith expected that the buoyancy of population and thus of demand would encourage rising prices and create a windfall increase in the quantity and value of the gross output from agriculture, a windfall which he assumed would benefit the landlords before the other income recipients of the soil, even though the landlords may not actively have been involved in raising that output, for example by investment. He therefore took rent to be the surplus over and above the returns to wages and capital, but more importantly he assumed that increments to the gross product would be enjoyed first by the rent holders and only later would other income shareholders take their share.

---

[7] A. Smith, *An Inquiry into the Nature and Causes of the Wealth of Nations* (London, 1900 edn), p. 134. See also W. J. Barber, *A History of Economic Thought* (London, 1967), pp. 38–9. See below, p. 19, for William Marshall's development of this idea.

Thus he assumed that rent was 'evidently the highest which the tenant can afford to pay in the actual circumstances of the land'.[8] The principal circumstance in mind was the landowners' control over tenure. As our discussion later in this chapter shows, and as is repeated at appropriate moments throughout the book, the control of tenure was not nearly as cut and dried as Smith assumed. At different times and in different places landlords had negligible powers. This circumstance and the possible conflict which it provoked in class relationships came sharply into focus when prices for agricultural products began to rise steeply in the second half of the eighteenth century. In chapter 10 we show that the course of rents lagged behind the course of agricultural prices by anything up to fifteen years.

Ricardo and his followers argued that rents represented the revenues from a farm after the costs of labour and capital as supplied by the farmer had been deducted. Note here that Ricardo also sharply defined proprietorial rights, in which the capital in terms of stock and that which was necessary for cultivation was owned by the tenant. To this extent Ricardo defined rent as 'that portion of the produce of the earth which is paid to the landlord for the use of the *original and indestructible* powers of the soil'.[9] The difference in rents between farms therefore arises from different qualities in the original land. But having established that idea, Ricardo then related the example of two farms which in terms of their original state were the same, but on one of which there were buildings, hedges, ditches, and fences, proper drainage had been introduced, manure had been applied, and so on. In both cases the exchange between tenant and landlord was called rent, but the one was naturally higher than the other. In the case of the improved farm a portion only of this rent was actually for the use of the 'original and indestructible powers', the other would be the return on the capital improvement. That which was for the original powers of the earth was 'pure rent' or, in today's language, economic rent. This rather blurred the reality of owning land and investing in land, and therefore Ricardo had to recognise that once permanent improvements had been made the original and indestructible powers of the earth had been changed, and the ensuing rent then recognised the return on the capital which had been employed in order to change that state. Here lay the distinction between the rental of a farm and the pure rent of land. However, permanent improvements became subject to the economic laws relating to rent, and could therefore be considered 'pure rent'. In fact, modern agricultural historians of the eighteenth and nineteenth centuries know that the empirical evidence cannot separate the pure rent of the original and indestructible

[8] Smith, *The Wealth of Nations*, p. 114.
[9] D. Ricardo, *The Principles of Political Economy* (London, 1973 Everyman edn with introduction by Donald Winch), p. 33, our italics.

powers from the practical rental which included landlord improvement. All that the archive can do, sometimes, is indicate separately the value of the repairs and of some of the improvements, such as drainage. Contemporary techniques of farm and estate administration and accountancy so rarely offer such complete information that we are bound to adopt a working definition of rent which is not purely Ricardian.

In the final analysis the three income streams from the cultivation of the earth were wages, profits, and rent. In distinction to the Physiocrats the net produce now allowed for a profit and thus also allowed for capital accumulation to accrue to the tenant. In other words there was more than one agent at work in ameliorating the original and indestructible powers of the soil. Long leases were originally preferred by the tenant because they gave him security and allowed the returns to his own capital to accrue to his benefit. In practical agricultural terms, however, as landlords increasingly replaced long leases by short leases and tenancies at will in the course of the nineteenth century, the loss of security of the tenants' returns on investment was replaced by tenant right. This was the compensation paid to the outgoing tenant by the incoming tenant in recognition of the income share of the capital investment of the former which would come to fruition later and be enjoyed by the latter. It was a system to encourage tenants to continue to invest even when faced by short-term security of tenure. Thus, it is no coincidence that the introduction and spread of tenant right came with the disappearance of long leases, in order to act as an encouragement to the tenants to enrich the soil by their own investment in the sure knowledge that they would reap a just proportion of the benefits. A related issue, therefore, was a greater definition of the meaning of capital, and its division into two elements, fixed and circulating. The former came with the land and therefore was remunerated through the rental – though it could be augmented, as at enclosure, with hedging and ditching, the costs of which were borne by the landowners – but the circulating capital was used up in the production process and was therefore rewarded by profit to the tenant. Tenant right sought to encourage the application of this capital by protecting the tenants' interest in the return.

Rent therefore developed as a form of net product, that which was left after the deduction of wages for labour and of a capital return and profit for the farmer. This residual was then known as the Ricardian surplus, and this surplus was not necessarily equal between farms because the original powers of the soil were not necessarily equal. Thus, 'rent is always the difference between the produce obtained by the employment of two equal quantities of capital and labour'.[10] On the best-quality soil, for the purpose employed, the rent will be maximised; on the worst-quality soil the rent will be zero. This comfortably gives us an explanation of why rents were not equalised, but there are further complications. In reality, when we view the contemporary archive, what should have been a clarification of income distribution is blurred because rent was meant to be this Ricardian surplus 'less' rates and local taxes. Some tenants did not appear to pay those rates and taxes, but others did. Some paid them only to be compensated by the landlords, but others were not. Some farmers sought to make owners responsible, and conversely some owners tried to pass the burden on to their tenants. While tenants usually paid local taxes and owners paid national taxes, this division was not rigidly applied. During difficult times owners could relieve the tenant of tax burdens, but during favourable times they might just as easily try to shift the burden back to the tenants. There was no obvious standard method of distribution. Hence Malthus's comment that: 'It sometimes happens that, from accidental and temporary circumstances, the farmer pays more, or less, than this; but this is the point towards which the actual rents paid are constantly gravitating.' This is yet another reason why the practical definition of a rack rent is so elusive.[11]

The practical weaknesses of the classical theories of income distribution, as applied to land rents, were that they depended on two assumptions, neither of which can be supported: first, that farmers carefully calculated the likely profits of a farm before agreeing to the rent which was asked; second, that were the landlords to set the rent so high that the tenant could not earn his usual return on capital and labour the tenant would move to another farm where better terms were on offer. The calculations needed to support these assumptions could not be made, even had farmers wished to make them.[12] Besides, setting the rent was a social exercise as well as an economic one, in which the confidence in the individual as a good tenant, or coming from families and generations of good tenants, was recognised in the bargain which was struck on the renewal of a lease or on the initial entry of a new family member. Local social standing could also play a role in setting the rent at a level diferent to that suggested by pure rent theory. James Loch, agent to the Sutherland estate, wrote in 1830 that 'Lord Stafford's rents ... have always been fixed at rather under the general average of the district ... I mean that the tenants should feel that they hold their lands on rather easier

---

[11] See the discussion on the distribution of taxes in J. V. Beckett, 'Landownership and estate management', chapter 6 in Mingay, *AgHist*, especially pp. 630–3. Malthus quoted in Allen, *Yeoman*, p. 174.

[12] Allen, *Yeoman*, pp. 181–4; G. Hueckel, 'English farming profits during the Napoleonic Wars, 1793–1815', *Explorations in Economic History*, 13 (1976), 331–45, shows on the basis of surviving accounts for eight farms that farmers lacked the basic accountancy skills that they would have needed to make some of the assumptions required by Ricardian rent theory.

terms than their neighbours. It is fit and proper that those who hold of a great man should do so'.[13] The idea of a fully articulated 'rack' rent is difficult to establish in the eighteenth century, though it does make more sense in the nineteenth century when archaic tenures and long leases gave way to more regular rent appraisals, notwithstanding a continuation of conventions based on social position. In practical terms, the idea that a rent was a residual after other claimants (wages and profits) had taken their share of the produce of the soil at best only partially explains the transaction which tenants struck with their landlords.

The abstract 'pure' rent was one thing; the practical rental was another. Eighteenth-century agricultural writers were not troubled by the philosophies of the Physiocrats or the search for economic order of Smith and others. Instead they took a wholly practical view. For example, they held strong views on methods of income maximisation: they were in little doubt that the ideal for a landowner was to be able to lease out his estate in large farms to well-informed tenants with plentiful capital. Such men and women would farm progressively and productively, and pay high (money) rentals for the land they worked. The much-publicised example of Thomas William Coke's estate at Holkham in North Norfolk seemed to bear testimony to the assumption that large farms on long leases (21 years) should be encouraged.[14] As an ideal it was probably indisputable, but as a reality it smacked all too readily of pie in the sky. There were so many constraints on the relationship between a landlord and his tenants which influenced rents that with the exception of high-profile agriculturalists like Coke – who was a masterly self-publicist – most landlords adopted a more pragmatic viewpoint. And for this they had good reason: whatever may have been the case at Holkham, elsewhere large farms did not bring in the greatest rents. As Nathaniel Kent noted, also of Norfolk, large estates were not necessarily let in large farms at rack rents: 'it is to large estates that we look for moderation in rents, as they are generally let upon a fair and consistent scale'.[15] In fact, small farms were more likely to yield high rents, pro rata, because they were worked more intensively and effectively. The advantages of large farms lay in their lower unit costs rather than their greater unit output. Just as large farms were not necessarily the answer to every landlord's prayer, so the long leases favoured by experts were seldom found in practice. Contemporaries

[13] Quoted by G. E. Mingay, 'The course of rents in the age of Malthus', chapter 6 of M. E. Turner (ed.), *Malthus and His Time* (London, 1986), p. 89. On the political reasons for having non-economic rents see p. 16 below.

[14] Parker, *Coke*. Large farms seem to have been attractive to corporate owners, such as Guy's Hospital, B. E. S. Trueman, 'The management of the estates of Guy's Hospital 1726–1900' (University of Nottingham, PhD thesis, 1975), pp. 209–11, 216a.

[15] Marshall, *Review*, III, p. 324.

debated at length the relative merits of leases by comparison with annual tenancies, a debate largely solved in favour of the latter as a result of economic conditions in the French Revolutionary and Napoleonic War years.

Coke may have had a high profile but was he also a good landlord? He was an excellent example of a landlord who rack rented his tenants, and it was for this that he enjoyed such a good press. Rack renting was a situation in which landlord and tenant agreed a rent which, from the landlord's point of view, reflected an economic return on his investment in land as an asset. From the point of view of the tenant the rack rent was a call or a cost upon the total income from agricultural production which still left him with an economic return for his labour and his other investments in production. Rack rents essentially represented an annual or twice-yearly economic assessment of the value of the land based on the laws of supply and demand. It was complicated, however, by less than uniform practice between tenants and landlords over who paid taxes and undertook repairs. Nevertheless, in general the more land there was available to rent, but the fewer the tenants seeking tenancies, the lower was the rent; but the less land there was available and the greater the number of potential tenants the higher was the rent, and this general principle held without even considering the quality of the land. It is true that in times of hardship, such as agricultural depression, a landowner might make concessions to a good tenant. However, in general, the rack rent was an economic measure of land value, from the landlords' point of view.

Agricultural experts approved of rack renting. The landlord, it was argued, offered security of possession, in return for which the tenant agreed to pay an equitable rent and to find the necessary capital to run the farm.[16] The disadvantage to the landowner was that he needed to keep a sharper eye open for malpractice than was the case with estates let by other forms of tenure. This meant that he needed a reasonably sophisticated structure of management which was inevitably a cost on the estate. The advantage was that the tenants, because they were 'racked' up to the highest money rent the farm could hope to sustain, needed to farm efficiently and effectively if they were to make a good living. Consequently the level at which the rent was set needed to be carefully determined if it were to act as an incentive to the tenant without potentially either bankrupting him, or forcing him to farm (or try to farm) in a manner designed to produce the greatest possible revenue with the least attention to the long-term good of the soil.

---

[16] David Low, *Landed Property and the Economy of Estates* (London, 1844), pp. 8–27.

The reality was that neither landlord nor potential tenant had any theoretical guidelines or manuals from which they could extract working formulae for setting rent levels. In theory, at least, the willingness of landlords to set rack rents reflected a desire to assume direct control of their estates. This in turn indicated a willingness to determine more closely the way in which their land was farmed, normally through carefully worded leases which included increasingly tightly drawn clauses relating to the arable rotations and the stocking patterns. To draw up and enforce such clauses, most owners needed to employ specialist stewards, and the increasing professionalisation of land agency during the eighteenth and nineteenth centuries was a reflection of these demands. Both in the manuals published to provide stewards with a guide to their jobs and in the way in which they were used by landowners, the need to control how an estate operated without day-by-day landlord involvement became paramount. The double-entry book-keeping system, designed to thwart venal stewards, together with the increasing reliance placed by owners on their stewards and agents (occasionally mistakenly) reflected this shift. In turn, agents were paid more money, and increasingly acted as the mouthpiece – they were always expected to act as the ears! – of the landlord.[17]

However sophisticated the means of running the estate, few landlords were in a position to rack rent their tenants to the full extent of their ability to pay. The desire or even the necessity to encourage good relationships with their tenants meant that landlords were often reluctant to push rents up to the highest possible levels. Under-renting, as much as over-renting, was a constant source of annoyance to agriculturalists. Nathaniel Kent wrote in 1775 that 'estates undoubtedly ought to be let for their fair value. The bad effects are equal, whether they be under-let, or over-let; in the one case the tenant is frequently negligent, in the other, he is discouraged.'[18] Thomas Robertson, reporting to the Board of Agriculture in 1796, argued that farmers should pay what he called 'an adequate rent'. His line of argument was much the same as Nathaniel Kent's:

> He who pays a small rent, and much more the owner, who pays none, having no sufficient spur to industry and ingenuity, cannot be expected to be good farmers; while, on the other hand, a more than adequate rent renders a farmer's profession, which at the best is not lucrative, one of the worst in civil society … Both too high rented, and too low rented farms agree in not giving proper employment to the cultivator, the one too much; the other too little.[19]

[17] Beckett, 'Estate management', pp. 55–72.
[18] N. Kent, *Hints to Gentlemen of Landed Property* (London, 1775), p. 95.
[19] Thomas Robertson, *Outline of the General Report upon the Size of Farms and upon the Persons who Cultivate Farms* (Edinburgh, 1796), pp. 56–7.

Arthur Young complained bitterly: 'landlords, who, through a false pride, will not raise [rents], when they easily might, do an inconceivable prejudice to their country... high rents are an undoubted spur to industry; the farmer who pays much for his land, knows that he must be diligent, or starve'.[20] Elsewhere he argued that 'landlords should be prepared to sacrifice popularity for the sake of five shillings per annum per acre'.[21] His plea evidently fell on deaf ears since according to James Caird, writing several decades later, there was 'not a county in England' where under-renting was not practised.[22]

Under-renting was socially and politically necessary,[23] but the pragmatic reasoning which lay behind the setting of rent levels drove Caird to despair. Rent was, he concluded,

> a capricious thing, often more regulated by the character of the landlord or his agent, and the custom of the neighbourhood, than by the value of the soil or the commodities it produces. There is not a county in England where this is not exemplified. On one estate we shall find land let at 20s per acre, and on the next, farms of the same quality and with the same facilities of conveyance, let at 30s.[24]

On a related theme, R. C. Allen has argued that because experience and convention became the watchwords for landlords and farmers alike in the setting of rents in some districts, during the course of enclosure a considerable redistribution of income occurred: 'rent increases bore little connection to productivity increases given the way in which rents were set in the eighteenth century'.[25] In his view it was landlords who benefited most clearly and comprehensively from the opportunity enclosure provided for renegotiating rents, especially since the resulting rise in rents could by no means be justified purely in terms of shared productivity gains. It was not that the landlords were better than their tenants at identifying and extracting the value of their shared asset, but that changes in the economic environment of eighteenth-century farming initially worked in favour of the tenants, and that advantage was halted and, to a large degree reversed, at enclosure.

Even if a landowner was willing to rack rents to the highest level they would reach, he still had to decide what this was. Landlords could, if they so

[20] A. Young, *A Six Months Tour Through the North of England* (London, 2nd edn, 1771), vol. IV, pp. 343–5, and quoted in Allen, *Yeoman*, p. 182.

[21] A. Young, *A Six Weeks' Tour through the Southern Counties of England and Wales* (London, 1768), p. 22. G.E. Mingay, *English Landed Society in the Eighteenth Century* (London, 1963), pp. 53–4.

[22] Caird, p. 477.

[23] See A. Offer, 'Farm tenure and land values in England, *c*. 1750–1950', *EcHR*, 44 (1991), 1–20, on a review of land as a positional asset.   [24] Caird, pp. 476–7.   [25] Allen, *Yeoman*, pp. 186–7.

wished, lay out farms on their estates and simply auction them to the highest
bidder. Such a practice was certainly used in Cornwall in the early
nineteenth century, and in Devon as late as the 1840s.[26] But agricultural
experts were at one in condemning this practice. Those farmers who
obtained a good bargain (that is, a rent beneath the economic level) were
held to lack encouragement because they could make a good living without
exerting themselves. Conversely, as we have mentioned already, those who
paid over the odds were likely to overcrop the land in a desperate attempt to
make a living before abandoning the lease and leaving the farm in a worse
state than that in which they found it initially.[27] Since they rejected auctions,
the agricultural experts had no alternative but to encourage landlords to fix
the rents, and to make every effort to ensure that the level was correct. In
William Marshall's words at the beginning of the nineteenth century: 'a
proprietor should spare no reasonable expense to come at the fair rental
value, the true market price, of his farms, at the times of letting'.[28]

   This, of course, begged the question, as Marshall well knew: 'let three
or four surveyors, or land valuers (all of them noted for being great
judges of land) go over a farm, separately, and their several valuations
will differ very materially'.[29] His solution was to have two or three valuers
'to settle, with sufficient accuracy, the rental value of farms'.[30] Elsewhere,
however, he showed a willingness to compromise. In criticising Young for
collecting specific rental figures for his report on Lincolnshire, Marshall
argued that:

> it is well known to every man who is acquainted with the values of lands, in
> various parts of the kingdom, that, not only in each county, but in each
> district, nay, in every parish, and every neighbourhood, there is a peculiar,
> yet fair, Market Price for its Lands, as for their products. And, in each, the
> current value is, in general, sufficiently known, on the spot; not only to
> occupiers, but to professional land valuers. Where this does not happen to
> be the case (a case that can rarely occur) an auction, or sealed bidding (which
> tho very improper, as a general means of letting farms might be admissible in
> a case of this kind) would ascertain the fact, not only sooner, but infinitely
> better, than a thousand volumes of crude, indefinite hearsays, collected at a
> distance.[31]

As Marshall was awkwardly aware, when it came to setting rents, no system
was foolproof.
   Nor did this problem lessen with time; indeed, it is nowhere better set out

---

[26] Marshall, *Review*, V, p. 535; H. Tanner, 'The farming of Devonshire', *JRASE*, 9 (1848), 487.
[27] Marshall, *Landed*, p. 389; Tanner, 'The farming of Devonshire'.
[28] Marshall, *Landed*, p. 387; Philip D. Tuckett, 'On land valuing', *JRASE*, 24 (1863), 6.
[29] Marshall, *Landed*, p. 388.   [30] *Ibid.*, p. 389.   [31] Marshall, *Review*, III, p. 121.

than in Philip Tuckett's prize essay for the Royal Agricultural Society in 1863, 'On Land Valuing'. Tuckett went straight to the heart of the matter, referring to the 'striking inequalities … constantly observable in the rentals at which farms are let throughout the country', while recognising that 'the art of land valuing is one that depends so entirely on the individual judgement and experience of the valuer, that it is really impossible to lay down any rules that can materially assist those who do not possess these requisite qualifications'.[32] Tuckett specifically rejected Ricardian calculations as the basis on which to value land,[33] and his proffered solutions were entirely empirical: 'the rent of land is regulated from time to time by actual experience, far better than it could be by the most elaborate calculations'.[34] For this there was a good reason:

> every experienced land-surveyor can readily compare in his mind almost any description of land with farms of similar quality in different localities, which he has previously valued and let, where there has been sufficient competition on the one hand, or difficulty in finding a suitable tenant on the other, to form a test of value. The negotiations connected with such lettings serve from time to time to confirm or correct the judgement, and afford a far more practical test of the value of the various descriptions of land, than any calculations that can be made.[35]

Tuckett emphasised the importance of using experienced land valuers, although he was presumably aware of Marshall's fears that, if asked for objective valuations, three or four surveyors were likely to reach very different conclusions.[36] Nor had the position changed in the 1870s. Elias Squarey, in a discussion of farm capital reprinted in the *Journal of the Royal Agricultural Society of England*, argued that,

> no precise formula can be adopted in fixing its amount, nor has any scheme, under which the landlord receives a proportion of the value of farm-produce, in lieu of a fixed money rent, ever yet worked permanently and satisfactorily. The ordinary tenant seems to prefer to take his chance of bad years as well as good ones, of low prices as well as high prices, whilst to the landowner it is obviously all important to know as nearly as may be the actual average income which is likely to accrue to him from his property.[37]

Yet it would be unwise to suggest that landlords, farmers, and land valuers were all working in the dark. Farmers, whether or not they had read Ricardo, had their own ideas as to how rent levels should be calculated, though at times their ideas have a classical edge to them. Thus Marshall

---

[32] Tuckett, 'On land valuing', 1–7, esp. 1.   [33] *Ibid.*, 6.   [34] *Ibid.*, 6–7.   [35] *Ibid.*, 7.
[36] Marshall, *Landed*, p. 388.
[37] E. P. Squarey, 'Farm capital', *JRASE*, 2nd series, 14 (1878), 440–1.

in 1818 quoted with approval the experience of the North Riding of Yorkshire:

> It has long been a prevailing opinion, that the produce of the farm should be equal to three rents; one for the landlord, one for the expenses of cultivation, and another for the farmer.

Which was not a far remove from Adam Smith's view fifty years earlier, but as Marshall then explained, time and practice had moved along:

> This might have been accurate some thirty or forty years since, when improvements were seldom made; and the system of three crops and a fallow was almost invariably pursued. It is at this time difficult to form an accurate calculation upon the subject, in consequence of the various improvements in agriculture which are taking place, and the various degrees according to which the disposition and purse of the farmer enable him to pursue them. In consequence of this change of system, as well as the great increase of taxes and wages, the land is cultivated at a much greater expense than formerly, and consequently ought to be much more productive to repay the farmer for his time and skill, and a reasonable interest for his capital. A well-managed farm, two-thirds of which is arable, should not produce less than five rents, and these rarely leave the farmer much more than one rent, for the present maintenance of, and future provision for his family.[38]

Marshall was summing up a shift in attitudes towards farm rent and revenue – in the 1770s the output of the farm was reckoned to produce three rents, but by the early nineteenth century output was increasingly thought to produce five rents.[39]

The corn scarcity in the 1790s which resulted in high prices on the one hand, and put strains on local poor rates on the other, persuaded Arthur Young to become fairly dogmatic over his functional definition of rent, and in general a more sharply defined capitalist attitude became apparent: rather than look for a multiple of the rent the farmer became increasingly concerned to secure a certain rate of return, usually 10 per cent, on his investment:

> Rent should always be calculated (for private use) in union with rates and tithe; for it must be evident at first blush, that a farmer can pay more rent where rates are 5 shillings in the pound, than where they are 15 shillings. The only safe and unobjectionable way of estimating the rent of land is to deduct

[38] Marshall, *Review*, I, p. 470.
[39] J. R. McCulloch, *A Statistical Account of the British Empire*, I (London, 1837), pp. 534–5; W. Stephenson, 'England', in D. Brewster (ed.), *Edinburgh Encylopaedia*, VIII (Edinburgh, 1830), p. 735; B. A. Holderness, 'Prices, productivity, and output', chapter 2 in Mingay, *AgHist*, pp. 179–80, who reports that in Norfolk between 1819 and 1843 the gross produce of a specific farm averaged 4.8 rents, which varied from 3.7 in 1833 to 6.4 in 1840.

the expences [*sic*] per acre (including 10 per cent. on his capital for his own profit) from the acreable produce; and the remainder is for rent, rates, and tithe (where not taken in kind), from this sum deduct rates and tithe; the remainder is the landlord's rent, and the farmer cannot afford to pay a penny more. By extraordinary capital; or by uncommon skill or exertions he may make more than 10 per cent. and in that case the difference is the fair remuneration for such capital, skill, or exertions.[40]

By another name this looks like the Ricardian surplus less rates and taxes.

By the 1830s, with the country in the grip of a major agricultural depression, the tension over the division of the spoils between the various calls on the income from agricultural produce was acute. When John Kemp of Southminster, Essex, was interviewed as a witness to the 1836 Select Committee he considered that a return of 10 per cent on the tenant's capital and also for his own labour was low, and another witness, John Brickwell of Leckhamstead near Buckingham, reckoned that farmers in his district were making only 5 per cent on the capital they employed; and R. H. Stares of Droxford in Hampshire, in considering this issue, concluded that 'a man ought not to have less than 15 per cent. for his capital employed'.[41]

Few farmers were sufficiently wealthy and educated to think in this way – the majority kept no records let alone understood the finer details of accountancy – but the way of thinking became well established. David Low argued in the 1820s that the landlord needed to regulate his demands on the tenant in such a way as not to exact so much in rent that the farmer skimped on capital investment.[42] The logic for the farmer was that in the event of financial difficulties he needed to protect his capital – in case he had to move on – at the expense of his rent. As Lord Sheffield learned in the post-Napoleonic War depression, 'neither capital improved and good husbandry nor the most rigid economy at the present price of produce will enable the tenant of land to pay the rent and other payments which are now imposed thereon, and he rather chooses if possible to save his remaining capital than longer to continue in the road to ruin'.[43] Marshall's own view was that:

[40] A. Young, *General View of the Agriculture of the County of Suffolk* (London, 1813), p. 16.

[41] *First Report from the Select Committee on the State of Agriculture: with Minutes of Evidence and Appendix*, BPP [79], VIII, part 1 (1836), Qs. 2214–20; *First Report*, Q. 402; *Third Report from the Select Committee on the State of Agriculture: with Minutes of Evidence and Appendix*, BPP [465], VIII, part 2 (1836), Q. 11755.

[42] D. Low, *Observations on the Present State of Landed Property, and on the Prospects of the Landholder and the Farmer* (Edinburgh, 1823), p. 67; J. Obelkevich, *Religion and Rural Society: South Lindsey 1825–1875* (Oxford, 1976), pp. 49–50; C. Shrimpton, 'The landed society and the farming community of Essex in the late eighteenth and early nineteenth centuries' (University of Cambridge, PhD thesis, 1965), pp. 330–1.

[43] Clements Library, Ann Arbor, Michigan, Sheffield Papers, Samuel Tuesday? to Lord Sheffield, 13 March 1816.

The due *proportion* between *rent* and *capital* depends on the existing state and circumstances of a farm, and the style of management in which it is intended to be conducted; as well as on the number and strength of an occupier's own family, and on their industry and frugality.[44]

The reality of the situation was that landlords had to set the rent at levels which would encourage tenants to sink their capital into farming but which would leave them with sufficient surpluses over and above the rent to enjoy a reasonable standard of living. On the Dudley estates in the early 1820s the landlord did this by first observing that the farms were in a dilapidated state, prompting a number of suggestions for improvements, and including a revaluation of rents. It was argued that the result of this would still allow the landlord to receive a 'full share of the produce of the soil' and in turn the tenant would still receive a sufficient remuneration for 'his labour, risk and capital employed'. This was the observation and argument, but the method of achieving it was left suitably vague. The resulting revaluation led to an adjustment of only 3 per cent in the rent, and since this was a decrease, *not* an increase, we are left to suppose that the intended share of the improvement which should have accrued to landlord did not take place to any great extent.[45]

We have hinted that the rent question was also complicated by the problem of what was included or excluded in making assessments, and whether necessary outgoings such as the land tax and poor rates were included, or whether the rent was assessed entirely separately from such considerations. Equally, contemporaries were just as unsure exactly how the rates and other local obligations related to rent. Marshall quotes the Board of Agriculture reporter for the West Riding who in investigating rent suggested that 'there was a long train of public burthens, over and above [the rent], which could not be easily ascertained', including land tax, tithe, roads, poor rates, church and constable dues. 'From all these things it may be supposed, that in many places the sums payable by the farmer to the church, the public, and the poor, are nearly as great as the nominal rent paid to the landlord.'[46] In addition, how was rent assessed in relation to the provision of capital, or the repair and upkeep of buildings? If any generalisation is possible it is that traditionally the tenant was responsible for paying all local taxes and providing the circulating capital, and the landlord provided the fixed capital.[47] National taxes were a matter for negotiation. Sometimes tenants were

[44] Marshall, *Landed*, p. 391.
[45] Quotations from T. J. Raybould, 'The Dudley estate: its rise and decline between 1774 and 1947' (University of Kent, PhD thesis, 1970), pp. 44–5. [46] Marshall, *Review*, I, pp. 368–9.
[47] Squarey, 'Farm capital', 431–2. On that blurred distinction see also B. A. Holderness, 'The Victorian farmer', in Mingay (ed.), *Victorian Countryside*, I, p. 233; B. A. Holderness, 'Agriculture, 1770–1860', in C. H. Feinstein and S. Pollard (eds.), *Studies in Capital Formation in the United Kingdom 1750–1920* (Cambridge, 1988), pp. 9–34.

required to pay the tax before deducting an equivalent sum from the rent. On some estates responsibility rested entirely with the landlord; on some entirely with the tenant; and on yet others it was shared between them. If we are not entirely clear about these issues we are not particularly helped by contemporaries. Marshall reports views from the West Riding on the size of the land tax, the tithes, and the expenses of keeping roads in repair, the contributions to the poor rates, and other expenses incurred by the church and the local constables. Whether or not these formed part of the rent is unclear, but what is concluded is that 'it may be supposed, that in many places the sums payable by the farmer to the church, the public, and the poor, are nearly as great as the nominal rent paid to the landlord'.[48] Landlords attempted to transfer many of these burdens to their tenants in prosperous times, while understanding that they might need to accept them back again when circumstances altered; but overall practice was so varied that it could differ from farm to farm. On Lord Lonsdale's estate in Westmorland the tenant of Burgh demesne covenanted to pay all taxes in 1723, but a similar clause did not regularly appear in leases until about 1732, and even in 1747 Londsdale was still paying taxes on Hilton Mill. By contrast, most of his tenants in Yorkshire had accepted responsibility for the Land Tax by 1716.[49]

The practice, as distinct from the theory, of capital provision, was equally varied. Sometimes the landlord left to the tenant the full liability for providing the capital. This was the case at Holkham, where Coke's farmers had to find the outlay on marling and draining.[50] Building repairs were usually shared, with the owner providing the materials and the tenant the labour. However, an alternative was for the tenant to take full responsibility for both materials and labour, and to be compensated by a rent reduction.[51]

The only reasonably accurate conclusion we can draw is that landlords spent a considerable proportion of rents on improvements and repairs. Table 1.1 is a composite assessment of landlords' expenditure related to rent received from 28 mainly substantial estates in England and one in Wales, and shows that the proportion of rent spent on repairs, fences, insurance, new buildings, and permanent improvements, increased from about one-quarter to nearer one-third between 1842 and 1892.[52] The table was

[48] V. M. Chesher, 'A social and economic study of some west Cornwall landed families, 1690–1760' (University of Oxford, BLitt thesis, 1956), p. 12; P. Roebuck, *Yorkshire Baronets 1640–1760: Families, Estates and Fortunes* (Oxford, 1980), p. 90; Marshall, *Review*, I, pp. 368–9.

[49] J. V. Beckett, 'Landownership in Cumbria, 1680–1750' (University of Lancaster, PhD thesis, 1975), p. 188.   [50] Parker, *Coke*, p. 155.

[51] Mingay, *English Landed Society*, pp. 177–8; F. M. L. Thompson, *English Landed Society in the Nineteenth Century* (London, 1963), pp. 235, 252.

[52] Reconstructed from the Royal Commission on Agriculture, 'Particulars of the Expenditures and Outgoings on Certain Estates in Great Britain and Farm Accounts', *BPP*, C. 8125, XVI (1896), pp. 54–8.

Table 1.1. *Landlords' expenditure as a percentage of rent received, 1842–92*

Date	The number of estates on which the calculation is based in each year	Aggregate of rent received – in £000s	Acreage from which rent received – in 000s acres	Percentages of rent received					
				Percentage of rent the landlord expends on repairs, fences, insurance, new buildings, and permanent improvements	Percentage of rent landlord expends on local rates	Percentage of rent the landlord expends on tithe, land tax, drainage rates, and miscellaneous outgoings	Percentage of rent the landlord expends in managerial charges	Total expenditure	Net income to the landlords
Weighted by rents									
1842	5	149	129	27.2	0.2	14.4	4.6	46.4	53.6
1852	6	198	156	31.4	0.4	17.0	4.1	52.9	47.1
1862	6	240	162	26.1	0.5	17.6	3.3	47.5	52.5
1872	14	457	301	26.0	0.6	16.4	4.2	47.2	52.8
1882	26	603	462	30.3	0.7	16.6	5.7	53.3	46.7
1892	29	538	479	31.1	1.0	18.6	6.4	57.0	43.0
Weighted by acreage									
1842		—	—	25.8	0.3	13.9	4.6	44.6	55.4
1852		—	—	30.1	0.4	16.6	4.0	51.1	48.9
1862		—	—	26.2	0.5	17.8	3.4	47.9	52.1
1872		—	—	26.6	0.6	15.9	4.2	47.3	52.7
1882		—	—	31.0	0.8	16.0	5.9	53.6	46.4
1892		—	—	31.3	1.0	17.9	6.9	57.1	42.9

Source: Reconstructed from Royal Commission on Agriculture, 'Particulars of the Expenditure and Outgoings on Certain Estates in Great Britain and Farm Accounts', British Parliamentary Papers, C. 8125, XVI (1896), pp. 54–8.

constructed from evidence presented to a Royal Commission investigating the late-nineteenth-century agricultural depression. This may have served to exaggerate the trend because it was not unusual for landlords to offer tenants the inducement of capital improvements if those tenants would remain in occupation even when the produce from the land was attracting rock-bottom prices. This was the case in the 1880s and 1890s. Nevertheless, the plough-back of rents through landlords' capital expenditure was never negligible, and customarily on the well-documented estates seemed to average about a fifth or a quarter, or occasionally as much as a third. On the Buckinghamshire and Bedfordshire estates of the Dukes of Bedford repairs alone as a proportion of rent represented 24 per cent between 1816 and 1825, and 39 per cent between 1826 and 1835. However, the proportion fell back to 28 per cent in the decade 1836–45, and only exceeded 20 per cent once more (1866–75) during the nineteenth century.[53] On only one out of nine large estates in Norfolk during the second half of the nineteenth century did the average expenditure during a five-year period exceed 20 per cent,[54] while on the Dytchley estate in Oxfordshire expenditure on repairs and improvements was over 20 per cent of the rental in 1846–7 but not again at this level until after 1866.[55] Something near or not much over 20 per cent was the norm for agricultural investment on the Clifton estate in Lancashire.[56]

The beneficial lease

Rack rents, for all the complications which surround them, offer the most accurate measure of the value of agricultural holdings, but large swathes of the country continued to be held in beneficial leases well into the nineteenth century and even into the twentieth century. In many counties agricultural

[53] Bedford, *Story*, pp. 218–25. The details of this estate are subsumed in table 1.1. Thus it will be seen that expenditure by the duke on repairs and allied items during the depression was not as great as it was for estates in general. See Royal Commission, 'Particulars of the Expenditures', p. 55.
[54] P. Roe, 'Norfolk agriculture 1815–1914' (University of East Anglia, MPhil thesis, 1976), p. 208. The tenth estate in Roe's sample was Holkham, where expenditure was 48.5 per cent and 21.2 per cent in the two half decades 1851–5 and 1856–60. A more extensive inquiry into Norfolk and Suffolk landlords' expenditure in the 130 years before the late-nineteenth-century depression, which also shows a lower level of outlay relative to gross rent than seems to have been reported to the Royal Commission, can be found in B.A. Holderness, 'Landlord's capital formation in East Anglia, 1750–1870', *EcHR*, 25 (1972), 434–47, especially the table on 439.
[55] J. R. Walton, 'Aspects of agrarian change in Oxfordshire, 1750–1880' (University of Oxford, DPhil thesis, 1976), p. 57.
[56] G. Rogers, 'Social and economic change on Lancashire landed estates during the nineteenth century with special reference to the Clifton estate, 1832–1916' (University of Lancaster, PhD thesis, 1981), p. 387. It is not our purpose either to question or to pursue this argument further, but it does point to a very real difficulty in using rents within national income accounting: the fact that they probably never accurately reflected the real value of agriculture, even if they must represent it relatively.

tenure embraced copyhold, customaryhold, and long or life leasehold tenures, which gave considerable powers over the land to the tenants, and were only slowly eradicated. These were ancient tenancy systems based on an entry fine, an annual rent payment, and often a service obligation to the lord. They did not reflect annual land values in the same manner as did rack rents.[57] For the most part payments were in two parts, an entry fine and an annual rent payment known by various terms including chief rent, lord's rent, reserved rent, and old rent. Because it had often been fixed years earlier and without subsequent review, the annual rent bore little or no relationship to the reputed economic value of the land. The fine was the principal element of the payment.

The fine was levied either when a new lease was granted or at the time of the death of one of the named 'lives' in the lease or after a stated period of years. While it was nominally based on the value of the holding as agreed between landowner and tenant, in practice it was rarely based on real economic information. To carry out a survey each time a fine was levied would have been prohibitively expensive. On small estates local knowledge facilitated realistic valuations, but on larger, remotely run estates, this was less often the case. The level of the fine could vary even while it was in force. On the Eyns estate in Cornwall in the late seventeenth century, it was calculated at twelve to fourteen years' purchase value for a new lease of three lives, six to seven years' when two lives were added onto a current lease, and two to three years' value for the addition of one new life. This, according to Christopher Clay, was reasonably standard in south-western England during this period. Some fifty years later he found the rate to have risen to between fourteen and sixteen years for a new lease, and by 1750 it stood at eighteen years' purchase value.[58]

The regional pattern varied. Land was more likely to continue to be held under the traditional leaseholds in the north-west, the west, and the south-west of England than elsewhere. However, beneficial leases continued to be found throughout the country well into the nineteenth century, including Norfolk, the home of the agricultural revolution. Land owned by a number of important institutions, including the Oxford and Cambridge colleges and the Church of England, continued to be let under beneficial and similar leasehold agreements until well into the nineteenth century. These tradi-

---

[57] For examples of the kind of copyhold services in operation, and also of the leasehold services, see J. H. Bettey, 'Agriculture and society in Dorset, *c.* 1560–1700' (University of Bristol, PhD thesis, 1977), pp. 202, 205–6. But if the custom in seventeenth-century Dorset is at all typical then generally the rent could not represent the true economic value of the land because there was no consistent pattern in the calculation of the valuation of copyhold tenements and therefore, equally, no consistent pattern in the value of entry fines and rents. *Ibid.*, pp. 215–21 and appendix 6, pp. 378–81.

[58] Cornwall AO, En 971/2, Survey of 1678; C. Clay, 'Lifeleasehold in the western counties of England, 1650–1750', *AgHR*, 29 (1981), 84, 87.

tional tenures had originally been granted as an inducement to the tenant to run the farm efficiently and productively. In return for a long and perpetually renewable lease, the tenant was persuaded to look after the property and to finance building and improvements. Occasionally the terms of such contracts were regulated. Elizabethan legislation limited the length of leases made by ecclesiastical bodies and by Oxford and Cambridge colleges to 3 lives or 21 years (renewable every 7) and this became the usual way by which church and college lands were held.[59] Copyhold and customaryhold tenures had fixed rents, and the only means of compensation to the landlord for inflation was to raise the level of fines imposed at entry or at death. Their efforts in this direction were not guaranteed success.[60] Indeed, it was the difficulty faced by many owners in imposing fines they regarded as adequately reflecting inflationary and other pressures which gradually made rack renting seem more attractive, although the problems of conversion – including the likelihood of overcropping and abuse in the closing years of a lease – meant that many landlords were cautious reformers.

As a result, the pace of change varied across the country. At Blunham in Bedfordshire the customary tenants held their lands on beneficial leases which were renewed in 1615/16 for 21 years. A general reletting of the estate occurred in 1655 and those leases were all for nine years at rack rents.[61] On the Grafton estates in Northamptonshire by the 1650s life leases, usually of three lives, had mostly been changed to leases based on a number of years.[62] However, in most places it was the eighteenth century before the changeover occurred. On the Leveson-Gower estates in Shropshire and Staffordshire after 1700 'there was a swing towards shorter term leases and letting at will. Entry fines therefore diminished or disappeared and rents rose.'[63] In

---

[59] See E. P. Thompson, 'The grid of inheritance: a comment', in J. Goody, J. Thirsk, and E.P. Thompson (eds.), *Family and Inheritance: Rural Society in Western Europe, 1200–1800* (Cambridge, 1976), pp. 332–3.

[60] Feudal tenures were abolished at the Restoration (12 Car.II c.24) but the battles over customary and other tenures went on much longer: see, for example, from modern accounts, N. Gregson, 'Tawney revisited: custom and the emergence of capitalist class relations in north-east Cumbria, 1600–1830', *EcHR*, 42 (1989), 18–42; R.W. Hoyle, 'Tenure and the land market in early modern England: a late contribution to the Brenner debate', *EcHR*, 43 (1990), 1–20; C.E. Searle, 'Custom, class conflict and agrarian capitalism: the Cumbrian customary economy in the eighteenth century', *Past and Present*, 110 (1986), 106–33; C.E. Searle, 'Customary tenants and the enclosure of the Cumbrian commons', *Northern History*, 29 (1993), 126–53. [61] Allen, *Yeoman*, p. 97n.

[62] R. Lennard, 'Rural Northamptonshire under the Commonwealth', in P. Vinogradoff (ed.), *Oxford Studies in Social and Legal History*, V (Oxford: Clarendon, 1916), pp. 32–3, 120.

[63] J. R. Wordie, 'Social change on the Leveson-Gower estates', *EcHR*, 27 (1974), 599 n4. Though on the Lilleshall part of the estate under the ownership of the Marquess of Stafford there seems to have been a reversion back to lifeleasehold in the mid-eighteenth century when the marquess, in a state of financial embarrassment, offered every tenant a lease for three lives provided they paid two years' rent in one. By 1813, one-third of the Lilleshall estate was on such life leases, and some still remained by 1833. E. Richards, 'James Loch and the House of Sutherland, 1821–1855' (University of Nottingham, PhD thesis, 1967), p. 164.

most of Northamptonshire and Bedfordshire leases for lives were still being renewed in the 1690s 'but after about 1710 the more usual practice is to replace them by a lease for some term of years at a rack-rent'.[64] In Nottinghamshire it was the second and third quarters of the eighteenth century before leases for lives were slowly replaced.[65] In East Yorkshire the copyholds were disappearing at the time of the French Revolutionary and Napoleonic Wars, but in the Holderness division of the county they 'continued in large numbers throughout the nineteenth century and into the twentieth century'.[66]

Across much of the Midlands a social transformation was in progress as a form of peasant proprietorship was replaced by direct control exercised by a landlord.[67] However, the converse could also be the case, to a degree. The copyhold cottages on the Dudley estates in the Black Country were replaced from the mid-nineteenth century with sitting tenants being offered the opportunity to buy out the freeholds. To this extent they became *de facto* and *de jure* peasant owners, although not all of them embraced the offer. A number of copyhold cottage arrangements remained until compulsory enfranchisement in 1926.[68]

Further north the changeover came much later. Two-thirds of eighteenth-century Cumbria was held in customary tenure, and so numerous were the tenants that they were regularly able to finance their defence in legal cases brought by landlords who wished to raise the level of fines.[69] An unspecified but archaic rent and entry fine system prevailed on the Percy estates in Northumberland until the mid-eighteenth century, but it was almost confined only to these estates.[70] Lifeleaseholds were still being granted at the end of the eighteenth century in Lancashire.[71] In the west of England lifeleasehold was widespread during the eighteenth century. Leases were guaranteed for the lives of three named individuals or for terms of 99 years terminable on three lives.[72] Customary tenures began to disappear rapidly in Dorset from 1670, but even so, during the eighteenth century, the copyholder was still in the majority; and even by the late eighteenth century, in so far as a sample of 49 Dorset manorial rentals indicate, 89 per cent of

[64] H. J. Habakkuk, 'English landownership, 1680–1740', *EcHR*, 1st series, 10 (1939–40), 16–17.
[65] G. E. Mingay, 'The East Midlands', Thirsk, *AgHist* (1984), p. 115.
[66] B. English, *The Great Landowners of East Yorkshire 1530–1910* (London, 1990), p. 163.
[67] Allen, *Yeoman*, pp. 99–101.   [68] Raybould, 'The Dudley estate', pp. 315–17.
[69] Beckett, 'Landownership in Cumbria', pp. 265–6; C. E. Searle, 'The Odd Corner of England: an analysis of a rural social formation in transition, c. 1700–1914' (University of Essex, PhD thesis, 1983), pp. 71–83.
[70] P. Brassley, *The Agricultural Economy of Northumberland and Durham in the Period 1640–1750* (London, 1985), p. 78.   [71] Marshall, *Review*, I, p. 274.
[72] Clay, 'Lifeleasehold in the western counties', 83–96; C. Clay, 'Landlords and estate management in England', in Thirsk, *AgHist* (1985), pp. 189–230.

Table 1.2. *Distribution of St John's College rentals, 1870–1920*
(also showing the pattern of enfranchisement)

		In £s				
Date	Reconstructed acreage	Rent charges and quit rents	Copyhold for lives	Money rents (leases)	Money and corn rents	Tenants at will
1770	?	258	167	2,164	1,272	439
1800	?	266	186	4,614	3,887	210
1820	?	314	207	6,788	5,820	127
1840	14,500	265	260	5,309	8,237	240
1850	—	212	309	6,040	9,242	797
1860	15,400	227	321	8,400	10,429	887
1861	—	243	312	11,919	8,020	926
1865	15,450	237	309	15,759	5,758	592
1870	—	237	334	22,675	3,149	913
1875	15,400	176	311	29,876	585	942
1880	15,900	166	300	31,347	493	916
		Copyhold for lives	Rack rents	Money and corn rents	Leases for years	Rent charges – mainly tithe
1882	—	300	24,773	506	105	5,089
1885	—	292	23,259	101	128	4,456
1890	15,950	—	19,114	—	128	3,270
1900	15,500	—	15,510	—	30	2,587
1910	15,400	—	15,075	—	19	2,532
1920	15,700	—	18,975	—	30	3,776

Note: The printed accounts changed in 1882. In addition to the post-1881 accounts above there are also entries for: houses on beneficial leases, houses on long leases, houses on rack rents and rents of small tenements. These must have been included in other descriptions of rents before 1882, and the tithes must have been included as well.
Source: Rentals directly transcribed from H. F. Howard, *The Finances of St John's College Cambridge 1511–1926* (Cambridge, 1935), pp. 313–35, and acreages reconstructed from pp. 286–93.

those rentals were still in copyhold, 6 per cent in freehold, and 5 per cent in leasehold.[73] While lifeleasehold dominated in Cornwall in the eighteenth century, it began to disappear rapidly from about 1780, but the pattern of this disappearance was uneven both temporally and spatially.[74] By the end of the eighteenth century lifeleaseholds were increasingly being abandoned in Shropshire.[75]

Nor was it in just a handful of areas of the country that rack renting was a

---

[73] Our thanks to J. H. Bettey (letter 21 January 1991) for his summary of Dorset tenures. See also his 'Agriculture and society in Dorset', p. 183.
[74] Our thanks to Sarah Wilmot (letter 14 January 1991) for her summary of the south-western counties. See also Chesher, 'West Cornwall landed families', pp. 127–9, 194, for details of selected Cornish estates where enfranchisement of archaic tenures in Cornwall into rack rents was introduced from the mid-eighteenth century.   [75] Marshall, *Review*, II, p. 232.

late development. 'Beneficial leasing' was widely practised on the estates of Oxford and Cambridge colleges, of bishops, and of cathedral chapters from the seventeenth century. The owner effectively passed over management of the property to a middleman, usually at a reserved rent representing only a proportion of the yearly value of the estate. The system prevailed on the properties of the Bishop and Dean and Chapter of Durham, who continued with the system of entry fines until well into the nineteenth century.[76] At King's College, Cambridge, the reserved rent was unchanged from the sixteenth to the nineteenth centuries. Beneficial leasing was conducive neither to efficient management nor to rack renting, but it was not until the mid-nineteenth century that the corporate estates began to wake up to the consequences. All but four of the twelve livery companies of the City of London repossessed their Irish estates from middlemen between 1817 and 1872.[77] St John's College, Cambridge, was active in the same way. In the mid-nineteenth century the college authorities began to convert beneficial leases to tenancies at rack rent. Table 1.2 gives an impression of the rate of change.[78] During this period the college held between 15,000 and 16,000 acres widely scattered over twenty English counties. There was buying and selling of parcels of land throughout the period, but in approximate terms the college held over 4,000 acres in Kent, over 2,500 acres in Cambridgeshire and 570 acres in the Borough of Cambridge, and over 1,000 acres in Essex, in Lincolnshire, and in Yorkshire.

Whether there was a geographical pattern in the enfranchisement of archaic tenures is not altogether clear. However, there is some evidence in the Property Tax returns of the early nineteenth century both on the magnitude of the tax yield from these tenures and also on their regional distribution. In the tax year 1808/9 the tax yield from unencumbered land amounted to £27.4 million, added to which there was a yield from houses and other tenement property, a yield from certain minor manorial profits, and finally a yield from the quit fines and other payments associated with archaic tenures. This last yield amounted to £109,761. In other words it formed a very small percentage of the whole yield from property but it was distributed in a way which may be indicative of the relative strength of

---

[76] Hughes, 'Northumberland', pp. 125–6, 132.

[77] O. Robinson, 'The London companies as progressive landlords in nineteenth century Ireland', *EcHR*, 15 (1962), 103–18. The problems caused by the use of middlemen, particularly for an institution which was reluctant to move positively into direct management, are discussed in R.B. MacCarthy, *The Trinity College Estates 1800–1923: Corporate Management in an Age of Reform* (Dublin, 1992). The inefficiency and mismanagement of corporate estates is emphasised by B. E. S. Trueman, 'Corporate estate management: Guy's Hospital agricultural estates, 1726–1815', *AgHR*, 28 (1980), 31–2.

[78] H. F. Howard, *An Account of the Finances of the College of St. John the Evangelist in the University of Cambridge 1511–1926* (Cambridge, 1935), pp. 178–9, 313–35.

survival of such tenures into the nineteenth century. The two largest amounts accrued to property owners in Oxfordshire and Cambridgeshire, at £36,908 and £27,285 respectively, or well over half the total yield for fines. This surely, mainly, or even exclusively relates to the income of the Oxford and Cambridge colleges which came from their possessions spread throughout the country. In other words, like the returns for property in general, the tax yield is registered in a single place – in this case Oxford and Cambridge – and not wholly or necessarily in the county in which the property was actually located. But apart from the Oxford and Cambridge colleges the ownership of property to which fines were attached suggests a heavy survival of old tenures associated with landowners who for tax purposes were resident in Berkshire (£17,721), Hampshire (£10,144), Norfolk (£5,622), Surrey (£4,105), and Kent (£2,983). We can only speculate on whether the lands on which these taxes were levied were also located in these counties. Only two other counties registered more than £1,000 of tax yield from this source (Cornwall and Staffordshire), and in as many as 14 English counties and all of the Welsh counties no such tax yields were registered at all. This may register the relative geographical distribution of survival of archaic tenures, with the clear exception of the Oxford and Cambridge colleges, which nevertheless still derived a large proportion of their incomes from local land. However, the fact that some counties appeared not to have any property which attracted this tax, including the whole of Wales, looks suspiciously like under-representation.[79]

In 1871 the Oxford colleges derived an income from rack rents of £151,465 and over £26,000 from beneficial leases and copyholds for lives and inheritance. The rack rents accounted for 102,259 acres, and the customary rents for 84,585 acres. Thereafter the trend to remove beneficial and other leases quickened. In 1883 rack rents accounted for £158,528 and other leases accounted for over £14,000, and by 1911 rack rents accounted for nearly £170,000 and other leases for only £1,500. In 1883 Balliol and seven other colleges no longer had any income at all from beneficial leases, but eleven other colleges did. Of these, Merton derived nearly 18 per cent of their combined rack rent and beneficial leases from this source, Magdalen College over 18 per cent, Brasenose nearly 36 per cent, and Christ Church 14 per cent. As late as 1911 six colleges still retained the remnants of beneficial incomes, and one other, Trinity College, became a new holder of a beneficial lease.[80]

[79] *Account of the Net Receipts of the Permanent, Annual, and War Taxes for the Years ending the 10th October 1811 and 1812; Accounts Relating to the Property Tax'*, BPP, VII (1812–13), p. 289.
[80] *Report of the Commissioners appointed to inquire into the property and income of the Universities of Oxford and Cambridge, and of the colleges and halls therein*, 'Volume I. Report including Abstracts and Synoptical

By 1914 very little land in England was still held in some form of archaic tenancy although it continued to be found on the Burton Constable estate in East Yorkshire in 1917,[81] and also in Cambridgeshire.[82] But the tide was running rapidly in the opposite direction. A series of Copyhold Acts in 1841, 1843, and 1844 made provision for voluntary enfranchisement of copyholds, while another series in 1852, 1858, and 1887, which was then consolidated in the Copyhold Act of 1894, allowed either the lord or the tenant to obtain compulsory enfranchisement.[83] Between 1841 and 1891 over 17,000 English copyholds had been enfranchised.[84] The final demise of copyhold came in the Law of Property Act of 1922 which enfranchised all copyhold land into freehold tenure from the beginning of 1926.

Archaic rents disappeared as the advantages of rack renting became increasingly obvious, but the decision to convert land out of beneficial and other forms of archaic leaseholds was a complex matter. It could only be accomplished across the holdings of most estates over an extended period, because entry fines would not all come up for renewal at the same time. Since the entry fine was large, a decision to change beneficial leases to rack rents inevitably meant a loss of income in the short term. At Magdalen College, for example, where the leases were set up on a seven-year basis, it was calculated that the process of converting tenures would take fourteen years to complete (1870–84), and that an income equivalent to 'something more than half the fine' would be lost.[85] In addition, a number of advantages inherent in traditional leasehold agreements would be relinquished. Because the tenancy was often passed down through a number of 'lives' it tended to remain in a family and was treated in much the same way as owner-occupied land. The risk that the land would be over-farmed and left exhausted when a son or grandson was next in line to become the tenant was minimal. The most onerous responsibility of anyone overseeing the tenancy

Tables, and Appendix', *BPP*, C. 856, XXXVII (1873), part 1, 'Volume II. Returns from the University of Oxford and from the colleges and halls therein', *BPP*, C. 856–I, XXXII (1873), part 2; L. L. Price, 'The estates of the colleges of Oxford and their management', *Transactions of the Surveyors' Institution*, XLV, paper no. 399 (1912–13), table II, 573–4. The enfranchising of beneficial leases on Cambridge college properties in general also occurred quite late in the nineteenth century, as reported by J. B. Loch, the bursar of Gonville and Caius in the discussion arising from L. L. Price, 'The accounts of the colleges of Oxford, 1893–1903; with special reference to their agricultural revenues', *JRSS*, 67 (1904), 655. See also *Report of the Commissioners appointed to inquire into the property and income of the Universities of Oxford and Cambridge, and of the colleges and halls therein*, 'Volume III. Returns from the University of Cambridge and from the Colleges and Halls therein', *BPP*, C. 856–II, XXXVII (1873), part 3. See also J. P. D. Dunbabin, 'Oxford and Cambridge college finances, 1871–1913', *EcHR*, 28 (1975), 631–47.   [81] English, *Great Landowners*, p. 162.

[82] H. Rider Haggard, *Rural England*, II (London, 1906 edn) pp. 40, 530, 552, 555.

[83] R. Megarry and H. W. R. Wade, *The Law of Real Property* (London, 1984, 5th edn), pp. 32–3.

[84] Quoted in English, *Great Landowners*, p. 162, citing B. W. Adkin, *Copyhold and other Tenures of England* (London, 1907), p. 88.   [85] Magdalen College Archives, CP3/13–14.

was to ensure that fines were paid on the death of one of the lives. The day-to-day supervision to protect the integrity of the land when associated with farms let at rack rents was largely absent on farms which were let for many years or a number of lives. Thus the necessity to supervise the land by the landlord under customary tenures tended to be far less than for land which was rack rented. This is why such tenancies were often favoured by institutions, because they received an income from the land but with minimal expenditure and supervision. They could also anticipate the annual average income which would accrue from entry fines, even if it was sporadic and payment was determined by the accident of death.

Paying the rent

Setting the rent was one thing, paying it – from the farmer's point of view – or extracting it – from the landlord's, quite another. The classic picture is that of the rent audit. In 1728 William Elmshall conducted the rent audit on the Deene estate in Northamptonshire, on behalf of the Brudenell family:

> Lord Cardigan dined early, and shortly after one o'clock the tenants started to stream into the house for the rent-audit. Two tables had been set ready with pens, ink, and paper, and a clerk sat at each. Elmsall presided at one table with the rental for Kirkstall before him, and his son at the other with the rental for the rest of the estate. There was 'a prodigious throng' and the entering up of the particulars in the books, the making out of the receipts, settling queries by reference to the bundles of leases which had been brought from Deene for the purpose, the counting of the little piles of gold and silver, took most of the afternoon, and ... according to the invariable custom on landed estates, the business of the day was surely followed by a dinner for the tenants.[86]

Rent audits of this type continued throughout the eighteenth and nineteenth centuries. Rider Haggard recalled his in 1899:

> Today was my rent audit. It is held at an inn in Bungay, where the tenants of this estate, which, although not large, is scattered, assemble once a year to pay their rent and dine. The ceremony begins about twelve o'clock, when the agent takes his seat in a small room in the King's Head at Bungay, and makes ready his papers and book of printed receipts. To him presently enters a tenant who produces – or does not produce, as the case may be – the rent he owes ... From the sum due is deducted the amount disbursed out of pocket by the tenant, but properly chargeable to the landlord, on account of rates or taxes and repairs. Next, having been offered and drunk a glass of

[86] Joan Wake, *The Brudenells of Deene* (London, 1953), pp. 242–3.

sherry, that tenant departs with a sense of duty done, a lighter pocket, and the instruction to send up Mr. So-and-so.[87]

Organised events along these lines were by no means the order of the day. In 1699 Lord Fitzwilliam told his land steward Francis Guybon that since 'harvest is in, or almost, ride among the tenants and get up what money you can'. Nor was this an unusual request. In October 1702 Fitzwilliam told Guybon: 'I have paid away all my ready money and am in debt. Ride among the tenants and tell them they must supply me now, it being an extraordinary occasion.'[88] Tenants were not usually over-anxious to part with their money. Sir Marmaduke Constable's long absence from his Everingham estates in Yorkshire was marked by steadily accumulating rent arrears, and a marked deterioration in estate affairs.[89] The *Gentleman's Magazine* complained about those landowners who effectively lived in London, 'and but rarely go into the country with any other design than to squeeze a supply of money out of their tenants'.[90] Much depended on the steward. Thomas Davis the steward to the Longleat estate from 1779 to 1807, commanded the respect of tenant and landlord alike. On one occasion at least, after suitably appraising the Marquess of Bath of his intentions, he was able to grant a rent abatement to one particularly valued tenant at a time when rents nationally were rising.[91]

When did tenants pay their rents? Leases and tenancy agreements normally stipulated that rents were due on the Quarter Days, but this was not normally when they were paid. The proper times for rents to be paid, in William Marshall's view, 'depend on the marketable produce of an estate, and on the season of the year, at which it goes, – in common course, and with the best advantage, – to market. A tenant should never be forced to sell his produce with disadvantage; nor, when he has received his money for it, ought he to be at a loss of an opportunity of discharging his debt to the landlord.'[92] He cited the case of Norfolk, where 'the latter end of February, or the beginning of March, appeared to be the most proper season for farmers to discharge their Michaelmas rents: and the month of June, for paying those which become due at Ladyday.'[93]

Marshall's complaint was that landlords gave insufficient thought to their tenants, failing to realise that rents should be collected when the tenants

[87] H. Rider Haggard, *A Farmer's Year* (London, 1987 edn), pp. 49–52.
[88] D. R. Hainsworth and C. Walker (eds.), *The Correspondence of Lord Fitzwilliam of Milton and Francis Guybon, His Steward 1697–1709* (Northampton, 1990), pp. 54, 112.
[89] P. Roebuck, 'Absentee landownership in the late seventeenth and early eighteenth centuries: a neglected factor in English Agrarian History', *AgHR*, 21 (1973), 1–17.
[90] *Gentleman's Magazine*, 7, (1737), 104–6.
[91] D. P. Gunstone, 'Stewardship and landed society: a study of the stewards of the Longleat estate, 1779–1895' (University of Exeter, MA thesis, 1972), p. 8.   [92] Marshall, *Landed*, p. 398.
[93] *Ibid.*, p. 399.

were best able to pay them, and that this required the tenant to have sound notice of rent day:

> The times of receiving rents are of considerable import in the management of a landed estate. Yet the subject, hitherto, would seem to have had but little thought bestowed upon it. Indeed, on most estates, there are no fixed days: neither the day, the week, nor the month of receiving is known to the tenants of many, until the pleasure of the receiver is signified to them in his precept. And what is still more vexatious to them, the appointed day, perhaps, will be altered, again and again!
>
> This is a crime which ought to disqualify a man from acting as a receiver of farm rents. How is a tenant to answer his payments, punctually, under such unreasonable conduct? He must either sell his corn and his cattle several weeks, perhaps, before it is necessary, and have a large sum of money to keep by him, he knows not how long, nor into whose hands it may fall, when his business calls him from home, – or he must meet the receiver, who has set him an example of impunctuality, with only part of his rent. Thus going on, six months after six months, or paying his rent in driblets, the year round; without coming to any regular settlement; until the account between them is rendered so intricate as to require legal assistance, perhaps, to settle it. If this should not be the case, the receiver's accounts become, by such irregular proceeding, so confused, with broken sums and arrears, that a proprietor, if he has resolution and patience to study and understand them, can have little satisfaction in settling them.[94]

Marshall considered it to be far more desirable to a proprietor, as well as to a tenant, that rent days should be fixed:

> The tenant knows, six months beforehand, the precise day on which he will be expected to pay the whole of his rent. He makes his arrangements accordingly; he takes every advantage of markets, and bargains for large sums to be payable the day before the rent day. He makes up his bag, sleeps with it under his pillow, and next morning takes it to the audit: – gets his receipt in full, returns home, with his heart at rest, and sets about making his money arrangements, for the ensuing rent day.[95]

This was the theory; the practice was rather more varied. In Kent in 1796 payments were half yearly, with Lady Day rent payable at Midsummer and Michaelmas rent at Christmas, so that the tenant was allowed 'one quarter's credit. In some few instances, a half year is given them, paying one half year under another.'[96] William Pitt, writing of Leicestershire and Northampton-shire in 1809, found a similar system in operation.[97] However, the position in

[94] *Ibid.*, p. 396.   [95] *Ibid.*, p. 397.
[96] Marshall, *Review*, v, p. 430, quoting J. Boys, *General View of the Agriculture of the County of Kent* (London, 1796), p. 34.

the early nineteenth century may have been tighter than in previous generations. In his discussion of Bedfordshire in 1808 Thomas Batchelor cited the case of Lidlington where, in the mid-eighteenth century, common practice was to pay half a year's rent at the time when a year and a half's rent had become due; 'but at present, it is customary with some of the principal proprietors, to receive half a year's rent, when it has been due only three months, by which means, it will be perceived, that an additional capital, equal to three-fourths of a year's rent, is necessary to stock a farm, and that the rent is raised £3 15s per cent. without any alteration in the nominal sum'.[98] The idea that landlords were tightening up was also recognised by Pitt when discussing Northamptonshire: while some landlords still allowed three months credit, others 'expect the rent within a month after becoming due'.[99] Yet on the Sledmere estate in East Yorkshire in the third quarter of the nineteenth century the rents due on Lady Day and Michaelmas Day were not entered into the accounts until the following July and January, effectively allowing the tenants the equivalent of four months' credit.[100]

Conclusion

If we were to rely upon Arthur Young, William Marshall, James Caird, and their fellow agricultural commentators, we would come to a rather strange view of rent. Their ideas and suggestions may seem straightforward, and often obvious, but as we have tried to hint in this chapter in reality the assessment and collection of rent was a complex, and sometimes rather sordid business. The contemporary ideal may have envisaged a landscape of large farms on which relatively wealthy tenant farmers regularly paid their rent to a landlord or steward who fixed the time of payment well in advance, but the reality was rather different. Large areas of the country, until well into the nineteenth century, were subject not to rack rents, but to customary and other archaic forms of tenure in which the real value of the holding was often untapped by the actual rent paid. Where freehold rents prevailed the assessment of rent levels was frequently a pragmatic gesture, determined by what the landlord thought he could extract – sometimes, what he could extract without doing permanent damage to his political interests – and the availability of tenants. Landlords had only a vague grasp of the theoretical constraints under which they were working, although Marshall for one was

---

[97] W. Pitt, *General View of the Agriculture of the County of Leicester* (London, 1809), p. 46; W. Pitt, *General View of the Agriculture of the County of Northampton* (London, 1813), p. 37.

[98] T. Batchelor, *General View of the Agriculture of the County of Bedford* (London, 1813), p. 32.

[99] Pitt, *General View of Northampton*, p. 37.

[100] B. English, 'On the eve of the Great Depression: the economy of the Sledmere estate 1869–1878', *Business History*, 24 (1982), 24–5.

well aware that even so-called experts could seldom agree any realistic guidelines on the processes of rent assessment. When it came to paying, the position was even more complex. The jockeying for position over what was or was not included in the rent (taxes, tithes, etc.), the regular efforts of tenants to stretch the timescale over which they paid their rents, and the decisions taken by landlords over abatements (chapter 3), ran counter to the best theory that could be invoked. The fundamental rural relationship may have involved the transfer of resources from one social group to another in the form of rent, but the mechanisms and customs cannot easily be reduced to a simple formula.

CHAPTER 2

Contemporary views of rent in eighteenth and nineteenth-century England

Landowners and tenants agreed the rent of a particular property, but as we have shown in chapter 1 the process of assessment and collection was by no means straightforward. Since by its very nature the agreement was a private one, between the landlord or his agent and the tenant, neither party was usually keen to discuss the matter openly. Contemporary attempts to collect rental data were frequently thwarted by the reluctance of farmers to make the information publicly available. Since it was only in the later nineteenth century that the government made any real attempt to collect rental data on a systematic basis the consequence was that contemporaries knew relatively little about rent levels, and even the gregarious Arthur Young regularly failed to coax specific figures out of hesitant farmers. What we show in this chapter is how little contemporaries knew about rents; indeed, we shall argue that it is only with the availability of estate records which have been subject to public scrutiny through the opening up of record offices in the second half of the twentieth century that the data have become available from which any sort of systematic analysis of rents can be attempted.

Perhaps not surprisingly with such a widely understood but secretive subject, contemporaries speculated even if they did not really know very much about the course of rents. It was only really in the eighteenth century that serious attempts were made to *collect* rental data, and this was initially as a result of the work of Arthur Young who, in numerous trans-national tours, faithfully recorded rental figures quoted to him from tenants and landlords from across the country, and through different agricultural regions.

Young was the first agriculturalist to gross up individual observations derived from regional tours into national estimates. In 1770–1 on the basis of the evidence he gleaned from his *Eastern Tour* Young suggested that the general average rent on 32 million acres of English and Welsh agricultural land yielded a rental income of £20.8 million, or 13 shillings per acre.[1] In the

[1] Quoted in Mingay, *AgHist*, p. 1111.

late 1760s he suggested an average regional rental of 10 shillings per acre in northern England, but 14 shillings for the eastern counties.[2] By the 1790s his average estimate for England was 15s 7d per acre.[3] Young was notoriously optimistic, and never afraid of lambasting landlords and farmers alike for failing to make the most of rental opportunities. He complained as he passed northwards from Aylesbury along the Buckingham road, 'This famous Vale [of Aylesbury] has received ample gifts from nature, but the efforts of art are all yet to be made: the landlords have fourteen shillings where they might have thirty and the tenants reap bushels, where they ought to have quarters.'[4] However, Young was not motivated by a desire to understand rents as a specific item of agricultural finance – they were part of a larger baggage of facts which he collected – and his figures therefore yield an unsystematic, even rambling database which it is, at the very least, dangerous to regard as a firm cross-section.[5]

Sir Frederick Morton Eden sporadically collected rental data in association with his inquiry of 1795 into *The State of the Poor*. While there is at least one quotation for most counties, the data actually refer to specific places. It would be unwise to attempt a county cross-sectional estimate from the resulting figures, not least because of the different types of land from which the rents are quoted. There are quotations for pasture in some places, arable in others, and both open and enclosed fields in yet others, and sometimes he is unspecific with regard to land use. Nevertheless some comparisons can be drawn. Arable was fetching 14 shillings an acre at Houghton Regis in Bedfordshire, but between 18 and 20 shillings at Maids Moreton in Buckinghamshire, and as much as 30 shillings at Blandford in Dorset. In contrast, pasture or grass or meadow was generally worth much more, from £3 an acre at Dunstable in Bedfordshire, down to £2 or less at Hesket in Cumberland, up to £6 in several places in Lancashire, but as low as £1 or less at Great Chart in Kent. In fact the quotations for all manner of lands throughout Kent were all on the low side.[6] Neither the generally high levels of these figures nor the relative distinction between arable and broadly pasture use, finds support in the national rent index and its regional components which are presented below in chapters 8 and 9.

Young and Eden were two individuals collecting rental material in a relatively unsystematic and unsophisticated way. The first real attempt to

---

[2] Quoted in R.C. Allen, 'The price of freehold land and the rate of interest in the seventeenth and eighteenth centuries', *EcHR*, 41 (1988), 43.
[3] Quoted in G. E. Mingay (ed.), *Arthur Young and His Times* (London, 1975), p. 183.
[4] A Young, *The Farmer's Tour through the East of England*, 1 (London, 1771), pp. 23–4.
[5] So much is clear from a perusal of the *Annals of Agriculture*.
[6] See the handy table constructed from Eden in D. E. Ginter, *A Measure of Wealth: The English Land Tax in Historical Analysis* (London, 1992), pp. 428–43.

collect material in any remotely methodical way came only with the formation of the Board of Agriculture in 1793, and the problems encountered by its reporters point to some of the very real difficulties that faced contemporaries who sought to extract information in a coherent manner.

The Board of Agriculture reports (1793–1816)

The Board of Agriculture was the first national initiative specifically concerned with agriculture. Promoted and chaired by Sir John Sinclair, a noted Scottish agricultural innovator, the Board helped to produce enthusiasm for improved farming and the exchange of ideas. Initially it needed information, and Sinclair's intention was to promote a statistical account of agriculture, on a parish-by-parish basis. After an objection by the Archbishop of Canterbury, who feared the survey would turn into an inquiry into tithes, Sinclair's original vision was changed to the production of a series of county reports. Many of the reports in the first round were produced quickly, but superficially, and Sinclair's hope of a general report arising from the individual county submissions did not come to pass. In any case, the surveys were of very varied quality, and for our purposes one of their more obvious weaknesses was in regard to rent: as the historian of the Board of Agriculture has written, 'one of the notable gaps in their investigations is rent. It is only used to give a description of the quality of a district, and even then Arthur Young apologizes for mentioning it at all.'[7]

In the second round of reports a concerted effort was made to persuade the reporters to collect information and comment according to a specified plan. One section was on rents. Arthur Young, who was Secretary to the Board and wrote a number of the second-round reports, was assiduous in collecting rental data in the counties he visited,[8] although Marshall, never much of a fan of Young, considered the Lincolnshire material to be of little use:

This would seem to be another subject to which the Reporter has not paid mature attention. He has filled nearly a sheet of paper with memoranda, loose and incoherent as sand, relating to the rents of lands in Lincolnshire; – generally, without describing their specific qualities or situations, further

---

[7] R. Mitchison, 'The Old Board of Agriculture (1793–1822)', *English Historical Review*, 74 (1959), 41–69, especially 52 quoting A. Young, *General View of the Agriculture of the County of Oxfordshire* (London, 1813), p. 36.

[8] A. Young, *General View of the Agriculture of the County of Lincolnshire* (London, 1813), pp. 46–58. Young's report was completed in 1799 and published as a second edition in 1813 with only the title page changed, Mitchison, 'Old Board', 51–2. For similar examples of his careful collection of rental figures see also Young's reports in the *General Views ... of Norfolk* (London, 1813), *Hertfordshire* (London, 1804), and *Oxfordshire* (London, 1813).

than by the name of some village, perhaps, which ninety-nine readers of a hundred never before heard of, and, unless in a few instances, without any authority given for the insertion of the respective rates of rents.[9]

Whatever Marshall may have thought, it hardly mattered, because few of the other reporters were anything like as rigorous. William Pitt writing on Worcestershire in 1813 provided only two or three average figures for the whole county, and no individual regional figures in the style of Young. Vancouver, reporting on Devon in 1808 is similarly vague. Worse still, many of the reporters provided no figures at all, so we have no rental data for Cambridgeshire, Derbyshire, Devon, Dorset, Durham, Gloucestershire, Nottinghamshire, Wiltshire, Worcestershire, and the East Riding of Yorkshire.

In the majority of cases rental material was provided in a format that must make us wary of using it. Several reporters noted the difficulty of being sure that they were repeating accurate figures rather than make-believe calculations. Pitt, writing of Leicestershire in 1809, argued that 'this subject [i.e. rents] can only be stated in a general way as minute enquiries of this kind are looked upon with suspicion, and considered as an over curious prying into private affairs'.[10] Similarly, Batchelor, writing of Bedfordshire in 1808, commented that 'the average rent of any particular parish is frequently as little known to many of the farmers who occupy it as to a person at a distance, as it is a question which would scarcely be asked among neighbours, in a direct way, without giving offence'.[11] Gooch, reporting on Cambridgeshire in 1811, noted that 'correct information on this subject, however desirable, is not attainable by an indifferent person, nor indeed can it be reasonably expected from those whose interests may be, and there is reason to believe has been, affected by such communication'.[12]

A second problem with the rental material provided by the Board of Agriculture reporters is that all too often it was given in vague and amorphous terms. At its worst, this type of reporting was epitomised by the reporter from the West Riding: 'it is difficult for us to say what may be the real rent of land'.[13] Even a respected agricultural writer like Nathaniel Kent, reporting from Norfolk in 1796, was unwilling to commit himself: 'respecting the scale of rent, it is the most difficult question to answer, with precision, of any the Board requires; for there is nothing so unequal in the kingdom, as the rent of land', although he did then produce a few figures.[14] Even Young found the effort too much on occasion, as in his 1797 report on Suffolk: 'to ascertain the rent of the several districts is impossible; nothing more is to be

[9] Marshall, *Review*, III, p. 120.   [10] From *ibid.*, IV, p. 215.   [11] *Ibid.*, IV, p. 584.
[12] *Ibid.*, IV, p. 634.   [13] *Ibid.*, I, pp. 368–9.   [14] *Ibid.*, III, p. 324.

expected than to guess, with some degree of approximation to the truth'.[15] In his second report on the county he admitted to the utility of ascertaining the rent of land in every county in the kingdom, but he also recognised some of the problems of finding it out. There was the obvious problem of deriving a county-based average figure for rent, and there was also a prior problem of collecting the individual observations from farmers. This involved the delicate matter of their suspicions when anyone asked for this kind of information, unless it had something to do with taxation.[16]

Other reporters estimated, in the absence of hard facts. Pitt, writing of Staffordshire in 1808, estimated average rents at about 20s an acre in 1796 and 25s in 1804, but added that these were speculative figures largely founded on his opinion that 'I have no doubt but the average value is increasing in consequence of progressive improvement.'[17] Similarly Boys hardly inspired confidence with his conclusion regarding Kent in 1796 that 'perhaps I may not be very wide of the truth, if I state the average rent of the county to be 15s per acre'.[18]

A third problem, and one which was the bane of almost every reporter's life, was that average figures for the county were often more or less meaningless. A few reporters simply offered an average figure without comment. Thus Mavor on Berkshire in 1813 recorded simply that the average was 21s an acre for every type of land.[19] Others offered a range. Worgan, writing on Cornwall in 1815, noted merely that 'the rental of the whole county may fluctuate between 5s and 50s per acre, of farms properly so called'.[20] Others tried following Arthur Young to provide 'representative' figures for the various districts within their counties. The variations, and with them the frustrations for the reporters, were considerable, and were usually expressed in terms of differences between types of land (arable, meadow, pasture), between size of holdings, and in relation to distance from towns. Across the country rents rose with proximity to towns, most notably, if not surprisingly, around London. Stevenson, writing of Surrey in 1813, noted that 'when we come within seven or eight miles of London the rent rises considerably running from 40s to £3. Still nearer the metropolis, the ground that is possessed in small quantities by cow-keepers, nurserymen, &c. lets for £6, £8, or sometimes £10 per acre.'[21]

---

[15] *Ibid.*, III, p. 427.

[16] In 1803 he had calculated that the 800,000 acres of Suffolk had annual rents which varied from 2.5 shillings per acre on the fens to 14 shillings on the rich loams, giving a county rental income of nearly £437,750. In 1813 he re-estimated on the same 800,000 acres annual rents of 4 to 18 shillings per acre and a county rental income of £538,664. A. Young, *General View of the Agriculture of the County of Suffolk* (London, 1813), pp. 15–20. Note that the 1831 Census of England and Wales reckoned that Suffolk was 918,760 acres in extent.   [17] Marshall, *Review*, IV, p. 30.

[18] *Ibid.*, V, pp. 429–30.   [19] *Ibid.*, V, p. 78.   [20] *Ibid.*, V, p. 536.   [21] *Ibid.*, V, p. 377.

London was not alone. Writing of rural Huntingdonshire in 1811, Parkinson noted that 'the rents run from 5s per acre, to 30s per acre; in a very few instances to as high as 40s in one instance to as high as 120s; but that it will be seen is in the neighbourhood of Huntingdon, where such rents are given for small pieces of land, for the conveniency of gentlemen, tradesmen, &, keeping a horse, cow, &c.'.[22] Plymley, writing of Shropshire in 1813, noted how

> land is measured by the statute acre, and it varies from 8s or less per acre, to 12s in districts where the roads are bad, and where the landlord has not interested himself in the improvement of his estates, or where the agent has gone on in the beaten track of superintendance; and from 15s to 20s per acre, and more, the farm together, in more favourable situations. Near towns land lets from £2 to £6 an acre; and in the manufacturing parts of the county small parcels of land also let high.'[23]

This interesting feature, a kind of Von Thunen style distance decay, was also noticed by Eden in the 1790s. Thus certain lands which he came across commanded £3 to £4 10s an acre near Monmouth, but only £1 at a distance, and grass was let at £3 near Frome in Somerset but between £1 and £2 at a distance. Land at a distance from Lichfield in Staffordshire was let on average for 30 shillings an acre, but for £3 to £4 near the city, and land which was contiguous to Hull in East Yorkshire was let for £4 to £5 per acre but dropped to an average of 30 shillings four to five miles from the city.[24]

In general, the rents around London were both more stable and also a good deal higher than in most, if not all other parts of England. In about 1800, not only were rents higher in the Home Counties, farm for farm and soil quality for soil quality, but within them there was also a sharp rent gradient away from London. For example a farm at St Pancras was let for 100 shillings per acre, another at Hendon for 54 shillings, and another at Pinner for 19s 4d. In Lewisham one particular farm was let for 50 shillings, while further out at Orpington another went for 11s 6d, and further away still one went for 10 shillings. In Essex, the farms controlled by St Thomas's and St Bartholomew's Hospitals let for 13s 9d, 10s 4d, 9s 8d respectively per acre from east London outwards to the Essex coast. Proximity to London was important, particularly because it was related to broad land use and the

---

[22] *Ibid.*, IV, p. 419.
[23] *Ibid.*, II, p. 233. On the Dudley estates in the mid-nineteenth century, 'The proximity of the large market in the industrial areas probably explains the higher rents', T. J. Raybould, 'The Dudley estate: its rise and decline between 1774 and 1947' (University of Kent, PhD thesis, 1970), p. 319.
[24] Ginter, *A Measure of Wealth*, pp. 428–43. On checking in Eden it appears that Ginter misquoted one of the Hull figures. He quoted the average rent four to five miles from Hull at £3 (p. 441), whereas the true figure of 30 shillings is taken directly from Eden, F. M. Eden, *The State of the Poor* (London, 1928 edn edited and abridged by A. G. L. Rogers), p. 357.

ability to exact higher rents for pasture, a factor which was directly
influenced by the demand for meat and dairy products.[25] By the time of the
agricultural depression in the 1830s one witness reported that the vicinity
around London was one of the few areas which managed to stabilise rents,
and still the rent gradient was evident. Closer to London the rents were
higher by about 5 shillings an acre, or one eighth higher than other rents just
a few miles further out.[26]

Rents were also affected by the nature of measurement and the unit of
account, particularly in the north. Writing of Lancashire in 1795, Holt noted
that:

> the rent of land is very variable in the different parts of the county, from 10
> shillings to 10 pounds per annum, the large acre, of eight yards to the rod;
> the latter enormous sum being frequently paid in the vicinity of large towns,
> for particular accommodation. The price paid by the farmer is from ten
> shillings for some barren lands, up to twenty, thirty, forty, and some (but not
> many) as high as eighty shillings per acre per annum (large measure) – which
> is somewhat more than two acres and one tenth, statute measure.[27]

In sum, the Board of Agriculture reporters collected a considerable
amount of general evidence relating to rents, although as some were aware
by quizzing farmers they could be less than certain as to the quality of their
data. In any case, because of the demand for the mythical average, the
material itself is too varied and too generalised to offer us anything other
than an indication of broad trends in the movement of rents over time. Yet if
the reporters achieved nothing more, they at least stimulated an interest in
rents which, coupled with what contemporaries recognised as the rapid
increase in rent levels during the French wars between 1793 and 1815,
persuaded others to follow where they had led.

Nineteenth-century contemporary estimates

The demand for statistics was gaining considerable momentum by the early
nineteenth century. Overtly there was the generation of data through the
emerging new national 'institutions', such as the introduction of the
decennial census in 1801, and covertly there was the generation of data
through other means, such as the introduction of income tax in 1799. On the
basis of the Property Tax of 1810/11 and 1814/15, McCulloch subsequently

---

[25] B. A. S. Swann, 'A study of some London estates in the eighteenth century' (University of
London, PhD thesis, 1964), pp. 151–2, 155.
[26] First Report of the Select Committee on the State of Agriculture; with Minutes of Evidence and Appendix, BPP
[79], VIII, Part 1 (1836), evidence of Francis Sherborn of Bedfont, near Staines, Middlesex, a
farmer of 1,600 acres, Qs. 3998–4000, 4015, 4090–3.   [27] Marshall, Review, I, p. 278.

came to a national rent estimate of 17s 3½d per acre in 1810–11 rising to 20s 2d per acre in 1814–15. At the county level in 1810–11 the highest rents (excluding Middlesex) were found in Leicestershire (just over 27 shillings per acre) and the lowest in Westmorland (just over 9 shillings per acre). There was a reasonably clear east/west gradient from low to high rents with a rough-and-ready distance decay from London to the north-west (see figure 2.1).[28] The broad progression from corn production, to mixed farming, and finally to grass-related output, from east to west across England may be an accurate reflection of general land values, especially as the nineteenth century progressed, but the distance decay from London may easily be a throwback from the more distant origins of early local taxation. By 1836, in the light of the problems faced by agriculture in the depression following the French wars, McCulloch estimated English rents at 17s 3½d per acre, which was a fall back to the same level as he suggested they had been in 1810–11.[29]

McCulloch essentially regurgitated the facts which others had gathered, a practice followed by many other nineteenth-century commentators. Depending on the source of the data there is the considerable problem of selection bias with which to contend. A case in point concerns the periodic editions of [George] Mulhall's *Dictionary of Statistics*, from which the broad trend of nineteenth-century agricultural rents can be discerned.[30] Other nineteenth-century 'arithmetists' also addressed the question of rent, although their data are often recycled or second hand, and therefore derived from their predecessors.[31]

James Caird, an authoritative voice in the second half of the nineteenth century, reported in 1850–1 on many agricultural matters, and while his descriptive perambulations around the country throw up some interesting facts, it is his summary tables which are the most useful.[32] In his opening pages we learn that Buckinghamshire rents ranged from 10 shillings per acre

[28] J. R. McCulloch, *A Statistical Account of the British Empire*, 1 (London, 1837), p. 531.
[29] *Ibid.*, p. 532. Note that the figures quoted for 1810–11, 1814–15, and 1836 are different from the estimates attributed to him and quoted in the *Royal Commission on Tithe Rentcharge: Minutes of Evidence* (London, 1934), p. 44.
[30] The actual trend more or less agrees with the one we have constructed, but the figures quoted for individual years are quite considerably higher than ours, and indeed higher also than those estimated by R. J. Thompson. Mulhall's figures are quoted in *Tithe Rentcharge*, p. 44. This source also summarises the equally high rents quoted by Christopher Turnor. Turnor was a substantial landowner in Lincolnshire who supplied R. J. Thompson with particulars of his estate. See Thompson, 'An inquiry', reference to Turnor on p. 58. There is, therefore, quite a lot of recycling of evidence to contend with in constructing an aggregate rent index from published sources. The *Dictionary of National Biography*, unnumbered volume for 1931–40 (Oxford, 1949), says that Christopher Hatton Turnor (1873–1940) came into his inheritance at Stoke Rochford Hall, with its associated lands in Lincolnshire, in 1903 on the death of his uncle. He owned 24,000 acres, 4,000 of which he took in hand at his inheritance. Even though the worst of the depression had passed it was not paying its way in rent.
[31] See the interesting summary in *Tithe Rentcharge*, pp. 44–5.   [32] Caird, p. 480.

for the lowest quality undrained clay lands under tillage, to 50 shillings per acre for what Caird called prime grazing lands. His county summary suggests an average rental of 26 shillings per acre, but in the light of the cross-county range this figure is almost meaningless.[33] He was sensitive regarding the definition of rent. He suggested that not only should it reflect the produce from the land but that this could then be simplified by reference to the broad staple stock of output – the corn and the grass. Thus rent was a function of derived demand, not from innate soil fertility, though the relationship of the two is perhaps closer than Caird wished to recognise. The average rental of the Midland and Western counties, those definably mixed corn and grass districts, he reported as 31s 5d per acre, in contrast to the chiefly corn-producing districts of the east and south-coast counties of 23s 8d per acre. The former varied from 42 shillings in Lancashire to 26 shillings in Derbyshire and Buckinghamshire, and the latter from 30 shillings in Lincolnshire and Berkshire to 17 shillings in Durham. Such harsh boundaries can only form approximate, but still meaningful regional disjunctures, although as Caird recognised with Wiltshire the 'chalk and cheese' distinctions have to be accommodated. In north Wiltshire the 'cheese' had an average rent of 35 shillings per acre, while the 'chalk' of the downland of south Wiltshire was valued at exactly half that at 17s 6d per acre.[34] Figure 2.2 is the map of county average rents which can be derived from Caird's data.

A national average may lose its significance and meaning given such disparate measures, but Caird's English average was 27s 2d per acre. He also pointed out that the regional differences had become adjusted and made more complicated as the transport network of England developed. Thus in Arthur Young's day there seemed to be a simple, and rough-and-ready relationship, with the distance from London, the distance decay to which we have already alluded. In 1770 average rents in Berkshire were 19s 6d per acre reducing gradually to 7s 6d in Cumberland.[35] Such a simple pattern prevailed into the nineteenth century, as we saw above in relation to the Property Tax of 1810–11 (figure 2.1), but it became less clear when the railway network developed. Rent was related generally to the derived demand for products, but the market conjunction of demand and supply was clearly adjusted more dramatically by the more or less once and for all change in supply conditions which came with the improved transport network. Francis Sherborn predicted this in his evidence to the 1836 Select

[33] *Ibid.*, pp. 2–3, 480.
[34] See also the significance of this during the late-nineteenth-century agricultural depression on the Longleat estate in D. P. Gunstone, 'Stewardship and landed society: a study of the stewards of the Longleat estate, 1779–1895' (University of Exeter, MA thesis, 1972), pp. 86–7.
[35] Caird, p. 479.

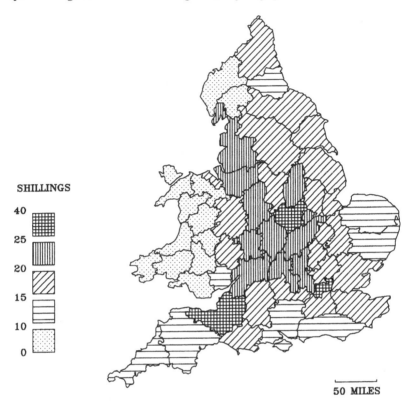

SHILLINGS

40

25

20

15

10

0

50 MILES

Fig. 2.1 Rent per acre, 1810–11

Committee on the State of Agriculture. He was a farmer from Bedfont in Middlesex, near Staines. In discussing the progressively higher rents that prevailed towards London he suggested that 'the railroads in progress will have a tendency to equalize the prices all over the country, which will take away the advantage, if we have any, of the vicinity to London'.[36] Yet figure 2.2 goes a stage further than simply to reflect the spread of the railways and industrialisation. It suggests that rents in the pastoral north and west had overtaken those in the grain-producing east and south. Our analysis in later chapters certainly confirms that rents in broadly pastoral counties rose much faster than those in broadly grain counties, but that it was not until the last quarter of the nineteenth century that they actually caught up. It will be seen, therefore, that our findings are somewhat at odds with Caird's. However, recognising that change both within and outside agriculture must

[36] *First Report*, Q. 4092.

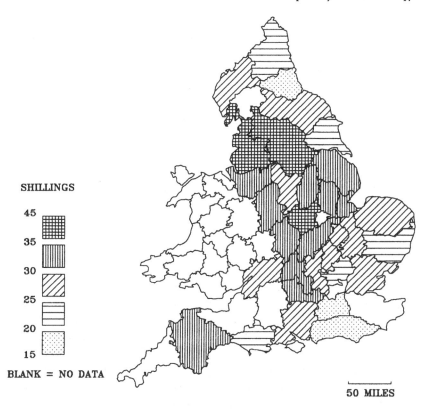

SHILLINGS

45

35

30

25

20

15

BLANK = NO DATA

50 MILES

Fig. 2.2 Rent per acre, 1850–51

sharpen views on rent, and although our intention in this book is to produce a national rent index, we will circumscribe our enthusiasm for a definitive index with greater discussions in chapter 9 of broad regional and land-use variations.

Prize essay writers in the *Journal of the Royal Agricultural Society of England* (*JRASE*)

The Board of Agriculture collapsed in 1822, and for the next two decades there was no single body in England responsible for the promotion of agriculture. This gap was at least partially filled with the formation in 1838 of the Agricultural Society of England and Wales (subsequently promoted to the Royal Agricultural Society). The Society published its transactions for the first time in 1840, and in an introductory essay Philip Pusey wrote of how the embryonic society would channel its exertions 'not so much in stimulating as in methodising the general desire for improvement'.[37] The aim of the society became 'practice with science', and to this end it promoted (among many other things) a series of essays on the agriculture of each county of England.

These essays were designed to develop the Society's aim, as expressed in its charter, of encouraging improvement,[38] and to do so by comparing current findings with the Board of Agriculture reports compiled a generation earlier.[39] C.S. Read, reporting from Buckinghamshire in 1855, noted that rents varied greatly across the country with land south of the Chilterns fetching 35 shillings an acre, the Chiltern range 20 shillings, the mixed loams of central Buckinghamshire 30 shillings, the Vale of Aylesbury 42 shillings, the dairy lands of the Oxford clays 22 shillings and the oolitic soils of the north of the county 28 shillings. He concluded that an overall average for the county was about 30 shillings an acre, an increase of no more than 2s 6d on the level of 1809.[40]

As with the Board of Agriculture reports, the material collected varied considerably and since the aim of the essays was essentially to study improvement and good practice, rental figures were of distinctly secondary importance. Some reporters made no mention at all of rents, including R.W. Corringham writing on Nottinghamshire in 1845, Samuel Jonas on Cambridgeshire in 1846, George Legard on the East Riding in 1848, and John Jephson Rowley in his prize essay on Derbyshire in 1853.[41] Others produced figures which can accurately be described only as vague. Thus George Buckland writing of the Kent chalklands in 1845 noted 'rents for arable farms from 30s to 45s; ... 2s 6d to 4s for marsh land per acre. The rents for pasture land are much higher'. Of the Weald he estimated rents at 'about 20s'.[42] Hugh Raynbird, writing on Suffolk in 1847 merely cited 'the authority of a gentleman' to the effect that the considerable differences in quality in the eastern sand districts ensured that 'land may be found on nearly every farm, the value of which to rent will vary from 5s to 28s per acre'. This is not very helpful, but except for some vague figures for the salt marshes, he gives no other direct evidence.[43] By contrast, in the same volume, Colbeck, writing on Northumberland, produced a map showing

[37] P. Pusey, 'Some introductory remarks on the present state of the science of agriculture in England', *JRASE*, 1 (1840), 21.   [38] *Ibid.*, clxx.
[39] P. Pusey, 'On the agricultural improvement of Lincolnshire', *JRASE*, 4 (1843), 288.
[40] C. S. Read, 'Report on the farming of Buckinghamshire', *JRASE*, 16 (1855), 310.
[41] R.W. Corringham, 'Agriculture of Nottinghamshire', *JRASE*, 6 (1845), 1–43; S. Jonas, 'On the farming of Cambridgeshire', *JRASE*, 7 (1846), 35–72; G. Legard, 'Farming of the East Riding of Yorkshire', *JRASE*, 9 (1848), 85–136; J.J. Rowley, 'The farming of Derbyshire', *JRASE*, 14 (1853), 17–66.   [42] G. Buckland, 'On the farming of Kent', *JRASE*, 6 (1845), 262, 284.
[43] H. Raynbird, 'On the farming of Suffolk', *JRASE*, 8 (1847), 261–329, esp. 264.

the physical characteristics of the county and the rent to be expected in each area.[44]

The problem with these essays is that the writers seem to have been under no instructions as to how they should construct the argument, and as a result few seem to have worried too much about what they may have seen as minor issues such as rent. For our purposes, however, this renders the material of little value. Indeed, the Royal Agricultural Society concentration on improvement left little room for such mundane matters. The first 25 volumes of its journal, 1840–64, contain only six indexed references to rents, and in some instances these are provided without any indication of acreage.[45] The second series of volumes, covering 1865–74, contains no indexed references to rents in England, and of the nine references for the years 1875–84 only one is identifiable to a particular area, in this case Derbyshire. Rent was simply not an issue, at least before that period for which we already have good data.

Conclusion

The debate over assessing and setting rents which we examined briefly in chapter 1 can now be set into the context of widespread vagueness about the pattern of rent in England, at least prior to the mid-nineteenth century. For all the expertise that went into farming, and into commentary upon farming, the question of rent levels – however central it may have been to the business calculations of individual farmers – remained largely unanswered, and sometimes unasked among commentators. The total stock of knowledge amounted to little more than the disparate and often unrelated evidence collected by individuals from Young to Caird, by the Board of Agriculture reporters, and by essayists in the Royal Agricultural Society's transactions. The collection and analysis of rental data really began only in the 1830s, and as we show in chapter 6 it was forced upon a slightly reluctant government by the need to understand the problems faced by the farming community in times of depression. In chapter 3, however, we review the current state of knowledge and the extent to which on a broad canvas historians have attempted to plot the course of rents over long periods.

---

[44] T. L. Colbeck, 'On the Agriculture of Northumberland', *JRASE*, 8 (1847), 422–7; see p. 190 below.
[45] For example see J. Grey, 'A view of the past and present state of agriculture in Northumberland', *JRASE*, 2 (1841), 159–60; C. S. Read, 'Recent improvements in Norfolk farming', *JRASE*, 19 (1858), 291.

CHAPTER 3

The current state of knowledge

Contemporaries knew relatively little about rents and there has inevitably been a knock-on effect for historians. Equally inevitably, historians have looked for ways of filling the gap in order to try to work out the trend in rents across time. In this chapter we look at the methods used to reconstruct the long-term pattern of agricultural rent, and in doing so we ask searching questions about the existing state of knowledge. Without much doubt modern agrarian historians know a great deal more about trends and patterns than Arthur Young, James Caird, and their contemporaries, but if we are to look with any certainty at the significance of rent for agricultural history, and for the economic history of industrialising England more generally, we need to be sure that our conclusions are anchored in rock and not in sand. To this end, we shall argue that modern attempts to reconstruct rental trends may have the parameters of the argument more or less right, within limits, but that a more systematic approach is required to ensure that we are building on reliable foundations which will not crumble.

Long-term trends

The starting point for any study of this nature must be the index of rents published thirty years ago by J. D. Chambers and G.E. Mingay and reproduced here as figure 3.1.[1] Chambers and Mingay used guesstimates. They worked from a 'small' sample of rents, skewed towards the eighteenth century.[2] On those grounds alone we have to be cautious about their findings because no attempt was made to collect data systematically, although there is no reason to believe that for this reason alone their work is seriously at fault.

---

[1] Chambers and Mingay, p. 167.
[2] Private communication with Gordon Mingay, for which we are grateful.

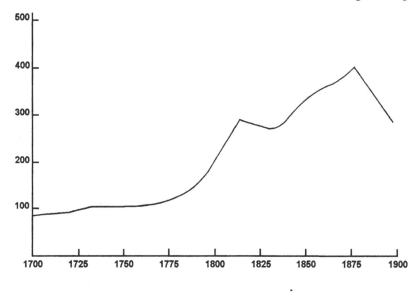

Fig. 3.1 The Chambers and Mingay rent index, 1700–1880

Figure 3.1 has a number of features. First, it shows a small rise in rents *c*. 1700 to *c*. 1730, followed by a levelling off to *c*. 1770. This levelling off was a consequence of the agricultural depression of the 1730s and 1740s.[3] However, this depression was regionally specific and some northern and western areas actually enjoyed rising rents throughout these decades. On the Swinburne estates of Durham and Northumberland rents rose over the period 1715–30 by two-thirds, and by 1750 they were more than twice the level of 1730. There was also a smaller, but continuous rise of rents on the Allgood estates and also on the Northumberland estate of the Earls of Carlisle, though in this case the occurrence of arrears from the 1730s onwards suggests the presence of a depression of sorts for the tenants.[4] Given these circumstances, it is not surprising to find that the overall effect of the agricultural depression is hardly noticeable in figure 3.1.[5] Although the depression was over by *c*. 1750, Chambers and Mingay argued that there was a time lag before rents rose, and that no sharp rent increases occurred until the 1760s or 1770s. In their view rents rose 40–50 per cent from *c*. 1750 to

[3] G. E. Mingay, 'The agricultural depression 1730–1750', *EcHR*, VIII (1956), 323–38.
[4] P. Brassley, *The Agricultural Economy of Northumberland and Durham in the Period 1640–1750* (London, 1985), pp. 76, 82. For examples from other Northumberland farms and estates see Hughes, 'Northumberland', pp. 270, 279, 282, 294, 303.
[5] For a discussion of the regional history of the depression see J. V. Beckett, 'Regional variation and the agricultural depression, 1730–50', *EcHR*, 35 (1982), 35–51.

c. 1790, the great majority of this increase being posted after 1770. This was for land not affected by enclosure.[6] The second clear trend from figure 3.1 is the steep rise in rents during the war years 1793 to 1815. Based on their conclusions from the work of Thomas Tooke and the reports prepared for the Board of Agriculture, Chambers and Mingay argued that while the rent of individual farms may have risen as much as three or even fourfold above the level prior to the outbreak of war in 1793, 'the more general figure seems to have been in the order of about 90 per cent'.[7] After 1815 the sustained upward rise of the two previous decades ended. The 1820s saw some landlords making considerable permanent reductions, and there was no widespread rise again until the later 1830s. Even with these reversals, by the later 1830s 'farmers in general were then paying rents which were still not far from double the pre-war level'.[8] After 1835 'rents definitely moved upwards to reach a peak in 1879' and 'The total gain in rents between 1815 and 1879 averaged between 25 and 45 per cent, but there were wide variations.'[9] This could not be sustained in the late-nineteenth-century depression, and Chambers and Mingay estimated that by 1900 the average level had fallen back to the levels of *c.*1815. They concluded that 'landlords really made their permanent gain from the doubling of rents which occurred during the wars of 1793 to 1815, for in the long run it was the 1815 rent, or thereabouts, which proved to be the level that could be held'.[10] This is the main message which comes from figure 3.1.

To date no one has attempted to supersede the conclusions drawn in figure 3.1. Indeed, it was reproduced in volume VI of the *Agrarian History of England and Wales*,[11] partly because no attempt was made in that volume to improve on the contemporary figures of Arthur Young and James Caird, supplemented by some general figures from the Rev. Henry Beeke for *c.* 1800, and from the Income Tax Schedule A returns.[12] No material was introduced from archival sources.

Only one serious attempt has been made to improve on figure 3.1, and this is to be found in the recent work of R. C. Allen.[13] However, his work is partial in that it is regionally specific to the Midland counties, although it has

---

[6] Chambers and Mingay, p. 112.
[7] *Ibid.*, p. 118. There are countless examples in contemporary literature demonstrating the great rise in rents during the war, some of which were itemised in chapter 2. Equally, there are numerous historians who have verified this trend. Thus on a sample of seven individual Northumberland farms rents increased by over 400 per cent in some cases from 1795 to 1810, and in all cases except one by as much as 100 per cent, Hughes, 'Northumberland', p. 209, and see also p. 241.
[8] Chambers and Mingay, p. 129.   [9] *Ibid.*, pp. 159, 167.   [10] *Ibid.*, p. 167.
[11] J. V. Beckett, 'Landownership and estate management', in Mingay, *AgHist*, p. 621.
[12] Mingay, *AgHist*, pp. 1108–9, 1111–13.
[13] R.C. Allen, 'The price of freehold land and the interest rate in the seventeenth and eighteenth centuries', *EcHR*, 41 (1988), 33–50, especially 42–4; Allen, *Yeoman*.

the benefit of covering a long time-span from the mid-fifteenth to mid-nineteenth centuries. Allen's data are of two sorts: individual farm observations, and village-wide assessments. In all there are over 1,600 separate observations, of which nearly 1,100 relate to individual farms and over 500 to villages. In the period from 1650 onwards, which most closely overlaps with our work, there are 900 farm and nearly 500 village estimates. Most of these are based on individual observations spread across the whole time period, but on occasions the data bunches in individual years. For example, for 1727 alone there are over 200 farm observations from 15 separate villages in Northamptonshire; for 1806 there are nearly 180 village-wide estimates covering the counties of Bedfordshire, Huntingdonshire, and Rutland; for 1811 Allen has a further 103 village-wide estimates for Northamptonshire; and there are 143 farm observations from Oxfordshire and Northamptonshire in 1844. Conversely, for some years there are no observations at all.[14]

Figure 3.2 shows the simple rent profile which can be constructed from these data, separating the farm from the village observations. They have been constructed not just as the mean of the separate observations in the individual years, but rather as the weighted mean employing the size of farm or size of parish/village as the weighting parameter. In addition, although Allen collected these data for a study based on the economic effects of enclosure, and this might suggest selection bias, in the event the only detectable partiality relates to the specific geographical confines of the study, and what he has produced is a rent index for the east and south Midlands. The data relate to an important adjustment in farming organisation – enclosure – and to an important distinction in farming – arable or pasture production. As a result we are able to study rents before and after enclosure, in enclosed and open situations, and in terms of broad land-use divisions. However, the relative paucity of continuous evidence before the 1770s persuaded Allen, in his published work, to rework the data into an index based on 25-year averages.[15]

The reconstructed index shows some patterns familiar from the work of Chambers and Mingay. The depression resulting from falling prices in the second quarter of the eighteenth century is plain to see. Although this was not as clear-cut in figure 3.1, it is no surprise to find it showing through in figure 3.2 given the location of the observations in the south and east Midlands where there was a concentration on arable production on heavy

[14] We are grateful to R. C. Allen for supplying us with his complete database and inviting us to use it. The counties for which he collected evidence are: Bedfordshire, Berkshire, Buckinghamshire, Cambridgeshire, Huntingdonshire, Rutland, Oxfordshire, Northamptonshire, Leicestershire, and Warwickshire.   [15] Allen, *Yeoman*, pp. 171–2; Allen, 'The price of freehold land', 43.

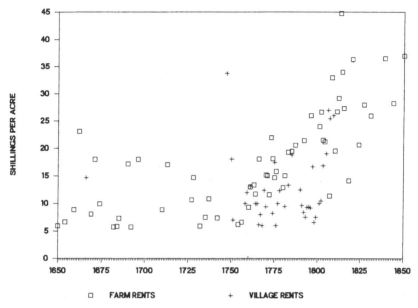

Fig. 3.2 A Midland Counties rent index, 1650–1850

clay soils. The late-eighteenth-century price and rent inflation is also clear, especially during the French wars of 1793 to 1815. The reversal in prices after the war can just about be seen, though apart from one or two outstanding years the number of observations diminishes rapidly after 1814.

Allen's data also reveal a clear relationship between size of farm and unit rents: in general the smaller the farm the larger the unit rent.[16] For a few selected years there are large numbers of farm observations which give the individual farm acreages and the rents paid. Figure 3.3 takes the form of a scattergram demonstrating the relationship between farm size and rent per acre for 1727. These observations are taken from over 200 farms in 15 Northamptonshire villages. While the graph is not a perfect hyperbola, there is nevertheless a clear demonstration that the large or largest unit rents occurred on the smaller or smallest farms, or at least that there was much more variation in rents on the smaller farms and conversely much more uniformity of unit rents on the larger farms. Figure 3.4 is a similar, but not as clear demonstration of the same effect involving 42 farms in five Oxford-

[16] We produce supporting evidence of this in chapter 6 in a discussion of the evidence from the late-nineteenth-century depression. We offer some explanations of why these patterns occurred.

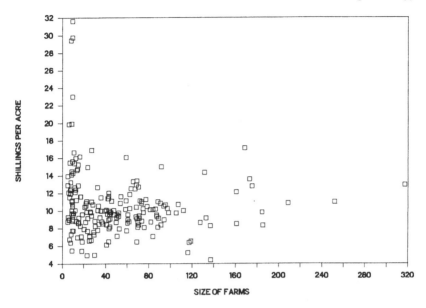

Fig. 3.3 Unit rents and farm sizes in Northamptonshire, 1727

shire villages and 101 farms in 17 Northamptonshire villages in 1844. To a degree, the higher unit rents on smaller farms may reflect the inclusion of dwellings which carry a disproportionately large share of the final rent, but the main reason will relate to the better quality land and the more intensive methods of production.

Allen's data can also be used to show the distinction between rents on arable land and on pasture (figure 3.5). Rents tended to be higher on the heavy lands relative to the light lands, but more importantly the rents on pasture tended to be higher than on arable down to 1750. This undoubtedly reflected the long-term decline in grain prices since the mid-seventeenth century as a result of which landlords on the Midland claylands attempted through voluntary enclosure or other means to increase the pasture acreage.[17] After about 1750 the difference between the pasture and the arable rents is neither consistent nor very great. However, this may be a reflection of the data since these interpretations are often based on single,

[17] For a specific example see J. V. Beckett, *A History of Laxton: England's Last Open-Field Village* (Oxford, 1989), pp. 107–14. For a general statement about land hunger in the Midlands with regard to extending available pasture see M. E. Turner, *English Parliamentary Enclosure: Its Historical Geography and Economic History* (Folkestone, 1980), chapter 6.

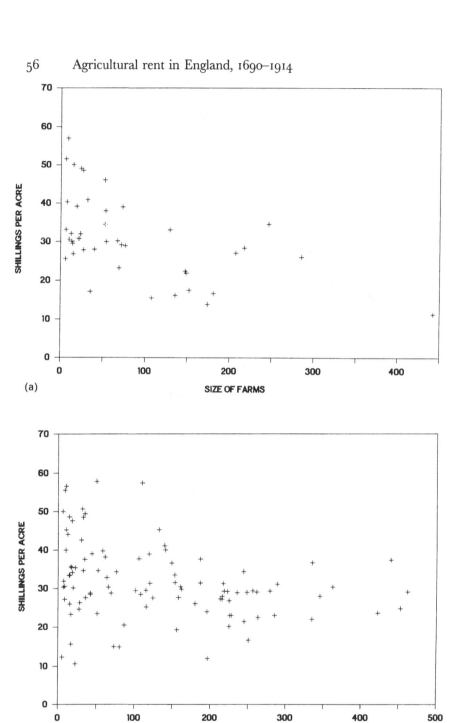

Fig. 3.4 Unit rents and farm sizes in (a) Oxfordshire, (b) Northamptonshire, 1844

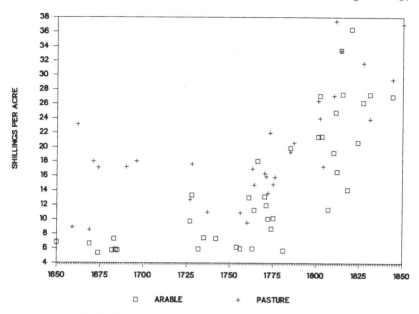

Fig. 3.5 Arable and pasture rents in the Midlands, 1650–1850

widely spaced observations: only from the 1770s are there regular annual multiple observations.[18]

The Chambers and Mingay and Allen indexes were attempts to construct national or very large regional profiles of changes in unit acre rents. A. D. M. Phillips has used rental data to look at several estates over large, and not

[18] Gregory Clark has constructed a rent index for the period from the early sixteenth century to the mid-nineteenth century, based on the evidence which was presented to the Charity Commissioners in the 1820s and 1830s. See G. Clark, 'Agriculture and the Industrial Revolution: 1700–1850', in J. Mokyr (ed.), *The British Industrial Revolution: An Economic Perspective* (Oxford, 1993), especially pp. 244–7, based on *Reports of the Charity Commissioners* (in 32 volumes (but volume XXXII in 6 parts), *BPP* (1819–40). The method of extraction and construction is not clear, however, and therefore the value of the index is open to question. For example, a superficial inspection of the Charity Commissioners' reports suggests that the charities were dominated by small 'estates' or farms. Even where the total acreage possessed by some charities was large, it was generally let in small farms. If on closer inspection this proves to be the case then, as figures 3.3 and 3.4 indicate, any index using this source is likely to be biased towards high unit acre rents, and therefore cannot be representative of agricultural land as a whole. In addition, the economics of letting this land is subject to opposing interpretations: since these rents were intended for subsequent charitable disbursement, it may have been incumbent on the trustees to rack rent to the absolute limit; but equally, since the trustees were third parties – neither payers nor payees, but middlemen without salary or profit from the transactions – they may have been less inclined to take their duties as seriously as would 'regular' landlords or stewards. Drawing on commentary from both the Charity Commissioners and also the 1894/6 Royal Commission, B. E. S. Trueman touched upon both of these possibilities, 'Corporate estate management: Guy's Hospital agricultural estates, 1726–1815', *AgHR*, 28 (1980), 31–2.

Table 3.1. *A nineteenth-century rent index*

	Annual average rent per acre in shillings	
Five-year periods	Rent index: Devon, Northants, and Northumberland	Rent index Devon and Northants
1800/1804	15.2	15.2
1805/1809	16.6	16.6
1810/1814	18.6	20.5
1815/1819	18.7	21.3
1820/1824	18.4	20.6
1825/1829	18.4	21.8
1830/1834	17.3	17.5
1835/1839	15.1	18.1
1840/1844	16.0	20.6
1845/1849	15.8	20.7
1850/1854	15.8	19.4
1855/1859	16.4	19.6
1860/1864	17.6	22.4
1865/1869	18.5	24.1
1870/1874	20.2	26.5
1875/1879	21.3	27.5
1880/1884	19.9	26.3
1885/1889	19.0	24.7
1890/1894	19.2	25.6
1895/1899	17.0	21.4

Source: Derived from A. D. M. Phillips, *The Underdrainage of Farmland in England During the Nineteenth Century* (Cambridge, 1989), pp. 156–7.

necessarily contiguous areas.[19] Table 3.1 presents the composite index we have derived from Phillips's research. It is based on a sample of estates from Devon, Northamptonshire, and Northumberland. The Northamptonshire data arise from splicing together the discontinuous records from nine estates, but there are data from the county throughout the series; the Devon data arise from splicing together the discontinuous records from five estates, and these begin in 1830–4; and the Northumberland data arise from splicing together the discontinuous records from five estates, which begin in 1810–14. The maximum acreage covered is 324,269 acres in 1870–4. Figure 3.6 translates table 3.1 into a graph. It shows that at a level where a smaller subset of the putative national index is taken, which is still nevertheless based on a large number of estates, the rent index which has been produced moves more or less in line with the current knowledge of the course of rents in the nineteenth century, including all of the familiar features – the inflation of rents during the French wars, the effects of the post-war depression, recovery in rents up to the nineteenth-century peak at the end of the 1870s, and finally the late-nineteenth-century depression. The significance of

[19] A. D. M. Phillips, *The Underdrainage of Farmland in England During the Nineteenth Century* (Cambridge, 1989), pp. 156–7.

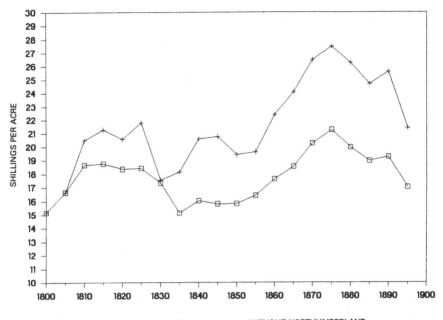

□ WITH NORTHUMBERLAND   + WITHOUT NORTHUMBERLAND
Fig. 3.6 A nineteenth-century rent index. Annual averages 1880/4–1895/9

drawing two profiles – one with and one without Northumberland – will be revealed in chapter 8.

Proxies

In the absence of a clearly constructed rent index which is based on a large dataset, and with relatively little good contemporary data, an alternative approach has been to look for proxies, which imitate rental trends and therefore offer a means of establishing the broad pattern across time.

An obvious starting point is the social surveys of eighteenth-century political arithmeticians such as Gregory King, Joseph Massie, and Patrick Colquhoun.[20] Their findings implied something about the position of

[20] From a wide literature see G. S. Holmes, 'Gregory King and the social structure of pre-industrial England', *Transactions of the Royal Historical Society*, 27 (1977), 41–68; P. Mathias, 'The social structure in the eighteenth century: a calculation by Joseph Massie', *EcHR*, 10 (1957), 30–45; F. M. L. Thompson, 'The social distribution of landed property in England since the sixteenth century', *EcHR*, 19 (1966), 505–17; P. H. Lindert and J. G. Williamson, 'Revising Britain's social tables, 1688–1913', *Explorations in Economic History*, 19 (1982), 385–408. Textbooks of the period often start with, or include a section on England c.1688 in which Gregory King's data are used as a cross-sectional summary of the economy and society in the final quarter of the seventeenth century. In this context see P. Mathias, *The First Industrial Nation: An Economic History of Britain 1700–1914* (London, 1969), pp. 23–31; P. Deane and W.A. Cole, *British Economic Growth 1688–1959* (Cambridge, 1969, 2nd edn), p. 2; D. C. Coleman, *The Economy of England 1450–1750* (Oxford, 1977), p. 6.

Table 3.2. *Income from agriculture, 1688, 1759, and 1801/3 (£ million)*

	Income 1688 (% of total)		Income 1759 (% of total)		Income 1801/3 (% of total)	
High titles and gentlemen	8.81	(16.2)	11.74	(17.6)	27.54	(13.9)
Agriculture	12.21	(22.4)	16.66	(24.9)	38.00	(19.1)
Labourers	4.27	(7.8)	4.20	(6.3)	10.54	(5.3)
Cottagers and paupers	2.04	(3.7)	1.25	(1.9)	2.60	(1.3)
Sub-total	27.33	(50.1)	33.85	(50.7)	78.68	(39.6)
Total of all incomes	54.44	(100.0)	66.84	(100.0)	198.58	(100.0)

Notes: 'Agriculture' excludes labourers and constitutes freeholders and farmers only. In 1801/3 the labourers were those engaged in husbandry, but in the other two years labourers included those both in husbandry and in commerce. In 1801/3 the cottagers and paupers were simply categorised as paupers.
Source: N. F. R. Crafts, *British Economic Growth During the Industrial Revolution* (Oxford, 1985), p. 13.

agricultural rent in the national income accounts. As N. F. R. Crafts has written, 'presumably rents, especially agricultural rents, must be represented as a large part of the incomes of the "High Titles and Gentlemen", but the amount cannot be pinned down accurately'.[21] Table 3.2 is a summary of these putative rents, set more widely in an agricultural framework, and with the national estimates of all income for comparison. It is based on Lindert and Williamson's revision of the original social tables, and further revised by Crafts into a much simpler format. We include the calculated incomes accruing to 'Agriculture', which by definition excludes labourers (they have a separate heading) but includes freeholders and farmers.[22]

Although these figures are indicative of long-term trends they clearly are not sufficiently specific to stand in place of a rent index. Another possible proxy is the records of taxation since, in proportional terms, taxes presumably reflected income. As such, and subject to suitable adjustments, tax records ought to act as a proxy for income which, in the case of landowners, would be predominantly from rent. If this assumption is correct, although taxation records may not furnish us with nominal rents, in a circular way they may provide us with a trend of rents. Although the theory is plausible, the practice depends on finding a suitable set of records. Ostensibly the eighteenth century Land Tax which, as its name implies, was essentially an extraction from the income of land, and the late eighteenth and nineteenth-century Income Tax, ought to provide a useful starting

[21] N. F. R. Crafts, *British Economic Growth during the Industrial Revolution* (Oxford, 1985), p. 12.
[22] If in the case of farmers a proportion of their incomes flowed away as rents to the landowners, then there will be double counting in these estimates. This seems highly unlikely. A more probable view is to assume that these income estimates are net.

point. We shall discuss each of these briefly, although neither quite fits the bill.

The Land Tax

The Land Tax, levied throughout the eighteenth century as a development of seventeenth-century assessments on land, might be expected to form at least a surrogate for landed income, or rather of the direct income or rent from the land. If the tax acquired from an income-bearing asset bears a reasonably steady relationship to the actual income from that asset, and if the income in turn bears a reasonably steady relationship to the changing value of the asset, then surely something like the Land Tax can be used as an index of that income and value? At first sight, since the tax was levied at fixed amounts at certain times, the answer is surely yes, since even when the rate of levy of the tax was changed from, say, four shillings in the pound to one, two, or three shillings these changes ought to be reconcilable.[23]

In reality such a construction turns out not to be possible. The Land Tax in its eighteenth-century form was set in the 1690s, but based on much older methods of taxing. It was designed to raise money to meet the emergency financial pressures of the Nine Years War, into which England had entered on the accession of William III in 1689. Initially it was designed as a tax on income, but like so many earlier schemes, the harsh reality of raising money from a reluctant public via an amateur and not over-efficient local government structure forced central government effectively to abandon such hopes. By 1698 it was effectively a tax on land, and the decision to revert to county quotas that year – whereby the government set the sum to be raised and left it to local administration to decide how to assess and collect the tax – brought an end to hopes of a realistic tax on incomes. Thereafter it was not reassessed. The quotas became fixed, and were raised at either 100 per cent, 75 per cent, 50 per cent or 25 per cent (expressed by government as 4, 3, 2, and 1 shilling in the pound). Each year the government passed a new Land Tax act, and rules and regulations were laid out about assessment and collection. As everyone knew, these rules meant very little; each county collected its quota by whatever mechanism it chose, which in some cases was one that had been in operation long before 1698. No allowance was made for inflation or ability to pay (in terms of population increase, or change in the levels of wealth). The result was that while the Land Tax was strictly

---

[23] Amongst a large literature see J. V. Beckett, 'Land tax or excise: the levying of taxation in eighteenth-century England', *English Historical Review*, 100 (1985), 285–308; J. V. Beckett and M. E. Turner, 'Taxation and economic growth in eighteenth-century England', *EcHR*, 43 (1990), 377–403.

speaking a tax on land – because within most counties the basic unit of assessment was land – it was not a levy on the actual income or value of land during the eighteenth century.[24] These misfortunes might not be so critical had the Land Tax represented real values in the 1690s, but even the chance that the tax bore some base relationship with the reality of property income in that decade is stolen from us. The government decision in 1698 to revert to quotas reflected a serious assessment problem. The 1693 Land Tax assessment – traditionally regarded as the beginning of the Land Tax proper although in reality it was only an extension of earlier practices – raised £1,922,713, the largest sum ever collected from a single annual extraordinary tax. Thereafter the sums collected slipped, until in 1697 the yield of £1,663,435 was just 89 per cent of the 1693 figure. In some desperation Parliament reverted to county quotas, fixing the sum raised from each county in 1693 as the sum to be raised thereafter on a four-shilling rate.

This decision might not have excluded the Land Tax as a proxy for rents had the sums raised in 1693 represented four shillings in the pound nationwide. No one doubted, however, that this was not the case, and figure 3.7, the county distribution of acres per county quota of the Land Tax in 1707, makes this abundantly clear.[25] In theory the distribution may properly have reflected the value of land at the time, and hence of agriculture and the distribution of rent, but given the extremes in the burden across counties this seems doubtful. In Middlesex £1 of tax represented less than one acre, but in Cumberland it represented 262 acres, and in Cardigan 323 acres. There was a decreasing burden, if we can put it in this way, north and west from London. The northern MPs had argued strongly in the 1690s that a national tax at a common rate (i.e. four shillings in the pound) was inequitable when comparing their relative poverty with the supposed wealth of southern England. When they lost the arguments their JPs, acting as Land Tax commissioners, took evasive action: 'Cumberland', as William Fleming MP noted in a letter to his father in Westmorland, 'will fare easily about the Land Tax in consequence of the prudent act of the commissioners in the first four shilling aid'.[26] Figure 3.7 shows that the Cumberland commissioners were not alone.

[24] From a large literature see J. V. Beckett, 'Local custom and the "New Taxation" in the seventeenth and eighteenth centuries: the example of Cumberland', *Northern History*, 12 (1976), 105–26; J. V. Beckett, 'Westmorland's "Book of Rates"', *Transactions of the Cumberland and Westmorland Antiquarian and Archaeological Society*, 77 (1977), 127–37; J. V. Beckett, 'Land tax administration at the local level 1693–1798', in M. E. Turner and D. R. Mills, *Land and Property: The English Land Tax 1692–1832* (Gloucester, 1986), pp. 161–79.
[25] Redrawn from D. E. Ginter, *A Measure of Wealth: The English Land Tax in Historical Analysis* (London, 1992), p. 310.
[26] Historical Manuscripts Commission, *The Le Fleming MSS* (1890), p. 350.

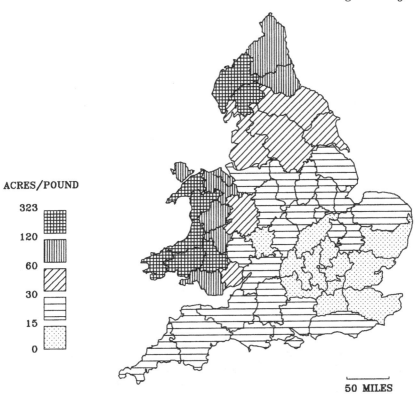

ACRES/POUND

323

120

60

30

15

0

50 MILES

Fig. 3.7 The county distribution of the Land Tax in 1707

This was the position in 1698, and we know enough about distance decay factors to suggest that it might be possible to construct a national index or a series of cross-sectional regional indexes of land income, land values, or rent. Realistically, however, we would need more than one 'reading' for this to be possible, and here we run into an insurmountable problem. After 1698 the government abandoned the Land Tax. True, it continued to raise the tax throughout the eighteenth century, and indeed in various forms until it was finally abolished only in 1963. But after 1698 the experiments of the post-Restoration period, which were designed to increase government revenue from direct taxes, were abandoned. Increasingly government sought to finance itself through indirect taxation, particularly excise duties, using the Land Tax as a regular income which could act as a boost (when levied at 4 shillings in the pound) in war time.[27] As a result, the county quotas

---

[27] See Beckett, 'Land tax or excise'; Beckett and Turner, 'Taxation and economic growth'.

remained untouched throughout the eighteenth century. Adjustments were possible within counties and within parishes, but not between counties. We know that as a result considerable variation arose between counties, and that even within counties major differences of valuation were allowed to persist.[28] In these circumstances, to try to use the Land Tax assessments to construct indexes of land income, land values, or rent, would be so complex, and so liable to gross distortion, that in our view the exercise would not be worthwhile, even if an adequate documentary record were shown to exist.

Property / Income Tax

It was not until the introduction of Income Tax at the end of the 1790s that we can obtain a reasonably firm impression of the income accruing from the land, in particular with the designation of Schedule A. We can follow a similar line of reasoning to the one we adopted in discussing the Land Tax, that is, if taxes extracted from the income from the land bore a relationship to the value of the land, that value would in turn be related to the rent. Unfortunately, there are problems with the source which reduce its value to us even though the returns 'include nearly all income accruing to individuals from the ownership of property, as well as the incomes of farmers and public servants'. To begin with, the tax was collected only for the years 1799 to 1816, and again after 1842: in other words it can offer evidence for less than two decades prior to a period in which, as we shall establish in later chapters, the rental evidence is relatively full. Second, it took some time to crank up the administrative machinery, and peak efficiency was reached only after 1808.[29] In other words the best-quality figures are for 1808 to 1816, and again beyond 1842, but in the earlier period at least, patriotism during a time of war may have counterbalanced to a great extent suspicions of widespread tax evasion. Third, we are dealing with grossed-up figures since individual returns have not survived.

Unfortunately for our purposes, the gross income accruing to the income tax under Schedule A, based as it was on the annual value not the actual income received by landholders, is somewhat different from the imputed if not defined concept of rent which we are employing.[30] Furthermore, that annual value is further compromised because it is an amalgam of many different tenurial occupations of, and hence incomes from, the land.

---

[28] In general see Ginter, *A Measure of Wealth*.
[29] P. K. O'Brien, 'British incomes and property in the early nineteenth century', *EcHR*, 12 (1959), 255–67, especially 256–7.
[30] For a discussion regarding the differences between gross incomes and annual values see Sir Josiah Stamp, *British Incomes and Property* (London, 1927 reprint), p. 16.

Although for the most part income assessed was the current rent being paid, on land where this was indeterminate, or where it failed to provide an accurate indication of income, the rack rent was used as the basis for determining income.[31] But therein lies further problems. For example, Patrick O'Brien discusses how the notion of rack rent was applied to properties which were clearly not racked at the time of the tax – including land which was in owner-occupation and property on which there were long leases.[32] In the case of land on which there was not a recent lease, it was accepted that where a lease had been bargained within seven years that would count as a lease for the current year. But on other lands the legislation allowed for a current valuation, based on local discretion and local measurement. As we saw in chapter one such 'discretion' was likely to be arbitrary and further to reduce any realistic chances of using income tax returns as a proxy for rent. Nevertheless, 'By one method or another an annual value in occupation was allotted to every holding of farmland in Britain.'[33]

But what can we do with that annual value? Figure 2.1 above mapped the distribution of the Property Tax for the tax year 1810–11, but using that part of the tax which was derived from agricultural rentals and then expressed in rent per acre. There is the warning that it records the location of where the tax was levied, not wholly the location of the land on which it was levied. Apart from the obvious examples of the Oxford and Cambridge colleges and some other large institutions whose properties stretched over large non-contiguous areas, it does not require a large leap in the imagination to suppose that this map represents roughly the diversity in agricultural rent through England and Wales.[34]

Evidently there are many provisos over using the early Income Tax returns as a proxy for rents, nevertheless they might offer some guidance on the course of agricultural returns, and examples are given in table 3.3. From 1842 the legal definitions of most schedules on the Income Tax can be equated with the same definitions employed earlier in the century, therefore seemingly there should be some continuity from the earlier to the later period.[35] On the basis of the Property Tax and in association with material supplied by the Chairman of the Board of Stamps and Taxes, J. R. McCulloch estimated that the average rental for England was 17.3 shillings per acre in 1810–11 rising to

---

[31] *Brewster's Edinburgh Encyclopaedia*, VIII, p. 735.   [32] O'Brien, 'British incomes', 257–8.
[33] *Ibid.*, 258.
[34] J. R. McCulloch, *A Statistical Account of the British Empire*, I (London, 1837), p. 531. That we cannot do much more than this with the Property Tax is owing to the short-sightedness of government and the civil service. McCulloch equates the 'voluntary destruction of so great a storehouse of curious information' as was contained in the original Property Tax Returns, as unparalleled, 'unless it be the burning of the Alexandrian Library', p. 530.
[35] See O'Brien, 'British incomes', 262. See also Stamp, *British Incomes*, especially chapter 1.

20.2 shillings in 1814–15. In McCulloch's calculations the arable property taxes and urban property taxes were intermingled, which must devalue his conclusions especially during this period of rapid urban growth.[36] However, the figures suggest that while Income Tax returns may not be easily or precisely employed as a surrogate for rent, they offer an indication of trend, if only for a handful of years. The average income from real property rose from £26 million to £40.2 million from the tax year 1806–7 to 1842–3, a rise of 55 per cent. This compares with a rise in unit acre rents, as established in chapter 8 below, of 44 per cent. The large difference in these figures does not obscure the fact that both these separate indications of land values, land incomes or rents point in the same direction, and indicate a rise of substantial proportions. However, rents were rising swiftly in the first ten years of the nineteenth century but that rise was not matched by the yield in tax revenues. Thus the income from land appeared to rise by 32 per cent from 1806–7 to 1814–15 whereas rents rose by almost 43 per cent, or to put it another way, practically all of the rise in rents which occurred before the 1840s took place during the French wars. Thus there appears to have been a substantial lag in the tax yield catching up with rental incomes.

This can be substantiated in other ways. The Board of Agriculture thought that across the country the rent rise from 1790 to 1814 was in the region of 84 per cent, and in some areas this may even have been a low estimate. A rise of the order of 100 per cent has been suggested by a number of historians.[37] From his work on Northumberland, Durham, Shropshire, and Northamptonshire F. M. L. Thompson suggested that rents approximately doubled between 1778 and 1815.[38] On Thomas William Coke's settled estates in Norfolk rents more than doubled between 1776 and 1816, and on farms held throughout the period on Lord Darnley's estate they rose by 100 per cent.[39] On the Grenville family estates at Stowe in Buckinghamshire between 1793 and 1815 rent rises totalled 90 per cent; on their Wotton estate they amounted to 87 per cent, and on their Burton Dassett estate in Warwickshire 105 per cent.[40] Such levels of increase were not repeated everywhere; some parts of the country saw rather less spectacular increases, and such was the variety of experience that individual farm rents rose by anything from 20–30 per cent to 300 per cent.[41] Nevertheless, the French

---

[36] McCulloch, A Statistical Account, p. 531.
[37] G. E. Mingay (ed.), Arthur Young and His Times (London, 1975), p. 46; J. V. Beckett, 'Landownership and estate management', chapter 6 in Mingay, AgHist, p. 622.
[38] F. M. L. Thompson, 'The land market in the nineteenth century', in W. E. Minchinton (ed.), Essays in Agrarian History, II (Newton Abbot, 1968), p. 35.
[39] Parker, Coke, p. 77; H. G. Hunt, 'Agricultural rent in south-east England, 1788–1825', AgHR, 6 (1958), 100.   [40] J. V. Beckett, The Rise and Fall of the Grenvilles (Manchester, 1994), p. 81.
[41] Beckett, 'Landownership and estate management', 622.

Table 3.3. *Income from Schedule A Property and Income Tax for England and Wales,*
1806/7–1848/9

Income from land assessed under Schedule A of the Property Tax	
1806–7	£25.9m
1808–9	£27.4m
1810–11	£29.5m
1814–15	£34.3m
Income from land assessed under Schedule A of the Income Tax	
1842–3	£40.2m
1845–6	£41.2m
1848–9	£42.3m

Source: Mingay, *Ag Hist,* p. 1111. See also J. Stamp, *British Incomes and Property* (London, 1927), pp. 49, 515. Some of these figures differ from those in Stamp. This arises from Stamp's inclusion of the uncommuted tithe.

war was a period of considerable rent increase, and for during the second half of the war, when the tax records are thought to be reliable, it looks as though the tax yield lagged significantly behind rent rises.

The war years represented a period when the question of tenure was vital in matters of income distribution. Ordinarily the differences in the degree of increase or decrease in rents can be explained partly in terms of differences in soil and farming types, partly by what Caird was later to call 'the character of the landlord or his agent, and the custom of the neighbourhood',[42] but partly because ongoing inflation meant that landlords with fixed long-term tenancies – i.e. leases or agreements with their tenants – effectively had to wait until the lease expired before they could raise the rent. In the meantime, those tenants with a fixed rent but rising unit incomes because of inflation, enjoyed rising real incomes while their landlords (with the reverse fixed income from their rents) experienced falling real incomes. The Ricardian rent surpluses therefore accrued more to the tenants than to the landlords. Twenty-one year leases signed in the 1780s were due for renewal in the first decade of the nineteenth century.

There were ways to break existing leasing arrangements, by the interposition of an enclosure act, for example, which in the usual form included a clause or clauses which made null and void existing leases at rack rent. R. C. Allen has suggested that enclosure was indeed a device as much for breaking leases and reversing the benefits of Ricardian rent surpluses as it was for any other purpose, and the fact that the years from 1800 to 1814

[42] Caird, pp. 476–7.

were the busiest in parliamentary enclosure history offers some support for this explanation. On the other hand we would not wish to overemphasise this point since, however much the agricultural experts may have extolled the virtues of long leases, they were far from universal.[43] It is true also, conversely, that those leases bargained during the inflation of the war years were protected in terms of landlord income once the post-war depression set in, although the level of protection was weak since if tenants could not pay they did not pay and in due course arrears increased. In any case, although a leading agriculturalist like Coke of Norfolk went on granting 21-year leases throughout the war years, increasingly he was a lone disciple.[44]

The tide was turning against long leases by the early years of the nineteenth century. Landlords were reluctant to grant them in a time of inflation. Thus between 1795 and 1812 Lord Darnley of Cobham converted his tenants in Kent from leases to tenancies at will, so that he could more effectively tap their growing resources, and in the same county on the Camer estates at Meapham, the Smith-Masters family let Westdown farm on a 21-year lease in 1792, reduced to a 10-year lease on reletting in 1815, and finally to an annual tenancy in 1826.[45] Added to this feature of landlord reluctance to continue with long-term leases, the post-war years were characterised by falling prices which discouraged tenants from taking on long-term commitments. In 1833 the Agricultural Distress Committee was told time and again that tenants simply did not want leases. With tenant right increasingly built into tenancy agreements, the protection to tenants offered by long leases was no longer essential.

The Property Tax can offer some valuable information and insights on the changing attitude to tenure because the trend away from archaic tenures and long leases is partly measurable in the returns. In 1808, 83 per cent of the income from cultivation came from tenant farmers (and 17 per cent from owner-occupiers), of which 85 per cent was valued on the basis of current rent, or by the looser definition employed based on a rent which had been contracted within a seven-year period. This evidence allowed O'Brien to observe that since 'It had proved administratively possible to value most agricultural land on the basis of a current rent', the move away from long

---

[43] R. C. Allen, 'The efficiency and distributional consequences of eighteenth-century enclosures', *Economic Journal*, 92 (1982), 937–53; Allen, *Yeoman*, p. 17. See also hints of this in Parker, *Coke*, p. 96. For basic statistics on the chronology of enclosure see Turner, *English Parliamentary Enclosure*, chapter 3, especially pp. 68–9.

[44] Parker, *Coke*, pp. 145–6, 151–2. Elsewhere in Norfolk this was not necessarily the case, P. Roe, 'Norfolk agriculture 1815–1914' (University of East Anglia, MPhil thesis, 1976), pp. 181–5.

[45] Hunt, 'Agricultural rent', 102–3; Chambers and Mingay, p. 47; M. Roake, 'The Camer estate, 1716–1852' (University of Kent, MA thesis, 1969), p. 222.

leases must have been well advanced, or as a minimum it at least argues for the prevalence of leases of less than seven-year duration for this period.[46]

Conclusion

What we have established in this chapter is the current state of knowledge about rents, and some of the difficulties of employing substitute measures for establishing the trend of rents. It is our contention that although indexes exist, they are, for one reason or another, not definitive. Equally, there are no easy ways of proxying the movement of rent. Consequently, what is known of rent trends tends to be derived from random and not necessarily systematic studies of landed estates, with conclusions grossed up to national levels. As we shall show in chapter 7, part of the problem is caused by the lack of consistency with which historians have extracted rental data from estate archives, but it also reflects an overall lack of agreement on what is being sought and what is being presented. Consequently we turn now from the known to the unknown, to ask in chapter 4 what the parameters for a rent index should be, and then in chapters 5 to 7 to draw upon the materials available for constructing a definitive rent index and an explanation of how we have utilised them.

[46] O'Brien, 'British incomes', 263.

The determining parameters of a rent index

We have argued in the preceding chapters that the existing state of knowledge allows us to understand the broad pattern of rent movement in England without providing a systematically compiled and rationally constructed index. Yet the data to do the job properly are available in a manner and form denied to contemporaries. Whereas reporters to the Board of Agriculture found farmers reluctant to discuss their rents, and presumably neither inquired after estate accounts nor would have been granted access to them if they had asked, the material is widely available to us today. The opening up of archives through the deposit of estate papers in public repositories, has provided a vast range of documentation which historians have not been slow to exploit. Over the past several decades a great number of estate biographies have been compiled, and from some of these we are able to extract useful rental material (chapter 7). In addition, contemporary commentators had no access to the wealth of material made available to the Royal Commission on agriculture in the 1890s, which collected rental material in a methodical way. In chapters 5–7 we shall discuss in some detail the material available and how we have used it to construct a rent index, but first we examine the different ways in which such an index might be constructed, in order to determine why we have proceeded in the manner outlined in subsequent chapters.

Almost certainly there is no such thing as an ideal rent index, although it is possible to think of ways to create an index which is ideal for certain purposes. For any one year a national index could presumably be constructed by taking the total rent of all English tenanted agricultural land and dividing by the total acreage involved. For a series of years this would create a unit acre rent on an annual basis. However, as economic conditions changed, the amount of land used for agricultural purposes would grow or contract, thus altering the quantity of marginal land included in the 'national farm'. This could not adequately be controlled for unless the amount of land in agricultural use was measured appropriately and regularly. Since this is unlikely, a method of creating a consistent data population would be to take a fixed sample or quantity of the agricultural land, and then the only worry would be the measurement of rents on a regular basis. The additional advantage of employing such a method would be the ease with which subsets of the land could be generated, according to soil type, climate, elevation, land use, type of landowner, tenure, and so forth, which could then be used in comparative analyses.

Unfortunately, the surviving historical data cannot be used to create the random sample desired. Many landowners kept few records of rent payments, and on small estates this was perhaps unnecessary, or never even thought about. Even on estates where records were kept, many have either been lost or remain uncatalogued. Even where rental data have survived there has been no attempt to develop a standard method for collecting and presenting the material. Each landlord invented his own accounting method. What we must do therefore is determine the limits within which we are working, and then assess the possible approaches allowed by the surviving archives.

Determining the chronological limits

It is important that the dataset on which any index is based is as representative of the total population of English rented land as possible. For this reason our material needed to reflect the geographical diversity of the land, and to include representative accounts of the holdings and the types of ownership patterns found nationwide. Ideally, the span of years covered by an index should be long enough to cover several economic cycles, thus including times both of prosperity and of depression and, equally important- ly, to cover the period of the so-called Agricultural Revolution.

The initial boundary dates were intended to be 1660 and 1914. Around 1660 the turmoil from the Civil War had ended, the restoration of the monarchy was under way, and the redistribution of property to those loyal to the Crown was taking place. The terminal date in 1914 marks the beginning of a troubled time for land and landed society in England. The First World War dealt a savage blow to the next generation of landlords. In addition, budgetary changes associated with death duties took effect from 1918. These factors marked the beginning of a shift out of property among existing landowners. F. M. L. Thompson has reminded us that 'between 1918 and 1921 something between six and eight million acres changed hands in England. Such an enormous and rapid transfer of land had not been seen since the confiscations and sequestrations of the Civil War.'[1] The period

[1] F. M. L. Thompson, *English Landed Society in the Nineteenth Century* (London, 1963), p. 332.

between c. 1660 and 1914, therefore, was a period of relative political quiet in England as far as landownership was concerned, aside from the cyclical economic rhythms which necessarily impinged on everyone engaged on the land. It was also the period from which we would expect to find good archival sources.

In the event, using 1914 as one boundary date proved feasible, but our attempts to stretch back into the seventeenth century were impractical. As a result of the widespread disruption in landownership arising from a combination of the Civil War and the Restoration, few rentals survive from as early as 1660. Landowners were more interested in consolidating and securing their land than in the technicalities of recording their income from it. In addition, the more sophisticated accounting practices associated with good rental data were still in an embryonic state. The double-entry bookkeeping system may have been invented with estate accounts in mind, particularly the need to protect landlords from the machinations of venal stewards, but it took many years to reach the larger estates, let alone smaller ones where no agents or stewards were required.[2] From a purely practical viewpoint we found insufficient surviving data to compile an index for the period earlier than 1690, and even then the quantity of material is smaller than we would have liked. It did, however, seem possible to construct a reasonable index for the period 1690 to 1914.

Other considerations

The chosen boundary dates were to a considerable extent determined by other considerations in constructing the index. The first was the need for the survey to encompass land from all parts of the country, held under a variety of tenancy sizes and conditions, and owned both privately and by institutions. A broadly based survey should ideally provide data to examine the effect on the scale of rents of various ownership patterns, both in terms of the size of and the type of ownership. Only such a survey will ensure that tenanted holdings are included from a wide variety of land uses and from the major farming systems, including extensive and intensive grazing of cattle and sheep, dairying, mixed arable/livestock systems, and various types of arable agriculture. Rents from all principal soil types, climatic areas, and

---

[2] S. Pollard, *The Genesis of Modern Management* (London, 1965), pp. 209–10. Despite its benefits the double-entry system spread only slowly and was still not universally employed in the late nineteenth century: B. English, 'On the eve of the Great Depression: the economy of the Sledmere estate 1869–1878', *Business History*, 24 (1982), 33. The pitfalls of trying to interpret eighteenth and nineteenth-century accounting practices and developments even on a well-managed corporate estate are outlined in B. E. S. Trueman, 'The Management of the Estates of Guy's Hospital 1726–1900' (University of Nottingham, PhD thesis, 1975), especially appendix B, pp. 520–9.

topographical zones should also be examined. Farm size and lease conditions tend to vary on a regional basis. To ensure a wide coverage, each sample series ideally should include a run for a minimum of 30 years to iron out any inconsistencies and avoid atypical data. A period of 30 years has the added advantage of touching upon parts of at least one each of the periods of prosperity and depression which can be traced through the whole period. Taken together the sample estates and their rentals needed to encompass all geographical regions of the country.

This presents us with a serious dilemma because of the differences between the manner of calculating rack rents and the payment for land held under beneficial leases. It would be unsound to create a single rent index using both rack rents and either the entry fine or the annual rent associated with beneficial leasehold properties. Once we recognised that land held in beneficial leasehold would need to be be excluded from the index, we had to seek ways of relating the rentals of this large sector of agricultural land to that held at rack rent which we were able to index. On any significant scale this proved impossible. Superficially there was a possible way to determine the relationship between the two types of tenure. This was to identify land which was held under an archaic tenancy agreement but which was then sub-let at a rack rent. This was a relatively common practice. The Duke of Devonshire, for example held land from the Duchy of Lancaster which he subsequently relet. On the Dudley estate, middlemen enjoyed rack rents on copyhold cottages where otherwise the lower beneficial rent accrued to the estate itself. This was one of the factors which motivated the move towards the enfranchisement of cottage copyholds, although in this case for the benefit of the sitting tenants.[3] The very fact that it was economically viable to sub-let suggests that land held under the ancient leasehold agreements was not let at its full economic value.[4]

The difficulties inherent in creating a composite agricultural rent index containing both the traditional and economic forms of rent are sufficient to preclude the use of the more ancient and customary forms of payments in the dataset. However, we recognise that by excluding land held under any of the archaic tenancy agreements we may possibly be making it more difficult

---

[3] Chatsworth House, *Trustees of the Chatsworth Settlement*, C. 80, Estate Survey; T. J. Raybould, 'The Dudley estate: Its rise and decline between 1774 and 1947' (University of Kent, PhD thesis, 1970), p. 317.

[4] In some cases Sarah Wilmot managed to obtain an annual value for life-leasehold property, although only for the year when the rent was converted. S. A. H. Wilmot, 'Landownership, farm structure and agrarian change in south-west England, 1800–1900: regional experience and national ideals' (University of Exeter, PhD thesis, 1988), especially pp. 461–2. A significant number of western county lifeholders actually paid fines at unrealistically low valuations before 1750, C. Clay, 'Lifeleasehold in the western counties of England, 1650–1750', *AgHR*, 29 (1981), 88. We thank both Sarah Wilmot and J. H. Bettey for helpful correspondence over this issue.

to obtain a balanced sample in terms of temporal and spatial coverage as well as of ownership type, as our brief résumé of the differential survival of these tenures in the eighteenth and nineteenth centuries in chapter 1 indicated. Thus otherwise valuable rental material has been excluded from the index, which is based only on rack rents. A separate index created by using a portion of the fine, a money equivalent for any service obligations, and the annual payment for the land from such leaseholds would be a useful complement to a rack rent index. However, the two concepts, though both pertaining to a payment for the use of land, are too distinct easily to combine in one series. Essentially archaic rents pertain to a time when the use of land represented a complex socio-political relationship between owner and tenant. Land held through the payment of a rack rent was more simply an economic relationship, and it is this economic payment as a measure of the mutually agreed value of the land that the rent index seeks to measure. One of the unforeseen consequences of our research has been to highlight the durability of beneficial leases, but it has proved a disadvantage in constructing an index because we have not been able to make use of beneficial rent payments. It has increased the problem of finding good rent series, particularly for the eighteenth century.

Basis for the dataset: farm, field, or estate

The index is intended to measure as completely as possible the economic value of rented agricultural land of all types and uses in England over the period 1690 to 1914. Consequently a database with a large number of examples from across the country was required, but at what level should these be collected: the farm, the field, or the estate?

Farm by farm

An obvious approach to the task would have been to locate farms for which a long run of rents was available and for which the size of the unit was known.[5] A number of advantages could be envisaged in creating a rent index using farms. Arguably such an approach would help to maintain consistency over a long chronology and across a stable geography. Theoretically it would have been possible more easily to remove any extraneous payments such as rates, taxes, and interest on loans with some

[5] For example, W. M. Hughes does this for a number of eighteenth and nineteenth-century farms for Northumberland: Hughes, 'Northumberland', pp. 190, 195, 209, 230–1, 236, 241, 260–4, and *passim.*

confidence, in a situation where consistency of practice could be guaranteed, or almost guaranteed. Non-agricultural land might have been eliminated by locating the farm or farms on maps, thus allowing a truer assessment or even a precise measure of the purely agricultural land to be made. Lease agreements, where they existed, would have provided information on the length of tenancy, the responsibility for repairs between the tenant and his or her landlord; the number of buildings might have been included; and any restrictive practices which might have affected the rent could have been included in a discussion of the meaning of rack rent, if not in its measurement.[6]

However, this approach has a number of disadvantages. First, there was the underlying assumption that conditions remained static, that the farm or farms remained the same size, with the same buildings, with the soil remaining in consistently good or poor condition, and with an unchanging relationship between tenant and owner. This is unrealistic. The state and usefulness of the buildings might vary over time; improvements to the farm such as underdrainage or irrigation, where this took place, would increase the value of the land and essentially change its quality; the chance that between the years 1690 and 1914 many of the farms so chosen would have been included in one or more acts of enclosure is very high, especially in the Midland counties; the size of the unit represented in the rental, where the rental represented a bargain between a tenant and a landlord, could have changed but with no actual change in individual farm size. For example, the actual tenant/landlord relationship could remain unchanged except to expand and include several farms for the same tenant through a process of combination and consolidation. In other ways the apparent rental relationship could remain unaltered and yet the unit of study could change. For example, fields could have been added or removed, or the farm could have been divided between two or more tenants. Our experience was that farmholdings changed regularly, in some cases with each tenancy. On the east Yorkshire estate of the Chichester-Constables we can be sure that only 7 out of 64 farms did not change size between 1850 and 1880, and only 9 of the 20 farms on the Langdale estate during the same period.[7] Whether or not this was typical, it suggests that a great deal of care and attention would have been needed to keep an accurate check on the size of individual farms, and to trace changes would require considerable research, even supposing that the requisite archives survived. We concluded that a farm-by-farm survey

---

[6] Such an approach was strongly espoused by Christopher Clay in personal discussion, for which we are grateful.

[7] M. G. Adams, 'Agricultural change in the East Riding of Yorkshire, 1850–1880, with special reference to agricultural labour' (University of Hull, PhD thesis, 1977), p. 261.

would probably result in a small sample of fully catalogued farms, but that the sample would have been skewed and biased in terms of a small number of locations, soil types, and farming systems.

Field by field

Another possible approach would have been to conduct the study at the level of the individual field. A search through the archives might easily uncover a continuous or near-continuous run of rentals for very small units, hardly worthy of the name farm. The accounts of local churchwardens or other trustees for the poor or other charities might easily allow the study of the tenancy of the lands under their trusteeship. In more accessible form the Charity Commissioners' reports (see footnote 18 in chapter 3 above) provide in readily available, printed form, rental information for parcels of land, generally relatively small, throughout the country over many years. Depending on the charity involved, it may be possible to trace the rental history of effectively a single field, if not annually, then certainly at regular intervals over a long period. The collection, or more likely the presentation of data by the Charity Commissioners was not always consistent, but at times they recorded information on other payments associated with the lease. The resulting data are available in one multi-volume source and it is reasonably easy to use, though the extraction of the data is laborious. However, the farming units represented by charity lands are not necessarily typical either of English farmland or farming, or of the main tenurial relationships. The lands were owned by registered charities, while the most typical land in England was in private ownership. Furthermore, the parcels of land involved were generally farmed either in conjunction with much larger holdings or on small, relatively non-self-sustaining holdings. Consequently the rent which accrued to such lands did not necessarily reflect that of other agricultural land. It was also possible that the land was not used exclusively for agricultural purposes. Perhaps most significantly, as we have demonstrated in general in chapter 3, if it was generally small areas which constituted the greater number of charity estates then they would probably have attracted higher unit rents than farmland in general. An index produced from charity estates alone might have the same trend as a national index, but the nominal level of unit rent in any particular year would almost certainly be higher.[8]

---

[8] The argument of this paragraph is supported by a spot check on entries in several of the volumes. *Reports of the Charity Commissioners* (in 32 volumes, in which volume XXXII is in 6 parts), *BPP* (1819–40). In general our conclusions regarding the skewed size distribution of charity estates is verified in the *Return of Owners of Land 1872–3*, *BPP*, LXXII (1874). See the reference to Gregory Clark's work in chapter 3, footnote 18.

Estate by estate

Although we considered the possibilities of creating a rent index using a farm and a field analysis, we eventually opted to work on the basis of individual estates. Such an approach seemed to us to offer a number of positive advantages. First, the estates which have surviving records seemed most likely to provide data in a relatively well-maintained and preserved state. Second, such a database should be capable of providing a mixture of large and small farms, from many if not most of the different agricultural soil types in England. Third, the area involved for each estate was large, generally over a thousand acres and often tens of thousands of acres, and consequently in terms of the fullest coverage of English farmland a rapidly growing dataset in terms of acres covered could be guaranteed. Once established this could be maintained throughout most of the period of study. Size in terms of acres covered was seen as a major advantage. While the different estates involved might vary over time, nevertheless it should be possible to maintain a large, if not growing coverage of England. The disadvantage of discontinuity might be outweighed by sheer volume.

Methodological problems and decisions

Although we decided to adopt an estate-centred approach, we were not unaware of the methodological problems that this presented. While contemporaries may have had little difficulty defining or recognising an 'estate', we could not expect to find any consistency in terms of the archives generated, or the presentation of material within them.

The survival of an archive is somewhat serendipitous. In his study of the Dukes of Devonshire, Newcastle, and Rutland in the period 1688–1714, O. R. F. Davies found that in the Devonshire archives in Chatsworth there was a good deal of material which related to the work of the land steward, and that there was estate correspondence and the Chatsworth building accounts, but no London accounts, few rentals for the period, and no abstract of accounts. In contrast he found that the Portland manuscripts of the Duke of Newcastle at Nottingham University contained no Welbeck estate accounts and few rentals, although there were valuations. In complete contrast, the Duke of Rutland's archive at Belvoir Castle contained an almost entire set of accounts.[9] In Norfolk, the Holkham estate rentals exist in a continuous series for the nineteenth century, but the same cannot be said of the estates in the county as a whole.[10]

[9] O. R. F. Davies, 'The dukes of Devonshire, Newcastle, and Rutland, 1688–1714: a study in wealth and political influence' (University of Oxford, DPhil thesis, 1971), pp. 6–7.
[10] P. Roe, 'Norfolk agriculture 1815–1914' (University of East Anglia, MPhil thesis, 1976), pp. 9–10.

This inconsistency of survival is probably not random; rather, it tends to reflect the attitude of the owner rather than the steward. A careful cost-conscious, debt-free landlord will often be found to have kept meticulous accounts, including rentals, but quite the opposite may be the case where a spendthrift was involved. Ray Kelch, in his biography of Thomas Pelham-Holles (1693–1768), Duke of Newcastle, was unable to reconstruct much detail about the financial income or inputs to the estate although he found plenty on outputs and the expenditure patterns of the duke. The estate stewards, whose duties involved collecting the rents from the tenants on the various parts of the estate, often immediately expended those rents in clearing debts, usually through paying the interest charges on existing mortgages. The duke anticipated his rents by borrowing from his stewards against the security of the next rent collection in order to maintain his lifestyle; and when a financial trust was created to manage the estate it was soon found that rental income alone would never disencumber the estate of its accumulated debts.[11]

Landowners with a penchant for excessive spending were prone neither to keep good accounts, nor to spend wisely. In 1826 Thomas Crawfurd urged the first Duke of Buckingham to have his estates run by 'men of business that will do their duty and establish a regular system of auditing, paying, and passing your accounts half yearly'. But Buckingham had little interest in numbers and, like Newcastle before him, did all he could to make his stewards return rents to London before they had met necessary outgoings, thus increasing his spending power while building up debts on the estate.[12] Sir Clifford Constable of Burton Constable in East Yorkshire refused to listen to any business, and knew so little of his estates that when financial problems arose in the years immediately prior to his death in 1870 he was powerless to put matters into some semblance of order.[13]

From such estates we have been able to collect little material. Rightly or wrongly – or, to be more precise, practically rather than theoretically – we have concentrated on those estates which have a systematically preserved archive, and usually this has meant well-run, often larger, private estates together with those institutions where administrators were responsible to trustees or some similar type of governing body. Thus, the sample of estates with surviving rental records which can be called upon is a biased sample. It

---

[11] R. A. Kelch, *Newcastle: A Duke Without Money: Thomas Pelham-Holles 1693–1768* (London, 1974), pp. 70–4, 21, 96–100.
[12] Huntington Library, California, STG Correspondence, 369/39, 441/47. Ironically the third Duke of Buckingham kept meticulous accounts but many of them were stolen by a venal steward in the 1870s, for which see J. V. Beckett, 'The Stowe Papers', *Archives*, 20 (1993), 187–99.
[13] B. English, 'Patterns of estate management in East Yorkshire, *c.* 1840– *c.* 1880', *AgHR*, 32 (1984), 47.

is self-selected, and we are wholly dependent on those archives where the material was not only recorded, but where it has also survived, and is accessible. Consequently, what can be collected represents a compromise some distance from the ideal, and the position is further complicated once we investigate the nature of estate accounting.

Where the income found in estate accounts included non-agricultural rentals, or land let under beneficial leases, or land for which no acreage could be found, and other unwanted incomes, it was necessary to exclude those incomes or rents. In some cases this was easier said than done. However, after some experience and familiarisation with estate accounts it became possible fairly quickly to assess their usefulness. For example, gradually a picture was built up of the trend in rents from the 'national farm' through the early construction of, and additions, to the national rent index. It became possible to make an initial assessment of whether the rents from a particular estate, and the trend in those rents, in association with the estate acreages, was producing plausible estimates of unit acre rents. If those rents were composites of rack and other kinds of rents, in which the beneficial rents were very extensive and important, they usually stood out when making this comparison. It was where these other rents were not particularly important that difficult decisions had to be made. Often, the safety-first line which we adopted was to remove these elements where they were clearly identifiable, or omit entire estates when there was any doubt. Fortunately, many estate accounts were kept in such a manner that such elements could easily be identified, and excluded, to leave only the agricultural rack rents in the database. The ideal estate rental separately listed non-agricultural elements and archaic rents, such as income from mines, urban or industrial properties, and beneficial lease rental income. The ideal estate archive also gave some indication of the acreages involved both in the agricultural and non-agricultural sectors. Surveys were particularly important in identifying these disparate components of the rental income. The need to guard against including non-agricultural rents in the dataset was a major problem when collecting on an estate-wide basis.

On many estates entirely separate accounts were kept for rents which derived from non-agricultural uses. This was particularly true of long-established rents associated with land which was also used for mineral extraction or for traditional industries. As industrialisation spread, however, quantities of land which had formerly been in agricultural use were increasingly allocated to industrial uses or were employed to satisfy the insatiable appetite of the burgeoning urban housing market. There were a number of more subtle problems. 'Cottages' could range from the individual homes of farm labourers to whole estate villages containing artisans and people in service occupations. The cottage rent was justifiably included if it housed the former but not the latter. In many cases labourers' cottages were rented as an integral part of a farm, and these were considered to be farm buildings, in which cases they were not deducted from the rental payment. However, when an estate listed cottages separately from the farms, there was a greater likelihood that these were part of the landlord's property which he rented out separately from the agricultural land, in which cases they should be and were excluded from the purely agricultural rents. However, even where it was not always possible to make this distinction, the cottage rents were very often associated with large estates and therefore with large acreages of agricultural land, and therefore the resultant influence they had on unit acre rents was small. For example the cottage rents on the Dudley estate represented only just over 1 per cent of the total of cottage and great rents in 1701, and in 1817 and 1836 they had risen to 4 per cent, to 6 per cent by 1850, and to nearly 10 per cent by 1924.[14] In this case the estate grew from 6,646 acres in 1824 to over 11,000 acres in 1883. We can only conjecture what this means concerning the acquisition of cottages when new lands were acquired, or indeed the relative value of the cottages to the land and how this varied over time but it does, perhaps, emphasise one of the recurring problems in preparing a rent index: the need for reliable and regular land and estate surveys.[15] Woods and plantations might also appear either as an integral part of a farm, or as separately rented land. Their purpose could be agricultural, providing shelter belts, or providing mast and other such feeds, or for hurdle making, or indeed for timber for commercial use, or they could be recreational or decorative.[16] However, in order to focus only on agricultural land where it was identifiable, the income from and the acreage of woods and plantations was excluded.

Rental data frequently contain hidden elements which may affect the overall shape of a rent curve. The assessed rent might, for example, include taxes, tithes, and rates, repayments of loans from the owner to the tenant, and interest on those loans. Where these were included the 'apparent' value

---

[14] Raybould, 'The Dudley estate', appendix 9, p. 584.
[15] *Ibid.*, and see also p. 46 for a conjecture regarding the sudden rise in rents which occurred apparently in 1811: 'There is little evidence to suggest that the dramatic increase in total rents for 1811 resulted from an extension of estate property', a statement which is still rather open-ended regarding the history of the estate. It would appear however that there was an increase in the number of cottages in the 1780s and 1790s associated with the enclosure of commons and wastes, thus perhaps explaining the increase in the contribution of cottage rentals before 1817 (p. 309), and from the mid-nineteenth century there was a move to enfranchise copyhold cottage tenures, though giving first refusal on the freehold to the sitting tenants (pp. 315–17).
[16] The value of such timber was often substantial and was almost always an integral part of estate income. For example, on the Sledmere estate the value of wood amounted to 21 per cent of the gross income in 1874, and 19 per cent in each of the years 1871, 1876, and 1877. English, 'On the eve of the Great Depression', 25, 28.

of the land was enhanced. The value of the land represented its ability to bear some of these costs as well as the unhindered bargain which the landlord had with his tenant, which is the most precise meaning we can come to for a rack rent. Often responsibility for these various components of the rent shifted between the tenant and the owner.

A particularly good example of the impact such hidden elements might have on the rent and the value of the land can be demonstrated by considering farm buildings, and in particular the repairs needed to maintain them in a satisfactory condition. The presence of appropriate buildings was an important feature of a good farm. For example, until the invention of milking bails during the twentieth century, dairying was dependent on stalls and a milking barn. During the depression of the late nineteenth century, particularly in arable farming, one way of attracting new tenants into empty farms was to construct buildings suited to dairying. Generally the rental of a farm reflected the state of the buildings. Thus, on a single farm, as the physical state of buildings deteriorated a corresponding fall in the real value of the farm could be expected. To protect this valuable feature of the farm, leases often explicitly specified the responsibility for repairs; it either rested with the tenant, with the owner, or jointly. Typically an owner would provide the materials not found on the farm and the tenant would provide the labour required for repairs and upkeep. The degree of responsibility assumed by the farmer for repairs was, in fact, an element in his rent. Thus, a tenant with complete responsibility for repairs would be expected to pay a lower rent than if a part of the cost of repairs was borne by the landlord. This, however, was rarely valued in monetary terms, and could shift according to the financial state of both the tenant and the landlord. Failure to maintain buildings could be used by the landlord to evict a bad tenant. On the other hand, a good tenant in financial difficulties could be forgiven the need to make repairs, which, in practice, was an abatement of rent.

Some accounts do record payments by the landlord for buildings and repairs, although only rarely do they give any indication of the share of costs undertaken by the tenant. Leases almost always provided details of the division of responsibility, and estate correspondence often adds details reflecting the attitude of the landlord towards tenants who failed to fulfil their part of the bargain. These subtleties may be overlooked when we are collecting rental material at the level of an estate. Ideally, data from farms on which the tenant was expected to undertake repairs should be offset against those on which this was not the case. Otherwise, particularly in difficult years when the landlord might relieve the tenant of some of the burden of repairs, we might not pick up the precise low point in the rent curve because this will have been blunted by an alteration of the terms of the agreement brought about to meet a particular situation.

The foundation of the new rent index is firmly rooted in the estate accounts of individual landed families, and yet we clearly cannot either ignore or overlook the relevant material which can be found elsewhere, particularly in the collections of data prepared for, and in conjunction with, the late nineteenth-century government commissions, and also the data acquired from other estates which have been studied in detail. These sources are outlined in chapters 6 and 7. A summary of both the primary and secondary data sources which have been incorporated in the rent index, with detailed provenances, is tabulated in appendix 1. This appendix takes the form of a set of biographical accounts, including a thumbnail sketch of the origin of the archive in question, the chronological completeness of the rents and the surveys each one contains, the geographical location of the lands from which the rents were due or received, and an indication of the size of the estate.[17]

This means, in effect, that although a considerable proportion of the data has been collected from archives the length and breadth of the country, it has been supplemented by material put together by other authors and scholars. This creates a minor methodological problem. *In the main* our data refer to single estates, or to large parts of large estates. For example, the property belonging to the Manvers family centred on Nottinghamshire but spilling into adjacent counties, includes the details from four separate 'collections', as they were termed, and also from two detached parts of the estate in West Yorkshire (Adwick) and in Wiltshire (Bradford). In this sense the Manvers property is treated as six separate properties, or estates, or archives. The same is true of the property owned by Guy's Hospital. This was located in three distinct places, in Essex, Lincolnshire, and Herefordshire, and we count this as three separate archives. Similarly the property owned by the Duke of Bedford was located in three distinct places: the family seat at Woburn, which included land in Bedfordshire and Buckinghamshire; the Tavistock estate, principally found in Devon; and the Thorney estate in the counties of Cambridgeshire, Huntingdonshire, and Northamptonshire. In consequence there are three entries for the Bedford estates. Conversely, the property belonging to the Earl of Yarborough in North Lincolnshire was regarded as four collections by the Earl and his managers, but because as much as 85 per cent of it was located in and around Brocklesby, the remnants (although quite sizeable in their own right)

---

[17] The actual data which were extracted are too large to include as an appendix, but since they constitute a volume of statistics in their own right, we have made it available for general use through the ESRC Data Archive.

at Grimsby, Irby, and Brigg have simply been lumped together with Brocklesby to form a single (though not contiguous) presence in north Lincolnshire. Our method means that estates can be located at least within specific counties, if not more closely to specific places.

When we come to use data collected by others, the position is more complicated. A number of estate owners who presented evidence to the Royal Commission of 1894–6 took up the option offered to them to remain anonymous.[18] Most of them did at least indicate in which counties their estates were located, but a handful of other important archives cannot be located so easily and specifically. These include the collected estates of the Oxford colleges, and the lands of St John's College, Cambridge, for both of which it was not possible to locate the land precisely. The estates of the Ecclesiastical Commissioners also presented difficulties. For the periods for which we have details, from 1880–92 and also from 1900–14, the sum total of their lands varied in size between 212,000 and 290,000 acres, scattered throughout England, albeit with some major groupings in some counties. It is impossible to disaggregate this material into specific counties, let alone more narrowly. A similar problem would have applied to the Crown Estate material but for the fact that the greater proportion of it is conveniently divided into six estates in six separate counties. We have included these six properties as six separate estates, but at the cost of losing several thousand acres from the rent index from those remnants of the Crown Estate which we cannot locate separately.

The net effect of taking into account these few variations in what we refer to as 'estates' or 'archives' is that the maximum number of estates included in any one year in the index, seventy-seven estates in 1888, rather falsifies the picture. If we joined the three sections of the Guy's estate into one single estate, and similarly if we joined together some of the other estates, such as the scattered Bedford estates, we would end up with fewer estates in total. Conversely, we could end up with many more estates in number if we could properly locate the diversified lands owned by the various Oxford colleges, the Ecclesiatical Commissioners, and others. Thus, the number of estates we refer to in chapter 7 must be regarded as an order of magnitude rather than a precise measure.

Conclusion

The conditions under which we have necessarily worked have ensured that we cannot produce an ideal rent index. Yet, while the historical data are by

---

[18] Royal Commission on Agriculture, 'Particulars of the Expenditures and Outgoings on Certain Estates in Great Britain and Farm Accounts', *BPP*, C. 8125, XVI (1896), pp. 20–33.

no means perfect, we are confident that by working within the parameters set out in this chapter it has been possible to collect information adequate for the purposes we have set ourselves. The sample of rentals is large in acreage terms because it is structured around estate accounts. By eliminating the influences from beneficial and similar leaseholds the data are largely free of certain considerations one normally associates with the traditional socio-economic obligations once existing between landlords and tenants. The rents will represent as near as possible the economic value placed on the land and the sample will be based purely on agricultural land. Obviously the index can only be as good as the data on which it is founded, and we have tried to recognise that there are problems we cannot hope to circumvent. We would argue that we have put together a database which in its overall coverage of English agricultural land is certainly much more comprehensive than anything previously achieved. We also believe that it is as close to being representative as can be expected without a much greater investment of time and resources, and that such an investment would be unlikely to produce more than marginal improvements on our findings.

CHAPTER 5

Constructing the rent index I: estate records

Having set out in chapter 4 the parameters within which we are working, we turn now to our methodology, and in particular to the way in which we selected estate records for inclusion in the database and then to the decisions we took about how and what data we should record.

We were fortunate in that we did not have to begin our study 'cold'; indeed, we enjoyed the benefit of a pilot study conducted some years ago by J. R. Wordie. The study was designed to uncover archival material relating to the administration of landed estates between the seventeenth and nineteenth centuries. As a result, Wordie listed the availability of rental material in record repositories across the country which he believed could be used to construct an index of rack rents of agricultural land.[1] In addition, we consulted a number of historians and historical geographers with specialist knowledge relating either to agricultural rents, or to related subjects. We requested, and were generously offered advice on our methods and suggestions regarding archival sources.[2] Finally, archivists in Record Offices around the country were kind enough to point us in the direction of other sources which might prove useful.[3] Our inquiries left us with a list of approximately 200 archives which merited further investigation. This generally involved visiting archive repositories to sample a selection of account books, rentals, and surveys of the estate records held in each, in order to ascertain whether or not the material was of sufficient quality to be included in our work. As a result, one-third of the archives in our original selection had to be rejected, generally because they did not have adequately

[1] J. R. Wordie, 'Pilot investigation into the sources available for the study of English landed estates between 1640–1840', *SSRC Final Report*, HR 4510, September 1978.
[2] Our numerous correspondents are thanked in the preface to this book, and mentioned hereafter specifically only where they have provided particular information.
[3] Anthony Smith of the Royal Commission on Historical Manuscripts was particularly helpful in guiding us through the National Register of Archives, and in giving us access to ongoing work at the Royal Commission on the archives of major landed families.

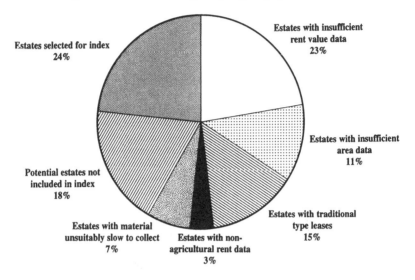

Fig. 5.1 English agricultural rents: details of estates surveyed

long rental series backed up by survey material containing acreages. A further 15 per cent contained land let under archaic tenures and 3 per cent involved rentals in which agricultural and non-agricultural uses were indistinguishable (see figure 5.1).

Estate selection

Having eliminated a number of archives which contained either insufficient or inadequate data the next step was to sample in more detail the papers available for the remaining estates. During this phase a further 7 per cent of the original group of identified archives was rejected because the material they contained was organised in such ways as to make their extraction unacceptably time consuming. This may have been because they were organised farm by farm and required laborious mechanical aggregation, or it may have been because each rental for each year or half year was contained in a separate book or ledger, and archival restrictions on the number of individual items which could be consulted at any one time suggested a disproportionate time would have to be devoted to that archive. These are just two of the reasons why some archives had to be rejected.

The material was originally recorded in a number of ways. Often complementary volumes of accounts and rentals of varying usefulness and complexity survived in an archive. Probably the most basic were the rental books which recorded the rental payments as the rents were collected. They contained many alterations, often without explanation, and the rents from the farms on the estate were only occasionally totalled at the foot of the page. One type of account book, often referred to as a 'cash book', recorded rents as they were paid. Within these cash books all receipts and expenditures for the year were listed according to the date of payment. For an investigation of the timing of rent payments, the ability of tenants to pay on time, and of other similar questions, they proved to be a good source. Occasionally it would have been possible to use cash books alone, particularly to construct schedules of rents received. However, again, it would have been a laborious business to extract the many individual transactions which took place, even on relatively small estates, and then to co-ordinate them yearly in order to achieve a short, let alone a long-run series of farm and estate rentals. Time was better spent on other sets of rentals which were kept in a more structured way. Some of these were organised annually by estate or for a number of years according to individual tenants or individual farms. While rentals arranged according to tenants or farms would have been ideal for a survey conducted farm by farm rather than on the basis of entire estates, or if the question of stability of tenure was under investigation, for the task we set ourselves it was prohibitively slow to extract such data. On many estates, particularly the larger ones, the rent information was entered annually into an account book to await audit. These accounts usually provided an abstracted annual total of previous arrears, assessed rents, rents due, rents received, and arrears still owing, arranged either by 'collection' or for the estate as a whole. Ideally the area of land, measured in acres, on which the rent was levied was also included, although all too often this was not the case. The accounts sometimes contained useful 'remarks' or 'observations' relating to changes in tenancies, additions or exchanges of land, abatements, increases in rents due to improvements, and other similar information. This proved useful in the detective work which was necessary, and which is outlined below, in piecing together the precise extent of estates as they changed over long periods. Payments made by the landlords towards rates, tithes, and taxes or repairs were also recorded. Such volumes were particularly useful and provided the bulk of our data.

During the sampling process a number of features had to be checked in each archive. It was important to assess the consistency of data over the span of the rent series. To presume the continuity of any one system of accounting during the entire period of a run of rents suggests a stability in estate management which was not often found. There was little standardisation of accounting practices, and it was common for the format to change regularly.

These changes most often took place at strategic times: at an owner's death; when estates went into or out of trusteeship; when a new owner took an active interest in improving or consolidating an estate; or when new agents introduced a different system of management. The excellent run of accounts for the Thoresby estate in Nottinghamshire began when the estate passed into the hands of a trust following the death of the 1st Duke of Kingston in 1725. For this reason, when coming afresh to an estate archive it was important initially to select a sample of documents containing a variety of rents and accounts from all periods in order better to judge whether there were strategic changes in accounting practices. When record office catalogues were sufficiently detailed to give such information, samples were also taken from each stewardship, and each time a significant change occurred in the composition of the estate.

It was important to evaluate the detail provided by the rental volumes. The final indexes of rents which we produced are of two sorts, one based on assessed rents and the other on rents received. These represent two distinct notions of value, the one the perceived value of the tenancy on entry, and the other the actual amount the tenant paid and the landlord collected. Not all archives recorded both kinds of rents. However, if arrears and allowances were also included alongside either of the two types of rental entry, it was possible to calculate the other, missing rental entry. The accumulation of arrears and the need to make abatements proved to be a useful indication of difficult times on the estate. Therefore, for their different purposes, where available, all these data were collected. Rentals which contained totalled abstracts of these classes of information were bonuses.

During the sampling phase it was necessary to ensure that surveys were available from which to indicate estate area. Occasionally acreages were recorded annually, but this was unusual. Normally a record of the total acreage for an estate at different dates gave an indication of the likely ease with which a reconstructed annual area could be calculated. Small alterations in size were generally easy to accommodate, while larger changes might have indicated a purchase or sale of land. These adjustments could also be accommodated as long as they were verifiable in the rentals. However, substantial changes in size might equally have come about by various purchases and sales over a long period, and these were almost always impossible to identify accurately when only a few land surveys existed. S. Wade Martins has admitted that it was difficult to work out precisely the history of land acquisitions on the Holkham estate in north Norfolk because they were not always recorded in the appropriate account books.[4] Even

---

[4] Wade Martins, *Holkham*, p. 87.

where a full record of purchase and sale was available through a meticulous search of the records, the often piecemeal nature of estate building meant that a full reconstruction of an estate would have occupied a disproportionate amount of the research time which was available. The pattern of estate building on the Audley End estate in north Essex demonstrates the complexity of the problem. Sir John Griffin acquired 3,257 acres when he took over Audley End in 1754. By the end of the 1790s he had added a further 2,622 acres both locally and in Norfolk, Suffolk, and Northamptonshire. In the parish of Walden alone he purchased 379 different parcels of property, 180 of which were acquired in the 1780s.[5] This pattern of estate instability was found quite frequently, in which cases, depending on the state of spatial and temporal coverage already achieved in the national index, it was often decided not to pursue the research further.

Other archives remained unresearched for less obvious reasons. In some instances an archive was abandoned because another archive met the guidelines of the study more exactly. When difficult choices had to be made, a large estate was usually preferred to a smaller one. An estate with earlier chronological coverage had preference over one for which the accounts began later. Sometimes an estate archive was excluded simply because another collection covered a greater area, had a longer time span, contained more surveys, had better organised material, or simply was more readily available. In East Sussex, archives from the Battle Abbey estate, the Abergavenny's Southdown estate, the Frewen estate at Brickwall, and the Glynde Place estate might have been included but were rejected in favour of the Ashburnham estate. The Southdown estate only had a good rent series from 1846; the Frewen estate at Brickwall is contiguous with the Ashburnham estate but had an incomplete run of rents; the Glynde Place archive lacked survey material; and Battle Abbey is more or less contiguous with the Ashburnham estate, but has a shorter run of rentals which are more difficult to use. In Devon, the organisation of the local record repository meant that a number of archives were problematical to use. Both the Acland and the Courtenay collections were stored away from the record office. Ordinarily, to transcribe annual rent data from a well-ordered account takes minutes at most, but often each entry was originally recorded in a separate volume, and if an estate was divided into a number of collections there could be several volumes to work through for each year. To order several hundred volumes from an outlying store as would have been the case for these Devon estates made little sense when this part of the country was reasonably well covered

---

[5] J. D. Williams, 'A study of an eighteenth-century nobleman, his house, household and estate: Sir John Griffin, 4th Lord Howard de Walden, 1st Lord Braybrooke, of Audley End, Essex, 1719–1797' (University of London, PhD thesis, 1974), pp. 385, 446–51.

by the Duke of Bedford's estate at Tavistock. Despite these constraints and omissions, we are satisfied that the final sample provides as reasonable a cross-section of English agricultural land for the period 1690 1914 as it is possible to achieve in the face of a time constraint.

To summarise, we had five major considerations in mind when deciding whether or not a particular estate might be included in the database. First, the requisite data had to be available: in effect a good set of rental data (preferably for thirty years or more) together with at least the barest indication of the area of land on which the rent was assessed, and the associated size of the rent. Second, we had to be sure that data in the original archives was accurate. The presence of a summarised abstract, and the inclusion of totalled columns on each page of the rent book was usually a determining factor, indicating as it did close attention to detail. Third, we had to consider the ease with which rental data which was beyond the scope of our research could be omitted, including urban and industrial rents. Fourth, we took into account the degree to which an estate met the specific needs of the project with regard to soil type, geographical location, the boundary dates of the rent series, the total holding size of the owner, and other features. This was primarily in order to satisfy ourselves that we were achieving a reasonably even geographical coverage across the country, and also that we could distinguish rack rents from other forms of tenure. Finally, when there was any opportunity of exercising a preference we generally opted to extract material from larger estates for the simple practical reason that substantial properties helped to provide a larger total coverage of acres.

This list of priority guidelines is neither absolute nor definitive. In his work on Northumberland W. M. Hughes was no less certain about the importance of sample or example selection, and although he was concerned with farms rather than estates, a number of his warnings have wider significance:

> The use of representative examples to illustrate the general pattern of rent changes in an area is a dangerous procedure unless those examples are very carefully selected . . . The criteria for selection has been simple – availability of continuous and full information being throughout the first consideration. It was next essential that nothing occurred on any of the farms in question in the way of boundary changes so significant as to make comparison of rents for the single holding at different dates unrealistic. When these two conditions had been fulfilled the final selection was determined by the necessity to ensure that the group selected, between them, covered as wide a range of results as possible. By this process it was hoped that the selection should be as representative of all the possibilities as feasible.[6]

---

[6] Hughes, 'Northumberland', p. 267.

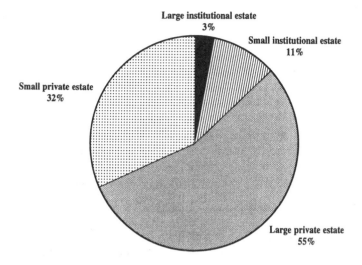

Fig. 5.2 Types of estate from which rental details extracted (by landownership type and size)

When we took all of these considerations, and others, into account, slightly under 25 per cent of the original group of archives was researched and material collected and collated for the project. As we could easily have predicted it was not possible to ensure an even geographical coverage in the survey for all periods, although we did manage to take samples from almost every county and from each major farming system and soil type (see figures 8.6 and 8.7 below). Temporal coverage was more of a problem, although as we indicate in chapter 8, from the second quarter of the eighteenth century the number of estates covered, and the total acreage they embraced, grew substantially to reach a maximum of 1.5 million acres in the 1880s. Our sample was always likely to grow larger the closer we came to modern times because of the general survival of records and the improving accountancy methods adopted by landlords. The distribution of usable archives was determined partly by the nature of surviving rentals in family archives and partly by the fact that institutional lands were less likely to be let at rack rents (see figure 5.2). When institutional owners maintained archaic rents, whatever the quality of their records and the consistency of their accounting practices, we had to discard their data. However, since even the most conservative landlords eventually adopted the rack rent the pool of usable archives inevitably expanded through time.

Rentals and account books were not specifically created to provide information on the rack rent of agricultural land. Many also contained data relating to other land uses or tenure types. Because the inclusion of such material could substantially affect the unit acre rent of the estate, it was necessary to remove it whenever possible. The exclusion of various non-agricultural and archaic elements altered both the size of the total rent and the total area on which it was assessed, and thus made the adapted numbers differ from those totals recorded in the estate archives. Each archive, in other words, had to be treated individually, and we were unable to adopt too many blanket rules for capturing data. The decision to discard material which could not be identified as a rack rent also constrained our use of much of the material collected by other historians, and which is otherwise available either in thesis or published form (see chapter 7).

Urban land, and land used for industrial purposes, for mineral extraction, or for quite exotic uses, could have a particularly distorting influence if included in a rent index. Two lakes which were used for recreational purposes on the Cockermouth estate in the Lake District extended to approximately 1,900 acres. They were removed from the total estate area. When mineral rights were let out on an estate the rents they attracted substantially increased the value of the agricultural land associated with them. The mineral exploration rents on the lands of the Bassetts of Tehidy in Cornwall represented about 44 per cent of their landed income in the 1720s and 1730s, but by the late 1730s the income from all of their mining activities, that is mineral extraction and mineral rents combined, amounted to 76 per cent of their total income.[7] Although on some estates mineral rents were recorded separately from those from agricultural land, such as on the Derbyshire estates of the Dukes of Devonshire, in yet other instances mineral rents were included in the general rental. By using information from the rentals in conjunction with surveys, these rents could sometimes be isolated and removed. This was possible on the Derwentwater estate owned by Greenwich Hospital in Northumberland where quarries, collieries, lime works, and smelting mills were individually identified and removed from the dataset. Sometimes these mineral rents were quite dominant. For example, the rentals on the Wharton estate of Lord Leconfield in Cumberland could only be integrated into the national index after more than 50 per cent of their total recorded rent was subtracted, thus eliminating the influence of land which was associated with mineral extraction and processing.[8] On other occasions the presence of mineral rents on estates was too great or too

[7] V. M. Chesher, 'A social and economic study of some west Cornwall landed families, 1690–1760' (University of Oxford, BLitt thesis, 1956), pp. 50–1, 60.
[8] Petworth House Sussex, Cockermouth estate accounts PHA 4296–383.

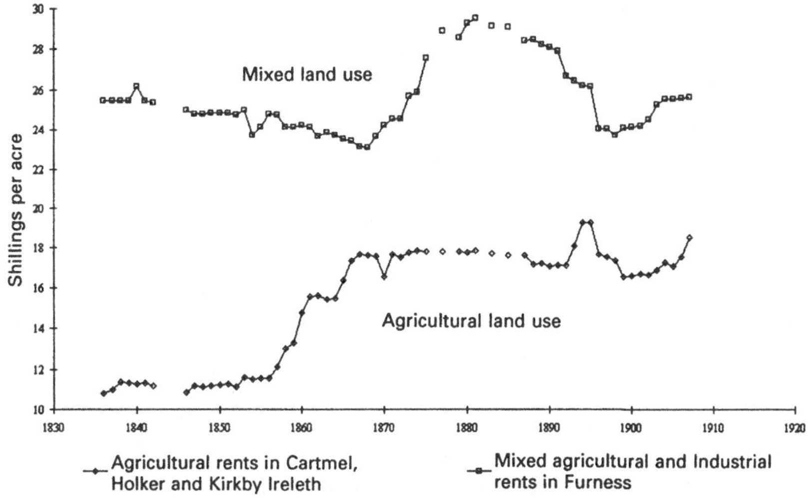
Shillings per acre
30
28
26
24
22
20
18
16
14
12
10
1830
1840
1850
1860
1870
1880
1890
1900
1910
1920
Mixed land use
Agricultural land use
Agricultural rents in Cartmel, Holker and Kirkby Ireleth
Mixed agricultural and Industrial rents in Furness

Fig. 5.3 The effect of industrial land use on the size of rent: Holker estate, Lancashire

dispersed to be identified precisely enough to be removed from the total rental and discarded, as was the case on the Leconfield Percy estate, again in Cumberland, and on the Greville estate in Warwickshire. When this was the situation, unfortunately but necessarily the material had to be rejected.

The rent associated with industrial land was similarly discarded wherever possible. The influence which the presence of the iron and steel works on the Furness portion of the Duke of Devonshire's Holker estate in Lancashire had on the agricultural rents could not be isolated, therefore the rents associated with this township alone could not be used without the danger of distorting the overall index for the rest of the estate (see figure 5.3).[9] Often in the records small-scale industrial land use was included along with the predominantly agricultural land rents. For the most part this could be identified and excluded, as on the Derwentwater estates, but on some estates this was not possible. On the Ashburnham estate in Sussex the record of rents included those attributable to charcoal burning. These could not be isolated, although they may conceivably have been included with the woodland rents which are separately distinguished. On the Badminton estate in Gloucestershire the recorded rents included some land used for brick making, and as in other examples this could not be disaggregated, and hence discarded. However, since it was apparent from the surveys associated with this estate that this was a small-scale operation, the inclusion

[9] Lancashire RO, Holker MSS, Furness portion.

of these industrial rents did not materially inflate the size of the assessed rents. It was considered an important archive both for its geographical location and for the long run of rents which it provided. The presence of mills presented a particular problem. Corn and provender mills were part of the agricultural economy and rightly should not have been excluded, but many mills were used for industrial purposes, for example for smelting and fulling, and other processing. Where the presence of mills was obviously for industrial uses the rent could easily and justifiably be excluded.

The presence of industrial and urban land, particularly when it was undergoing development in a formerly agricultural area, caused more problems. This was particularly so with land in the West Riding of Yorkshire. In the Sheffield area, both on Earl Fitzwilliam's Wentworth Woodhouse estate and also on the northern estates of the Duke of Norfolk, there was land which was undergoing rapid urban or industrial development. This could not be included in our work. A survey of the Fitzwilliam estate in 1870 revealed the increasing division of the land into urban and industrial plots which were then let on 99 and 200-year leases.[10] Similarly, on the Duke of Norfolk's estate, a survey of 1861 recorded that lands 'should be disassociated from those Farms [in Brightside, Bierlow, and Attercliff] as opportunity presents itself and let at a higher price as accommodation land'.[11] Both of these archives were excluded from the dataset because it was impractical to separate the land which was in the process of conversion for urban development from the land which remained in agricultural uses. The Norfolk northern estates were further complicated by the inclusion of the mining rentals along with the agricultural income.[12] The decision to discard these two Sheffield estates was relatively straightforward, but in other cases the decision was more difficult.[13]

On the Holme Pierrepont estate of the Manvers family in Nottingham-

[10] Sheffield AO, Wentworth Woodhouse MSS, WWM.A 1648/1 Working Survey. See also J. T. Ward, 'The Earls Fitzwilliam and the Wentworth Woodhouse Estate in the nineteenth century', *Yorkshire Bulletin of Economic and Social Research*, 12 (1960), 19–27, for an indication of the various rents which constituted the final income of an estate in an industrial and urban area. By the end of the nineteenth century the incomes from his mines far exceeded the earl's income from his agricultural rents, 26.   [11] Sheffield AO, ACW S 109/8, survey 1861.
[12] Sheffield AO, ACM S 152, Accounts, 1692–93.
[13] See the discussion in chapter 7 below regarding the Shropshire and Staffordshire estates of the Leveson-Gowers and Dukes of Sutherland where we suspect the discontinuities in the rents analysed by different historians may be due to the inclusion or exclusion of industrial lands. On occasions agricultural land could also present problems. In his study of Northumberland W. M. Hughes was better able to identify the influence of rough grazing on the overall level of rents by concentrating on individual farms. The inclusion of this particular land use clearly reduced the overall rent per acre quite drastically. Hughes, 'Northumberland', pp. 190, 195. This was a problem we found with the Duke of Northumberland's estate where much of his land was composed of rough grazing in the Cheviots. In chapter 7 below we return to a consideration of this estate, but in the end we excluded it from the survey.

shire, the expansion of Nottingham transformed the rural parish of Sneinton into an industrial suburb. On enclosure (in 1796), the proportion of the total rent in the Manvers accounts arising from Sneinton rose from 5.8 per cent in 1795 to 15.2 per cent in 1800.[14] By 1800 parts of Sneinton were being developed for overspill housing from Nottingham, and therefore the rentals for the parish had to be excluded from the project. The material from the Hatfield estate had to be rejected because urban land around Hertford and Hatfield was so intermixed with farmland that it could not be easily identified, isolated, and excluded.[15] An attempt was made to find a way to sample the farms on the estate but the influence of metropolitan London caused such a great variation in unit acre rents between large and small farms that it proved impractical to extract a suitable sample.

Archaic rents also had to be extracted from the rents, particularly where they constituted a significant proportion of the total sums involved. On estates where this type of leasing dominated, the rental collections often had to be rejected. This was the case with the Oxford and Cambridge colleges for most of the period, for many of the better-known public schools, and for the estates of the Church of England.[16] For much of our period the two types of letting, the beneficial and the rack rents, existed side by side on a single estate. If the two types of tenure were separated in the rental or if one predominated in specific areas of the estate, the process of identification and exclusion was relatively easy. However, where such payments were scattered throughout the rental, the archive was rejected or only used for the period after the conversion to rack rents had been made. In order to obtain a good spread of estates, both chronologically and spatially, even some of those records with a considerable extent of outmoded tenures had to be employed and the archaic rents meticulously identified, isolated, and excluded. On the Tavistock estate of the Duke of Bedford in Devon and Cornwall whole parishes were excluded because such tenancies predominated.[17] For other parishes on the estate only farms let at rack were included. The situation became more complex as the archaic leases fell in and were converted to rack rents. From 1820, the areal extent of the various parts of the Tavistock estate was included in the rentals, and it was then simply a matter of subtracting the area involved and thus excluding the relatively

[14] Nottingham University Manuscripts Department, Holme Pierrepont Collection, Accounts 1795 and 1800.   [15] Hatfield House, Hertfordshire, Hatfield estate accounts 1857–1914.
[16] For a discussion of the Oxford colleges see chapter 6 below.
[17] The Tavistock estate was very much dispersed. While most of it was in west Devon around Tavistock itself, there were enclaves also in north Devon near Barnstaple, and in north Cornwall around Launceston. See P. V. Denham, 'The Duke of Bedford's Tavistock Estate. 1820–1838', *Reports and Transactions of the Devon Association of the Advancement of Science*, 110 (1978), 19–51, a list of places is given on 20–1.

small number of archaic holdings. But for the period before 1820 a different procedure had to be adopted. That part of the rental which identified variations in the rent was used individually to identify properties switching from archaic to rack rents, and the areas of those properties were calculated from the 1820 rental.[18] Complex though this process may seem, it was even more problematic on the Longleat estate in Wiltshire and Somerset. Only very limited acreage data existed for this estate, and so to use the material it was necessary to extrapolate the areas involved when leases were converted from archaic to rack. In the cases of both Tavistock and Longleat the extra effort involved was justified because both estates helped to bridge gaps in the chronological and spatial coverage.[19]

On some estates, larger farms were let at a rack rent while small holdings and cottages remained in beneficial leases. In such cases, and the Badminton estate provides an example, the aggregative contribution of such small properties was so small that the problem of relating the area under rack to the appropriate recorded rents was far less critical to the desired outcome of producing unit acre rents.[20] The inclusion or exclusion of free rents, that is those rents which were charged in lieu of feudal services and which were not associated with a specific area of land, mostly made almost no difference to the unit acre rent because they were generally very small proportions of the total rents. On the Castle Howard estates in Yorkshire these free rents contributed only a fraction of a percentage of the annual total rent, a mere £8.65 in 1750.[21] This was not always the case however; the Duke of Devonshire's Bolton Abbey estate proved the rule because free rents regularly amounted to about £500.[22] These had to be subtracted annually from the total rent.

Recording the rents

Once it was established that the archives of an estate could be included in the survey, rent material was entered into an individually designed matrix on a standard spreadsheet. Extraneous material such as non-agricultural rents could then easily be extracted and missing elements in the rental record could be calculated. When, for example, rents assessed, arrears, and allowances were given, the otherwise missing rents received could be easily

[18] Devon RO, Bedford Tavistock Estate T 1258/M/ER 15A&B – 129.
[19] Longleat House, near Warminster, Wiltshire, Longleat Estate Archives, Estate Accounts.
[20] Badminton House near Chipping Sodbury and Gloucester RO, Badminton Estate Archives, GRO & House D, QB, PB, QP.
[21] Castle Howard, near Malton, North Yorkshire, Castle Howard archives, Account Book for 1750.
[22] In 1785 they amounted to over £520, and also in 1894. Chatsworth House, Archives of the Trustees of the Chatsworth Settlement, Account Books for 1785 and 1894.

calculated and inserted. Any land which was untenanted, and therefore in hand, was excluded.

The aim was to create a tailor-made matrix for each estate to facilitate recording of the data. The account book or rental formed the template for the matrix with data entered as it appeared across the page of the volume. When different formats were encountered the flexibility of the spreadsheet enabled the matrix to be altered. Half-yearly payments could be combined automatically to form annual rents. These rents could then be entered annually, generally working from a benchmark year for which the area of the estate was known.[23]

A number of other considerations affected the layout of the matrix. For each archive the information available in any given year had to be determined. In the very best ordered accounts they would show the acreage on which the rents were collected, the arrears due, the rent assessed, the rent due, the rent received, the amounts allowed in rent rebates and also those allowed or payable for taxes, rates, and tithes, and finally the amounts spent by the landlord or the tenant on building, repairs, fencing, drainage, and other expenses, and whether or not these were deducted from the rent. But that was the ideal archive. Most accounts were less informative and recorded the assessed rent: that is, the rent agreed between the tenant and landlord and variously called the 'rent due' or 'rent agreed', or simply 'rent'; and the rent received, that is, the rent actually paid by the tenant to the landlord and variously called the 'cash received', 'net rent', or simply 'rent'. The total rent due was also usually recorded. This last entry was the assessed rent, plus the outstanding arrears and any additional sums which were due to be paid by the tenant. Obviously it was important to try to determine what exactly was involved in these calculations. The way in which the various sums of money moved over time helped to determine which of the two possible rents had actually been recorded by the accountant, the rent due or the rent received. In the case of the Greenwich Hospital estate the absence of regular alterations – normally typical of received rents – suggested that the figures were in fact the assessed payments. For a number of estates it was possible to calculate any missing rents in a series. This was obviously the case when they were recorded over a long period. Most commonly, it was the rent received which was not recorded. If the assessed rent, the arrears paid and due, and any elements which were allowed but included in the assessed rent, were all recorded, it was relatively easy to calculate the rent received by determining what

---

[23] Wherever practical, those records which were better presented were the first to be used so that the accounting practices of the estate administration became familiar and then any problems with the data could be accommodated at a point where the records were easiest to use.

components were customarily subtracted from the assessed rent and what arrears were due and remained to be paid.

In chapter 4 we have already indicated that for some estates with widely scattered component parts – for example, the Manvers and the Bedford estates – we decided to treat these component parts as individual estates or archives. This is part of a wider problem over identifying estates. We had to decide whether or not these large and scattered estates should be divided by region or county, or whether they should be studied as single entities. This depended both on the geographical coverage and also on the way estate material was organised. If more than one soil type or farming region was present it was sometimes possible to separate the estate into component regional parts – the Bedford estate is a prime example. Recording the rents by parish could help with the reconstruction of the estate acreage. Entering the data at parish level made it possible to anticipate whether a change in the size of rent was due to an overall rent reassessment or to an alteration in the size of an estate. At parish level it was easier to isolate such alterations accurately. If the survival of the records was patchy, or if the estate was divided at various times and run by different agents or for different members of the family, it was possible that the rents of a number of parishes would only be available in some years. By recording the data by parish or rent 'collection' this could generally be accounted for and the acreage varied accordingly. The Manvers estate material was recorded by individual 'collection' and thus yielded six separate archives. Four estates in particular which might have been recorded in this way were the Longleat estate in Wiltshire and Somerset, the Leconfield estate in Yorkshire, the Ashburnham estate in east Sussex, and the Cornwallis estate in Kent and Sussex. Dividing each of these into parishes might have provided more data for separate regional indexes, but in the end a number of factors determined that we treated them each as single estates.

A number of elements were frequently included in the assessed rent whose actual size might not have been apparent from the rental. In some instances the rental or accounts gave details of payments made by the landowner which were related to the management of the estate. These most often included payments of taxes, particularly land and property tax, and payments for improvements and repairs to the estate. Allowances and abatements of rent were periodically recorded in the rental. Occasionally, the landlord made loans to the tenant, and both the principal sum and the interest might be added to the tenants' annual rent. These nebulous, but significant, elements in rent payments varied considerably, not only temporally and spatially, but even from tenant to tenant on a single estate. By varying the amount of the payment that each tenant was expected to bear, the landowner was able to alter the actual rent without changing the quoted rent of a holding. Thus, in times of distress, the landowner might exclude or allow the tenants the tax and tithe payments, and not enforce covenants concerning the repair of fences, ditches, and buildings. This would reduce the financial burden on the farmer without actually reducing the book rent paid for the farm. In some instances these allowances were understood rather than written. Furthermore, the payments were often spread between the owner and the tenant, and the rental rarely indicated what proportion of the total payment was being allowed. It is not just difficult, but often impossible, to allow for these various elements in the rent index.

Once a matrix had been created and all decisions had been made concerning material which was to be included or excluded, the value of the rent was recorded. Usually the material which had to be excluded was removed annually. Some data, particularly payments of archaic rent, varied so little over time that they were only periodically checked and removed for groups of years. If no extraneous sums of money had to be subtracted, the abstracted or summarised figures often included in the accounts, and which were the easiest type of archive to transcribe, were used wherever these existed. When no summaries existed, the rents had to be transcribed and totalled together parish by parish from wherever they appeared in the rentals. In rare cases, such as the Lilford estate of the Earl of Powys, the rents were collected laboriously, entry by entry. However, this was only done when the archive was required to bridge a particular void in the overall survey, usually of a spatial nature.

The findings from each archive were graphed, both to provide a check on the accuracy of data transcription – sharp inflections in a rental trend might indicate an error in transcription – and also to highlight any sudden alteration in the rent trend, which could be investigated further by an inspection of the rentals or account volumes.

Finally, in some cases we adopted the unit of account which was employed by the estate accountant in the first place (whether farm or parish rather than estate or collection). This was the case when regular payments such as tithes, archaic rents, or non-agricultural rents had to be subtracted from the annual rent totals of some parishes. The accounts for the Badminton estate contained entries for both rack and archaic rents in each parish. In the summary attached to this archive these had been totalled. Therefore the matrix for the estate was arranged by parish so that only the rack-rent element was extracted. The Chatsworth matrix was also organised by parish, but rental information survived for some parishes for only a few years, and only limited survey material was available. To ensure a proper match between rents and the land area on which the rents were collected, only a sub-set of the estate was extracted, and this was determined by the survival of survey material. On the Earl of Derby's estate at Knowsley in Lancashire, for which the unit of account was the township, thirty-three places had rents based largely on archaic leaseholds. As a result, only a sample of one-third of his Lancashire property could be included. The matrix produced for the Dalemain estate of the Hasell family in Westmorland and Cumberland was organised by farm, but the actual accounts were recorded in terms of holdings. In this case a sample of farms enabled a stable area of approximately half the estate to be collected efficiently. In regard to some archives difficult but pragmatic decisions had to be taken, and otherwise excellent collections had to be put to one side because they failed to satisfy one or more of the critical criteria.

Reconstructing estate acreages

When assessing individual achives it was sometimes obvious that locating the acreage would be a problem, in which case the size of the total rent, when graphed over time, could provide essential clues to the expansion or contraction of property. An unexpected rise or fall in total rental income might suggest the purchase or sale of a parcel of land, and thereby indicate a date around which to concentrate the search for acreage information. Sometimes the rentals themselves eased this position by giving the acreage details, and it was vital to make a careful inquiry in the case of estates with good rental runs to be sure that acreage material was not overlooked. In the case of the Higham Ferrers estate of Earl Fitzwilliam in Northamptonshire this proved particularly critical since a gap in the acreage data was filled when a volume mistakenly catalogued as a rental turned out to be a survey.[24] Observations and remarks in the rentals also added information which was useful for calculating the acreage. Where these occurred they often included information concerning both the changes affecting the apparent size of an estate, such as land sold or purchased, land newly leased at rack instead of for life, changes in farm sizes through the addition or subtraction of one or more fields, and events which indicated a change in the rent without necessarily affecting the area. These could include rent abatements, reductions or increases of rents, writing-off rent arrears, and changes in rent associated with new leases or tenants.

For a small number of estates, particularly during the nineteenth century, the area was recorded annually. The Powys estate at Lilford in Northamp-

---

[24] Northamptonshire RO, Higham Ferrers archives, F(WW), Rental of 1807.

tonshire was unusual in that the acreages were recorded in the rentals as early as the mid-eighteenth century.[25] More usually it was only as the nineteenth century proceeded, and particularly towards the end of that century, that this practice became common. The rentals from the Tavistock estate of the Duke of Bedford contain acreages from 1822 onwards, and those for Lord Leconfield's estates included areas for Yorkshire from 1838 and for Cockermouth in Cumbria from 1860. Rentals of the Barking Hall estate of Lord Ashburnham in Suffolk included this information from 1830, and the Guy's Hospital printed accounts for their three estates in Herefordshire, Lincolnshire, and Essex contained annual acreages from 1840.[26] However, apart from the series from Lord Leconfield's Cockermouth estate, and for the Powys estate, no archive contained the acreage annually for the entire run of the rents we have used.[27] In general, acreage material was rather more difficult to find than rentals, and consequently a number of techniques had to be devised to reconstruct the areas of the estates involved.

The simplest archives to use when calculating the acreages were those which recorded the area frequently, say at intervals of between about five and twenty years. In such cases it was generally possible to locate the more precise dates when any alterations in estate size occurred by looking at the lists of tenants in the rental. Often these were assigned a unique number and therefore occupied a particular place in a rental from year to year. If the number changed one year in line with a change in area, and if there was no positive indication that the change was simply a redistribution of the land already included in the acreage, it was reasonable to assume that at least part of the total change occurred in that particular year. Graphing the assessed rents for the period also helped to estimate the point of change. Once

---

[25] Northamptonshire RO, Powys Estate archive, POW 3–6. It was unfortunate that the rentals for this archive were not conveniently totalled. They had to be added entry by entry for each year, and thus in spite of the presence of all of the essential elements needed for the survey, the archive was only used for a short period between 1741 and 1781.

[26] The Herefordshire estate material can be found in Hereford and Worcester RO, Guy's Hospital archives, Herefordshire Account, C99/III/308. The evidence which the hospital brought to the Royal Commission in the 1890s covered all three of its estates, in Hereford, Essex, and Lincolnshire. It included annual acreages, rents, arrears (when over £200), temporary abatements (where applicable), the cost of improvements such as new buildings (where applicable), and various remarks, annually from 1801 to 1893. The acreages which were printed appear to be estimates for the period from 1801–30 for Lincolnshire, 1801–41 for Essex, and 1801–40 for Herefordshire, but they appear to be precise measurements thereafter. Royal Commission on Agriculture, 'First Report of Her Majesty's Commissioners Appointed to Inquire into the Subject of Agricultural Depression: Minutes of Evidence with Appendices', C. 7400, XVI (1894), pp. 423–7.

[27] Though this occasionally occurs for estates which have appeared in print in one shape or form, notably in the biography of the Bedford estate by the Duke of Bedford, *A Great Agricultural Estate* (London, 1897). In addition, the evidence which was brought before the Royal Commission of the 1890s and outlined in chapter 6 below almost always provided annual acreage details.

located in time, the size of the increase or decrease was used to adjust the area assigned to the property in the appropriate rental. On the Pitt-Rivers estate in Dorset and Wiltshire the area was recorded on four dates between 1850 and 1900. From this information it was relatively easy to calculate the yearly changes in area by a combination of the techniques outlined above. These simple techniques could often be used to calculate the area with reasonable certainty for twenty or thirty years on either side of the more detailed measurement. The advantage was that rentals were often usable well in advance of the first detailed estate survey. This allowed us to carry the rental and land area details of Lord Ashburnham's Barking Hall estate in Suffolk back in time from 1830, through an increase of approximately 200 acres in 1820 and then on back to 1790.

A more complex reconstruction process was necessary when the estate area was known only at long intervals, particularly when a substantial increase in area occurred between two surveys. On the Duke of Devonshire's Bolton Abbey estate approximately 3,000 more acres of land were recorded in a survey of 1869 than in the previous survey of 1790. On closer inspection it turned out that this was the net result of the estate acquiring about 6,000 acres, but selling about 3,000. Once all of the acreages which represented land in-hand, land on which archaic rents prevailed, and lands which attracted non-agricultural rents, had been identified, isolated, and extracted, the next step in the reconstruction of this estate was to graph the assessed rents for the period (see figure 5.4). The graph identifies several key dates when irregular movements or inflections in trend suggest the possible sale or purchase of land. For example, in 1807–8 the rent increased by £1,425; in 1831–2 there was a fall of £503; but there were further increases in 1833–4, 1845–6, 1857–8, and 1859–60, of £570, £1,931, £255, and £457. A number of other techniques could then be applied to the material to isolate alterations in the estate. The simple expedient of listing the parishes and their areas from two surviving surveys made it possible to see whether whole parishes entered or left the estate, or if the land owned by the estate in a parish changed greatly in size. Table 5.1 shows the most important alterations in parish size and the size of rents on the Bolton estate.

Once the approximate year when the estate changed size had been identified, the rentals and accounts could often help to isolate the acreage involved. For this task, it was useful to have a selection of types of accounts and rentals ranging from the rough rent collection book to the audited account. All could be searched for clues. Those arranged by parish often provided the most expedient means of co-ordinating the date of change with the magnitude of change. If land in a parish was known to have been bought

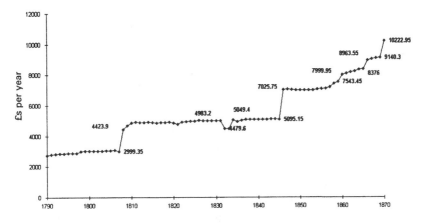

Fig. 5.4 The value of assessed rents for the Bolton Abbey estate (to identify points when there were major alterations in the rental)

Table 5.1. *Changes in parish size and variations in annual rent on the Bolton Abbey Estate, 1790–1870*

Changes in parish size	
Parishes	Additions (+) or subtractions (−) in acres
Barden	− 446
Bolton	− 868
Langstroth Dale	− 1,953
Beamsley	+ 269
Draughton	+ 832
Embsay	+ 495
Fewston	+ 3,621
Hebden	+ 183
Grassington	+ 125
Rilston	+ 147
Storriths	+ 738
Littondale	+ 220

Variations in the annual rent			
Date	Causes of change	Change in value (£)	Change in area (acres)
1807–8	Purchase and rent increase	+ 1,425	+ 1,061
1831–2	Sale	− 503	− 2,036
1833–4	Purchase	+ 570	+ 253
1845–6	Purchase and rent increase	+ 1,931	+ 640
1857–8	Purchase	+ 255	+ 390
1859–60	Purchase	+ 457	+ 2,146
1860–1	Purchase	+ 96	+ 1,939
1869–70	Revaluation of rents	+ 1,083	− 16

Source: Chatsworth House: Archives of the Trustees of the Chatsworth Settlement, Bolton Abbey Accounts

or sold, the rentals could be scanned in search of the inclusion or removal of the parish or for a sudden change in the rents of the land in the parish. If the rent subsequently moved in line with the trend on other land on the estate, the amount of change known to have occurred in the area of the parish could reasonably be assigned to that date. This method was employed as the principal means of determining the areas involved in any change in estate size. The Bolton Abbey estate again offers an illustration of the point. The increase in rent and thus in area in 1807–8 was, in part, caused by the purchase of 832 acres in the parish of Draughton. In 1831–2 over 2,000 acres were sold, largely from the parishes of Langstroth Dale and Littondale. Over 2,000 acres were purchased in the parish of Fewston in 1859–60.[28]

A number of other factors had to be considered when calculating the estate acreage. Land 'in hand' occasionally presented a problem. If the accounts assigned a sum of money to represent what the rent would have been if the land was let then it was included in the series. If not, both the rent and the area were omitted. Such untenanted land quite naturally affected the rent, but the incidence of land in hand was especially great at times of agricultural distress when unit acre average rents necessarily declined. Failure to remove the acreage of land taken in hand would therefore increase the apparent magnitude of the fall in the rent index by increasing the size of the denominator in the arithmetic. The rents for two Hampshire estates during the late-nineteenth-century agricultural depression owned by Lord Bolton illustrate this problem. On the Wallop estate, much of the land was untenanted and the acreage involved could not be determined. On the Hackwood estate, in contrast, there were fewer farms taken in hand and their area could be determined. This decision to remove from consideration land for which there were no longer tenants in occupation was an important consideration. Our aim has been to quantify the economic value of agricultural land as portrayed in rents. By definition this has to involve the value to both tenants and landlords, so where landlords could not attract tenants it has been necessary to exclude unoccupied land. For this reason, the rental data from the Wallop estate during the late nineteenth-century agricultural depression were excluded.

Generally, finding or reconstructing estate areas was less difficult than deducting the inappropriate rents. In part this was because the areas remained fairly constant over time while the size of the rent might change annually. Some historians have deliberately manipulated the archives to achieve what amounts to the same thing. Thus O. R. F. Davies took a fixed area of land on the Duke of Devonshire's Cavendish estate in order to show

---

[28] Chatsworth House, Archives of the Trustees of the Chatsworth Settlement, Bolton Abbey accounts.

a rise of 63 per cent in rents between 1617 and the 1670s.[29] Roy Sturgess analysed the course of agreed rents on the Sandwell estate in Staffordshire from 1853 to 1889, but he did it in two ways. He recorded the actual agreed rents, and then on the assumption of an average rent on a fixed acreage (the acreage in 1853), he estimated what the agreed rent would have been. Thus in 1889 the actual rent was £4,516 but would have been £6,125 if the 1853 acreage had pertained. Sturgess adopted the same methodology for the Chortley estate rentals from 1875 to 1900 based on the fixed acreage of 1875, for the Weston estate from 1813 to 1858 based on the 1813 acreage, and for eleven farms of constant acreage on the Farley estate from 1876 to 1888.[30] Richard Perren proceeded similarly when working on the Lilleshall and Trentham estates of the Dukes of Sutherland. He isolated the farms which paid at least £50 annual rental in 1893 then traced their average rents over the period 1870–1900.[31]

Despite these various checks and balances it is impossible to test and verify the acreage data with complete confidence. Inevitably not every exchange of land or minor land transaction could be identified. However, each estate was considered individually on its own merits, and a large range of documentation was searched to arrive at the closest approximation to the actual rents which applied to the actual acres of agricultural land.

Conclusion

At the end of the process of data extraction, adjustment, and final entry into the database, rents were rounded to the nearest pound and areas to the nearest acre. In this chapter we have outlined the methodology we adopted to arrive at this situation from more than forty separate archives. This database was the starting point from which a rent index could be constructed. As appendix 1, table A1.1, shows, for only a brief period from 1718 to 1723 did the contribution of this new archival evidence to the final rent index fall significantly below 50 per cent, and again in the 1880s when the evidence from a national inquiry is available, and finally again in the period 1901–14 when the evidence from the vast estates of the Ecclesiastical Commissioners is available. However, in only two of those years, 1720 and

---

[29] O. R. F. Davies, 'The dukes of Devonshire, Newcastle, and Rutland, 1688–1714: a study in wealth and political influence' (University of Oxford, DPhil thesis, 1971), pp. 144–5.

[30] Unfortunately Roy Sturgess did not record the acreages in his thesis, and therefore an otherwise usable data series mostly remains tantalisingly close but not close enough for inclusion in the rent index. R. W. Sturgess, 'The response of agriculture in Staffordshire to the price changes of the nineteenth century' (University of Manchester, PhD thesis, 1965), pp. 41, 62, 87, 89. In correspondence (1 May 1992) Roy Sturgess was unable to recall the acreages in question.

[31] R. Perren, 'The effects of agricultural depression on the English estates of the dukes of Sutherland, 1870–1900' (University of Nottingham, PhD thesis, 1967), pp. 294, 301.

1723, did the contribution of the new evidence fall below 30 per cent of the whole. Nevertheless, this means that other evidence was available and it made no sense to ignore it. We turn to these other sources in chapters 6 and 7.

CHAPTER 6

Constructing the rent index II: government inquiries

Until the nineteenth century the movement of rent was of little or no direct interest to government. This situation changed only when the incidence of agricultural depression raised questions to which answers were sought by a more systematic analysis than had previously been attempted. It was when the landlords' incomes came under the most severe threats that Parliament mounted large-scale inquiries and looked seriously at the agricultural base of the economy. In the course of the nineteenth century this happened on two occasions: first, in the agricultural depression which came in the two decades after Waterloo; and second, and more intently, during the agricultural depression which set in during the late 1870s and arguably did not recede until the First World War. These inquiries, particularly the 1890s Royal Commission and a series of private surveys carried out in relation to it, offer us a core of material which we can use in constructing a database.[1]

During the French Revolutionary and Napoleonic Wars there was a period of over two decades of inflationary price movements in Britain. It was caused by a number of factors, not least the wars, but it was also due to a scarcity of food. This was related to successions of harvest deficits and also to problems over external supply. Then in 1797 there were mounting fears of a French invasion. This provoked a run on the country banks by people wanting to redeem their bank notes for gold coins. This developed into a convertibility crisis as the drain on gold locally was transmitted by the country banks to London banks and the Bank of England as they tried to redeem their gold deposits to meet the crisis. The drain of gold had every likelihood of handicapping the government in its bid to prosecute the war, and therefore it suspended cash payments and effectively came off the gold

[1] Royal Commission on Agriculture, 'First, Second, and Final Reports of Her Majesty's Commissioner Appointed to Inquire into the Subject of Agricultural Depression: with Minutes of Evidence', *BPP*, C. 7400 (1–3), XVI (parts 1–3), 1894, C. 7981, XVI (1896), C. 8021, XVII (1896), and C. 8540–1, XV (1897).

standard. This suspension lasted until 1821. The result was over twenty years of almost continuous credit expansion, the proliferation of new banks, and the printing of paper money. This, probably more than the food scarcities, accounted for the inflation of the war years.[2] While inflationary market prices caused distress to the purchasers, it was a period of rising incomes for farmers, who in turn were able to pay high and rising rents. So much will become evident below. Yet there is an argument which says that rents did not rise high enough during the war for landowners to take a fair proportion of the rising income which arose from the inflated prices for farm production. Some years later a Mr Calthrop, a general merchant with some specialism in corn from Spalding in Lincolnshire, noted that 'I know farmers that amassed extensive fortunes by farming then.' Nevertheless, both farmers and landlords, but perhaps especially farmers, enjoyed rising incomes during the wars.[3]

One particular question, conceived during the war decades and debated subsequently, was the extent to which landowners and owner-farmers took advantage of cheap credit conditions in order to invest. Although this was a period of high nominal interest rates, there was also a general price rise. Thus the real interest rate fell as other prices rose. These cheap money conditions led to an extension of the mortgage market and a general invigoration of capital development within agriculture which was reflected in the number of enclosures which took place during the war years. In the deflationary decades which followed Waterloo the mortgagees were obliged to repay at the original high nominal rates, and these repayments were translated into high and rising real interest rates. Mortages could be renegotiated, and clearly for a large mortgage it was worthwhile renegotiating to a lower interest rate, but on smallish mortgages the legal costs of renegotiation left the mortgagees stranded with both high nominal and high real interest repayments.[4] In addition, the revision of the corn laws from 1815, and then further revisions in the 1820s, against a background of falling market prices, did not adequately provide farmers, and therefore their landlords, with the protection of their incomes that they required. This, and

[2] See M. E. Turner, 'Corn crises in the age of Malthus', in M. E. Turner (ed.), *Malthus and his Time* (London, 1986), pp. 112–28; M. E. Turner, 'Agricultural productivity in England in the eighteenth century: evidence from crop yields', *EcHR*, 35 (1982), 489–510; L. S. Pressnell, *Country Banking in the Industrial Revolution* (Oxford, 1956).

[3] *Second Report from the Select Committee on the State of Agriculture*, BPP [189], VIII, part 1 (1836), Q. 7901. On the idea that farms may have been underlet during the war see Hughes, 'Northumberland', pp. 263–5.

[4] M. E. Turner on 'Costs, finance, and parliamentary enclosure', *EcHR*, 34 (1981), esp. 243–4. See also *First Report from the Select Committee on the State of Agriculture*, BPP [79], VIII, part 1 (1836), Qs. 886, 1268; *Second Report*, Qs. 7902–3; *Third Report from the Select Committee on the State of Agriculture*, BPP [465], VIII, part 2 (1836), Q. 11312.

other considerations, helped to promote a series of Parliamentary Select Committees in the early 1820s to investigate the 'depressed' or 'distressed' state of agriculture, as the language of the time put it.[5] A second period of agricultural introspection occurred in the 1830s, first with a Select Committee in 1833;[6] second, a more extensive House of Commons Select Committee in 1836 appointed to inquire into the 'State of Agriculture and into the causes of the Distress which still presses upon some important branches thereof';[7] and third, a House of Lords Select Committee in 1837.[8]

Agricultural depression in the 1830s

The level and the trend of agricultural rent was just one of the many concerns of all of these committees, and the 1836 Select Committee is probably the most informative for our purposes. The committee met under the chairmanship of Charles Shaw-Lefevre, later Viscount Eversley, and included Lord John Russell, Sir Robert Peel, the Marquess of Chandos, and 32 other members, including James Loch, at one time chief land agent to the Dukes of Sutherland, and by this time the MP for Wick.[9]

The witnesses called before the 1836 Select Committee were an assortment of agricultural and land-related practitioners: farmers, valuers, land surveyors, stock appraisers, farmers who had other occupations such as acting as maltsters, millers, and general corn merchants, and one estate manager who was also a banker. Some were very large farmers, such as Henry Morton of Denham in Buckinghamshire, Francis Sherborn of Bedfont, near Staines in Middlesex, and Christopher Comyns Parker of Woodham Mortimer in Essex. They farmed 2,000, 1,600, and 'Rather more than 2,000' acres respectively. Parker's main occupation is difficult to pin

[5] Report from the Select Committee on Petitions Complaining of Agricultural Distress, BPP [255], II (1820); Report from the Select Committee to Whom the Several Petitions Complaining of the Depressed State of the Agriculture of the United Kingdom were Referred, BPP [668], IX (1821); First Report from the Select Committee Appointed to Inquire into the Allegations of the Several Petitions Complaining of the Distressed State of the Agriculture of the United Kingdom, BPP [165], V (1822); Second Report, BPP, [346], V (1822). See also A. R. Wilkes, 'Adjustments in arable farming after the Napoleonic Wars', AgHR, 28 (1980), 90–103; A. R. Wilkes, 'Depression and recovery in English agriculture after the Napoleonic Wars' (University of Reading, PhD thesis, 1975).

[6] Report from the Select Committee Appointed to Inquire into the Present State of Agriculture, BPP [612], V (1833).

[7] First Report [79], Second Report [189], Third Report, BPP [465], VIII, parts 1 and 2 (1836).

[8] Report from the Select Committee of the House of Lords on the State of Agriculture in England and Wales, BPP [464], V (1837).

[9] On Charles Shaw-Lefevre see Dictionary of National Biography, XVII (Oxford, 1921–2), p. 1388. See also the section below and note 19 on the 1890s Royal Commission for family continuity in the Chairmanship of another committee when Shaw-Lefevre's nephew chaired the 1894–6 Royal Commission. On Loch see Dictionary of National Biography, XII, p. 26; see also E. Richards, The Leviathan of Wealth (London, 1973), pp. 19–34; E. Richards, 'James Loch and the House of Sutherland, 1821–1855' (University of Nottingham, PhD thesis, 1967).

down; he was a farmer, estate owner, land agent, tithe assessor, banker, and political activist, in each capacity working with some distinction.[10] John Houghton of Sunning-Hill in Berkshire and Dinton in Buckinghamshire was a farmer and was particularly well qualified to talk about rents in his capacity as a receiver of rents in Lincolnshire, Buckinghamshire, Middlesex, Surrey, Berkshire, Sussex, Northamptonshire, and Suffolk. Thomas Bennet of Woburn was the steward to the Duke of Bedford. One of the most notable witnesses was the famous underdrainer, Mr James Smith of Deanston in Perthshire. In answer to the question regarding his occupation he claimed he was an occupier of 200 acres, and also a manufacturer and improver by thorough draining and subsoil ploughing. Another celebrated witness was John Ellman of Glynde in Sussex, the son of the even more famous agriculturalist, also John and also from Glynde, both of whom also had given evidence to the 1821 Select Committee.[11] In the main, however, the witnesses were farmers, both occupying owners and tenants. They were men of considerable practical knowledge with a vested interest in the outcome of the inquiries, an interest so strong that we may suspect it coloured their opinions, though not the generality of the agricultural depression and the attendant distress which they described.[12]

In the main the proceedings were conducted in a very informal manner with very little information submitted in tabular form. When a similar exercise was carried out in the 1890s it became usual for pre-prepared hard numerical evidence to be presented. This was not usually the case in the 1820s or 1830s. The question-and-answer responses involving Mr Umbers of Leamington Spa were not untypical. His family farm was about 260 acres in 1794, and this had increased to about 700 acres in the 1830s. He could not recall the rent in 1794 when the farm was occupied by his father, nor could he recall what it was in 1816 when he took it over himself. But when pressed he did suggest that the rent in 1816 was about the same as the rent he now paid in 1836. In the meantime however there had been a rise and then an abatement in that rent. He confirmed that the rent in 1816 was above the rent in 1794 and therefore the rent in 1836 was also above the rent of 1794, by his estimation by about 7 or 8 shillings per acre. The current rent was about 30 shillings per acre on one farm and 23 shillings per acre on another. He

[10] J. Oxley Parker, *The Oxley Parker Papers: From the Letters of an Essex family of Land Agents in the Nineteenth Century* (Colchester, 1964).

[11] James Smith answered questions on rent in the *Third Report*, 1836, Qs. 15078–81. See also A. D. M. Phillips, *The Underdraining of Farmland in England during the Nineteenth Century* (Cambridge, 1989), pp. 158–60, 228. On the Ellmans see S. Farrant, 'John Ellman of Glynde in Sussex', *AgHR*, 26 (1978), 77–88, especially 87.

[12] A number of witnesses appeared before more than one of the committees itemised above, but most of them only appeared once. In the 1837 House of Lords Committee John Rickman, the 'demographer', was one of the witnesses.

finally agreed that the rent in 1794 was about 24 shillings per acre.[13] If we suppose that Mr Umbers was not being evasive, but genuinely had difficulty in recalling the details of his past, and was not aided by any written records, then it helps to explain the problems faced by the Board of Agriculture reporters when collecting evidence on rents and other hard facts – as distinct from reporting local traditional practices – which we touched upon in chapter 2.

There are numerous specific references to the course of rents on particular estates or in particular locales throughout the Select Committee Reports, as well as many references to rent arrears, abatements, and adjustments. But the evidence is too diffuse, uneven, and uncoordinated for it to be arranged into a database for their times. However, in chapter 11 we return to this evidence when we place the new rent index in historical context.

The Royal Commission on Agriculture – 1894–96

By the later 1830s conditions in agriculture were improving, and it did not become a serious subject for either government or individual concern until the depression of the closing decades of the nineteenth century. By the third quarter of the nineteenth century the UK economy was devoid of any legislative agricultural protection whereas under the Corn Laws, finally repealed in 1846, it enjoyed an enormous psychological if not actual economic protection. In addition it had become devoid of any physical protection afforded by either its isolated island state, or its distance from available supplies of food products. Under the old Corn Laws, arguably, there was never a threat from Europe of a great influx of European corn because the countries on the mainland were undergoing industrialisation and experiencing their versions of the demographic transition. They were not generating surpluses for export to Britain on any great scale except perhaps the Russians, who continued to export in quantity until the First World War.[14] At a greater distance, the extensive new agricultural lands of the New World, and Britain's southern hemisphere colonies in Australasia and South Africa were not ready by the mid-nineteenth century to enter the international food market on any significant scale, and neither was South America, especially Argentina. Moreover, in Britain's island state there was

---

[13] *Second Report* (1836), Qs. 8637–47.
[14] See A. S. Milward and S. B. Saul, *The Development of the Economies of Continental Europe 1850–1914* (London, 1977), pp. 477–9, showing the dominant position of Russia in the world grain trade in the second half of the nineteenth century. The country provided between a quarter and a third of the world trade in wheat, and at all times well over one-half of the barley, oats, and rye.

a large degree of natural protection against the influx of many perishable products. During the second half of the nineteenth century this situation changed.

The mid-1860s' 'Contagious Diseases' legislation gave a measure of protection to the livestock industry because it disallowed the entry of live animals into Britain, though the main purpose was to control the spread of disease and not directly to offer economic protection to producers.[15] In the following decades, with the advent of iron-clad, steam-driven ships, refrigeration, and the development of the tin can, the products of the far-flung agricultural world came within easier reach. The opening up and sanitising of North America and its indigenous peoples led to the greatest influxes, and North American grain imports caused the most alarm and provoked inquiries.

In a Parliament still dominated numerically by the landed interest, agricultural affairs continued to enjoy a high profile. The landlords sought to protect the interests of their clients, the tenant farmers, who were faced with new and cheap competition (there was in fact an international deflation of commodity prices in general from the 1870s to the turn of the century). Britain had long since lost the ability to feed its own people from its own agricultural resources – the country had been in constant wheat grain and wheat flour deficit from about the 1770s – but in the last quarter of the century the small influx of foodstuffs which heretofore had closed the deficit gap on home production became an avalanche. This had a dramatic effect on prices. As tenant incomes were squeezed they were forced to pass a proportion of their losses to their landlords. They defaulted on rents, the landlords allowed abatements, at first on a temporary basis, but as arrears mounted the abatements *de facto* became permanent and were made *de jure* by negotiated rent reductions or remissions. Land values declined, rents fell, farms were left vacant, and a great many people asked why.[16] The result was an outpouring of literature which gives us our first really consistent set of rental material.

Several sets of data were assembled. First, the government set up a Royal Commission which, in the course of the 1890s, collected a large quantity of the kind of material which can be recycled for our purposes. Second, the depression provoked wide-ranging concern from many different interest groups which themselves generated data which we can employ. In this

---

[15] R. Perren, *The Meat Trade in Britain 1840–1914* (London, 1978), pp. 84–5, 108–13.
[16] In this context see the letter from the firm of Norton, Trist, and Gilbert to *The Times*, 20 April 1889, p. 11, and reprinted in 'A century of land values: England and Wales', *JRSS*, 54 (1891), 128–31. See also G. H. Peters, S. T. Parsons, and D. M. Patchett, 'A century of land values 1781–1880', *Oxford Agrarian Studies*, 11 (1982), 93–107; A. Offer, 'Farm tenure and land values in England, c. 1750–1950, *EcHR*, 44 (1991), 1–20.

context there was the first long-run rent series for the nineteenth century produced by R. J. Thompson in 1907 and the inquiry into land values by the firm of estate agents, Norton, Trist, and Gilbert. Third, some of those people and institutions who suffered as a direct result of the depression produced their own analyses of what had gone wrong, among them the 9th Duke of Bedford who wrote an introspective appraisal of his family estates and their development during the nineteenth century, and L. L. Price, the Treasurer of Oriel College, Oxford, who first investigated the effects of the depression on the income of his own college and then extended his analysis to the university as a whole.[17]

If the evidence on rents from the 1830s agricultural inquiries is superficial and sketchy and hardly capable of contributing a great deal to a national rent index, the experience of a further sixty years of public inquiries and Royal Commissions meant that by the 1890s something quite different was constructed. Until the 1870s contemporaries only had recourse to the proxy evidence of taxation from which to approach the question of landed incomes, but from the 1890s they began to acquire hard data.

By a parliamentary order dated 14 September 1893 a Royal Commission was set up 'to inquire into the Agricultural Depression prevailing in that part of Our United Kingdom of Great Britain and Ireland called Great Britain, and whether it can be alleviated by legislation or other measures'.[18] The Commission met under the chairmanship of George John Shaw-Lefevre, the First Commissioner of Works and Public Buildings. There were sixteen other members of the Commission including Viscount Cobham, and Sir Robert Giffen, an Assistant Secretary at the Board of Trade.[19]

The witnesses who presented oral and written evidence were said to represent landowners, land agents, and tenant farmers and were variously described by occupation as tenant farmers, land agents, and landowners.

---

17 Thompson, 'An inquiry'; Norton, Trist, and Gilbert, 'A century of land values'; Bedford, *Story*; L. L. Price, 'The recent depression in agriculture as shown in the accounts of an Oxford college, 1876–90', *JRSS*, 55 (1892), 2–36; L. L. Price, 'The colleges of Oxford and agricultural depression', *JRSS*, 58 (1895), 36–74, including a discussion; L. L. Price, 'The accounts of the colleges of Oxford, 1893–1903; with special reference to their agricultural revenues', *JRSS*, 67 (1904), 585–660, including a discussion; L. L. Price, 'The estates of the colleges of Oxford and their management', *JRSS*, 76 (1913), 787–90; L. L. Price, 'The estates of the colleges of Oxford and their management', *Transactions of the Surveyors' Institution*, 45 (1912–13), 542–603.
18 For this and other details, including membership, see Royal Commission on Agriculture, 'First, Second and Final Reports'.
19 Shaw-Lefevre was later created Baron Eversley (in 1906). The viscountcy associated with the family became extinct when uncle Charles died without surviving sons. In economic theory Giffen is attributed with developing the idea of the so-called 'Giffen good' whereby for an inferior good, under certain income conditions, the demand curve is forward sloping. Under those certain conditions, theoretically, it is observed that a rise in the price of bread, for example (Giffen's example was potatoes in post-Famine Ireland), calls forth an increase in consumption, not, as normal theory suggests, a decline in consumption.

They included the Treasurer of Guy's Hospital, representativies of county agricultural and commercial interests such as the Farmers' Union and Chambers of Commerce, the Surveyor-General to the Duchy of Lancaster, the Secretary to the Duchy of Cornwall, auctioneers, bankers, MPs, some of the appointed Assistant Commissioners to the Commission (for which see below), and many others. One of the witnesses was E. G. Strutt, agent to Lord Rayleigh of Essex. The Strutts were firmly connected to the Parker family, also of Essex, and this provides a link with the 1836 Select Committee at which Christopher Comyns Parker had presented evidence.[20] Of special interest to students of agricultural history will be some of the major late-nineteenth-century writers who presented evidence. These included R. Hunter Pringle (also an Assistant Commissioner), Hugh Raynbird, Elias Squarey, Arthur Wilson Fox (also an Assistant Commissioner), Albert Pell, Clare Sewell Read,[21] Sir Robert Giffen (a full member of the Commission but also a witness), Major P. G. Craigie, Sir John Bennet Lawes, W. C. Little (another full member of the Commission), L. L. Price, R. Henry Rew (also an Assistant Commissioner) and R. E. Turnbull. In all there were nearly 180 witnesses.

Apart from the witnesses who were called, the Commission also adopted the standard nineteenth-century practice of appointing regional Assistant Commissioners with the task of reporting from selected areas of England and Scotland 'on the condition and prospects of agriculture in those districts'. The choice of district was informed by a letter/questionnaire to the Inspectors of the Land Department under the Board of Agriculture.[22] The Assistant Commissioners included some notable personalities from British agrarian history, including Arthur Wilson Fox and R. Henry Rew. In addition, the principal landed proprietors were requested to provide details of estate expenditure, of outgoings and deductions from rentals since 1872.

The Royal Commission is a rich source, not only of opinion, but more usefully of hard facts. Table 6.1 is a summary of a large part of that evidence. It has been compiled from 29 estates distributed amongst 22 English and 1 Welsh county from which the evidence was drawn.[23] They ranged from the more or less contiguous 49,000 acres of the Earl of Ancaster's Lincolnshire

[20] Sir William Gavin, *Ninety Years of Family Farming: The Story of Lord Rayleigh's and Strutt and Parker Farms* (London, 1967).

[21] See J. R. Fisher, *Clare Sewell Read 1826–1905: A Farmers' Spokesman of the Late Nineteenth Century* (University of Hull Occasional Papers in Economic and Social History, 8, 1975).

[22] The answers to which are tabluated as Appendix D in the Royal Commission on Agriculture, 'First Report'.

[23] In fact 30 estates formed the evidence in this part of the inquiry but the 588 acres of Lord Fitzhardinge's Middlesex property have been excluded for two reasons. First, the data reported for this estate include only this single indication of the size of the estate for the single year 1894; the evidence for the other estates indicates their changing structure. A second reason for exclusion is given in note 25 below.

Table 6.1. *Rents due and received for major English estates, 1842–92*

	Rent due			Rent received		
Date	Acres 000s	Rent £000s	Rent/acre Shillings/acre	Acres 000s	Rent £000s	Rent/acre Shillings/acre
1842	85.5	110.5	25.9	128.7	148.6	23.1
1852	113.1	135.3	23.9	156.3	197.8	25.3
1862	118.1	186.5	31.6	161.7	240.0	29.7
1872	273.1	420.0	30.8	301.6	456.8	30.3
1873	289.1	446.1	30.9	317.6	484.7	30.5
1874	291.3	451.2	31.0	319.8	487.4	30.5
1875	291.7	454.0	31.1	320.2	489.3	30.6
1876	315.8	477.0	30.2	344.4	512.0	29.7
1877	316.3	485.0	30.7	345.3	523.6	30.3
1878	347.4	533.1	30.7	370.9	554.7	29.9
1879	341.6	524.8	30.7	370.7	477.1	25.7
1880	377.7	559.8	29.6	414.1	532.7	25.7
1881	437.6	612.5	28.0	479.6	584.6	24.4
1882	432.0	602.3	27.9	473.9	615.5	26.0
1883	431.7	598.8	27.7	488.2	649.0	26.6
1884	429.2	585.9	27.3	485.6	623.8	25.7
1885	425.8	577.4	27.1	482.0	565.5	23.5
1886	428.4	560.5	26.2	484.5	573.8	23.7
1887	426.8	551.1	25.8	483.0	535.9	22.2
1888	426.3	541.4	25.4	482.4	553.4	22.9
1889	432.2	544.3	25.2	488.1	579.7	23.8
1890	433.4	542.3	25.0	489.7	561.3	22.9
1891	433.4	545.4	25.2	489.7	569.1	23.2
1892	434.7	548.7	25.2	490.9	548.9	22.4

Source: Reconstructed from Royal Commission on Agriculture, 'Particulars of Expenditures and Outgoings on Certain Estates in Great Britain and Farm Accounts', *BPP*, C. 8125, XVI (1896).

and Rutland estate, and the 50,000 acres of the Duke of Bedford's estate in the east and south Midlands, down to a little over 2,400 acres from the single Welsh estate in Flintshire owned by the Duke of Westminster. If we combine the disparate estates of individual landowners then the largest belonged to the Duke of Bedford. At 75,000 acres, in more or less three equal portions, it was spread over the counties of Bedfordshire and Buckinghamshire; Cambridge, Northamptonshire, and Huntingdonshire; and Devon, Cornwall, and Dorset.

The main evidence was presented in a form which gave the acreage of the estates let to tenants, the agreed rents or rents which were due, and the actual rents received. The full range of these data was recorded for most years from the 1870s to the 1890s, with often a retrospective look back to the 1850s, and in a few cases back to 1842. However, because of some incompletenesses in the submissions the sum of the acreages for estates where rents were due does not necessarily always match the sum of acreages where we have entries for rents received. From 1872 onwards, however, there are data which are common to rents due and received for as much as 250,000 acres. We have not attempted to weight the estates in any way, to take regard of environmental characteristics of location, of land use, or to weight on the basis of any other factors or superficial descriptions other than by size. In any case this is unlikely to be possible on anything other than an exceedingly superficial basis. The computed rent per acre in table 6.1 is our calculation. It is not the mean rent based on up to twenty-nine separate estate-based average rents per acre; rather it is the aggregate of all rent due or received divided by the aggregate of all the acres to which they applied.

It is possible only partially to conduct independent checks on the data presented in the Royal Commission. Notably we can check the consistency of the evidence for the Bedfordshire and Buckinghamshire estates of the Dukes of Bedford because the 9th Duke subsequently constructed his own estate history, as well as having furnished evidence to the Royal Commission. A comparison of the evidence and the subsequent history reveals that the 'rents received' as quoted in his book resemble closely the supposed equivalent data which was presented to the Royal Commission. The chronological overlap in the two sources begins in the 1870s. While the two sets of monies do not precisely match one another at first, they do so to within 1 or 2 percentage points, or a few hundred pounds. But later, for the years of the depression in the 1880s and early 1890s, the differences in the two reported rents differ by up to 5 per cent or more. Except for 1890 the quotation in the Royal Commission was always higher, at least partly because the figures for the duke's town property were included without distinction in the evidence presented to the Royal Commission. Conversely, the areal extent of the duke's estate in the two sources was reported in quite the opposite direction: in his estate history the duke quoted acreages which were between 4 and 11 per cent higher than the equivalent acreages presented to the Royal Commission. No explanation of these discrepancies is available, but the overall consequence is that the calculated rent per acre was always higher in the Royal Commission evidence, in most years from 1882 to 1892 by 10 per cent, but as high as 20 per cent in 1891.[24]

The average size of the 29 estates in the Royal Commission evidence was 16,700 acres. This is calculated by counting each of the detached parts of the largest estates, like the several Bedford properties, as separate properties. This is not a particularly meaningful conclusion in a study of rent since in all cases this results from the aggregation of many separate farms on which there were large variations in the rents which were exacted. In all cases the unit rent on the smaller farms was greater than on the larger, and in casual

[24] Bedford, *Story*, p. 65n.

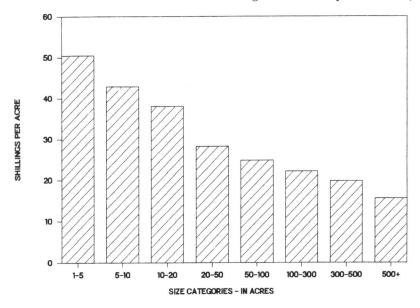

Fig. 6.1 Rent per acre and size of farm, 1894

terms at least this gradient in rent per acre worked in a fairly uniform fashion. Figure 6.1 is a summary of the farm distribution evidence. It is based on 5,330 farms on 28 of the estates covering 460,000 acres and yielding £498,000 in rent in 1894.[25] The farm-size categories were determined by the Commission, indicating that the original data were presented in a systematic way.[26] Occasionally dwellings were included in these distributions and their inclusion may partially explain the higher unit rents on smaller properties, though a more significant reason for the range of unit rents is due to the land quality involved. Small tenants could not contemplate the inclusion of too much, if any, marginal land on the property they rented, therefore they paid more per unit because they extracted more per unit from good quality land using relatively intensive farming methods. The smaller or smallest farms in some parts of the country were farmed as smallholdings or market gardens.[27] In the evidence from North Devon a witness prepared an

---

[25] Of the 30 estates which form the evidence, the data for the Duke of Richmond's 14,000 acre Goodwood estate in Sussex were not presented in a way adequate for them to be included here, and the 588 acres of Lord Fitzhardinge's Middlesex estate included dwellings, and these contort dramatically the unit acre rents when compared with other parts of the country.

[26] Farm holdings were categorised into eight size groups: 1–5 acres, 5–10, 10–20, 20–50, 50–100, 100–300, 300–500, and 500 acres and above.

[27] For example around Liverpool, for which see, Royal Commission on Agriculture, 'Garstang and Glendale: Reports by Assistant Commissioner Mr Wilson-Fox', C. 7334, XVI, Part 1 (1894), p. 18.

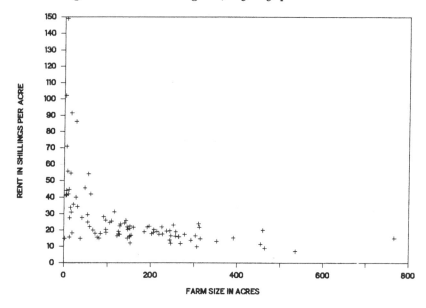

Fig. 6.2 Farm size and rent in North Devon, 1894

appendix of 103 individual farm rents for an estate of over 17,000 acres with a yearly rent, in May 1894, of over £15,000. They clearly show this special distribution of rents from large to small which when graphed takes the form of an hyperbolic shape (figure 6.2, and see also figures 3.4 and 3.5 above).[28] The average rent for the whole sample was 18.2 shillings per acre.

There were sound economic reasons for the identifiable rent gradient, not least that to take on a large farm required a tenant to enter a rental contract with a large personal contribution towards total capital. A spokesman for the Ecclesiastical Commissioners found that during the depression the larger farms were the hardest to let for this very reason. They attracted a lower unit rent to begin with, but they were also associated with the largest rent abatements or rent reductions.[29] Nationally, the number of farms of 300 or more acres declined between 1885 and 1915 by 14 per cent, and Welsh

[28] Royal Commission on Agriculture, 'North Devon: Report by Assistant Commissioner Mr R. Henry Rew', C. 7728, XVI (1895), pp. 65–6. The number of farms included in the graph has been reduced to 97 by excluding 4 very small farms, each less than 5 acres, where houses and/or cottages and gardens were included. Such small holdings have a calculated rent per acre of up to £33. In addition, two farms of over 1,000 acres each have been excluded. They were let respectively at 8 and 13 shillings per acre. The overall average rent including all farms was 17.5 shillings per acre.

[29] Evidence of Alfred de Bock Porter, Secretary and Financial Adviser to the Ecclesiastical Commissioners, 'First Report', Qs. 474–97.

commentators were in no doubt that small farmers suffered less than their larger neighbours in the depression.[30] Size of farm, therefore, was only one of many factors in the equation of economic survival: as the observation from a Lincolnshire witness emphasised, 'the bare mention of the amount paid per acre is no guide to value, for soil, situation, and size of farms are all factors which must be reckoned with'.[31]

There was also an evident regional dimension to the incidence of depression, as might be expected given its relatively arable emphasis. This regional character was expressed through the generally higher rents in the relatively pastoral west (and north) in contrast to the depressed rents of the arable east. Those depressed rents hit large and small farms alike and therefore the differentials between farm sizes were less pronounced in the east. These patterns are revealed in figures 6.3 and 6.4 which have been constructed from the evidence in the Royal Commission. The distinction between east and west, between arable and pastoral, is not hard and fast: much of the south Midlands was mixed agriculturally, and parts of south Derbyshire might be better placed in the arable east. Certainly the Tithe Commissioners defined Derbyshire as arable for its purposes, although this was surprising given the extent of pastoral uplands in the county.[32] Nevertheless, to the extent that a distinction can be made, figure 6.3 distinguishes between nearly 2,000 farms in the east comprising 216,000 acres which yielded £218,000 in rent, and over 3,300 farms in the west comprising 244,000 acres which yielded £280,000 in rent. Marginal adjustments of the estates as between east and west make little difference to the clear message in the graph. Figure 6.4 compares the 41,000 acres of an unnamed Norfolk estate which included 110 farms, which we might label as the arable extreme, with the 18,000 acres of Lord Fitzhardinge's Gloucestershire estate which included 188 farms, which represents the pastoral extreme, with the Duke of Bedford's 25,000-acre estate in Bedfordshire and Buckinghamshire which included 186 farms, which represents the margin between east and west, between arable and pastoral.[33] The patterns are unmistakable and the generally larger arable farms of the east and the

---

[30] HMSO, *A Century of Agricultural Statistics: Great Britain 1866–1966* (London, 1968), p. 19; D. W. Howell, *Land and People in Nineteenth Century Wales* (London, 1977), pp. 71–2.

[31] Quote from, Royal Commission on Agriculture, 'Lincolnshire: Report by Assistant Commissioner Mr Wilson Fox', C. 7671, XVI (1895), p. 19; see also Caird, p. 482.

[32] See J. V. Beckett and J. E. Heath, *Derbyshire Tithe Files 1836–50* (Chesterfield, Derbyshire Record Society, 22, 1995), pp. xviii–xix.

[33] We have deduced that the Norfolk estate illustrated here is Holkham. This deduction is based on a comparison with John Bateman, *The Great Landowners of Great Britain and Ireland* (Leicester University Press edn, 1971, being a reprint of the fourth and last edition of 1883). The work was first published in 1876 but it was extensively revised and expanded in 1878, further corrections being added in the third edition in 1879, with final corrections in 1883.

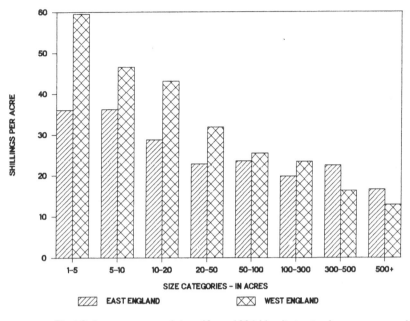

Fig. 6.3 Rent per acre and size of farm, 1894 (the distinction between east and west of England)

smaller grass farms of the west help to pick out the distinctions. The overall average farm size was 86 acres, on the eastern estates it was 111 acres, but on the western estates 72 acres.

Some of the evidence in the foregoing paragraphs from the Royal Commission was almost certainly repeated in the subsequent work of R. J. Thompson which will be discussed below, although he also communicated directly with some of the landowners concerned. From the 29 estates which we have summarised here he certainly acknowledged in his own work the Bedford estates. He also included data from estates other than the 29 which we have described here, estates which were reported quite separately in the Royal Commission evidence. These included the Ecclesiastical Commissioners, and also Guy's Hospital.[34] Witnesses representing these estates gave evidence separately in the inquiry and presented that evidence in different formats. The Guy's material covers the rent received by the hospital for the years from 1801 to 1893, and the Ecclesiastical Commissioners' material comes from the narrow period 1880–92. The Guy's submission was particularly detailed, presenting separate sets of accounts for the estates in Lincolnshire, Essex, and Herefordshire, including up to 6,401, 8,790, and

[34] Thompson, 'An inquiry', 58–9.

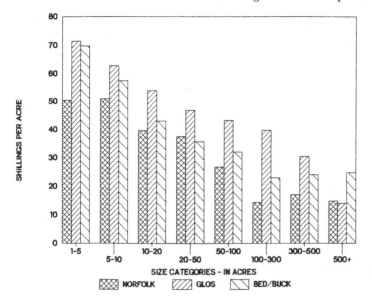

Fig. 6.4 Rent per acre and size of farm, 1894 (examples from Norfolk, Gloucestershire, and Bedfordshire/Buckinghamshire)

9,475 acres respectively. This particular semi-public, originally charitable, institution has been the subject of quite detailed analysis. J. C. Steele, the first superintendent of the hospital had already written an account of the effects of the agricultural depression on the estate and its income in the *Journal of the Royal Statistical Society* in 1892.[35] The finances and management of the estate have been studied in some detail in more recent times by B. E. S. Trueman.[36]

As a single estate the property of the Ecclesiastical Commissioners was the largest in the 1890s inquiry. In 1892 the Commissioners possessed a little under 279,000 acres, 'in nearly every county in the kingdom ranging

[35] In an article in the *JRSS* which was read on the same occasion (16 Feb. 1892) as a similar paper by L. L. Price on Oriel College, Oxford. J. C. Steele, 'The Agricultural Depression and its effects on a leading London hospital', *JRSS*, 55 (1892), 37–48; Price, 'The recent depression', 2–36; and the discussion which followed the presentation of the two papers, 49–55.

[36] B. E. S. Trueman, 'Corporate estate management: Guy's Hospital agricultural estates, 1726–1815', *AgHR*, 28 (1980), 31–44; B. E. S. Trueman, 'The management of the estates of Guy's Hospital 1726–1900' (University of Nottingham, PhD thesis, 1975). Trueman was concerned with wider aspects of the financial and general management of those estates which provided the income for the hospital. Whilst he carried his analysis back into the eighteenth century, he inadequately itemised the changing size of the estate over the period. In this respect the data in the 1890s inquiry, as far as the history of the extent of the Guy's estate is concerned for the nineteenth century, are more useful than the seemingly equivalent data in Trueman's study.

from 52,000 acres in Durham to some six acres in Shropshire'.[37] The amount of rent due in 1892 was £310,061. Annual acreages and rents were listed in an appendix to their main evidence to the Royal Commission. In 1880 the estate extended to over 212,600 acres providing a rental income of £308,885, but at its income-bearing height in 1882 the rents provided £350,013 from a property of 236,000 acres. The actual gross rents received, however, took into account allowances to tenants and irrecoverable arrears which were written off. In 1882 these allowances and arrears amounted to £48,977. In terms of acreage this is the single largest estate represented in the evidence to the Royal Commission, but unfortunately the data it furnished cover only a short period. Furthermore, unlike the relatively discretely located estates of private owners, the thousands of acres in the control of the Ecclesiastical Commissioners covered the whole of the country, however thinly they did so at times. This is all the more reason to bemoan the fact that the rental data were presented for such a short period. The estate comprised 3,000 holdings of over 2 acres, 58 of which exceeded 500 acres, including 7 of over 1,000 acres each.[38] The average rent due varied from 29 shillings per acre in 1880 to 22 shillings per acre in the early 1890s, and the rent per acre received after allowances and the deduction of irrecoverable arrears varied from nearly 27 shillings per acre in 1880 to 21 shillings per acre in the late 1880s and early 1890s. If the sheer coverage of land under the control of the Ecclesiastical Commissioners can be taken to offer a sample of English rents in its own right, then it can be compared with the aggregate of the 29 other estates which made up the bulk of the evidence to the Royal Commission. In terms of rent per acre the two samples are roughly comparable. The rents on the church lands were marginally lower. Taken together, these two samples, if only for the narrow period 1880–92, furnish data on both the rent due and the rent received on something between half a million and well over 700,000 acres of England, or something close to 2 per cent of the land mass, and in excess of this as a proportion of the effective agricultural area.

The Royal Commission also made a serious attempt to investigate the ramifications of the depression at the farm level, by utilising the observations of its assistant commissioners on those farm accounts which were made available to them. These data were presented throughout the several volumes of evidence in the Royal Commission (and therefore furnish a very large and detailed database including details of outgoings and income) and

---

[37] Royal Commission on Agriculture, 'First Report', Q. 369.   [38] Ibid., Qs. 374–8.

Table 6.2. *Summary of rents received from up to 69 tenant farms in England, 1875–1894*

Year	No. of accounts	Acreage of farms	Total rent including tithe rentcharge £	Average rent (Shillings) per acre
1875	4	2,217	3,753	33.88
1876	5	3,057	4,515	29.50
1877	6	3,351	4,861	29.00
1878	6	3,351	4,957	29.75
1879	7	4,188	5,420	25.83
1880	9	5,563	6,470	23.25
1881	12	7,075	9,085	25.67
1882	13	7,757	9,350	24.08
1883	14	8,491	10,184	24.00
1884	17	13,121	15,504	23.67
1885	21	16,507	18,416	22.33
1886	24	16,887	19,098	22.58
1887	29	20,935	21,778	20.75
1888	31	21,528	22,087	20.50
1889	35	23,051	22,773	19.75
1890	40	25,222	24,388	19.33
1891	40	25,621	25,154	19.58
1892	42	26,270	24,524	18.67
1893	48	27,554	25,997	18.83
1894	22	12,297	12,563	20.04

Note: The figures in column 5 were originally given by the Royal Commission in shillings and pence.
Source: Royal Commission on Agriculture, 'Final Report ... Appendix', *BPP*, C. 8541, XV (1897), Appendix III, p. 50.

they were also summarised as an appendix.[39] They are further summarised here as table 6.2. They relate to up to 69 tenant farms of varying sizes scattered throughout England. A large proportion (50 out of 69) were located in the eastern and east Midland counties, with as many as 14 from Essex and ten from Lincoln alone; six refer to south Midland counties, nine to southern, and only four to northern counties. In this particular sample there are none from the whole of the western side of England, from the Scottish border down to Land's End. In summary therefore they are almost certainly dominated by arable farms. Because the evidence was not presented in a standard format the summarisers had to make certain adjustments. For example, the amounts for rent, tithes, taxes, and rates were frequently aggregated in one sum. In order to approximate the rent they

[39] Summary to be found in Royal Commission on Agriculture, 'Final Report', Appendix III, p. 50, and detailed accounts in Royal Commission on Agriculture, 'Particulars of the Expenditure and Outgoings on Certain Estates in Great Britain and Farm Accounts', *BPP*, C. 8125, XV (1897).

made a deduction of 12.5 per cent on account of rates and taxes. In some cases remissions of rent escaped notice and therefore what we are left with is a mixture of accounts of both the rents payable and the rents actually paid. A full interpretation of what table 6.2 reveals, therefore, is not easy, but the recognised disaster which hit arable farmers in 1879 through a collapse of their incomes is evident – it translates into a fall in rent of 13 per cent in one year. It was then followed by a larger, if uneven, fall in rents amounting to 28 per cent in the next 13 years. When we review the findings of the new rent index in a later chapter we shall see that our appraisal of the national rent index reveals a rent per acre for rents received of 28.4 shillings per acre in 1878, 25.4 in 1879, and 20.1 by 1893. The comparable figures in the sample of farms in table 6.2 are 29.75, 25.8, and 18.8. The trends are the same even if the magnitudes of change are slightly different – they were more extreme in the sample of farms. This is to be expected given the emphasis of location of those farms in the arable east.

Overall the Royal Commission of the 1890s furnishes the historian with a considerable database itemising rents due and rents received, yet we need to have a feel for the possible biases which were in place when the data were collected. The inquiry investigated agricultural depression and therefore it seems to have concentrated on the most depressed parts of the country. This implies a bias, though not an exclusive bias towards the arable eastern half of the country. For example, the evidence from the whole of the Duke of Bedford's agricultural property necessarily included also that extensive part of his estate located in the West Country which did not experience the depression to the same degree as his eastern estates. His agreed rental on a relatively unchanged acreage in the West Country actually increased by 4 per cent from 1879 to the early 1890s, while the equivalent agreed rents fell by 11 per cent in the east Midlands (with a modest drop in acres), and on his home estate centred on Bedfordshire and Buckinghamshire they fell by 33 per cent (though accompanied by a 25 per cent reduction in acres). The ability of an estate owner to cross-subsidise net losses with net gains was a luxury not all landowners could share. It all depended on where the lands were located and under what broad agricultural regimes. The Treasurer of Guy's Hospital gave evidence relating to the Hospital's three principal estates, in Herefordshire, Lincolnshire, and Essex. He shows that there was an all-round reduction of rents even though the hospital held lands in the pastoral west. In the 1880s the reductions amounted to 30 per cent in Herefordshire, where the rents also included the tithe paid by the tenants, but in Lincolnshire the reduction was 38 per cent which, with a further reduction of 8 per cent for the tithe, amounted to a total reduction of 46 per cent. In Essex the fall in rents amounted to 47 per cent, but since the tithe was paid by the hospital in this case, effectively the loss of revenue to the Governors was of the order of 60 per cent.[40] In contrast, the Secretary and Financial Adviser to the Ecclesiastical Commissioners reported that there had scarcely been any rent reductions in Cheshire and Lancashire, and little in Cumberland, or in Devon until recently.[41] The reductions and abatements were worst in Huntingdon, Nottinghamshire, Lincolnshire, and, perhaps surprisingly, Somerset.[42] The lands of the Ecclesiastical Commissioners were widely spread and therefore perhaps the trend in average rent per acre across their interests was representative of the country as a whole. But that is not the point. If this evidence to the Royal Commission is used alone in the construction of a national rent index it may give a more depressed picture for the agricultural sector as a whole than was in fact the case. We hope to show that a more representative geographical selection of evidence presents the same trend but with milder inflections in that trend.

Late nineteenth-century contemporary estimates

We turn now to the contribution to rent history made by R. J. Thompson and by a number of concerned individuals in the late nineteenth century. As individual appraisers perhaps they should be included in chapter 2, yet their motives for studying rents related more to specific circumstances, in this case the depression of the 1890s, than to the general spirit of inquiry of agricultural writers and journalists such as Arthur Young and others. Thompson made available his findings in a lecture to the Royal Statistical Society in December 1907, which was subsequently published in the society's journal. The worst of the late-nineteenth-century agricultural depression had passed, but agriculture was not yet even in a state of recovery let alone good health. In other words, his work was as much inspired by thoughts of the depression as was the work of the Royal Commission.

Table 6.3 is a summary of the data which Thompson collected. It includes four separate estimates. The first was based on about 72,000 acres from estates in Lincolnshire, Essex, Hereford, and North Wales, and this is available for the period 1801–1901; the second was from estates totalling over 120,000 acres in Lincolnshire, Hereford, Buckinghamshire, Bedfordshire, Cambridge, Essex, and North Wales, and available from 1816–1900; the third was from estates totalling between 390,000 and 400,000 acres distributed across more than 24 English counties and 1 Welsh county, and available from 1872 to 1900. The fourth was based on evidence presented many years later by Sir Charles Howell Thomas, the Permanent Secretary

[40] Royal Commission on Agriculture, 'First Report', Q. 1635.   [41] *Ibid.*, Qs. 425–6, 429.
[42] *Ibid.*, Qs. 391–402.

Table 6.3. *A composite rent index for the nineteenth century based on R. J. Thompson*

Date	1st sample Rent	2nd sample Rent	3rd sample Rent	4th sample Rent	Total acres	Composite indexes 1st	Composite indexes 2nd
		All in shillings per acre					
1801	11.7	—	—	—	62,655	11.7	14.5
1802	10.8	—	—	—	62,655	10.8	13.4
1803	10.9	—	—	—	62,655	10.9	13.5
1804	11.2	—	—	—	62,655	11.2	13.8
1805	11.2	—	—	—	62,655	11.2	13.8
1806	11.2	—	—	—	63,325	11.2	13.8
1807	11.3	—	—	—	63,620	11.3	14.0
1808	11.7	—	—	—	64,320	11.7	14.5
1809	11.7	—	—	—	64,320	11.7	14.5
1810	12.3	—	—	—	64,320	12.3	15.2
1811	13.5	—	—	—	65,320	13.5	16.7
1812	14.5	—	—	—	65,320	14.5	18.0
1813	14.9	—	—	—	66,320	14.9	18.5
1814	15.0	—	—	—	66,320	15.0	18.6
1815	15.2	—	—	—	66,320	15.2	18.8
1816	14.6	18.0	—	—	175,741	16.7	20.7
1817	14.4	18.8	—	—	177,848	17.1	21.2
1818	15.9	19.3	—	—	177,848	18.0	22.4
1819	15.4	18.8	—	—	178,225	17.5	21.7
1820	15.4	18.7	—	—	178,431	17.4	21.6
1821	14.8	18.3	—	—	178,430	17.0	21.0
1822	13.6	17.2	—	—	178,788	15.8	19.6
1823	14.8	17.5	—	—	178,990	16.5	20.4
1824	16.1	18.2	—	—	179,298	17.4	21.5
1825	16.8	18.5	—	—	179,525	17.8	22.1
1826	14.9	17.2	—	—	180,727	16.3	20.2
1827	15.0	17.3	—	—	180,949	16.4	20.3
1828	15.4	18.3	—	—	181,252	17.2	21.4
1829	14.8	17.8	—	—	181,518	16.7	20.7
1830	15.3	18.3	—	—	181,718	17.2	21.3
1831	15.8	18.7	—	—	182,050	17.6	21.8
1832	15.2	18.3	—	—	183,200	17.1	21.2
1833	15.3	18.4	—	—	183,915	17.2	21.4
1834	15.2	18.3	—	—	184,181	17.1	21.2
1835	15.5	18.5	—	—	184,459	17.4	21.5
1836	15.3	18.7	—	—	184,659	17.4	21.5
1837	15.8	18.5	—	—	184,546	17.5	21.6
1838	15.8	18.4	—	—	185,655	17.4	21.6
1839	15.3	18.4	—	—	185,831	17.2	21.4
1840	15.6	19.1	—	—	186,392	17.8	22.0
1841	16.5	19.8	—	—	186,858	18.5	23.0
1842	16.3	19.8	—	—	190,744	18.5	22.9
1843	16.4	20.1	—	—	190,898	18.7	23.2
1844	16.7	20.3	—	—	190,471	19.0	23.5
1845	16.7	20.5	—	—	190,673	19.1	23.6
1846	17.1	20.8	—	—	190,778	19.4	24.0
1847	16.7	20.5	—	—	191,015	19.1	23.6
1848	17.3	21.1	—	—	191,456	19.6	24.3
1849	16.1	20.3	—	—	191,760	18.7	23.2

Table 6.3. (cont.)

Date	1st sample Rent	2nd sample Rent	3rd sample Rent	4th sample Rent	Total acres	Composite indexes 1st	2nd
		All in shillings per acre					
1850	16.3	20.5	—	—	192,069	18.9	23.4
1851	16.0	19.8	—	—	192,586	18.4	22.8
1852	16.5	20.3	—	—	193,055	18.8	23.4
1853	16.6	20.1	—	—	193,563	18.8	23.3
1854	16.7	20.3	—	—	193,798	19.0	23.5
1855	16.8	20.8	—	—	193,891	19.3	23.9
1856	17.1	21.8	—	—	193,950	20.1	24.9
1857	17.5	22.9	—	—	194,552	20.9	25.9
1858	17.8	23.3	—	—	194,571	21.2	26.3
1859	17.8	23.1	—	—	194,959	21.1	26.2
1860	18.0	23.0	—	—	194,302	21.1	26.2
1861	18.2	23.4	—	—	193,445	21.5	26.6
1862	18.1	23.3	—	—	193,961	21.4	26.5
1863	18.2	23.5	—	—	193,348	21.5	26.7
1864	18.2	23.3	—	—	194,379	21.4	26.6
1865	18.4	23.2	—	—	194,468	21.4	26.5
1866	18.5	23.3	—	—	194,325	21.5	26.7
1867	18.6	23.8	—	—	194,509	21.8	27.1
1868	18.8	24.6	—	—	194,886	22.4	27.8
1869	18.9	24.8	—	—	194,751	22.6	28.1
1870	18.8	24.0	—	—	195,609	22.0	27.3
1871	19.2	24.3	—	—	195,700	22.4	27.8
1872	19.4	24.8	28.5	—	611,659	26.7	28.4
1873	19.8	25.3	28.8	—	614,767	27.0	28.8
1874	20.0	25.5	29.0	—	616,890	27.2	29.0
1875	20.1	25.5	29.1	—	617,106	27.3	29.1
1876	20.1	25.4	29.3	—	618,510	27.4	29.2
1877	20.3	26.1	29.8	—	619,303	27.9	29.7
1878	20.5	26.4	29.5	—	620,457	27.8	29.7
1879	20.2	19.8	26.7	—	620,223	21.5	26.0
1880	18.4	21.3	26.3	—	618,554	24.4	25.9
1881	18.6	20.5	25.9	—	609,537	24.0	25.5
1882	18.2	23.5	27.1	—	603,860	25.3	27.0
1883	17.5	23.3	27.3	—	597,245	25.4	27.0
1884	16.9	22.3	26.5	—	593,465	24.5	26.1
1885	16.7	18.0	24.1	—	593,809	22.0	23.3
1886	16.3	20.9	25.3	—	594,869	23.4	24.8
1887	15.8	17.0	22.4	—	593,529	20.6	21.8
1888	15.5	19.5	23.0	—	592,550	21.4	22.8
1889	15.5	20.1	23.3	—	592,921	21.7	23.1
1890	15.6	19.5	23.1	—	593,772	21.5	22.8
1891	15.2	19.5	23.0	—	590,834	21.4	22.7
1892	15.6	18.5	22.4	—	592,876	20.8	22.1
1893	14.7	17.0	22.0	—	564,374	20.0	21.3
1894	15.0	15.9	21.4	—	571,324	19.5	20.7
1895	14.5	16.1	21.3	—	571,416	19.4	20.6
1896	14.6	17.0	20.8	—	580,643	19.3	20.5
1897	14.2	16.9	20.5	—	580,850	19.0	20.2
1898	14.4	17.0	20.5	—	580,372	19.0	20.3

Table 6.3. (cont.)

Date	1st sample Rent	2nd sample Rent	3rd sample Rent	4th sample Rent	Total acres	Composite indexes	
						1st	2nd
		All in shillings per acre					
1899	14.6	17.1	20.0	—	589,533	18.8	20.0
1900	14.6	17.2	20.1	—	589,814	18.8	20.1
1901	—	—	—	20.7	290,000	20.7	20.7
1902	—	—	—	20.3	290,000	20.3	20.3
1903	—	—	—	20.5	290,000	20.5	20.5
1904	—	—	—	19.9	290,000	19.9	19.9
1905	—	—	—	20.4	290,000	20.4	20.4
1906	—	—	—	20.6	290,000	20.6	20.6
1907	—	—	—	20.6	290,000	20.6	20.6
1908	—	—	—	20.8	290,000	20.8	20.8
1909	—	—	—	20.8	290,000	20.8	20.8
1910	—	—	—	20.8	290,000	20.8	20.8
1911	—	—	—	20.8	290,000	20.8	20.8
1912	—	—	—	21.1	290,000	21.1	21.1
1913	—	—	—	21.3	290,000	21.3	21.3
1914	—	—	—	21.3	290,000	21.3	21.3

Note: The first index arises from the weighted average of the four individual series of rents per acre, weighted by the number of acres in each sample. The second index further weights the first two samples by a factor of 1.24, for reasons explained in chapter 8 below.
Sources: Samples 1, 2 and 3: Thompson, 'An inquiry', 587–625.
Sample 4: Royal Commission on Tithe Rentcharge. Minutes of Evidence (London, 1934).

at the Ministry of Agriculture and Fisheries, to the Royal Commission on Tithe Rentcharge in 1934, but which he attributed to the research of Thompson. This last estimate refers to a single estate of 290,000 acres covering the period 1901–14, though the details are available up to 1933, and we should note that it also formed a large proportion of the land in Thompson's third sample.[43] Given the county locations specified, the relatively small number of large estates involved, and Thompson's own acknowledgements to what we might call his benefactors, we strongly suspect that Thompson's evidence in sample three is not much more than a refinement of the evidence presented to the Royal Commission. This is not precisely verifiable because Thompson assured those who supplied him with information that, 'The information has been supplied on the understanding that the particulars should not be published in such a way as to enable any particular estate to be indentified.' However, it is almost certainly the case

[43] Thompson, 'An inquiry', 82–4, for the period up to 1900; and Royal Commission on Tithe Rentcharge: Minutes of Evidence (London, 1934), First day of evidence, 25 October 1934, pp. 22, 44–5, and reprinted in H. A. Rhee, The Rent of Agricultural Land in England and Wales (London, 1946), pp. 34 and 42.

that there is considerable overlap with the Royal Commission evidence since he cites the assistance of the Duke of Bedford, the Royal Commission itself, the Ecclesiastical Commissioners, and Guy's Hospital, among others.[44] We may deduce that the evidence from Herefordshire which has been subsumed in estimates one and two refers to the lands belonging to Guy's Hospital, and that estimate number three is Thompson's own analysis of the Royal Commission evidence.

We suspect that there is a regional, and hence a land-use, bias in Thompson's three estimates. The Royal Commission was biased towards estates in eastern England; Guy's Hospital had two-thirds of its land concentrated in Lincolnshire and Essex, and from Thompson's list of acknowledgements of those who furnished him with information, cross-referenced with the biographical entries in Bateman's *Great Landowners* in 1883, it is clear that the east of England is again well represented in these estimates. For example, the Duke of Bedford, as we have already indicated, had land in many places, including an extensive estate in Devon, but nearly 70 per cent of his land was along a line from Lincolnshire to Hertfordshire and centred on Bedfordshire; 97 per cent of the Duke of Newcastle's land was located in Nottinghamshire, and the remainder in adjacent counties; the Marquess of Ripon had land in Yorkshire and Lincolnshire; 65 per cent of the Marquess of Northampton's English lands were in Northampton-shire; Lord Carrington held lands in Buckinghamshire and Lincolnshire; the Earl of Onslow was mainly represented in Surrey and Essex; and Christopher Turnor had a 21,000 acre estate in Lincolnshire. The evidence from the Ecclesiastical Commissioners is more representative geographi-cally – they owned land almost everywhere, though the largest acreages were in Durham, Yorkshire, Lincolnshire, Kent, Cambridgeshire, and Nottinghamshire, with sizeable holdings also in the west in Wiltshire, Somerset, and Worcestershire. Just about the only individual landowner mentioned by Thompson who did not have the lion's share of his estate in eastern or east-central England was the Earl of Jersey, whose address was Bicester in Oxfordshire where he possessed nearly 6,000 acres, but whose biggest single estate was 10,000 acres in Glamorgan. He also owned nearly 2,000 acres in Middlesex and 1,000 and 500 acres respectively in Warwick-shire and Kent.

These estimates may not be accurate to the nearest acre, but they surely make the important point that along with the Royal Commission's findings, many of which we believe to have been duplicated in Thompson's work, there was a significant concentration of data from the relatively arable east

[44] Thompson, 'An inquiry', 58.

of England. A rent index which purports to be a national index, but which is based on this evidence alone, will tend to deepen the profile of depression and drive down the average rent in an exaggerated way. The problem was clearly illustrated earlier in the broad regional differences in rent per acre depicted in figure 6.3.

There is obviously nothing like a depression to provoke a searching review of estate finances. In the Royal Commission findings, and in the work of R. J. Thompson, we have two sources which purport (whatever our misgivings) to examine the question from a national viewpoint, but others undertook the same exercise on a more limited scale, including the 9th Duke of Bedford. The timing of his estate biography is not without significance. He began work on it following a speech he made to the Thorney Unionist Association on 13 May 1896. Thorney was the second of his three major English estates. It stretched over the counties of Cambridgeshire, Northamptonshire, and Huntingdonshire. This part of the east of England had just emerged from an agricultural depression, probably the deepest in its history, though in 1896 they could hardly imagine they had entered a period of recovery. To all engaged in agriculture it surely felt as though the depression was still present. Whilst having every sympathy for the ways in which agricultural fortunes had fluctuated variously for landlords, tenants, and labourers, Bedford was, nevertheless, quick to establish that for the Thorney estate, as for the separate Woburn estate in Bedfordshire and Buckinghamshire, the possession of property for a landlord involved heavy annual losses. Yet the English system of landholding and inheritance, and the social as well as the economic position and commitment of great landowners needed to be defended against the forces of change because the very social structure which he, and others like him, was born into, was not a recent creation, but 'a social structure [already] tested by stress of change'.[45] Thus:

> Relief from agricultural depression accordingly must be sought, not in the extermination of the great landlord; nor in the artificial manufacture of a peasant proprietary without either capital, or hereditary aptitude in the management of land; not in protection; nor in the production of cabbages, jam, eggs, duck or fruit. A principal source of relief to agricultural depression is to be found in the restoration of confidence and the consequent attraction of more capital into land; in the encouragement of good farming; and in the obliteration of such barriers to the wider distribution of landed interests as are raised by the existing artificial and costly system of land transfer.[46]

[45] Bedford, *Story*, p. 4. The introduction, pp. 1–11, in general provides the background which we have sketched in here.
[46] *Ibid.*, p. 6. See also J. S. Anderson, *Lawyers and the Making of English Land Law 1832–1940* (Oxford, 1992), the most recent study which debates the perceived monopoly and thus iniquitous practices of the legal profession in the operation of the land market.

The duke complained about a whole collection of burdens as he saw them from a landlord's point of view, but including the burden of his class that they, the landlords, were regarded as 'a parasitical class, feasting on others' labour, reaping where others sow; and that it is the national duty of the State not to defend their rights like those of other citizens, but to eradicate them as vermin whose existence is incompatible with public welfare'.[47] The introduction to his history continued in such a vein; it was a denunciation of the forces of political and social change, and a justification for the continuity of his class. Without using direct language, he was surely reacting to the recent but abortive political debate regarding land reform and its ultimate goal of land nationalisation. His parting shot in his introduction was related to 'the ominous prospect of confiscation', and a grim future if 'the wild proposals for the compulsory distribution of property are realised'.[48] His history thus became a defence of his class, an explanation that a good proportion of his rental income was always spent on capital improvements which tenants and labourers both enjoyed, and also on many other expenditures which added to the standard of life of his local rural community, whether it was through the provision of churches and schools, pensions and allowances, gifts and other charitable causes, all of which expenditures continued at their customary high levels even in the nine years when the Woburn estate suffered net deficits on its rental income. In addition, he argued, he provided cottages, whose costs of maintenance far outstripped the rents he received for them; an allotment system; and, during the difficult years of the recent depression, he allowed annual remissions of rent, and more than one revaluation of rents. All in all, he argued, the rent he received was certainly not a profit from his land. With average net incomes at Thorney of marginally over 2 per cent over and above his outlay of capital for new works, and barely 1 per cent at Woburn, against the foregone income from other possible investments, landlordism, he argued, was hardly a just return on anyone's capital. Far from being the parasite of some contemporary popular legends, he was closer perhaps to the knight in shining armour.

The late-nineteenth-century debate about land reform and its ownership is not without importance for the interpretations which might be put on the rent index, and the underlying agricultural history which it represents, but for the moment the importance of the Duke of Bedford is that, alone of his peers, he has produced data for two of his three estates. The third estate, Tavistock in Dorset and Devon, we have separately extracted from the archives. We have already commented on the inclusion of the duke's land in

[47] Bedford, *Story*, p. 8.   [48] *Ibid.*, p. 11.

R. J. Thompson's inquiry, and yet we are frustratingly unable to separate the precise estates from Thompson. Nevertheless, the data from the duke's history of Thorney and Woburn will be included in the rent index for much of the nineteenth century. It is probably not without significance that his history does not include details from the Tavistock estate. As a west of England estate it did not experience the late-nineteenth-century depression to the same degree. While throughout the nineteenth century the rent per acre was larger on both of the eastern estates, by the 1890s this differential had pretty well disappeared. The western rents held up well and, given the general deflation of the last three decades of the century, in real terms those rents may have improved. These broad trends are shown in figure 6.5, a comparison of the rent per acre on the duke's three principal estates for most of the nineteenth century.[49]

J. C. Steele, in his work on the Guy's Hospital accounts, made the distinction between the hospital, which was founded on a real property bequest and which therefore derived the bulk of its income from land, and other hospitals, and indeed charities in general, which existed on voluntary contributions. Guy's Hospital, therefore, 'suffered materially from the continual agricultural depression', which Steele specifically related to the diminished value of the arable land. From the hospital's point of view, the difference between a declining gross rental income and a more static if not rising estate liability and outgoing produced a net rental income which on the Essex estates yielded a decline from the 1870s to the early 1890s of nearly 60 per cent.[50] As we have already indicated from the Royal Commission data, and as is itemised also in Steele's account, the relatively arable east of England estates experienced the worst of the depression.[51] With the declining net income the governing body of the hospital was compelled to compromise its service to patients, to borrow money, to accept private subscription, and generally to publicise the plight of a curative institution which catered for the poor. The only way the hospital was able to square the circle of resource constraints and still cater for the same annual throughput

---

[49] *Ibid.*, pp. 218–24, 230–7; Devon RO, Bedford Tavistock Estate T 1258/M/ER 15.A&B – 129. Note that for the Woburn estate a distinction was made between the acreage of the agricultural estate and the woods and plantations, but this distinction was only made from 1873. Before that date, annually, a combined figure was always quoted. Woods and plantations amounted to 4,293 acres in 1873, reducing gradually to 4,274 acres in 1881, and then more swiftly to a low point of 3,879 acres in 1887, and recovering to 4,000 acres in 1895. For comparability the overall acreages recorded annually from 1816 to 1872 have been reduced by 4,000 acres. Timber was always an important feature of Woburn's income, especially during periods of railway building when the Woburn estate provided timber for sleepers. On the trend of the timber income an allowance of 4,000 acres does not seem too great, and may even be on the low side.
[50] Steele, 'The agricultural depression', 37–48, especially 39–40.
[51] Steele was not subsequently the witness who represented Guy's before the Royal Commission. This duty fell to Edward Harbord Lushington, the Treasurer of the Hospital.

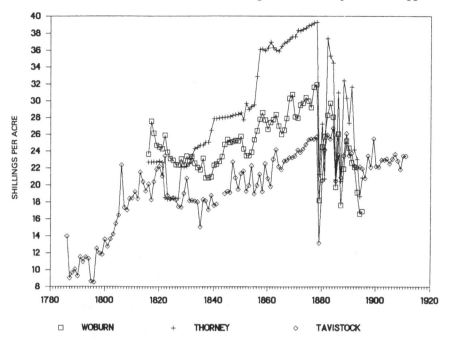

Fig. 6.5 Rent per acre on the Duke of Bedford's estates, 1785-1910 (comparison between Woburn, Thorney, and Tavistock, based on received rents)

of patients was to reduce the average period of in-patient residence from nearly forty days per patient in the mid-1870s to twenty-seven days by the mid-1890s.[52]

The case of the Oxford and Cambridge colleges perhaps has parallels with Guy's Hospital in that a large proportion of the colleges' income was derived from landed property, and the ability to raise other funds through other kinds of investment was limited. The move towards rack renting by the corporate estates raised the question of what was a reasonable bargain for a rack rent, reasonable both from the point of view of the lessee and the lessor. Those tenancies which were converted at otherwise fruitful times after the depression of the 1830s had a relatively short-lived period of prosperity before the late-nineteenth-century depression took a severe hold. At St John's College, Cambridge, the annual average college revenue from 1844–50 was £21,569, of which £12,061 came from rack rents, and already the dismantling of old-style tenures had begun. By 1882 the college revenues had risen to nearly £38,000, of which nearly £25,000 now came from rack

---

[52] Steele, 'The agricultural depression', 41, 48.

rents, and well over £5,000 from newly acquired urban property. There is a suggestion that the college, probably accidentally, applied excessively the notion of rack renting. We say accidentally because probably the new rents looked sensible and correctly competitive in the climate of the 1840s, 1850s, and 1860s, but on reflection from the viewpoint of the final quarter of the century they may have looked like famine rents. The difference between a competitive rent and a famine rent is only ever identified when the tenant finds he has little margin out of his own revenues with which to pay the rent. As the historian of the college finances put it, 'the rents . . . were certainly on the full side and left little margin for bad years'.[53] Arrears on rent, often liberated as abatements of rent, mounted from the late 1870s, and farms were taken in hand as new tenants could not be attracted.[54] The college held land across much of the country, but there was a concentration of property in the eastern counties where the depression hit hardest. The high point of rents from money leases (which included some non-landed income) was over £31,000 in 1879 and 1880, but this rapidly gave way through abatement and rent reduction on the landed portion of the estate to a low point of under £15,000 in 1896.[55] The college income from rack rents, which stood at almost £25,000 in 1872, only slowly recovered from that low point in the mid-1890s. Even as late as the early 1920s it stood only at £20,000. The college had woken up to the realities of modern living and from the 1890s it developed its portfolio of interests to include houses on building leases, and revenues from its securities.[56] To this extent it paralleled private landlords, who, by the 1890s, were busy transferring their resources from land into stock, shares, and art collections. By 1894 Lord Leicester's portfolio was valued at £500,000, and in the same year the Duke of Bedford's equities portfolio accounted for about 16 per cent of his gross annual income.[57] Other families kept afloat by selling artefacts, among them the Fawkes family of Farnley Hall in Wharfedale, who sold part of their art collection in 1890 to offset the effects of falling agricultural prices.[58]

Even though the late-nineteenth-century depression was severe, if a private or quasi-public institution like a university held its lands in a particular locale, such as the west of England, it could almost regard the

[53] H. F. Howard, *An Account of the Finances of the College of St. John the Evangelist in the University of Cambridge 1511–1926* (Cambridge, 1935). See pp. 178–9 for the discontinuation of beneficial leases from the 1840s, pp. 112–13 for the course of arrears from 1770–1881, and pp. 203–5 for an account of this period of the college's history.   [54] *Ibid.*, pp. 226–9.   [55] *Ibid.*, pp. 328–31.
[56] *Ibid.*, pp. 244–5.
[57] Appendix to Wade Martins, *Holkham*; D. Spring, 'Land and politics in Edwardian England', *Agricultural History*, 58 (1984), 22–5.
[58] M. Sharples, 'The Fawkes–Turner connection and the art collection at Garnley Hall, Otley, 1792–1937: a great estate enhanced and supported', *Northern History*, 26 (1990), 131–59; D. Cannadine, *The Decline and Fall of the British Aristocracy* (New Haven, Conn., 1990), pp. 112–25.

depression as a figment of the imagination. But for others, like Guy's, who had a concentration of their property in the east of England, the effects of the depression were all the more severe. The middle road was where an institution had sufficiently far-flung investments that some portions of their estates could effectively subsidise others during bad times.[59] Some major private landowners were clearly in this position.[60] The Oxford and Cambridge college estates, whose individual properties were more or less randomly acquired through benefactions rather than purchases over long periods, may furnish evidence of accidental survival strategies during bad times. The precariousness of an institution whose main business was learning but whose principal form of revenue was the uncertainty of rent from land was vividly brought to light by the Treasurer of Oriel College in the late nineteenth and early twentieth century. It was the ramifications of the depression which provoked his research, but by 1892 when he first presented his findings the crisis was already abating. The college, and the university, had successfully survived. In terms of acreage and comparative income wealth, Oriel was a middling college. It had lands and landed interests in 11 counties, though its principal income was concentrated close to Oxford. The college had a little under 6,300 acres in 1881 of which 5,300 acres were let at rack rents. Minor land transactions in the last quarter of the century had little effect on this acreage – there were some sales and some purchases, and some lands were converted from beneficial leases. A little over 2,700 acres was located in Oxfordshire, and nearly 2,650 acres in Berkshire. The rest was spread over Yorkshire, Lincolnshire, Buckingham-shire, Somerset (especially), and Kent, with small acreages in Northampton-shire and Wiltshire. The college experienced a general decline in all rents (including non-agricultural rents) from nearly £10,500 in 1877–8 to nearly £7,500 in 1890, but this was during a time when the acreage of land let at rack rent increased modestly, and therefore in other circumstances the

---

[59] This was at least hinted at by Price, 'The recent depression', 4.

[60] For example, this was the case on the Duke of Bedford's estates, as we have hinted at already. See also T. W. Fletcher, 'The Great Depression of English agriculture, 1873–1896', reprinted in W. E. Minchinton (ed.), *Essays in Agrarian History*, II (Newton Abbot, 1968), especially p. 245 where Fletcher states that the Earl of Derby's Fylde rents in Lancashire actually rose, and by as much as 18 per cent from 1870–1 to 1896. The antithesis of Fletcher's general analysis can be found in G. Rogers, 'Lancashire landowners and the Great Agricultural Depression', *Northern History*, 22 (1986), 250–68, where he found that the depression was real enough in the very same county as Fletcher's study. It may not have shown itself in rent reductions, though certainly there were rent abatements and a history of accumulated rent arrears. Nevertheless, while the depression did not go unnoticed in the western counties of England, there was a clear enough regional dimension to the excesses of the depression. For example see F. M. L. Thompson, 'An anatomy of English agriculture, 1870–1914', in B. A. Holderness and M. E. Turner (eds.), *Land, Labour and Agriculture, 1700–1820* (London, 1991), pp. 211–40, esp. pp. 223–7, for a demonstration of the different regional consequences of the depression in terms of rent additions or deductions.

college would have expected to obtain a rising revenue. The general decline in rents was made up by a combination of a major decline from Oxfordshire properties from just over £4,100 in 1877–8 to a little over £2,700 in 1892, an even bigger decline from Berkshire properties from approximately £4,300 in 1877–8 to a little over £2,700 in 1890, but a rise on the Somerset properties from nearly £1,700 in 1877–8 to nearly £1,750 in 1890, when the acreage in that county modestly fell (though the proportion which was rack rented increased).[61]

The depression was not nearly so severely felt on Oriel's Somerset property, although this was partly because a proportion of it was let in market gardens and other non-farm properties.[62] On the purely farm side, even the Somerset lands experienced the depression. In general however, the most serious fall in rents occurred on arable lands. A cross-estates subsidy partially softened the extent of the depression for Oriel, but did not completely negate it. The reduced net income sometimes took the form of transferring the burden of the tithe rentcharge from the tenants to themselves. Overall, the decline in estate rent income amounted to 28 per cent over the course of the depression from 1876–7 to 1890, but on agricultural lands alone it amounted to 40 per cent. Furthermore, as a result of the University Commission of 1872, a public inquiry into the administration of the Universities of Oxford and Cambridge, the anticipation had been for a continuation in the rise of income, a decline in the system of beneficial leases and their substitution by a rack rental system, and therefore a rise in nominal rent income. In terms of forward planning therefore, the depression neutralised the effects of enfranchising the beneficial leases.[63] The accumulated rent arrears at Oriel were rapidly formalised as permanent losses by a yearly system of rent abatements. Yet the charges on the college such as rates, interest on borrowing for past estate expenditure, current estate expenditure, especially as beneficial leases ended and properties required modernisation, did not decline by the same amount. This further widened the gap between gross and net income.

Conclusion

Contemporary interest in rents was largely geared to individual estates, and to individual fortunes. Only in the serious conditions of the late nineteenth

---

[61] Calculated and simplified from Price, 'The recent depression', 8–9, and see also 10–11.
[62] Price, 'The recent depression', especially 14, 17, 23, and 27–35.
[63] A problem which was more generally encountered at the university. See Price, 'The colleges of Oxford and agricultural depression', esp. 44–9; Price, 'The accounts of the colleges of Oxford, 1893–1903', esp. 597–601.

century was data gathered with any consistency, and then, as we have suggested, there may be a problem of bias towards the arable east of England, where there is good reason to believe that the depression was deepest. The Royal Commission was concerned with depression rather than with agriculture more generally, and this tended to influence its proceedings and its findings. The data from the Duke of Bedford's estate, and from those properties in the north and west of England which formed part of the evidence, and more generally where regional cross-subsidisation took place, may help to correct these regional imbalances. Despite these biases, the range and quality of the rent material available for the late nineteenth century is such that we could not possibly ignore it; indeed, one of the reasons why the rent index appears to include so much more data for the last quarter of the nineteenth century than for earlier periods is precisely because of the quantity of data thrown up by the several surveys outlined here. In the national index the evidence from the Royal Commission comprises c. 200,000 acres of the whole in the 1870s, or about one-quarter, rising dramatically to 48 per cent in the 1880s. This includes over 500,000 acres in 1881, and over 600,000 acres in 1888. The peak year for acreage is 1892 with a contribution of 630,474 acres, and in terms of the proportion of contribution the Royal Commission evidence represents 50 per cent of the whole in both 1889 and 1890. A large part of this contribution from 1880 to 1892 was the diffuse estate of the Ecclesiastical Commissioners which alone accounted for between one-fifth and one-quarter of the index in those years.[64]

---

[64] In the final rent index we could have relied more heavily on the data of the Royal Commission. It took evidence relating to some estates for which we have acquired data independently, including Woburn and Chatsworth. If we had set aside this independent evidence and relied solely on the Royal Commission, for the period 1872–92 it would have accounted for over 40 per cent of the rent index, and always over 60 per cent from 1880 to 1892. At its peak it would have accounted for 65 per cent of the rent index in 1880, and a peak acreage of 796,041 acres in 1892.

CHAPTER 7

Constructing the rent index III: other studies

Our own analysis of archival material, coupled with the evidence collected by and in connection with the late-nineteenth-century Royal Commission, has provided the greater part of the data from which we have compiled a rent index. However, we commented in an earlier chapter that many large estates, in particular, had been the subjects of biographies.[1] We turn in this chapter to considering whether any of the materials in these studies can be added in a satisfactory way to the database. While any conclusions will be regionally specific (except perhaps in the case of large and scattered estates), the least we can do perhaps is to attempt to build up an impressionistic picture. Since contemporaries were often uncertain about the calculation of rent, there is little likelihood that historians collecting rent material will have acquired data which can easily be compared. None the less it may be that material collected for individual estates across long time spans offers us a way of shadowing a rent index to ensure that we have the correct framework.

For the mass of landowners there is barely the odd estate history to rely on, let alone a collective story to be told.[2] Yet from these individual biographies there are some families and some estates which have been

---

[1] Of individual biographies see, Parker, *Coke*, and Wade Martins, *Holkham*, on the Cokes of Holkham; Bedford, *Story*, on himself; R. A. Kelch on the Duke of Newcastle in, *Newcastle: A Duke Without Money: Thomas Pelham-Holles 1693–1768* (London, 1974); the Oxford Colleges on themselves, as in L. L. Price, 'The recent depression in agriculture as shown in the accounts of an Oxford college, 1876–90', *JRSS*, 55 (1892), 2–36; L. L. Price, 'The colleges of Oxford and agricultural depression', *JRSS*, 58 (1895), 36–74, including discussion; L. L. Price, 'The accounts of the colleges of Oxford, 1893–1903; with special reference to their agricultural revenues', *JRSS*, 67 (1904), 585–660, including discussion; L. L. Price, 'The estates of the colleges of Oxford and their management', *JRSS*, 76 (1913), 787–90; L. L. Price, 'The estates of the colleges of Oxford and their management', *Transactions of the Surveyors' Institution*, 45 (1912–13), 542–603.
[2] Two of the exceptions include Sir William Gavin, *Ninety Years of Family Farming: The Story of Lord Rayleigh's and Strutt and Parker Farms* (London, 1967); J. Oxley Parker, *The Oxley Parker Papers: from the Letters of an Essex family of Land Agents in the Nineteenth Century* (Colchester, 1964).

picked over more than once. Potentially we could piece together the longest continuous single series for a family and its estate by splicing together the researches of the several biographers of the Leveson-Gower/Sutherland estates in Staffordshire and Shropshire.[3] Four scholars have worked on the family archive in the production of doctoral theses. Yet once we look in detail at their interpretations of the financial records, the hazards of relying on the research of others soon becomes clear. For the Trentham estate J. R. Wordie extracted the rents due and rents paid for 1703, and for every year from 1717 to 1839. In addition, for all but four of the years from 1700 to 1716 he also collected evidence of rents due.[4] For the same estate Eric Richards extracted the half-yearly rents due and rents received for the period from Michaelmas 1776 to Lady Day 1867 inclusive (less one or two missing entries and one major gap from 1805 to 1812).[5] Where there is a chronological overlap in their research the rents reported by Wordie and Richards should be comparable. For the period 1777 to the late 1790s this is the case, although there is never a perfect match. Almost invariably for the period before the late 1790s the Richards rent quotations are 2 or 3 per cent higher than the equivalent ones from Wordie, but for 1798 this difference was nearly 11 per cent. Subsequently the Richards figures are always higher, and from 1824–39 they are higher by 10 per cent or more, and as high as 25 per cent in 1825. Equally large discontinuities are revealed when Wordie's rendition of the Lilleshall estate rents in Shropshire for the years 1700 to 1839 are compared with Richards's reported rents for the years 1812–65.[6] There is no ready explanation for these large differences though Richards recognized the need for great caution in the interpretation of the accounts.[7] The most likely explanation for the lack of comparability is that Richards included a proportion of the rental income which came from the industrial properties attached to the estate, which in the 1820s and 1830s amounted to about 20 per cent of the total estate income at Lilleshall.[8]

For the late nineteenth century on the Trentham part of the estates it is possible to make a similar comparison between quotations of 'agreed' rents and rents 'due' as extracted and quoted by Roy Sturgess and Richard

[3] J. R. Wordie, 'Rent movements and the English tenant farmer, 1700–1839', *Research in Economic History*, 6 (1986), 193–243; E. Richards, 'James Loch and the House of Sutherland, 1812–1855' (University of Nottingham, PhD thesis, 1967), especially pp. 338–44; R. Perren, 'The effects of agricultural depression on the English estates of the dukes of Sutherland, 1870–1900' (University of Nottingham, PhD thesis, 1967), especially pp. 291–301, 424–9; R. W. Sturgess, 'The response of agriculture in Staffordshire to the price changes of the nineteenth century' (University of Manchester, PhD thesis, 1965), especially pp. 492–535, and appendix pp. 40–92.
[4] Wordie, 'Rent movements', 225–30.   [5] Richards, 'James Loch', pp. 341–4.
[6] Wordie, 'Rent movements', 231–5; Richards, 'James Loch', pp. 338–40.
[7] Richards, 'James Loch', p. 153n.
[8] E. Richards, '"Leviathan of wealth": west Midland agriculture, 1800–50', *AgHR*, 22 (1974), 100.

Perren. Finding comparability is elusive. For all the years between 1870 and 1880 Perren's 'rents due' figures exceed the 'agreed rents' quoted by Sturgess. The differences vary from 19 per cent for 1875 to 41.5 per cent for 1873. As with Lilleshall in the earlier period we have a similar explanation for these differences: there is the likelihood of inclusion of industrial property rents in Perren's schedules and/or the subtraction of an allowance for such rents in the Sturgess schedules.[9] With this estate, as with others, there are some doubts over the inclusion of non-agricultural elements in the rent rolls, and obviously in industrial parts of the country these could be quite substantial. On the Dudley estates in the Black Country the income accruing to the estate in 1833 was just over £111,000, of which £91,000 came from mineral and industrial income and only £20,000 from agricultural rents.[10] On the Longleat estate, although it was predominantly in Wiltshire, the property included coal deposits in Somerset, and lead mines in Shropshire. The receipts from agricultural rack rents amounted to about 60 per cent of total estate income in the second half of the nineteenth century.[11] Agriculture was the most important element of income, but industrial earnings were far from trivial and need to be carefully removed before the data can be deployed in an agricultural rent index.[12]

These examples highlight the very considerable difficulties we faced in using the research work of other scholars in compiling the database within the parameters set out in chapter 4. Hewers in these same seams have usually been interested in total estate income (and expenditure) but not necessarily in its disaggregated forms, such as income from rents alone. The primary aims and objectives of other historians has of course determined the use they have made of the material. This also accounts for a further major problem we have encountered in using this work, the identification of estate acreages in conjunction with rental figures. As we noted in chapter 5, without the relevant acreage figures we have been unable to use otherwise excellent rental material. Others have hinted at the extent of the estates they have studied, but such details have not always been systematically extracted in the manner which is vital to our work.

Norfolk has always figured prominently in the historiography of the

[9] We are grateful to Richard Perren for suggesting this possible difference. We are also grateful to Roy Sturgess for his help in other matters.

[10] T. J. Raybould, 'The Dudley estate: its rise and decline between 1774 and 1947' (University of Kent, PhD thesis, 1970), p. 149.

[11] D. P. Gunstone, 'Stewardship and landed society: a study of the stewards of the Longleat estate, 1779–1895' (University of Exeter, MA thesis, 1972), especially p. 86.

[12] On the Wentworth Woodhouse estates in south Yorkshire the same problem arises, see P. Nunn, 'The management of some south Yorkshire landed estates in the eighteenth and nineteenth centuries, linked with the central economic development of the area (1700–1850)' (University of Sheffield, PhD thesis, 1985).

Agricultural Revolution, and within Norfolk the Coke family, Earls of Leicester, have always been celebrated. It comes as no surprise therefore that one of the major estates whose rents and rental history have been reviewed in the literature is the Coke estate at Holkham in north Norfolk. Two studies cover the estate history in the eighteenth and nineteenth centuries, but the problems of using the material they contain become clear when we examine the period for which they overlap. R. A. C. Parker's book covered the period 1707–1842, while Susanna Wade Martins wrote on Holkham between 1790 and 1900. On only two occasions do the rental figures extracted by Parker cover an extended period, for 1814–24 and 1820–42, and these years are also covered in Wade Martins's work.[13] For the years 1814–24 the reported rents are described by Parker as 'rents due', but as 'rent collected' by Wade Martins. Between 1814 and 1820 inclusive (apart from differences in arithmetic rounding), the rental figures quoted by Parker and Wade Martins agree, but for 1821 the Wade Martins figure is the higher by 2 per cent, and for 1822 the margin of difference is an alarming 10 per cent. The two studies also give different figures for 1823. These were difficult years when even the Holkham tenants ran into financial problems, and Parker seems to have deducted sums of money which were allowed to tenants, representing a proportion of forgiven rents.

These differences highlight the recurring question of what is a rent. If Parker and Wade Martins have extracted what all historians have considered to be rack rents at Holkham the figures should represent what the land will bear, but what the land will bear is also dependent on the ability of the tenant to pay as well as on some notion of explicit value. Neither at Holkham nor anywhere else are historians liable to have treated these apparent subtleties in like manner. In times of agricultural plenty when rents due and rents paid are virtually the same it really does not matter, but in times of agricultural crisis it does matter whether or not allowances or forgiven rents and arrears are taken into account. Since the position is not always made explicit in estate accounts, historians have needed to make assumptions which may, or may not, have been consistently applied.

Even if we could reconcile the rental figures, there would still be a major problem in trying to use the Holkham rental quotations, especially during the eighteenth century. The estate was evolving, but we do not know

---

[13] The only other rents quoted by Parker are for six discontinuous years between 1629 and 1706, and then only for a specific portion of the estate. Isolated references also appear elsewhere in the book: Parker, *Coke*, pp. 4, 146, 153; Wade Martins, *Holkham*, pp. 87, 270–2. The Coke family held lands in Suffolk, Buckinghamshire, Oxfordshire, Somerset, London, Staffordshire, Kent, Dorset, but their main interests were in Norfolk. The estate at Hillesden in Buckinghamshire, for example, was sold to the 1st Duke of Buckingham in 1823, for which see J. V. Beckett, *The Rise and Fall of the Grenvilles* (Manchester, 1994), p. 143.

precisely on what acreage the rents were assessed. All we can be certain of is that during the eighteenth century there was an increase in rents on the Coke estates which carried over until after the Napoleonic Wars. This increase arose for several reasons: a rise in nominal rent per acre; an increase in the size of the estate; and adjustments of tenure which brought some settled land into possession.[14] The gross rents accruing to the Coke family rose from £5,525 in 1706 to £9,102 in 1720, to £11,565 in 1730, to £12,629 in 1740 and to £14,400 in 1749, but they then fell dramatically to £12,096 in 1755 before rising again to £13,665 in 1759.[15] The major fall and major rise were due mainly to the selling and buying of land, but exactly how much land this involved is not clear. All we really know is that there was a bid to consolidate the estate in the vicinity of the Norfolk property.[16] On the occasion where the rents can be isolated for a constant land area, the gross rents in Norfolk rose by 44 per cent between 1718 and 1759.[17] In view of the *relative* stability of general prices during the period this rise in rents opens up interesting questions about adjustments in tenure and the course of agricultural productivity, but without offering definitive answers. Parker is happy to settle for an explanation based on underlying agricultural progress, although he also indicates a problem with rent arrears.[18] Equally significant may be the elimination of ancient tenures coupled with adjustments to what was an historic situation of under-renting. As far as we were concerned the discrepancies between the evidence presented in the two books and the absence of regular estimates of estate size were such that the only way forward was to revisit the Holkham archive and to extract the rents afresh. This we did for three periods, 1708–17, 1722–54, and 1775–1900. We also reconstructed the size of the estate, though the coincidence of rents and the certainty of estate size has only allowed us to use this material from 1775 onwards. For the period when our estimates coincide with the annual estimates of Wade Martins, from 1790–1900 inclusive, the total rent collected according to our research was £4,172,203 and according to Wade Martins it was £4,171,441. This is a remarkable coincidence, though it does hide some important differences. The two estimates do not perfectly coincide in any single year. Throughout the period they are within a few percentage points of one another, but in 1796 Wade Martins's figure is higher by 13 per cent, and then in 1797 lower by 13 per cent. In 1821 and 1822 a similar disjunction occurs of plus 11 and minus 13 per cent, and in 1877–79 Wade Martins is 21 per cent higher, then 14 per cent lower, and finally 12 per higher than us. The only way, therefore, in which we might claim that our estimates are superior is that we have taken them back to 1775.

[14] Parker, *Coke*, p. 4, and see also p. 77.   [15] *Ibid.*, pp. 5, 22, 26–7, 37.
[16] *Ibid.*, pp. 27, 37–8.   [17] *Ibid.*, p. 39.   [18] *Ibid.*, pp. 39–40.

Of the other large estates whose rents have been extracted by historians one of the most notable is that of the Sykes family of Sledmere House in East Yorkshire. Indeed, like so many other well-documented archives this one has been worked over by two historians. Barbara English has extracted an annual series from the late 1860s to the early 1890s, while Michael Adams has produced a discontinuous schedule of rents and acres for the period from 1850 to 1880. Each study, however, is based on a different composition of the estate farms. For example, in the case of Adams it is based on farms of an annual rental of at least £30. His data therefore cover a sample of 18,000 to 20,000 acres whereas English has data for nearly 30,000 acres. Therefore, in view of what we have established in chapters 3 and 6 about smaller farms attracting higher unit rents, it comes as no surprise to learn that where the two overlap the rents per acre on the larger English sample are higher than the rents per acre on the smaller Adams sample, which has deliberately excluded the smaller farms. From our analysis in earlier chapters these smaller farms would have attracted higher unit acre rents. As a result, the English data produce an estimate of average rent in 1870 of 21.5 shillings per acre, but the equivalent rent derived from Adams is 18.3 shillings per acre. In 1878 the equivalent average rents were 29.1 and 27.0 shillings per acre.[19]

What these examples reveal is a basic methodological problem which is central to our work. In studying landed estates scholars have been interested in rents as an indication of wealth, and in land sales as evidence of financial problems. Generally they have not needed to relate rental data to acreage because this has not been a central concern of their work. Even some brief and general studies of agricultural rent have adopted this line of argument: thus David Grigg, in examining agricultural rent and expenditure for three extensive estates in nineteenth-century Lincolnshire used estate acreages only for 'the first year' of his series, 'and later additions to the estate have been excluded'.[20] Since many landed estates do not have the quality of data to permit anything more systematic than this, we should not be surprised if historians have frequently used disconnected figures for long time spans in order to discuss income or estate size, and relatively few attempts have been made to trace the financial histories of estates which are directly linked to acreages on an annual basis over a long period.[21]

[19] B. English, 'On the eve of the Great Depression: The economy of the Sledmere estate 1869–1878', *Business History*, 24 (1982), 23–47, esp. 23–4; M. G. Adams, 'Agricultural change in the East Riding of Yorkshire, 1850–1880: an economic and social history' (University of Hull, PhD thesis, 1977), pp. 262–3.

[20] D. B. Grigg, 'A note on agricultural rent and expenditure in nineteenth-century England', *Agricultural History*, 39 (1965), 147. Correspondence with David Grigg has established that he did not extract acreages when he conducted his researches, with a strong suspicion that the available estate evidence would not have permitted this in any case. Our thanks to David Grigg for his help.

[21] In studying seventeenth and eighteenth-century Cumbria one of us (J. V. Beckett) was unable to

B. E. S. Trueman's study of the Guy's Hospital estates looks in exhaustive detail at financial management, but he was interested primarily in income and expenditure, and we cannot reconstruct adequately from his material the changing size of the estate.[22] Even the well-crafted story of a single family has usually been constructed for reasons which only obliquely touch on our own objectives. The estate history of the Strutt family in Essex is full of interesting personal incidents and familial connections, but it only occasionally affords insights into the economic management of the property. Rents are touched upon only occasionally. On an estate of 5,257 acres in 1781, increasing to 5,835 acres in 1816, rents rose from 13s 1d per acre to 22s 9d per acre. This evidence may more or less verify our own findings, but it cannot add much substance to a rent index because only for isolated years is it possible to make the calculation of rents per acre. The same is true of evidence from the same estate for the late nineteenth century when all of the distresses which hit eastern England corn farms were critical issues on the Strutt family farm. Thus there was a history of arrears, farms in hand, and, tellingly, a decline in rent per acre from 25s 5d to 15s 3½d between 1882 and 1896.[23]

Finally, there is a considerable amount of data collected by A. D. M. Phillips in the process of researching a book on underdrainage. We outlined these data in chapter 3 (table 3.1 and figure 3.6). Unfortunately we cannot employ them in the index because it is clear that of the 14 estates which he researched in Devon and Northamptonshire, two of the major ones have also been included in the index we describe in subsequent chapters (the rentals of the Fitzwilliam family at Higham Ferrers in Northamptonshire, 1800–14, and the Tavistock rentals of the Duke of Bedford's Devon estate, 1870–1914). It is not possible to isolate these estates and use the remaining 12 estates. Nevertheless, since Phillips's data is probably the most comprehensive of modern times so far we compare his broad findings in table 7.1 with a simplified preview of the new rent index.

Only occasionally, therefore, do existing studies help us in compiling a rent index. To those outlined in this chapter, and which we have used for illustrative purposes only – some of which we have discarded but others we have made some use of – we could add a number of others which we have

find satisfactory data for rent per acre on even the largest landed estates: J. V. Beckett, 'Regional variation and the agricultural depression, 1730–50', *EcHR*, 35 (1982), 35–51, esp. 37. We could cite numerous other examples of historians being able to do little more than patch together a picture of estate finances from scattered data: for example, David Howell, *Patriarchs and Parasites: The Gentry of South-West Wales in the Eighteenth Century* (Cardiff, 1986), pp. 82–9; J. D. Williams, 'The finances of an eighteenth-century Essex nobleman', *Essex Archaeology and History*, 9 (1977), 113–27.
[22] B. E. S. Trueman, 'The Management of the Estates of Guy's Hospital 1726–1900' (University of Nottingham, PhD thesis, 1975).
[23] Sir William Gavin, *Ninety Years of Family Farming: The Story of Lord Rayleigh's and Strutt and Parker Farms* (London, 1967), pp. 8–9, 82–5.

Table 7.1. *Two nineteenth-century rent indexes compared*

	Phillips' index	New index
	Rent per acre in shillings (Annual averages)	
1800/4	15.2	13.4
1820/4	20.6	20.4
1840/4	20.6	19.4
1860/4	22.4	24.3
1880/4	26.3	27.1
1895/9	21.4	21.9

Sources: Chapter 8 and appendixes below; A. D. M. Phillips, *The Underdrainage of Farmland in England During the Nineteenth Century* (Cambridge, 1989), pp. 156–7.

managed to incorporate into the rent index. Yet it remains true to say that generally the material is too disparate, too inconsistent, and too patchy for inclusion. Although there have been many attempts to use rental material, few of them have been sufficiently systematic to produce results which can satisfactorily be utilised in terms of illustrating long-run changes in agricultural history, or in attempts at reconstructing the national income accounts. Even those historians who have used archival material have seldom employed it in such a way that the broader conclusions which we seek can be drawn. Hardly anyone has deliberately specified the acreage on which rents have been collected. Instead, they have concentrated on the size of incomes.

Conclusion

This is a depressing conclusion from our perspective, but it also highlights the fact that rent, as a subject in its own right, has been neglected in British, or more narrowly English, agrarian history research. However, as one of the more contentious areas of estate management, and as a critical element for most landlords in the composition of estate incomes, rents can hardly be ignored. Nor have they been. The problem for us is that precisely because rent has formed part of wider investigations of financial management it has yielded very little in aggregate terms to contribute to a national or regional rent index. While we have attempted to make use of scattered data from individual studies, where appropriate, we have had little option but to discard most of what is currently available for the simple reason that it fails the quality tests we outlined in chapter 4.

Yet some of this material has been of great value, especially in the early eighteenth century when the sample of estates with usable sources is thin, and also at the very end of the period in order to substantiate what by then is a large database anyway. The data which we have extracted and employed are of two sorts: those which can be specifically located geographically, if necessary; and those which are less easy, or impossible, to locate. In these contexts we have employed Wordie's rents for the Lilleshall and Trentham estates of the Leveson-Gower, later Sutherland, family dynasty in Stafford-shire and Shropshire. These are available for most years from c. 1720 to 1840, along with the Wolverhampton rents of the same family for 1730 to 1755.[24] Attached to the same family was the Stittenham estate in West Yorkshire, for which rentals are available in Perren's thesis for the period 1870–1900.[25] The Audley End rentals in Essex have been employed for the period 1754–91, extracted from Williams's thesis; the Woburn and Thorney rentals from the Bedford estates for 1816 to 1895 have been taken directly from the Duke's autobiographical account; and the Sledmere estate rentals in East Yorkshire are available for the period intermittently from 1869 to 1892 through the work of Barbara English.[26] These rentals can be fixed fairly precisely in location. To these can be added the rentals from the Oxford colleges and St John's College, Cambridge. As beneficial leases gave way to rack rents in the second half of the nineteenth century on college lands, so the number of acres which could be included in the database increased substantially. The Oxford college material is available for 1871, 1883–1903, and also in 1911, and the St John's College material for the period 1882–1914.[27] The accumulated rents on 290,000 acres spread throughout England, for the estates of the Ecclesiatical Commissioners are available from 1900 through the research of R. J. Thompson, thus adding to the accounts for the same estate available through the Royal Commission for the period 1880–92.[28] In addition there are a few anonymous and small estates located in Cambridgeshire, Devon, and Yorkshire and available intermittently for the period 1870–1914.[29]

---

[24] Wordie, 'Rent movements', 235.   [25] Perren, 'The effects of agricultural depression', p. 430.
[26] J. D. Williams, 'A study of an eighteenth-century nobleman, his house, household and estate: Sir John Griffin, 4th Lord Howard de Walden, 1st Lord Braybrooke, of Audley End, Essex, 1719–1797' (University of London, PhD thesis, 1974), pp. 466–73; Duke of Bedford, *Story*, pp. 218–39; English, 'On the eve of the Great Depression', 23–4.
[27] For the Oxford Colleges see the many items by Price in note 1; for St John's College, Cambridge, see H. F. Howard, *An Account of the Finances of the College of St. John the Evangelist in the University of Cambridge 1511–1926* (Cambridge, 1935), pp. 313–35.
[28] The estimates attributed to him and quoted in the, Royal Commission on Tithe Rentcharge: Minutes of Evidence (London, 1934), p. 44; Royal Commission on Agriculture, 'First Report of Her Majesty's Commissioners Appointed to Inquire into the Subject of Agricultural Depression: Minutes of Evidence with Appendices', *BPP*, C. 7400, XVI (1894), Appendix A, table VII, p. 420.
[29] In fact some of these data are available up to 1934. H. A. Rhee, *The Rent of Agricultural Land in England and Wales* (London, 1946), pp. 41–3.

We conclude, albeit reluctantly, that the inconsistency of data collection by historians and others means that we can use their material only intermittently in the present project, a conclusion which gives added urgency and meaning to the need for a definitive rent index. R. J. Thompson in 1907 commented with remarkable understatement that: 'On the whole ... the statistical evidence of the general trend of rents in the past century is very meagre.'[30] In broad summary the material from these printed sources represents between 34 and 86 per cent of our total sample (by acreage) in the early period 1717–32 when there are relatively few new estates in our database. From 1733 to 1753 their contribution is never as much as 20 per cent of the total sample; from 1754 to 1774 it is always over 20 per cent but only in two years as much as 30 per cent; from 1775 to 1779 it is below 20 per cent, and from 1780 to 1793 it reduces from 24 to 10 per cent; from 1794 to 1815 it is always below 20 per cent; from 1816 to 1839 it hovers around 25–30 per cent; from 1840 to 1892 it is on or around 20 per cent; and from 1893 to 1900 it is on or around 30 per cent. Finally, from 1900 to 1914, when the Ecclesiastical Commissioners material is available and is so large and important, this source alone is practically 60 per cent of the total index.

In the next chapter we bring together all of the evidence: from the new estates we have researched; from the official government inquiries of the late nineteenth century; and from the printed (including unpublished) sources discussed in this chapter; to produce a definitive rent index for the period 1690–1914.

[30] Thompson, 'An inquiry', 58.

CHAPTER 8

An English agricultural rent index, 1690–1914

Despite the problems described in earlier chapters, we have collected a considerable body of data with which to construct a representative index of English agricultural rent. At its greatest extent in the 1880s our database contains material from nearly eighty estates across the country, and over the entire period 1690–1914 we have collected evidence from more than 100 estates (see appendixes). At its maximum, in the third quarter of the nineteenth century, the database includes rents from nearly 1.3 million acres of agricultural land in England. This was a little over 4 per cent of the total land area, but it was upwards of 5.5 per cent of the agricultural area – the area of crops, rotation grass, and permanent grass fluctuated from 23.4 to about 25 million acres according to the June Returns. In this chapter we present our main findings through a series of graphs and tables which provide indexes of rent. At each stage we explain the likely constraints on and limitations of our findings, particularly in the chronological and geographical context. In an ideal world the rents from every estate would be extracted (where they survive) and fed into a database, but we suggest that in the non-ideal conditions under which we have worked the overall results of our work provide a best-possible guide to English agricultural rent between 1690 and 1914. In the second half of the chapter we shall argue, with reference to other estimates, that the index is effectively definitive, and at its most defective it cannot be more than marginally out of true for the greater part of the period.

A national agricultural rent index, 1690–1914

In figure 8.1 we present an index of rents assessed for the period 1690–1914, and figure 8.2 is the comparable index of rents received. The summary data from which these graphs have been constructed are given in appendix 2. The broad shape of the curve is much as we would anticipate, but there are significant improvements on the Chambers and Mingay index which has

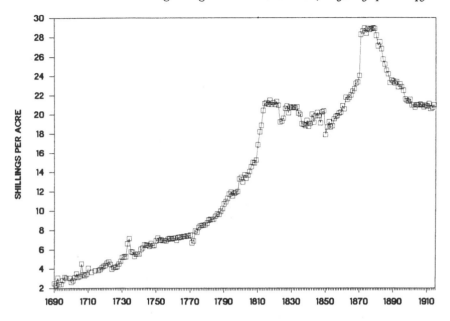

Fig. 8.1   Index of agricultural rent assessed in England 1690–1914 (shillings per acre)

guided historians for three decades, notably over the trend of rents in the eighteenth century. In the longer term, from the 1690s to *c.* 1880 we show a distinctive pattern in the profile of English agricultural rent through three full cycles each composed of a plateau followed by a rise. The first plateau, which was actually slightly upward sloping, lasted from 1690 to 1730. During this time rents actually doubled from 2 to 4 shillings per acre. Proportionately this is a dramatic increase but its importance is diminished because of the low base from which it commenced. Then from 1730 to 1750 unit acre rents doubled again, this time from about 4 shillings to 8 shillings per acre, and for the first time the change is readily noticeable in the profile. The Chambers and Mingay index is flat during this period, and the new findings must raise searching questions about the agricultural depression of the second quarter of the eighteenth century.[1] In later chapters we make important points about the geographical location and depth of the depression. From 1750 to about 1790 we find another slightly upward sloping plateau, but rents only increased by 10 per cent at most, and then from about 1790, until a peak rent

[1] For the Chambers and Mingay index see Chambers and Mingay, p. 167. On the depression see G. E. Mingay, 'The agricultural depression 1730–1750', *EcHR*, 8 (1956), 323–38. J. V. Beckett, 'Regional variation and the agricultural depression, 1730–50', *EcHR*, 35 (1982), 35–51.

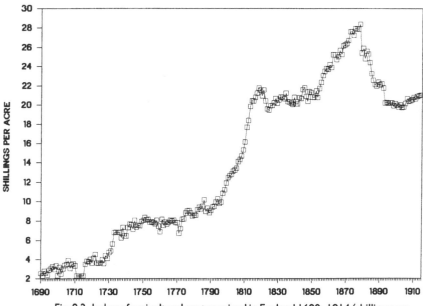

Fig. 8.2 Index of agricultural rent received in England 1690–1914 (shillings per acre)

in about 1810 to 1815, rents nearly trebled from what was no longer a low base. This period is coincident with the first period of serious and sustained inflation to hit the British economy since the Price Revolution of the sixteenth century, and the relationship between the inflation in rents and the general price movements of the period will be explored in chapter 10. From 1815 to 1850, apart from a fall in the immediate aftermath of the French wars, rents remained roughly level. From 1850 to *c.* 1880 rents increased by about 30 per cent in a remarkably steady fashion, before plummeting between *c.* 1880 and the mid-1890s to a level which effectively turned the clock back to the experiences of the 1830s and 1840s. Thereafter, beginning midway through the Edwardian decade, the semblance of a recovery had begun in the years leading up to the First World War.

These are the bare facts. We need to reiterate the point that the index represents an amalgam of many separate estate profiles which by a method essentially of scissors and paste have been joined together in a weighted fashion in which the method of weighting is by estate size. We are satisfied that no single estate has had a significant distorting influence over the whole period, and even across relatively short sub-periods we are satisfied that only one estate has had an influence which may have affected the average profile. This exception is the Duke of Northumberland's 164,000 acres encompassing much of the mainly harsh environment of the Cheviot Hills, and Scottish border country in general. We have data for this estate covering the narrow period 1850–70.[2] Its inclusion in the national index has a profound effect on the trend of rents. In 1850, on the basis of about 440,000 acres, when the average rent received per acre from all other estates was 21 shillings per acre, on the Northumberland estate it was 11 shillings per acre. When these Northumberland rents are included in the national index the average rent falls to 18 shillings per acre. In appendix 2 and in figures 8.1 and 8.2 the index is constructed to exclude the influence of this particular estate. The significance of figure 3.6 in chapter 3 should now be apparent. Our treatment of A. D. M. Phillips's data on that occasion very clearly reveals the influence of the Duke of Northumberland's estate, and others locally, on any attempts to construct a rent index.

We should also repeat that one of our major difficulties has been to determine the relationship between what a farmer agreed to pay to the landlord (rent assessed) and what in any given year he actually paid (rent received). Farmer X might agree to pay £100 a year rent, and while he might do so in many of the years in our sample, in others he might fail to pay the full amount, for whatever number of reasons, which we have discussed in earlier chapters. Thus in any particular year the rent assessed may be £100, but the rent received by the landlord and paid by the tenant might be £90 or, if the farmer is catching up on past arrears, it might even be £110. Figure 8.1 therefore represents the bargain which was set between landlords and tenants. It reflects their joint appreciation of the annual value of the land when the tenancy commenced, but it will not necessarily portray the practical reality of how much money actually changed hands.

The rent received in figure 8.2 represents a slightly different set of calculations. Here we are looking not at the agreement between the two parties as to the sums due and payable, but at the sums received by the landlord on an annual basis. It might usefully be regarded as the best and most sensitive indicator of the circumstantial joint perception by farmers and tenants of the value of the agricultural land in any particular year. As J. T. Ward has pointed out, 'An index based on rents actually received is therefore likely to give a much better indication of the reaction to changing circumstances than one based on contract rents.'[3] It reflected the tenants'

---

[2] Details of the Northumberland estate were originally taken from F. M. L. Thompson, 'The economic and social background of the English landed interest, 1840–1870, with particular reference to the estates of the Dukes of Northumberland' (University of Oxford, DPhil thesis, 1956), appendixes VIII and XI. See also Hughes, 'Northumberland', pp. 190, 195, for other examples where the rough grazing so prevalent in north and west Northumberland had similar effects on average rents.

[3] J. T. Ward, 'A study of capital and rental values of agricultural land in England and Wales between 1858 and 1958' (London University, PhD thesis, 1960), p. 72n.

ability to pay rather than the agreed annual value of the land. Ability to pay is obviously determined by various considerations, but we cannot easily build in an allowance for individual farming failures due to mismanagement or incompetence. What we can look for are longer-term movements affecting a broad spectrum of the farming community. In times of agricultural depression we would expect to find a high and rising incidence of rent arrears. In some cases the accumulation of arrears over time could and did result in landlords writing off outstanding rents, or making allowances for such arrears, and in the most extreme circumstances bargaining afresh the agreed rent in a downward direction. This certainly may have been the case where long leases prevailed, but with the movement towards annual tenancies by 1815, it was relatively easy to alter the financial bargain to which tenants and landlords agreed. Non-economic factors such as loyalty and long service, and also political considerations, will of course have continued to influence the bargain. In any one year the rent paid might be a composite of the tenant's appreciation of the value of his tenancy, and of a partial or full repayment of his debts, although the non-economic considerations would not readily be detected. Where it was a full repayment of debt this could be identified in the rentals. This very rarely happened in practice. Instead the full debt might never be redeemed, or it may have been paid off over a long period. In any one year, from the point of view of the tenant, the rent actually paid to the landlord might not be regarded as the considered value of his tenancy, because it might contain an element of unpaid rent from previous years, but it might also not be the considered financial value of the tenancy because it might hide non-economic factors. These are considerations which we can highlight but not pursue any further, although we shall return to the subject when we examine rent arrears.

If all archival material gave us both rent assessed and rent received, we could relate the two on a single graph, but the material is not so consistent. For some estates and in some periods we do have quotations both for rent due and rent received, but on other occasions only one of the two has survived. Consequently, within figures 8.1 and 8.2 the absolute acreage of the land to which they apply is not the same in every year, and neither is the precise geography of the land covered.

We have shown in previous chapters that the quality and quantity of surviving material improves through the period with which we are concerned. Figures 8.3 (a) and (b) demonstrate this graphically by showing a long-term view of the chronological build-up of the archives we have used. The acreage of land on which the rent indexes are based is quite small early in the period, but it increases in an uneven but near-linear fashion, until by the 1880s both of the main rent indexes are based on over one million acres

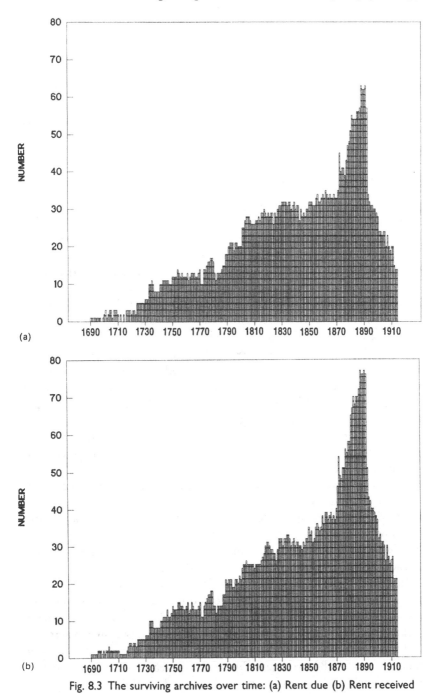

(a)

(b)

Fig. 8.3 The surviving archives over time: (a) Rent due (b) Rent received

of agricultural land. What now follows is a more detailed examination of the database and the resulting rent index which it provides. We discuss first the chronological and second the spatial cover we have achieved. We move on, third, to look at the incidence of rent arrears, since this opens up the important distinction between times of relative feast and relative famine. Fourth, we look at the extent to which we can define separate regional indexes of rent movements. In chapters 9 to 11 we will explore the broader context of our findings.

Chronological cover

The distinction between rents due and rents received has been well made, and in reiterating Ward's view that the bottom line in the relationship between tenants and landlords is the ability to pay, it comes as no surprise that the survival rate for rentals is greater for rents received than it is for rents due. Figure 8.4 (a) and (b) gives the chronological build-up of data from which the index of rents received has been constructed. This is arranged both by the monetary value of the rents received and also by the acreage from which those rents accrued. From these two measures it is a simple step to an index of rent received per acre (figure 8.2). The survival rate of records for the early part of the period is poor. The earliest estate to enter the index is the 6,500 acres at Castle Howard, North Yorkshire. The rentals survive from 1690 and continue until at least 1914 with minor gaps between 1711 and 1715, 1747 and 1749 and one major gap between 1758 and 1769. The rent per acre for Castle Howard is shown in figure 8.5. The records of the Emanuel Hospital estate at Brandsburton in East Yorkshire run continuously from 1695 until 1914. These two estates represent the longest running records in the survey.

For the period from 1690 until the early 1730s the index of rent received is based on six estates at most, but coverage thereafter improves. From 1741 it is based on at least 10 estates each year, rising to 20 or more almost continuously from 1790, 30 or more from about 1830, with a peak of over 50 in most of the last quarter of the nineteenth century. The absolute peak is formed by the data from 77 estates in 1888 and 1891.

In terms of acreage, from 1717 onwards the index of rent received is based on at least 10,000 acres, rising to over 40,000 acres from 1724, to 90,000 from the 1750s, and to over 100,000 acres from the mid-1770s onwards. From the first decade of the nineteenth century at least a quarter of a million acres are included, rising to over half a million acres from 1850, and to over one million acres for 1881 to 1892 inclusive. At its greatest monetary extent we have a total of £1.5 million of rent received in 1883, which covered

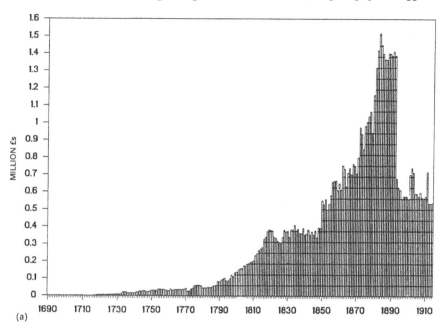

(a)

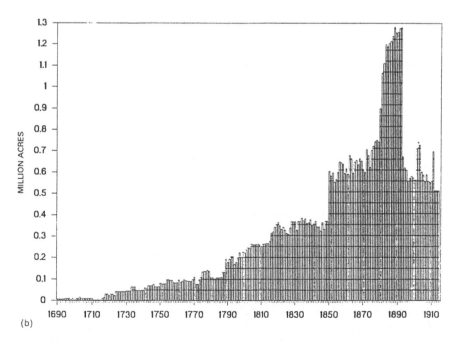

(b)

Fig. 8.4 The chronological history of rent received, 1690–1914: (a) Rents
(b) Acreages

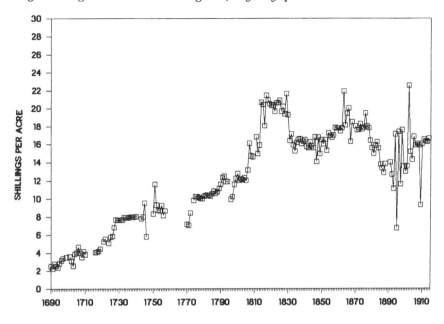

Fig. 8.5 Castle Howard: rent received per acre, 1690–1914

1.2 million acres, and at its greatest areal extent we have £1.4 million of rent received in 1887 representing 1.3 million acres. This was about 4 per cent of the total land area of England, though something over 5 per cent of the agricultural land. Table 8.1 summarises in a very broad fashion the attributes of the data which constitute the index of rent received. It summarises the number of estates which contributed to the data base in broad chronological terms (mainly in quarter centuries), and the changing average size of those estates.

In the first 70 years the average size of the estates was between 6,000 and 7,000 acres, rising to 9,000, 11,000 and 12,000 acres as more, and therefore larger estate collections were added to the database. Average estate size peaked at 17,000 acres by the early twentieth century, but there is no consistency in this across the sample of estates. We have already demonstrated that the inclusion of the Northumberland estate in the third quarter of the nineteenth century had a dramatic influence on the index. In addition, and for quite different reasons, the inclusion of three other estate collections distorts the overall usefulness of representing average estate size in table 8.1. First, the largest single influence on the rent index is the estate of the Ecclesiastical Commissioners, but like other institutional landlords it

Table 8.1. *Average estate sizes in the rent index*

Period	Number of estates	Average size (in acres)	Average size after adjustment (see text) (in acres)
1690–1715	2	6,021	6,021
1726–50	9	6,319	6,319
1751–75	14	6,746	6,746
1776–1800	17	9,149	9,149
1801–25	26	11,285	11,285
1826–50	30	12,202	12,000
1851–75	39	16,246	13,122
1876–1914	48	17,046	11,462

Source: See text.

was not an estate in the same way as we consider the property of private landlords. The size of the ecclesiastical property fluctuated according to their pattern of buying and selling, and at its greatest extent it covered over 270,000 acres in the 1880s. These acres may have been numerous, but they were spread thinly across the country. Consequently the church estates probably represent the widest geographical coverage of any single archive in the data. For the short period that it is available to us, this estate comes closest to having not simply the best geographical cover, but the only cover which truly represents England. Second, the data which were presented in evidence to the Royal Commission on Tithe Rentcharge in 1934 by Sir Charles Howell Thomas, the Permanent Secretary at the Ministry of Agriculture and Fisheries, referred to a 'single estate' of 290,000 acres which covered the period 1900–33. Sir Charles attributed these data to the researches of R. J. Thompson. For reasons stated in chapter 6 we are almost certain that these data are also from the estate controlled by the Commissioners.[4] The third distorting influence comes from the inclusion of the composite estates of the Oxford colleges. Like the lands of the Ecclesiastical Commissioners they might well be the most representative lands for which there are data in the late nineteenth century. However, for the purposes of table 8.1 their maximum extent of 140,000 acres in 1911 and their average extent of 92,000 acres from the 1880s for those parts for which we have reliable data – rack-rented land – distorts the picture which is being conveyed. The final column in table 8.1 therefore presents the changing

[4] After a thorough review of Bateman we are reasonably certain that this single estate was not in private hands. On the basis of size, the subject matter of the Royal Commission on Tithe Rentcharge, and R. J. Thompson's earlier use of information from the Ecclesiastical Commissioners, the obvious conclusion is that this is the estate of the Ecclesiastical Commissioners. Thompson, 'An inquiry'; Royal Commission on Tithe Rentcharge: *Minutes of Evidence* (HMSO, London, 1934).

average estate size without the influence of these exceptionally large and mostly scattered estates. In the main this final summary of average size represents single estates associated with fairly precisely located lands in particular places or, more usually, particular counties.

Otherwise the estate sizes range from a minimum average size of a little over 1,000 acres for the Wiltshire (Bradford) and Yorkshire (Adwick) properties of the Earls Manvers, to a maximum size of 47,000 acres for the estates of the Earls of Yarborough in Lincolnshire, along with about 45,000 acres which belonged to the Dukes of Portland spread across the adjacent counties of Nottingham, Derbyshire, and Lincolnshire, with a detached residual portion in Worcestershire.[5] In addition, there were four other estates with a long-term average size of over 30,000 acres – of the Earls of Leicester at Holkham, the Egremont family estate at Petworth in Sussex, the estates of the Earls of Pembroke at Wilton in Wiltshire, and the Sykes' family estate centred on Sledmere in East Yorkshire – and a further three of over 20,000 acres – the Dukes of Bedford, specifically their Woburn estate, the Marquess of Bath at Longleat, and an anonymous estate in Yorkshire.[6] The index is also influenced by the bunching of very large estates in the second half of the nineteenth century, particularly for those estates which presented evidence to the Royal Commission. The average size of the estates giving evidence to the Royal Commission was over 16,000 acres.

The profusion of large estates need not have a distorting influence on the resulting rent index because within each estate there were large and small farms, the large farms with low unit acre rents countered by the small farms with large unit acre rents. In other words we should not assume that large estates automatically meant large farms.

We should stress that the index is not the result of a single unchanging dataset. The lack of consistency both in the data which have survived and in the very process of survival, has determined that it is a conglomerate of a random sample of English properties, combined with quite specific government investigations which were conducted at various times, and interleaved with the work of others. On periodically reviewing the accumulation of material we specifically tried to unearth new records to fill gaps in the chronological record, and, more importantly, in the spatial coverage. The

---

[5] There is a problem of identity regarding this last estate. The information is summarised in the Royal Commission, but in this case the owner took up the option which was offered to remain anonymous. The four counties in which the estate was represented were listed, but not differentiated in terms of separate acreages. With the help of Bateman and knowledge about the break up of the Portland estate in the 1870s, we have deduced that this is the residual estate belonging to the Duke of Portland.

[6] This was one of the few estates summarised in the Royal Commission which were entered anonymously and which we cannot identify through related sources.

extent to which this infilling process was possible was very partial, and therefore the indexes are essentially based on the relatively random survival of usable materials. There is no way of guaranteeing that the rents collected are typical of contemporary rents in general, but equally there is probably no such thing as a typical rent per acre. The environmental, let alone economic, variations, even in a country as small as England warn against the search for the mythical average, and there can be no assurances even about the vaguest notions of typicality.

The geography of survival

In the same way that the sample of estates included in the exercise increased over time so the geographical coverage of those estates broadened. We demonstrate this in figures 8.6 and 8.7. Figure 8.6 takes three broad cross-sections in time and plots by county the location of the estates which make up the sample of rents received. These are not simply locational maps assigning the rental data to appropriate counties; they are also density maps measuring the number of acres for which we have rental information as a proportion of the county area. The 'counties' are those that existed in the eighteenth and nineteenth centuries, with the three Ridings of Yorkshire, and the three divisions of Lincolnshire distinguished.

The three cross-section dates in figure 8.6 are not particularly significant in historical terms; they are merely chosen at regular intervals. The inclusion of an estate in any particular map depended on a rental surviving in the decades either side of the dates chosen. Thus the map for 1750 includes those estates where there is at least one surviving rental for the period 1740–59. In practice, however, apart from the odd random appearance and disappearance of estates in the sample, most estates have a presence in the two relevant decades of some substance. Thus the measurements in the map for c. 1750 are effectively the annual average acres per estate with surviving rentals over a period of twenty years, arranged by counties and by density of survival. Figure 8.7 adopts the same procedure but for the ten years of the 1880s alone. This is the decade where the number of estates in the sample is at a peak and therefore represents the maximum coverage in the rent index. In the maps for c. 1850 and the 1880s the estates belonging to the Oxford colleges and the Ecclesiastical Commissioners have been excluded because they are too widely scattered and the sources from which they have been extracted do not allow us to assign their acres to specific counties. In a few cases an estate involved land in more than one county, which cannot be distinguished at source. In these instances the

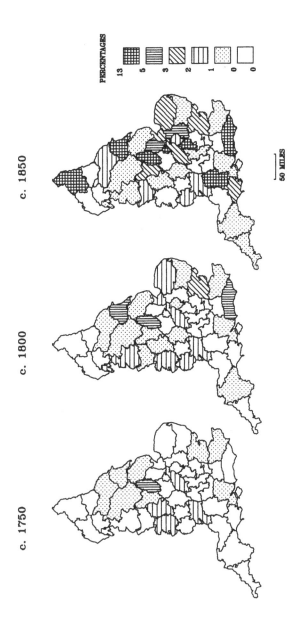

c. 1750

c. 1800

c. 1850

PERCENTAGES

13

5

3

2

1

0

0

50 MILES

Fig. 8.6 Density and distribution of rents received, c. 1750, c. 1800, and c. 1850. Absence of shading indicates no information available.

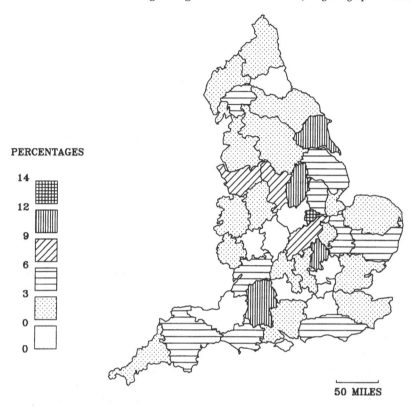

PERCENTAGES

14
12
9
6
3
0
0

50 MILES

Fig. 8.7 Density and distribution of rents received in the 1880s

relative county distribution of lands as indicated by Bateman in 1883 has been used to separate and weight the county distributions.[7]

There are data for 13 of the 43 English counties by *c*. 1750. At its greatest coverage this accounts for over 4 per cent of Nottinghamshire, arising from the various estates of the Manvers family, and over 1 per cent each of Gloucestershire, Northamptonshire, Shropshire, and Staffordshire. The absence of any rents from many of the counties of the south-east Midlands and East Anglia (apart from a presence in Essex) means that the broadly arable part of the country may not be as well covered as the mixed and broadly pastoral areas. There are no data for the West Country. In total, less than one-half of 1

---

[7] For example, the Woburn estate of the Duke of Bedford according to Bateman's summary of great landowners was mainly located in Bedfordshire and Buckinghamshire in the ratio 9:91. The duke's Thorney estate in Cambridgeshire, Northamptonshire, and Huntingdonshire was distributed in the ratio 80:14:6.

per cent of England is accounted for in the surviving sample by the mid-eighteenth century, or about one-half of 1 per cent of the farming area. By c. 1800 a good deal of infilling in the database has taken place. The sample of rents touches 23 of the 43 counties. However, modern-day Cumbria and Northumbria, and the Home Counties, are still not covered, but there is a presence in Devon, and the East Midlands and East Anglia are well covered. The data at this date account for over 4 per cent of both Nottinghamshire and Sussex, nearly 4 per cent of the East Riding of Yorkshire, and nearly 3 per cent of Essex. In total, nearly 1 per cent of England is covered in what appears to be a reasonable-looking spread across the major farming regions.

By c. 1850 only 13 counties are *not* covered, leaving gaps in modern Cumbria, parts of the south-west Midlands, and in the counties to the immediate north and south of London. Over 13 per cent of each of Northumberland and Rutland is covered at this date. Rightly speaking, Northumberland should be excluded for reasons explained earlier in this chapter, but it is included to show in another way just how large an influence the estate of the Duke of Northumberland can have. Nearly 9 per cent of Bedfordshire is covered, and nearly 7 per cent of Wiltshire. In total, between 1.5 and 2 per cent of England is accounted for (excluding and including the single Northumberland estate). At its greatest extent in the 1880s (figure 8.7), the geographical coverage includes over 3 per cent of England, and for only nine counties is there no coverage . Over 13 per cent of Rutland is covered, over 10 per cent of Wiltshire and the East Riding of Yorkshire, nearly 10 per cent of Nottinghamshire, over 9 per cent of Bedfordshire, and over 5 per cent of four other counties – Cheshire, Derbyshire, Northamptonshire, and Sussex – and the Lindsey division of Lincolnshire. Throughout the whole period from 1690 to 1914 only eight counties are not touched at all by the data which can be reliably assigned to specific locations. These are Berkshire, Durham, Hertfordshire, Leicestershire, Middlesex, Somerset, Surrey, and Worcestershire, as well as the Isle of Wight. However, these maps do not include the properties of the Ecclesiastical Commissioners, the Oxford colleges, and St John's College, Cambridge, properties which were extensive but which we cannot reliably locate in specific counties. With their inclusion in the main index however, we can be reasonably confident that at some stage every corner of England is represented.

The validity of the findings

In our view the rent index has been defined and researched in such a way as to be definitive. If we are right, it seems pertinent to ask how close others have come to defining accurately the course of rents. How, in other words, do their conclusions, usually based on smaller and sometimes more distinct collections of data, hold up in the light of these findings?

For the late seventeenth and eighteenth centuries the material is not sufficiently comprehensive for us to offer dogmatic conclusions. Gregory King assessed the arable, meadow, and pasture of England and Wales at a rent of 7.33 shillings per acre. Our single observation for the period puts the average figure at or around 3 shillings per acre, but clearly we are able here to do little more than make informed guesses. R. C. Allen estimated unit rents in the south Midlands, based on the weighted average of pasture, light arable, and heavy arable, at a little under 10 shillings per acre for the last quarter of the seventeenth century.[8] Clearly this makes our single observation look even more precarious, and suggests that we should not claim very much for it. However, as the eighteenth century proceeded, especially into the second and third quarters, our sample thickens both in acres and in geographical distribution, and we have greater confidence in the figures. Allen's average rents for the south Midlands rose from 10 to 11 to 12 shillings per acre over the course of the first three quarters of the eighteenth century; by contrast, we find that average rents never reached double figures over this same period.[9] It could be the case that Allen's figures, which are derived from a regionally specific context, reflect quality farming conditions which were above the national average.

For the 1770s and beyond we can raise questions about Arthur Young's rental findings. Young thought a reasonable average for northern England was 10 shillings an acre, and for the eastern counties 14 shillings an acre.[10] He was notoriously optimistic; just how much so becomes clear by comparing these estimates with our figures for the 1760s of between 6.8 and 8.1 shillings per acre. Young, we recall, regularly argued that land was under-rented,[11] but our findings suggest not only that he was wrong, but that his calculations were probably based on the overall value of good-quality arable or grass, with little allowance for poorer land and unproductive waste.[12] Although his order of magnitude is not so different from Allen, this tends only to reinforce our argument that Allen's self-selected samples may reflect quality farming rather than average farming conditions. Nor does the position change in the 1780s and 1790s. The index shows average rents at generally less than 9

[8] R. C. Allen, 'The price of freehold land and the rate of interest in the seventeenth and eighteenth centuries', *EcHR* (1988), 42–3.
[9] *Ibid.*, 43.
[10] A. Young, *A Six Months Tour Through the North of England*, IV (London, 1771) p. 341; A Young, *The Farmers Tour through the East of England*, I (London, 1771), p. 456.
[11] For which see G. E. Mingay's commentary in *Arthur Young and His Times* (London, 1975), pp. 45–8.
[12] Allen, 'The price of freehold land', 43n.

shillings for the 1780s and between 9 and 11.9 shillings for the 1790s. Young estimated an average of 15s 7d per acre for c. 1790.[13] For the same period Allen's south Midlands average is over 16 shillings per acre. During the 1790s the index rises from a low of 9 shillings per acre to 12s, with an annual average for the decade of just over 10 shillings per acre. More than other contemporary or modern estimates, this can be reasonably compared with Pitt's estimate for the 1790s of 12.5 shillings per acre. Henry Beeke's estimate for 1800 of 14 shillings per acre compares much better with our own of just over 12 shillings per acre for that single year.[14] We conclude that Young in the eighteenth century and Allen in the twentieth, have produced figures which are far too high as *averages* and may well reflect the best-quality land and the most progressive farming.

For the years of the French war the findings can be compared with figures produced by J. R. McCulloch. On the basis of evidence from the Board of Agriculture, McCulloch reckoned that average rents between 1791 and 1804 had risen by 39 per cent.[15] Our own estimates for those years suggest a rise of 40.4 per cent (from 9.4 to 13.2 shillings per acre). McCulloch further argued that average rents in England rose from 17.3s per acre in 1810–11 to 20.2s in 1814–15. These figures are close to the index estimates of 16.1s and 17.7s for 1810 and 1811 and 20.5s and 20.4s for 1814 and 1815.[16] He also argued that the average rent in England in 1836, at the bottom of the long post-war depression, was on or around the level it had reached in 1810–11, or 17.3 shillings. This is a little under our own estimate of 20s for 1836 and the adjacent years of the mid-1830s, but the broad history of rents told by McCulloch, for all practical purposes, is the same tale that we tell.[17]

Estimates for 1850 by McCulloch and James Caird suggest an average rent for cultivated land in England and Wales of 22 shillings and for England alone of a little over 27 shillings per acre.[18] Our estimates for the 1840s and 1850s, decades when rents were largely stable, is 20 to 21 shillings per acre. An estimate for 1872–3 suggests that the average rent for agricultural land (without rough grazing) was 28 shillings per acre (or 25 shillings with rough grazing). This was an estimate for medium to large-sized farms. The average rent for all holdings – in which the high unit rents on small holdings which were associated less with self-contained farms, and inevitably have a large influence on average rents – was reckoned at 34.5 shillings per acre without

[13] Mingay, *Arthur Young and His Times*, p. 183.
[14] Pitt's estimate from Allen, 'The price of freehold land', 43; Beeke's estimate from Mingay, *AgHist*, p. 1111.   [15] J. R. McCulloch, *A Statistical Account of the British Empire*, 1 (London, 1837), p. 533.
[16] *Ibid.*, p. 531. We noted in an earlier chapter that McCulloch's calculations may include urban property, which would tend to push his estimates up.
[17] *Ibid.*, p. 532.
[18] *Ibid*, p. 531; Caird, p. 480.

Table 8.2. *The trend in agricultural rent: a comparison*

Time	National index		South Midlands' index	
	Shillings/acre (all rounded to first decimal place)	Index	Shillings/acre (rounded to first decimal place)	Index
1675–99	2.8	13.7	9.8	31.3
1700–24	3.2	15.7	11.1	35.6
1725–49	6.3	30.4	10.7	34.3
1750–74	7.8	37.9	12.6	40.3
1775–99	9.5	46.1	16.4	52.6
1800–24	17.4	84.7	26.6	85.5
1825–49	20.6	100.0	31.2	100.0

Note: The first observation for the national index covers the period 1690–9.
Sources: This chapter; R. C. Allen, 'The price of freehold land and the interest rate in the seventeenth and eighteenth centuries', *EcHR*, 41, 1988, 43.

and 30.75 shillings with rough grazing.[19] The index for the early 1870s suggests an average rent of 27 to 28 shillings per acre. Finally, an official estimate made in 1919 on the basis of a very small sample of farms covering fewer than nine thousand acres put the average rent per acre in 1913–14 at a little over 26 shillings.[20] The index offers a much lower figure of 21 shillings per acre.

While there is a good deal of variation in these nominal estimates of agricultural rent, the index helps to give us a clear picture of trend over time and at the same time to show a closer relationship with other indexes than was the case with nominal estimates. Table 8.2 compares the index with Allen's data for the south Midlands. In both cases the table represents annual average rent, corresponding to time periods determined by Allen. We have constructed the index using a terminal rather than a starting base on the understanding that the most recent evidence is the most robust in terms both of the number and reliability of observations. From the quarter decade 1725 to 1749 the two indexes move very well together.

During the French wars between 1793 and 1815 a number of historians have estimated a rise in rents of 90–100 per cent. This clearly was of the right magnitude since the index shows a rise of 106 per cent between 1793 and 1815, levelling out thereafter. It also confirms the variations in rent changes which ranged from between 50 and 175 per cent across different counties.[21]

For the nineteenth century we have several long series against which the

[19] A. W. Ashby's introduction to H. A. Rhee, *The Rent of Agricultural Land in England and Wales* (London, 1946), pp. 31–2.   [20] *Ibid.*, p. 38n.
[21] Mingay, *Arthur Young and His Times*, p. 46; J. V. Beckett, 'Landownership and estate management', in Mingay, *AgHist*, p. 622; F. M. L. Thompson, 'The land market in the nineteenth century', in W. E. Minchinton (ed.), *Essays in Agrarian History*, II (Newton Abbot, 1968), p. 35.

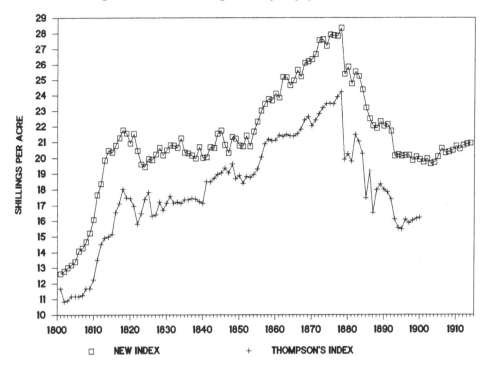

□   NEW INDEX   +   THOMPSON'S INDEX

Fig. 8.8 A comparison with R. J. Thompson's rent index

rental material can be contrasted: R. J. Thompson's investigations for the whole of the nineteenth century; the evidence from Schedule A Income Tax; J. R. Bellerby's estimate of gross farm rents, which although it includes the whole of the UK was nevertheless dominated by England; and the index which can be derived from the land-auction sales of the nineteenth-century estate agents, the firm of Norton, Trist, and Gilbert. These comparisons are presented in figures 8.8, 8.9, 8.10, and 8.11, and are discussed in more detail in the following paragraphs.

The specific comparison with R. J. Thompson's research involves splicing together two of his four schedules of long-term rent: the first was his assessment of rent received on between 62,000 and 72,000 acres from estates in Lincolnshire, Essex, Herefordshire, and North Wales, over the period 1800–1900; the second was his assessment of rent received from estates totalling between 110,000 and 120,000 acres in Lincolnshire, Hereford, Buckinghamshire, Bedfordshire, Cambridgeshire, Essex, and North Wales, for the period 1816–1900. There is a danger of overlap in the comparison since it is certainly the case that some of Thompson's material is also

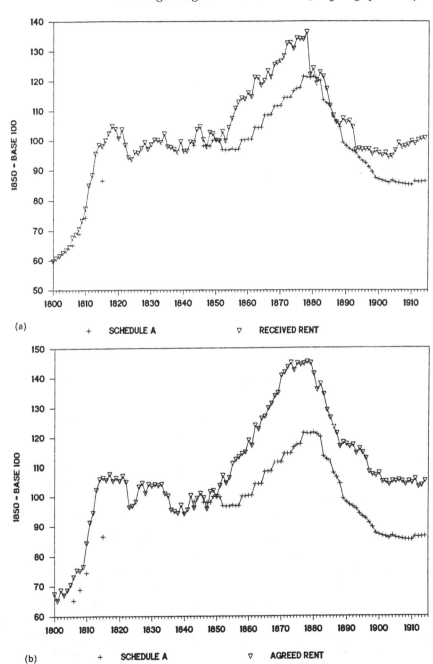

(a)   +   SCHEDULE A   ▽   RECEIVED RENT

(b)   +   SCHEDULE A   ▽   AGREED RENT

Fig. 8.9 A comparison with Schedule A Income Tax returns

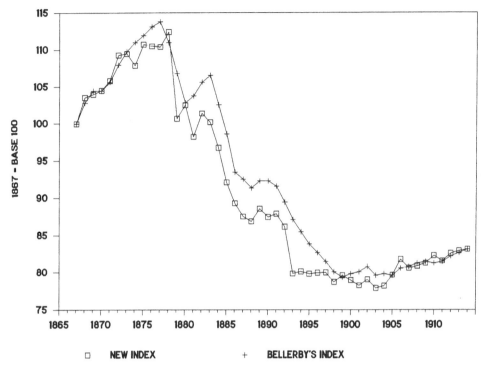

Fig. 8.10 A comparison with Bellerby's gross farm rent index for the UK

included in the new index. In particular this would have been so if we had also included two other rent samples for the period after 1870 which Thompson constructed (see table 6.3 for a full digest of his four samples). Even so, the fact that the new rent index is several shillings per acre greater than the one derived from Thompson has to be explained. A possible reason has been pointed out by J. T. Ward, who spliced together the various series prepared by Thompson,[22] and in so doing picked up the fact that where a weighted combination of the first two series overlapped with a third (from 1872) there was a disparity in average rents of the order of 1:1.24. Ward suggested that this arose from the differential composition in the farms included in the various series and that this in turn suggested that the earlier series were more dominated by larger farms which produced smaller unit rents. As a result Ward weighted the first two series by a factor of 1.24 to produce an annual index from 1857 to 1938. Ward's resulting composite rent index is usually slightly higher than the new one. Thus comparing

---

[22] For which see chapter 6 above.

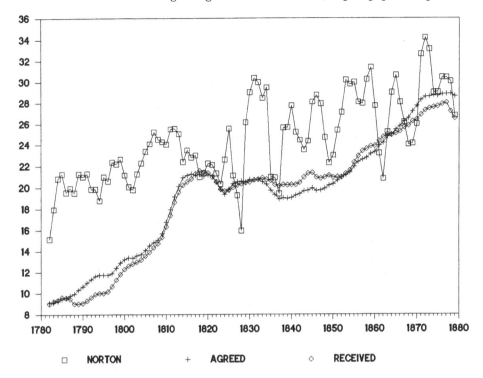

Fig. 8.11 A comparison with the Norton, Trist and Gilbert rent index

Thompson – with Ward's version of Thompson – with the new index, shows that the new index is a good deal higher than Thompson's, but slightly lower than Ward's adjusted index. In absolute terms the new index is closer to Ward's version of Thompson, although in all three cases there are no serious differences in the trend of rents. Thus in 1875 the unadjusted Thompson index produces an average of 23.5 shillings per acre, Ward's adjusted Thompson index produces 29.1 shillings per acre, and the new index 27.9 shillings per acre. In 1895 the figures are, 15.5, 21.3, and 20.1 shillings per acre respectively (note that these figures will not be found in table 6.3 which is a composite index which includes all four of Thompson's samples). Ward's adjustment helps to reconcile the new index with Thompson's work.[23]

The Schedule A Income Tax returns refer to the putative land values (and tithes) assessed for property and income tax purposes, which we assume (here and earlier, in chapter 2) bore a relationship with the rents which were

[23] Ward, 'A study of capital and rental values', esp. pp. 74–80.

paid for those lands. The comparisons we make are of two kinds; the trend of the two indexes of rents – received and agreed – are each compared with the trend of land values.[24] For the years 1806, 1808, 1810, and 1814 15 the land values are based on the property taxes of those years, and for the years from 1842 they are based on the income tax returns. The inclusion of the tithes in these returns is marginal, especially from the 1840s onwards, and in any case hardly affects the trends which we are comparing. The trend in both of the rent indexes precisely mirrors the trend of land values until about 1850, after which date rents began their relentless rise to an eventual peak in the late 1870s. During this period of rising rents the index of the income tax returns rose, reflecting the improvement in land values, but it rose less steeply, and in a stepwise motion. This came about because the reassessment of land values, and hence of income tax returns, occurred every three or four years. On the downturn of rents after 1879 the trends of rent received and the Income Tax returns are almost identical until the trend reversed again in the 1890s. Again, because there was a lag in the reassessment of tax, the trend of land values took a while to catch up with the improvement in rents.

Comparison with Bellerby's gross farm rents for the UK in figure 8.10 requires little further comment. Although there is a good degree of interconnection between all of these series – Bellerby was partly guided by Schedule A, and was informed by Thompson's work as to trend – we can justifiably emphasise the extraordinary robustness of all the comparisons with the new index.[25]

The Norton, Trist, and Gilbert material (hereafter NTG) is available annually from 1781 to 1880.[26] Over the century they sold (and possibly resold in some cases) 876,000 acres. Their business was conducted by auction and no estate which was sold privately is included in their evidence. Landowners invariably preferred secrecy in their land transactions, relying on agents and stewards to negotiate appropriate deals.[27] Consequently, whenever possible they avoided bringing land to auction. When they did so it was frequently to establish market value, with a private sale following.[28] Thus there was no

[24] The values are taken from Sir Josiah Stamp, *British Incomes and Property* (London, 1927 reprint), pp. 49, 515.

[25] J. R. Bellerby, 'Distribution of farm income in the United Kingdom 1867–1938', *Proceedings of the Journal of the Agricultural Economics Society*, 10, no. 2 (1953), 127–44, esp. 131–2; J. R. Bellerby, 'Gross and net farm income in the United Kingdom', *Proceedings of the Journal of the Agricultural Economics Society*, 10, no. 4 (1954), 356–62, esp. 357–8.

[26] Norton, Trist, and Gilbert to *The Times*, 20 April 1889, p. 11, and reprinted in 'A century of land values: England and Wales', *JRSS*, 54 (1891), 128–31.

[27] For which see J. V. Beckett, 'The land market in nineteenth-century England: the sale of Burton Dassett, 1826–36', *Warwickshire History*, 9 (1993), 2–11.

[28] P. B. Barnes, 'The economic history of landed estates in Norfolk since 1880' (University of East Anglia, PhD thesis, 1984), pp. 180–6.

recognisable open 'market' in land sales, so that whatever the auction figures may be they cannot properly represent the entire market in land sales and transfers. If anything, of course, they represent a restricted market and hence probably an inflated price whenever such sales took place. This may be reflected in our comparison, though we should add that the rental figures quoted in NTG are not derived from the value of the land sales but are in fact the quoted rents on the lands at the time of auction.

At their busiest NTG sold just over 71,000 acres in 1827 by auction, though the next busiest year was 1836 when just under 25,000 acres were sold. At their least busy they sold just 358 acres in 1781, and did not sell as much as 10,000 acres in any single year until 1818. Therefore this was not a large sample of land, and it raises the question of who would use the firm in the first place, especially in view of their London location. Therefore it is not possible to claim that the NTG material is particularly representative. However, one estimate has suggested that during a Napoleonic wartime peak of land transfers probably no more than 170,000 acres per year were sold by auction between 1810 and 1814 – and the chances are that it was a good deal less – and this figure might represent upper and lower limits of between 50 per cent and just 10 per cent of all land transfers that had taken place.[29]

Figure 8.11 plots the average rent per acre from the NTG sample together with the new estimates of both rents received and rents agreed. At first sight the comparison is not a good one. In the 1790s the NTG index fluctuates around 20 shillings per acre – making even Arthur Young appear to underestimate the contemporary average rent – rising to almost 26 shillings by the end of the French wars. In contrast the new index languishes around 10 shillings per acre rising to 16 to 20 shillings by the end of the wars. If we ignore the unlikely sharp year-to-year fluctuations which arise from the small sample base of the NTG index, we can argue nevertheless that it comes into line with the new index during the post-French wars depression into the 1820s. Thereafter the new index is mostly much lower – by 8 to 10 shillings per acre in the third quarter of the nineteenth century – before the two indexes once again come together on the eve of the Great Depression in the late 1870s.

These trends suggest that in periods of depression or impending depression the indexes tend to converge, but during buoyant periods land coming onto the auction market seems to have been considerably more valuable than the generality of land. Given the limited nature of the evidence from land sales we would not wish to press this conclusion too far, particularly as a substantial proportion of English land was not realistically

[29] This was a speculation by Thompson, 'The land market', 36.

part of the pool of available supply. However, according to NTG, land which was 'free of or easily freed from settlement' came onto the market or changed hands 'once in a generation, or at most in every two generations'.[30] Our comparison suggests that this land was more highly valued, perhaps because it was more fluid. Thus what we might have here is the important difference between land which was, and land which was not, available on the market. In general, the new index is probably based on estates which included settled land, although it would have been difficult to pursue this distinction for the purpose of our research. This may become useful in substantiating empirically the view that land as a positional asset offered the landowner an advantage which was greater than the actual flow of money rent.[31] The positional asset was greatest for settled or encumbered lands and therefore landed society, and this was land which was not generally available on the market, a fact reflected in lower and non-competitive rents. By contrast, unencumbered land was akin to a fixed supply of land, but only parts of it became available on the market at any one time, and then only at long intervals. This restricted supply was reflected both in the higher market price paid, and in the higher rental charged.

This comparison and analysis of the land market can be extended up to the First World War. The NTG data include the average price per acre of the land which was sold by auction, and from this a land prices series can be constructed. A similar series has been constructed by J. T. Ward for the period 1857 to 1957.[32] Ward arranged the data into five-year moving averages, and for comparative purposes we have adjusted the NTG annual series and annual rent index accordingly. The aim is to compare the trend of land prices for property coming to auction – which, if our previous assumption is correct, was almost invariably land which was more highly rented – with the trend of the prevailing agricultural rents represented in the new rent series. The results are shown in figure 8.12.

For the period 1857–78 the Ward and NTG land price series overlap, although NTG was almost always higher.[33] For the period c. 1815 to the 1860s the NTG land sale price series is more or less in harmony with the rent

[30] Norton, Trist, and Gilbert, 'A century of land values', 129.
[31] In general see A. Offer, 'Farm tenure and land values in England, c.1750–1950', EcHR, 44 (1991), 1–20. In particular see also J. D. Williams, 'A study of an eighteenth-century nobleman, his house, household and estate: Sir John Griffin, 4th Lord Howard de Walden, 1st Lord Braybrooke, of Audley End, Essex, 1719–1797' (University of London, PhD thesis, 1974), pp. 303ff.
[32] J. T. Ward, 'Farm sale prices over a hundred years', The Estates Gazette, Centenary Supplement, 3 May 1958, 47–9.
[33] This reflects the fact that continuously in the heart of this overlap, from 1862 to 1874, the Norton, Trist, and Gilbert average price was between 1 and 9 shillings per acre higher than the prices Ward extracted from the contemporary Estate Exchange, possibly reflecting the more local or home counties business of Norton, Trist, and Gilbert, which was a London-based firm. In addition, the Norton, Trist, and Gilbert index is very volatile, even with a five-year average.

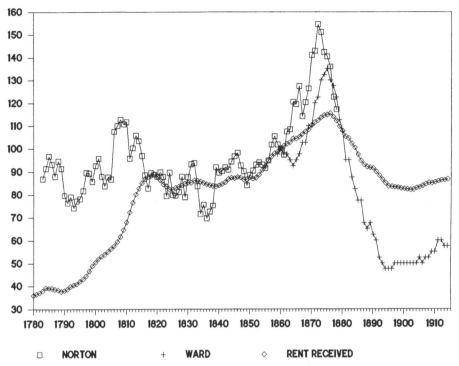

Fig. 8.12 The average price of land and the movement of rent, 1780–1914

index. This is consistent with the general association between rents and purchase prices where the rents (in terms of the number of years' purchase, meaning the number of rent equivalents) determined the purchase price. Before c. 1815 however, as we have already seen, the NTG land price index represents land for which the average rent was high by contemporary standards. From 1860 or shortly thereafter, the two land sale price series take off relative to the index of rents, reflecting what was probably a peak in the volume and value of land transfers in the late 1870s. Conversely, on the downturn during the agricultural depression land purchase prices tumbled, not necessarily because land flooded the market but rather because the demand for land had subsided. Since landlords were also faced with losing and not replacing tenants in these years, or at the very least of giving substantial rent reductions, they discovered that the value of their main asset was further debased.[34] The more enterprising landlords did not take this lightly, and some of them began to farm the land directly. Edward Strutt's management of the family estate in Essex is one of the best chronicled

[34] In this context see P. J. Perry and R. J. Johnston, 'The temporal and spatial incidence of agricultural depression in Dorset, 1868–1902', *Journal of Interdisciplinary History*, 3 (1972), 297–311, esp. 299–300.

examples.[35] The estate was 9,000 acres in extent in 1876 of which 854 were farmed in hand, but the acreage in hand rose to 2,344 acres by 1882, to 3,596 acres by 1888, and to 4,315 acres by 1896. The Strutts became more the gentleman farmers and less the rentiers. So successful was their move during the depression that there proved to be no turning back when the recovery began, and the acreage in hand grew to nearly 6,000 acres by 1914.

Recovery, both in rents and in the land market, began in the mid-1890s. F. M. L. Thompson has indicated a general association between fluctuations in the volume of land sales and the building cycle of the 1870s and 1890s.[36] Sale prices therefore relate rather harmoniously with the movement of rents providing there is reasonable, although not necessarily perfect, stability in agriculture. But during excessive inflationary or deflationary times sale prices are able to adjust rather more quickly to prevailing circumstances than are rents. Perhaps the interesting feature of this comparison is that these differences in adjustment existed even during the late nineteenth century when annual tenancies dominated. This reinforces what we already know, that land was a positional asset, the acquisition of which was as important, if not more important, in social terms than the income it provided. This led to large swings in prices but relatively small swings in rents, to the point that during buoyant times for agriculture tenancies may indeed have been under-rented.

Conclusion

We have presented in this chapter our major findings. In our view, for the most part, the data from which the index was compiled is sufficiently representative of England in both chronological and geographical terms. While the material is weaker for the eighteenth than for the nineteenth century, we do not believe it would have been possible to add substantial additions of good quality data. Within the parameters we outlined in earlier chapters we believe that our conclusions are based on a best-possible input even if at times the coverage seems thin. Furthermore, in the second part of the chapter we have tested the evidence against other measures, both nominal and trend, and on all counts we would argue that the new index is a substantial improvement on what has gone before. Young writing in the eighteenth century and Allen in the twentieth have produced estimates for the eighteenth and early nineteenth centuries which differ from the new index. We suggest they may each have been too optimistic, or perhaps concentrated too much on better quality land. For other times contempor-

[35] Sir William Gavin, *Ninety Years of Family Farming: The Story of Lord Rayleigh's and Strutt and Parker Farms* (London, 1967), pp. 81–2, 235–7.   [36] Thompson, 'The land market', esp. 47, 49.

ary estimates and historians' calculations overlap reasonably closely with the new index. We contend that the new index provides a comprehensive analysis of rents for the period 1690–1914 even if for the earlier years it is not everything that we might have liked. In chapter 9 we discuss the problems faced by tenants in paying their rents on the basis of what we have established regarding the level of rent arrears, and we attempt a partial regional analysis of the trend in agricultural rents.

Rent arrears and regional variations

The rent index we have described in chapter 8 has provided us with national data over a period of more than two hundred years, and the tests that we have applied suggest that the findings are definitive within the parameters we established at the outset. Before we proceed in chapters 10 and 11 to examine the implications for agricultural and economic history more generally, the index offers us other data from which we can trace agricultural trends: in particular, in relation first to times of plenty and times of dearth; and second to regional variations in the long-term rental trends. We examine these questions in this chapter.

Integrating rent due and rent received

One of the major questions which we have had to address is the mismatch between those archives which reveal rents which were *due*, and those which reveal rents which were actually *received*. Where an archive gives both it is possible to construct two indexes which refer to the same geography and chronology, and which therefore share a common acreage. In these cases the observation for each year is a unique event because, as with our separate indexes for rents due and rents received, the sample of estates which are represented each year changes according to the random survival of the records. However, even though the schedules of rents due and rents received from common acreages may appear as a chronological patchwork, they do share one important parameter arising from the original research method employed. This was the desirability, which became a necessity, of having relatively long runs of records. As a result, there is a good deal of yearly continuity in the annual survival of the measurements of rent.

Figures 9.1 and 9.2 summarise the trends in the extent of the archives and the growth of acres covered where rents due and rents received coincide. In just seven years through the whole period, years which are all grouped early

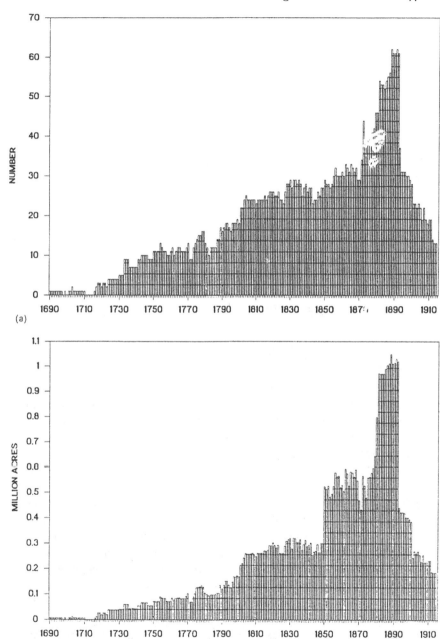

(a)

(b)

Fig. 9.1 Rents due and rents received: (a) Number of archives. (b) Extent of common acreage

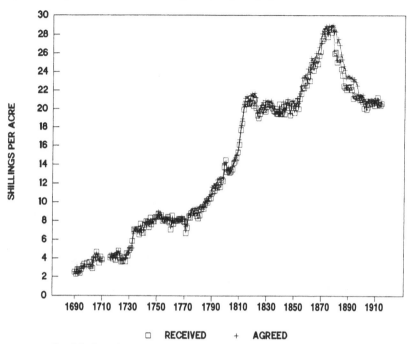

□   RECEIVED   +   AGREED

Fig. 9.2 Rent Indexes: rent due and rent received from common acres

on, the two types of rent do not occur at all together for any particular estate. For most of the first 30 years the only estate for which both rents due and rents received coincide is Castle Howard, but from about 1720 onwards the number of archives or estates where we do have both figures multiplies rapidly. By the 1740s there are up to ten such examples, and for the whole of the second half of the eighteenth century, except in two years, there are at least ten archives and as many as 19 by 1799. Throughout the nineteenth century, there are at least 20 such archives in every year, and over 30 for most years in the second half of the century. At the peak of survival, over 60 examples are included for each year from 1888 to 1892 inclusive. In the few years of the twentieth century covered by the index the number of archives of this nature falls to a low of 13 in each of 1913 and 1914. In every year from 1718 onwards over 20,000 acres are covered by the coincidence of rents due and rents received, over 50,000 from 1741, over 100,000 acres continuously from 1786, and at least a quarter of a million acres from 1803 to 1900. By 1850 the common coverage extends to half a million acres with over 900,000 acres from 1881 to 1892. The high point occurs from 1886 to 1892 when more than one million acres are covered for both rents due and rents received.

Rent arrears

At its simplest, the difference between rents due or assessed and rents received measures the arrears of rent, and the trend of such arrears over time measures in general the ease or difficulty tenants found in paying their rents, and the ease or difficulty faced by landlords in maximising their rental income. This apparent clarity may be partially obscured by those tenants who were persistently late payers regardless of the prevailing economic climate, or by those dutiful tenants who caught up with arrears and who sometimes paid over and above the agreed rent in doing so. In addition, some arrears may have arisen through general mismanagement by landlords of their affairs. Whatever the improvements in estate management during the eighteenth century, we showed in chapter 1 that examples of poor estate management can be found in all periods. These provisos apart, a trend of rent arrears may act like a thermometer to gauge the general health of agriculture, the 'Feast and Famine' within the agricultural sector. In plotting the fluctuations in agricultural prosperity in this way, particularly the very short-run movements, an index of rent arrears provides vital information. Indeed, it may even be more useful than an assessed rent series, because it points to the ability of tenants to pay. Assessed rents point to the market value of rent in optimum agricultural conditions, but in a depression the tenants responded by failing to pay part or all of their rents, and the landlords responded, *force majeure*, by agreeing to abatements. Initially, in a downturn in the economy, assessed rents will be higher than the sums actually paid, but when it became clear that a depression was deep and lasting, and when landlords perceived that tenants would not be able to pay, they took the more radical step of forgiving arrears and reducing rents.

But the question is, how best can we portray the history of rent arrears? We think there are two methods. The first is portrayed in figure 9.3 and is seemingly the logical approach since it measures arrears as they were recorded in the rentals. Therefore, the graph is the product of a direct transcription, appropriate weighting to take into account the mixture of large and small estates, and some simple arithmetic. The second, and as it turns out the preferred method, does not directly transcribe arrears at all. This second method is depicted in figure 9.4.

The first, and in our opinion the false measure of 'Feast and Famine' in figure 9.3 satisfies many of the expectations from the historiography. This includes the agricultural depression of the second quarter of the eighteenth century, and the Great Depression at the end of the nineteenth century. Less dominant, but still self-evident, is the post-Napoleonic Wars depression which supposedly lasted through much of the 1820s and 1830s. When we

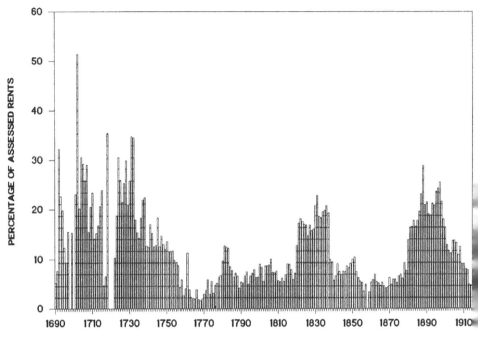

Fig. 9.3 Feast and famine: rent arrears as a proportion of agreed rents

discuss the second method of portraying arrears, and in later chapters when we discuss the rent index in detail, we present evidence to suggest that neither the eighteenth-century depression (particularly) nor the post-Napoleonic Wars depression were as severe as traditional historiography has led us to believe. Over the whole period there appears to be what we might call a normal background of arrears of around 5 per cent.

This first measure of 'Feast and Famine' measures the recorded arrears as a proportion of the agreed rent. Ostensibly it seems to capture the difference between the agreed rent and the received rent. Yet arithmetically it has been calculated without any reference to the schedules of received rents. The second measure, in contrast, is derived from a calculation involving the recorded rents but not the recorded arrears. It is the difference between the agreed and received rents, but only for those estates where both measures coincide. The large level of arrears portrayed in 'Feast and Famine' in figure 9.3 is rather surprising in view of the fact that when the agreed and received rents are put together, as in figure 9.2, they look remarkably similar. While they seem to tell the same long-run tale, and while they seem to move almost identically, in fact they are not precisely the same. Putatively the difference

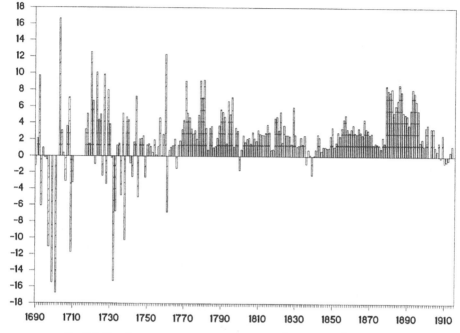

Fig. 9.4 Putative rent arrears, as percentage of rent agreed

between them is the level of annual rent arrears (or indeed in some cases where more rent was paid than was due it may suggest that accumulated rent arrears were being paid off). This is what figure 9.4 captures. It is the difference in the two rents as a proportion of the agreed rents.

There are choices, therefore, in the way which we depict the history of rent arrears. But those choices do not exactly mirror one another, and are not interchangeable. Therefore we seem to be confronted with a measurement problem, and this in turn becomes a problem of historical interpretation. One of the methods is sending false messages about rent arrears. In the first years both methods are based on only a small number of separate estate rentals. When we review those separate rentals we find quite a variation across estates. We also find reason to argue that the measure of putative arrears is more meaningful and accurate than the measure we first produced in 'Feast and Famine'. The reason is simple, and can be easily demonstrated. Until 1750 the recorded arrears on the Manvers estate at Adwick in south Yorkshire were negligible, both in nominal terms and as a proportion of the agreed rents – the standard method we have employed in 'Feast and Famine' – but on other Manvers' estates the recorded arrears as proportions of agreed rents varied from an annual average of 2 per cent at Holme

Pierrepont to 7 and 8 per cent at Beighton and Thoresby, and to nearly 21 per cent on the Crowle estate in Lincolnshire. Such a persistently high level of arrears points to a measurement problem. Nor is this a lone example. At face value the average recorded rent arrears on the Castle Howard estate for the decade 1701–10 were 31 per cent of the level of agreed rents, and over the period 1724–50 the equivalent annual average recorded rent arrears on the Badminton estate stood at an astonishing 130 per cent of the agreed rent. In the first year when the data are available for Badminton the accumulated arrears were £1,850 while the assessed rent was £865.

What these examples point to is the difference between accumulated arrears, and freshly acquired arrears. Wordie encountered this same difficulty in his study of the Trentham and Lilleshall rentals in Staffordshire and Shropshire. The accumulated arrears at Trentham in 1703 stood at £1,112 against a rent due of £852.[1] Mingay illustrated the problem on the Myddleton estate at Chirk Castle in Denbighshire, showing that the accumulated arrears totalled £6,274 and £4,941 in 1749 and 1750 respectively when the gross rental was £2,854.[2] Other examples abound. On Lord Monson's estate in Lancashire accumulated arrears totalled £7,548 in 1741 from an annual rent roll of £4,127.[3] On the Greenwich Hospital estates in Northumberland the problem of accumulated arrears persisted throughout the eighteenth century. At the end of 1745 these arrears stood at £6,283 against a rent received for that year of £6,965. The situation certainly improved thereafter, but by 1790 accumulated arrears still stood at £3,938 against rents received of £18,029, and then during the post-Napoleonic Wars depression the accumulated arrears rose to between £9,000 and £15,000 over the period 1815–25 when rents received stood at between £33,000 (with a 15 per cent abatement) and £43,000.[4] On the Sutherland estate at Trentham the high level of arrears and accumulated arrears evident in the early eighteenth century was tolerated through much of the nineteenth century: in 1813 arrears amounted to 22 per cent of the agreed rents but thereafter only fell below 15 per cent in six years before 1854, with peaks of 41 per cent in 1833–4 and 34 per cent in 1850.[5]

---

[1] J. R. Wordie, 'Rent movements and the English tenant farmer, 1700–1839', *Research in Economic History*, 6 (1986), 225 specifically, and in general 225–35. See also examples of the same problem for the 1690s on the Kingston and Devonshire estates in O. R. F. Davies, 'The Dukes of Devonshire, Newcastle and Rutland 1688–1714' (University of Oxford, DPhil thesis, 1971), p. 168.

[2] G. E. Mingay, *English Landed Society in the Eighteenth Century* (London, 1963), pp. 127, 56, and 125–30 in general.

[3] P. J. Bowden, 'Agricultural prices, wages, farm profits, rents', in Thirsk, *AgHist* (1985), p. 82.

[4] Hughes, 'Northumberland', comparing pp. 80 and 82, and for other examples in the county p. 230.

[5] R. W. Sturgess, 'The response of agriculture in Staffordshire to the price changes of the nineteenth century' (University of Manchester, PhD thesis, 1965), p. 503.

These examples demonstrate the importance of distinguishing between arrears accruing in a particular year, and the carry-over or accumulation of arrears from year to year, an accumulation which in some cases would never have been paid off and may eventually have been written off by landlords, or 'forgiven', in the language of the day. This means that figure 9.3, whilst an accurate transcription, is not so much a record of new arrears, but rather a record of new and old, forgiven and unforgiven, and probably, for part at least, irredeemable. Quite why such accounting arrangements were used and persisted we do not know, although they probably arose from a combination of inefficient collection, the unwillingness of landlords to accept that arrears could not be recovered, and problems with tenants which were resolved by allowing arrears to build up. We suspect that there was a radical shift in attitudes anyway in the relationship between landlords and tenants from the balmy days of benign dictatorship in the early eighteenth century to the more business-conscious world of the nineteenth century in which, amongst other things, the tenants fought with the landlords over the issue of tenant right and the compensation they regarded as theirs for their unexhausted capital improvements at the end of their tenancies. The replacement of leases for years by annual agreements may also have had some effect on the build-up of arrears.

Our alternative measure of 'putative' arrears, by ignoring accumulated arrears, offers a realistic way of capturing the level of new arrears on an annual basis. It may understate the true level of difficulty facing tenants, because accumulated debts must have had a bearing on the security of tenure, but it avoids the yearly carry over of accrued arrears which in many cases had to be written off.[6] Individual tenants must occasionally have experienced a bad year or two, but then made up ground with an extra payment, and sometimes an extended period of difficulty may have led to abatements and no making up of arrears. In really dire circumstances, as occurred certainly during the late-nineteenth-century depression the rents may have been renegotiated downwards. The course of action will have depended on various considerations, among them the number of tenants involved, and the general trend of agricultural conditions. However, we suggest that although our method of portraying arrears will probably understate the true level of difficulty facing tenants the trend and the impact of relative depression and recovery, it is more accurate than if we were to show all arrears without distinction. We recognise of course that this method of depicting agricultural distress or relative riches

---

[6] So much is clear from Wordie's tables of rents where periodically arrears were, indeed, written off.

will hide the large variations which were encountered from estate to estate.[7] The long-run level of new rent arrears only exceeded 10 per cent of rents due on three occasions, and mostly it was on or under 5 per cent. The late-nineteenth-century depression stands out as a period when arrears were persistently on or over 5 per cent, and therefore in terms of our basic agricultural history it emerges as the deepest depression of the entire period. The post-Napoleonic Wars depression does not stand out particularly forcefully, and in the years of high farming the level of arrears was remarkably steady at about 4 per cent. John Bateman estimated a level of ordinary arrears in the nineteenth century of about 6 per cent per annum and our own figures, although mostly lower than his, nevertheless support the suggestion that generally arrears were not a major problem either for tenants or landlords.[8] The putative arrears show that the depression of the second quarter of the eighteenth century is now not particularly pronounced either in magnitude or longevity, and indeed where in figure 9.4 the arrears dip below the zero line they suggest that tenants attempted to pay back some of their recent, current, or accumulated arrears when conditions improved.

The full impact of the role of the rent index in illuminating the good and bad times in English agricultural history will be discussed at length in chapter 11. The importance of the sub-periods which have become familiar in the historiography will be clarified, but it is worth emphasising here just how our use of putative arrears may affect and revise views inherited from a familiar historiography. Our comparison of feast and famine, in which the famine of the second quarter of the eighteenth century seems perfectly clear (figure 9.3), is now less clear in the light of our illustration and discussion of putative arrears (figure 9.4). Any understanding of the course of agricultural rent requires an appreciation of the role of arrears, and, as we have suggested here, there is a real need to distinguish between annual and accumulated rental debts.

Regional index of agricultural rent, 1690–1914

Although in global terms England is a relatively small country, in soil and farming terms it embraces an enormous range of regional and local

---

[7] For example see the large variation in arrears on East Anglian estates in the post-Napoleonic period, variations from a high of 15 per cent of gross rental to a low of 3 per cent, P. Roe, 'Norfolk agriculture 1815–1914' (University of East Anglia, MPhil thesis, 1976), p. 11. See also a few examples in A. Offer, 'Farm tenure and land values in England, c. 1750–1950', EcHR, 44 (1991), 6.

[8] John Bateman, The Great Landowners of Great Britain and Ireland (Leicester University Press edn, 1971, being a reprint of the fourth and last edition of 1883), p. xxv.

differences. By good fortune the new index may happen to include a cross-section of the nation and represent England as a whole, but if this is the case it is pure chance. The data are drawn from estates which included fen, heath, and moor within their borders as well as those located in prime arable or best pasture country. In what follows we seek to break down the index along regional lines in order to test assumptions and assertions about variation in rental levels according to farming conditions.

As a generalisation, the lighter soils of eastern England where rainfall is not particularly heavy are noted for arable, particularly corn production, and the heavier soils of the west of England, where rainfall is relatively heavy, are noted for their pasture. The clay vales of the Midland counties were adaptable to both pasture and arable, although the extent to which this happened often depended on the availability of convenient supplies of chalk to break up the soil, as in the shadow of the Chiltern Hills. It could also depend on whether the land was enclosed or in open fields. The lighter soils of the Midlands were adapted for arable use.

These broad brush strokes on the agricultural canvas are hardly in dispute, but when the detail is added the picture is complicated by an enormous range of local variations. In the mid-nineteenth century James Caird seemed certain about the agricultural regions of England and Wales. The corn-growing counties were those lying in the east and south incorporating Northumberland and Durham, most of Yorkshire North and East Riding, pretty well the whole of Lincolnshire, Huntingdonshire, Bedfordshire, Hertfordshire and Middlesex, most of Berkshire, half of Wiltshire, the whole of Dorset, and all other counties lying east of this ragged line. Mixed and pastoral farming was to be found in the Midlands and western counties. Although this division may seem crude, Caird justified it in terms of rent levels. He suggested that, broadly, the mixed and grass counties enjoyed a rent which was 30 per cent greater per acre than the rent of the corn counties.[9] Caird's views have never seriously been tested, but data collected for the index can be disaggregated to provide some rough-and-ready assessments of his viewpoint.

From the writings of William Marshall in the eighteenth century through to the agricultural discussions of Caird in the nineteenth century, and on to the work of modern scholars, the regional agricultural diversity of England has been well understood. The likely impact on rents, both through time and at particular disjunctures, was also well known. Thomas Crawfurd, chief accountant to the 1st Duke of Buckingham, wrote to a fellow steward in 1822 in terms which show just how clearly contemporaries understood the

[9] Caird, map in frontispiece and table on p. 480.

differences, especially those whose work brought them into contact with different farming systems:

> the farmer on arable land has been suffering ever since 1813 but in this last year his loss has been ruinous and I am sorry to say 9/10 of them are not worth a shilling if they were now to be sold up and their arrears of rent and debts paid, these I call the first class from their priority in distress. The second is arable and pasture farms. The price of stock till this last year has been a saving one and consequently the farmer has only suffered half in former years that the arable farmer has done, but now that both stock and corn is so much below the price at which it be reared and growed the farmer is at present placed on the same level as the arable farmer, but has not so long been a general sufferer. The third class is the breeder and grazier. They have suffered severely by a fall in their stock of nearly 10 per cent independent of paying rent taxes etc. from the land whereon the cattle have been grazing for the last two years. The fourth class is the Dairy Farmer and Milkman, their sufferings have been but trifling compared with the others and where they have been situated within the reach of the London market butter has always been at a saving price and cheese, calves etc. has not fallen more than 1/4. This class, with a little abatement, might by struggling and where they are not over rented go on; as they have not even participated in the general distress which has with the other classes existed for years. From the foregoing statement of facts you will perceive my ideas respecting abatement of rent when the farms have been let fairly by survey and valuation at the high times price and are as under.
> The first class 25 per cent will I fear hardly enable them to go on.
> The second class 20 per cent. The probability being that both stock and corn will not continue at the present low prices.
> The third class 15 per cent. The produce of grazing farms is not likely to continue at the present price. The meat market can never have foreign competition.
> The fourth class 5 to 10 per cent. Where butter is a principal that has always been a saving price, but calves and cheese have fallen also 1/4 within these two last years.[10]

Crawfurd was an experienced agent, who recognised the need to disaggregate the various branches of agriculture for rental purposes. His observations give substance to our attempts here to examine regional patterns.

Although contemporaries and historians have been aware of regional differences, only in recent times has more sophisticated regionalisation been attempted beyond the rather crude efforts of Caird. This has been primarily in the work of scholars such as Eric Kerridge, Joan Thirsk, and Hugh

---

[10] Huntington Library, STG Correspondence, box 441–28, Thomas Crawfurd to Tobias Ledbroke, 5 February 1822.

Prince. Kerridge based his classification mainly on farming techniques over the period 1500–1800, and Thirsk incorporated broader issues of the agrarian economy in her distinctions, including an appreciation of the social structure of regions. However, from our point of view the sum total is the same, because in neither case can the level of detail which they identified be matched by the rent data.[11]

At best it might be possible to rationalise the detail into broader-based and more simplified regions. Thirsk recognised three broad agricultural types for the period 1500–1640, none of them purely arable, or even more narrowly of dominantly corn production within an arable regime. First of all she recognised a range of activities which were recognisably mixed farming (essentially sheep and corn, or more generally stock and corn). These were relatively dominant in parts of the Midlands, the downs, and much of the east coast. Secondly there was a pasture region which she called wood pasture in which stock keeping, rearing, fattening, and dairying were dominant, and with at least one subregion in which there was also some corn growing. In these regions there was also pig keeping and horse breeding. These regions occupied those parts of the Midlands which were not mixed farming, and also the eastern and southern counties which were not mixed. The exception in the east was the fens. The third category of farming region was called open pasture, and this was dominated by cattle and sheep rearing on the fells and moors, as well as smaller pockets of rearing and fattening, and included fish and fowl activities in the fens of the Wash and Somerset. This third category was found west of the Pennines, along the Welsh border, in the west country, the north-west Midlands, and in the fens.

For the period 1640–1750 Thirsk constructed farming regions which adopt the same broad-brush approach but with rather more variations within categories: much of the south, central, and east Midlands, east Yorkshire, much of Norfolk, the chalklands of southern England, and much of the south coast in general she defined as one or other variety of arable in which corn and livestock were mixed (mainly but not perfectly matching the mixed-farming types of the earlier period); the western counties, including everything west of the Pennines, along with the London Basin, the North York Moors, the Weald, and much of Suffolk she defined as one or other variety of pastoral type region. Much of the country in the north-west Midlands, Essex, that part of the north-eastern counties east of the Pennines which she had not already specified as pastoral (or in the case of much of Yorkshire as arable), and the

<hr />

[11] E. Kerridge, *The Agricultural Revolution* (London, 1967), frontispiece, and reproduced along with Thirsk's own agricultural regions in J. Thirsk, *England's Agricultural Regions and Agrarian History, 1500–1750* (London, 1987), pp. 24, 28, and 31. H. C. Prince, 'The changing rural landscape, 1750–1850', in Mingay, *AgHist*, pp. 21, 81.

fens, she defined as intermediate types with corn and livestock. It is hardly possible to do justice to the many variations which Thirsk has identified, but the essence is captured in this summary.[12] Hugh Prince's reconstruction of the farming-regions of England in the period from 1750–1850 makes no real attempt to rationalise Thirsk's detail. His summary of William Marshall's evidence for the period 1794–1814, and his clever piecing together of the evidence from the *JRASE* Prize Essays produces two maps which in essence are soil and surface geology maps, not farming-region maps, although of course the one is an influence on the other.

For our purposes these different maps are not particularly helpful, and we have had to reach a series of compromises in identifying farming regions to show whether or not those regions produce different unit acre rents. Our compromises allow us to produce two regional rent indexes, and hence to begin the task of establishing whether there was a significant difference between the rent per acre broadly of the arable and broadly of the pasture counties as originally postulated by Caird.

The method of weighting such disparate land uses is embodied in the more or less random survival of the rents which accrued to them. In the basic equation of rent per acre, the rent of land devoted to crops was higher per unit than the rent paid for the equivalent extent of moorland. Yet what proportion of England was devoted to the main land-use types, and how are those land uses represented in the rent sample which has been assembled? These are necessary questions to pose but they have no ready answer. Even in the best sets of rentals and surveys the actual use of the land on which rents were paid was rarely given. Besides, over time, notwithstanding any restrictions in their lease agreements and the natural restrictions of the environment, farmers could and did change the emphasis of their farming strategies. Even when the natural environment did not change, the economic environment often did. In times of depression poor yielding soils might be abandoned to former uses and some farmers might even shift their interests out of crops and into grass, but in times of agricultural or general economic buoyancy what was otherwise economically marginal land appeared less marginal and the tide of agricultural development crept up the hill slope and onto the moors and fens. The closest we might come to an appreciation of the farming coverage of the rent data is by way of dissecting its main component parts in an attempt to postulate a set of crude regional indexes.

[12] See the greater detail in Thirsk, *AgHist* (1984), pp. xx–xxi. We point out, however, that the reprint of this map in Thirsk, *England's Agricultural Regions*, does not contain the key with which to interpret it (p. 31). The unwary reader may mistakenly think that the key which accompanies the map for the period 1500–1640 (p. 28) is also applicable to this map of later farming regions.

If an estate could be identified as the ideal representative for a particular agricultural region, and as long as the surviving rental data for that estate covered most of the period of the study, it could stand alone as a type example. Unfortunately, not only is it impossible to be certain about the representativeness of any single estate, but also few of them have yielded data covering the whole of the period under review. Alternatively, it is possible to envisage splicing together the data from a few identifiably typical regional estates, although the problem here is to define the typical. The national rent index may already do this by bringing together a representative cross-section of the English farming landscape, but if it does, it does so by accident. We could assume that some of the estates from which data were collected are typical of their regions unless otherwise shown not to be, in which case there are a few candidates which may serve the purpose: Castle Howard in North Yorkshire and the Emanuel Hospital estate at Brandesburton in East Yorkshire are obvious candidates for the arable east; the Badminton estate in Gloucestershire might represent the pastoral west; and the Manvers estates in Nottinghamshire together with the Leveson-Gower estates in Staffordshire and Shropshire might represent the intermediate regions based on mixed farming. In any event, in a broad cross-section of England it might be thought that at least the two main farming types would be covered by these estates – the dominantly arable and the dominantly pasture: Badminton for pasture, Brandesburton for arable, Manvers for mixed, but veering towards the arable, and Leveson-Gower also for mixed but now veering towards the pastoral.

In theory this sounds fine, but land use did change during the period, especially in the Midland counties. There was a tendency in the eighteenth century towards greater pastoral activity, especially in connection with enclosures, to be followed by a countervailing move to extend the arable in the French wars, again often associated with enclosures. In addition, the large estates we have included in the database covered many parishes or townships with whole varieties of land use. Figure 9.5 demonstrates this complexity very well by showing T. L. Colbeck's appreciation of both the topographical and resulting land use complexity of Northumberland in the 1840s. On to this is superimposed the enormous variation in the yearly value of the land per acre.[13] The tithe files and accompanying maps of the 1830s and 1840s are replete with similar local variations showing the complexity of land use and farming practices. Derbyshire is predominantly an upland county and therefore mainly devoted to pastoral farming, but in every parish, however inhospitable, a few oats were grown and sometimes a little

[13] T. L. Colbeck, 'On the Agriculture of Northumberland', *JRASE*, 8 (1847), 422–37.

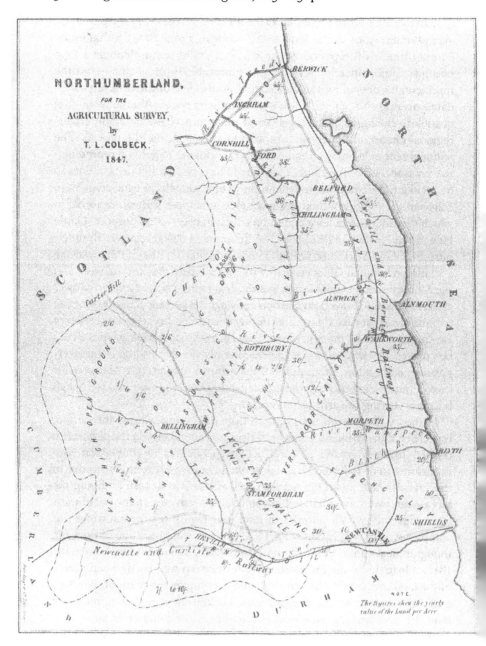

Fig. 9.5 The variation in land use and land values in Northumberland, c. 1847

barley, while the south of the county was characterised by rich, high-yielding clays and gravels.[14]

In the futile search for precision, we end up instead with the oversimplification of regional land use defined by Caird, juxtaposed with the greater but not perfect complexity of farming regional types produced by Thirsk, and in both cases an inability to accommodate whatever land use changes occurred over the period. Nevertheless, we adopt both and produce two different regional evaluations of rent per acre. The first quite simply takes Caird's twofold division of pasture and corn counties, and in the second we simplify Thirsk's threefold division to identify the broad geography of the pasture counties, the arable counties, and what she termed the integrated, or mixed counties.

Caird's twofold division of England and Wales can be applied fairly simply to the rent data since his line of demarcation falls neatly along county borders. Even the data from some of those estates whose owners cannot be identified in the Royal Commission can be included in this classification because in many cases there is at least an indication of the county of origin. However, we have deleted the data derived from some estates which cannot be identified by county, and we have also eliminated those years for which there are data available from only one estate sample. The effect of imposing this second constraint is particularly felt in the early years of the period. Thus from 1690 to 1720 there are no observations for the counties of the Midlands and the west, and there are also gaps for the southern and eastern counties. However, from the 1730s we have at least three observations in the two broad regions. For most of the eighteenth century there are marginally more observations in the west and south, and by the 1790s the two regional samples include 100,000 acres or more each year. Throughout the nineteenth century there are at least 10 estate observations each year in each broad region, rising to over 30 in each during the 1880s, by which time over 400,000 acres are covered in each.

Figure 9.6 links Caird's simple twofold regional farming division to the rent data. The trends of the two resulting rent indexes are identical, and before about 1810 the actual magnitude of the two indexes are also more or less identical. If anything, up to about 1790, the corn-based rents were usually marginally larger than the combined mixed-farming and pasture rents. However, from the 1790s, those combined rents were always above the corn rents, and as the nineteenth century proceeded the gap between the two increased. Around 1850 the combined mixed and pasture rents were rarely as much as 20 per cent greater than the corn rents, and therefore this

[14] J. V. Beckett and J. E. Heath (eds.), *Derbyshire Tithe Files 1836–40* (Chesterfield: Derbyshire Record Society, 1995), esp. pp. xxxiii–liii.

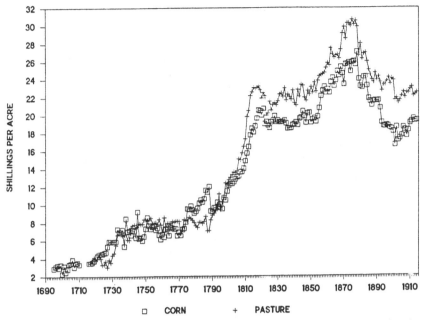

Fig. 9.6 Corn and pasture rents compared: based on Caird's agricultural regions

was less by some margin than the difference which Caird himself had estimated. The rents differed because the relative good fortunes of the two main farming systems fluctuated over time.

The difference and the trend in that difference is demonstrated in figure 9.7, which depicts the mixed and pasture rents as a percentage of the corn rents. This can be likened to a terms of trade index between the two farming systems. The trends in the eighteenth century show two main movements: from about 1730 to about 1760 there is a strong suggestion of rising landlord incomes per acre in the mixed farming and pasture districts relative to those in the corn districts (the terms of trade move in favour of pasture and this is shown as a rise in figure 9.7); but from 1760 to 1790 there was a reversal in the terms of trade trend to reveal rising unit acre arable incomes relative to others (shown in figure 9.7 as a downturn). This may be picking up real adjustments in the relative fortunes of corn and pasture, or it might easily be a reflection of the narrow sample base or biased sample base through much of the eighteenth century. The relative movement of rents in the 1790s, however, is unambiguous. Apart from short-term fluctuations the strong move in the terms of trade towards pasture-based rents from about 1790 to 1815 gave way in the long term to a plateau, or slightly rising plateau which

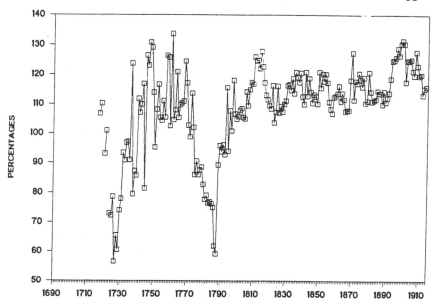

Fig. 9.7 Pasture rents as a percentage of arable rents: based on Caird's agricultural regions

suggests that pasture rents were 10 per cent higher than corn rents in about 1830 rising to as much as 30 per cent higher at the height of the late-nineteenth-century depression.

Adopting Thirk's regions may uncover local and regional differences with clear messages for agricultural history, and it will overcome the starkness of Caird's simple twofold structure. To do so requires a modest amount of creative accounting with further slimming down of the database. We lose those large estates for which the data are not distinguished by county, and we also lose some of those estates which were anonymously submitted to the Royal Commission because we cannot locate them within counties. As far as possible though, we have located accurately the remaining estates in one of Thirsk's three broad regions. In this exercise we must bear in mind that Thirsk's regions reflected her appreciation of the agricultural geography of the period 1640–1750, but we are using those same regions projected across the next century and a half. The agricultural geography will have changed, but we will not be picking up those changes. Nevertheless, at the simplified and indicative level at which we are operating we think that there is still something of value in this exercise.

The act of reducing the database, however, has important repercussions on the chronological and geographical coverage. It is only from the last quarter of the eighteenth century that a reasonable sample of estates in each region survives the slimming-down process. By this period the rent data covers at least 50,000 acres in each of the three regions. For most years in the nineteenth century there are at least ten and upwards of twenty estates represented in each region, and at its peak in the 1880s the coverage accounts for over 300,000 acres of, broadly, corn country, nearly 200,000 acres of an intermediate corn and pasture country, and nearly 300,000 acres of, broadly, pasture country.

The loss by this dilution of coverage compared with the same exercise using Caird is countered by the gain in detail by adding a third farming division, although a comparison of the Caird and Thirsk regions exposes a major discontinuity. Some of Caird's pasture and arable country is redefined by Thirsk as belonging to an intermediate farming regional type; and some of his arable country changes complexion entirely to become pasture country in Thirsk's broad definitions. Conversely, some of Caird's pasture becomes arable country on Thirsk's map. We suggest that this may be less a true impression of the changing agricultural geography of the period 1640–1750 to c. 1850, and more a reflection of the problems which arise in defining farming regions.

Without insider knowledge of each and every estate this exercise in regionalisation was always going to be something of a lottery, but figure 9.8 shows the three profiles which emerge. Just about all the time the arable and intermediate rents were greater per unit than the pasture rents until the last quarter of the nineteenth century when, during the agricultural depression, the slump in corn rents was greater than the slump in all other rents. Give or take short-term fluctuations, the trend in all three rent profiles was more or less the same, but while in the 1790s the arable rents were at least twice as high as the pasture rents, by the 1830s and 1840s they were barely a fifth higher. Thus while the direction of the trends in the three profiles suggests a considerable degree of continuity across the agricultural landscape, we can demonstrate important variations in relative movements. Identifying such variations may have little value for much of the eighteenth century when the database is relatively narrow, but throughout the nineteenth century the sample base is large and the relative trends may have some substance for our interpretation of agricultural history.

We can best demonstrate this through indexes of relative rental movements, figure 9.9 (a–c). In figure 9.9a the pasture rents are taken as a percentage of the arable rents. The ensuing terms of trade effect sees the advantage in unit rents move almost inexorably towards pasture for a century from the 1790s, but it is not until the early 1870s that the level of pasture rents

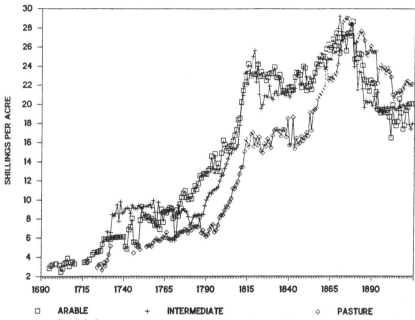

□   ARABLE   +   INTERMEDIATE   ◇   PASTURE

Fig. 9.8 Rent per acre for arable, intermediate and pasture regions: based on Thirsk's farming regions

equalled and then passed the corn rents. This movement is replicated in trend though not in degree in the relationship between the rents from the broad arable region and those from the intermediate farming region (figure 9.9b, though we would emphasise that the scales on these various graphs are different). The terms of trade relationship between the rents in the intermediate region and the rents in the pasture region now follows as in figure 9.9c; that is, while the terms of trade for intermediate rents improves with respect to arable rents, it gets worse with respect to pasture rents. Thus what we see is akin to a filter taking place from one pole of land use, the arable, through to the other pole, pastoral farming, as the relative fortunes of these farming systems changed as the nineteenth century proceeded.

This may have implications for English agricultural productivity and the impact of the so-called agricultural revolution. It adds weight to the evidence for the long march in improving arable productivity, but now within a more integrated agricultural system which saw pastoral farming products become increasingly important. But in terms of gross rental income, the importance of the latter did not supersede the importance of the former until it was almost too late for the agricultural industry as a whole. By the time pasture incomes relatively dominated the scene, agriculture had been deserted to its fate as the poor sector of the British economy. Pasture

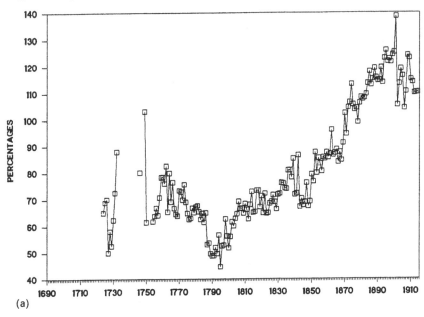

(a)

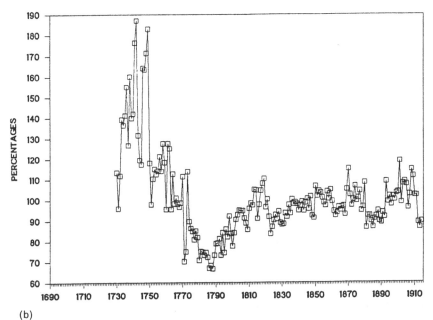

(b)

Fig. 9.9 Relative rent movements by region: (a) Pasture: arable (b)
Intermediate: arable (c) Intermediate: pasture. Based on Thirk's farming
regions

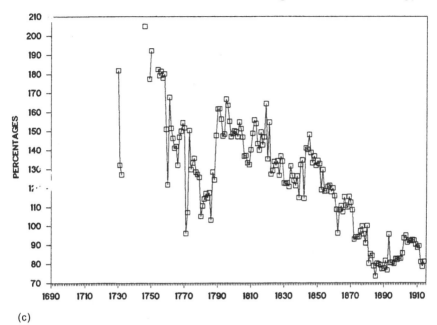

(c)

Figure 9.9 c

lingered on relatively successfully, even in the face of mounting pressure
from imports as technological changes in transport and food processing
broke the protective barrier offered by Britain's isolated island state, because
the market for home-produced livestock production remained relatively
buoyant. Home-produced meat rose throughout the late nineteenth century
and up to the First World War, and though its proportional contribution to
total meat production declined from 86 per cent in 1872 to 68 per cent in
1892 the volume of home production was still rising. In 1912 the home
producer was still contributing 58 per cent of home meat supplies.[15] In real
terms, the gross incomes of livestock producers probably continued to gain
throughout the late nineteenth century, or at least did not fall.[16] Taken
together these factors projected back in time help to explain why so-called
pasture rents rose more swiftly than other rents throughout the nineteenth
century, eventually overtook all other rents by the late 1870s, and declined
less fast in the Great Depression. A greater refinement of the data and a
closer identification of the precise location of the pasture lands would not

[15] R. Perren, *Agriculture in Depression, 1870–1914* (London, 1995), p. 8; Perren, *The Meat Trade in Britain
1840–1914*, p. 3.
[16] M. E. Turner, 'Output and prices in UK agriculture, 1867–1914, and the Great Agricultural
Depression reconsidered', *AgHR*, 40 (1992), 50.

necessarily produce the seemingly predicted continuous rise in pasture rents from *c.* 1880, or more likely a levelling off in rents, because farming was a living organism and such refinements would also identify lands relatively poorly suited to pasture which had converted to pasture and diluted the magnitude of the buoyant incomes to livestock producers.[17]

Conclusion

In this chapter we have been able to develop two further themes which arise from the rent index. First, our technique of analysing the data for arrears has enabled us to use the material advantageously in looking for the peaks and troughs within the agricultural cycle over long time spans. This has not led to any radical new interpretations, but we have been able to distinguish between the ongoing level of arrears running at about 5 per cent annually, and higher levels which correspond to dips in the long-term trend of agricultural prosperity. Consequently we now have every reason to feel confident that we can identify periods when prosperity or depression in agriculture are likely to have had wider repercussions for the economy, or are themselves likely to have arisen as a result of fluctuations in that economy. Second, our regional analysis of rent – although necessarily somewhat crude – has made it possible to reconstruct something of the pattern of division between farming areas across the country. We cannot endorse Caird's summary of the difference between arable and pasture rents, because we have not been able to identify his 30 per cent difference (in favour of the pasture rents) between the rent of the corn counties and the rent of the pasture counties. Instead, on the basis of Thirsk's broad agricultural regions we find that it was not until the final quarter of the nineteenth century that unit rents in the pastoral west exceeded those in the arable east. This is not necessarily a surprising finding except in the light of Caird's summary, because corn, after all, remained the staple of the English diet, the farmer's profits, and the landlord's rent, and was not seriously challenged by overseas competition until the last three decades or so of the nineteenth century.

---

[17] See F. M. L. Thompson, 'An anatomy of English agriculture, 1870–1914', in B. A. Holderness and M. E. Turner (eds.), *Land, Labour and Agriculture, 1700–1820* (London, 1991), pp. 224–6, who, on a county basis using Schedule A Income Tax returns as a proxy for rent, identifies only Westmorland, Cornwall, Cheshire, and Cumberland as counties which gained in average rents in the period 1872–3 to 1892–3. By the same analysis *all* counties then suffered a decrease in rents down to 1910–11 during a time when the rent index shows that rents at least stabilised or increased modestly. Thompson says his findings will be partly influenced by a time lag while income tax assessments adjusted to the realities of the real world. Thus with the continued fall in prices in the early 1890s the picture from Schedule A looks less bad than in fact it was in the first period, but worse than it was during the second period.

CHAPTER 10

The rent index and agricultural history I: the long term

How does the new index of rents influence our understanding of the fortunes of agriculture in the period 1690–1914? In this chapter and the one which follows we attempt to assess the index against the broader history of agriculture, and in particular we look in some detail at the pattern of prosperity and depression. We shall attempt to link changes in agricultural practice, and in output and productivity, to the rent index, in order to establish the relationship between rent levels and broader changes in agricultural practice. We are well aware that the correlation is not straightforward. Rents did not rise or fall merely in step with alterations in output: the pattern of change was much more complex than this, but rental data is particularly useful for identifying booms and slumps and our concern will be to look for links with agricultural change more generally.

Why did rent levels change over time? We may identify several main causes. The first is competition for land. Clearly rack-rented land will be subject to rental fluctuations according to demand for farms generally, and for particular types of farm (either in terms of size, or soil, or culture, or proximity to markets, etc.). Agricultural experts opposed the letting of farms simply to the highest bidder but had few ideas as to how to establish what a reasonable rent should be (chapter 2). Yet as the eighteenth century passed into the nineteenth, and as tenancies for leases and lives were converted to tenancies on medium-term leases, or became tenancies at will, rack-rented farms could indeed have become subject to market forces, with rents varying appropriately. We should not exaggerate this progress, however, since landlords wanted to hold on to their existing tenants: they knew them; they had confidence in them; they had grown content with the security derived from what was often a long association with a steady income; and good replacements could not always easily be found. In such relationships tenants did not necessarily receive, or ask for, leases, since the question of eviction rarely entered the equation. This natural trust between landlords and their tenants is not something which can be easily modelled, but also it cannot be ignored. Nevertheless, in time, economic forces played a role. This could work in several ways: there could be an active demand for farms in some periods, but in others there could be a veritable desertion of the land, and in yet others there could be a differentiation in demand. For example, during the late nineteenth-century depression the demand for large farms slackened, but the demand for small farms increased, enhancing the existing differential pattern in rents.[1]

Second, rents reflected price trends, since these will have affected the ability of the farmer to pay. We shall see that there is a clear correlation between prices and rents, but with time lags while landlords and tenants alike adjusted to altered conditions by renegotiating rents. This adjustment took several forms, the most noticeable of which was the movement during and after the Napoleonic Wars away from long leases (usually of terms up to 21 years) in favour of annual 'at will' tenancies. Landlords learnt from the inflation of the years 1793 to 1815 that tenants would reap the financial benefits while rents were rising, but that they were not able to sustain the losses when depression set in. As a result, tenancy at will, with a suitable system of compensation (tenant right) became the standard means of letting freehold agricultural land almost everywhere, despite sustained opposition from agricultural writers and other experts. The tenant compensation, or tenant right, encouraged farmers to invest in the soil. Where it was practised they were secure in the knowledge that if, for some reason, they were not taken on again when the old tenancy ran out, the unrewarded portion of their investment which would benefit the incoming tenant would be compensated.

Third, rents moved in relation to output and productivity, particularly the latter since it was in the landlords' best interests to try to cream off excess profits from their tenants if and when they saw what was being produced. Productivity changes depended on a number of factors, among them the introduction of new crops and rotations, changes in manuring and land organisation, labour inputs, and weather conditions. However, while it was clear what affected productivity measuring it was far more difficult. No figures were collected by government until the agricultural returns began in 1866 (and data on crop yields were not included until 1884), and the mechanism whereby productivity change was reported from farmer to landlord remains something of a mystery. How did the landowner or his agent assess productivity and output unless they had access to the farmers' accounts? Although farm account books show that some farmers kept quite

[1] For illustrations of the differential rents on small and large farms see chapter 3 above.

detailed records of the ratio of grain harvested to seed sown, it seems unlikely that regular reviews of farmers' accounts featured in rent renegotiation. The one thing that farmers, agents, and landowners would always be aware of, however, would be market prices for raw produce or processed foods, and also complaints of hardship from farmers. But would the farmers beat a path to the agents' door to seek congratulations on a bumper harvest, or on the successful adoption of an innovation which raised productivity?

The difficulties involved in measuring productivity changes are most clearly expressed by the impact of enclosure. Throughout the period some form of enclosure was taking place somewhere, even if the best-known phase of the movement clearly coincided with the period of parliamentary enclosure between c. 1760 and c. 1830. The difficulty in making allowance for enclosure is twofold. First, we need a multiplier to convert productivity increases which may have resulted from enclosure, into rent increases. Second, ideally, we would wish to estimate, in a national index, the likely annual effect of enclosure, taking into account the extent and quality of land being enclosed (as a proportion of the cultivated acreage) and the knock-on effect in terms of rent. It has been estimated by M. E. Turner that by 1801 corn yields in enclosed parishes were 20 to 25 per cent higher than in open-field parishes, but R. C. Allen has set the figure rather lower at 5.6 to 13.7 per cent.[2] At a crude level both estimators tried to control for soil and other environmental characteristics. Both estimates suffer from the problem that the parishes and places involved were not studied before and after enclosure. Instead the open-field parishes formed a group or groups in isolation from the enclosed parishes.

Even if we can find ways of allowing for such differences, the problem is still to find a suitable way of converting yield changes into rent changes. The typical rent increase which followed enclosure seems to have been between 50 and 100 per cent, but can we automatically assume that a relationship existed between enclosure, productivity gains, and rental increases? On the contrary, the evidence seems to suggest that in the arable and pasture districts of the Midland counties the post-enclosure rent increases were much larger than the Ricardian surpluses (revenues minus labour and capital costs) dictate that they ought to have been. Consequently a share of the rent increase effectively took the form of a transfer of income from the farmer to the landlord, so that enclosure has to be seen as a way of redistributing existing income. In turn this suggests that rents were below

[2] M. E. Turner, 'Agricultural productivity in England in the eighteenth century: evidence from crop yields', *EcHR*, 35 (1982), 489–510; M. E. Turner, 'Crop distributions, land productivity and English parliamentary enclosure', *Journal of Economic History*, 46 (1986), 669–92; Allen, *Yeoman*, p. 136.

equilibrium on open-field land. While farming on these lands was controlled by antiquated customs, rents necessarily were set partly according to time-honoured conventions and experience. Yet there was also a mixture of tenures to contend with. By the eighteenth century some land was already racked, but there was also the survival of customary tenure. With this in mind Allen has suggested that enclosure was not necessarily motivated by the pursuit of productivity gains *per se*. Rather, it was a method employed by landlords in order to renegotiate existing tenures. Why should they wish to do this? One very important reason relates to the general price history of the times. Prices, practically all prices, began to rise from the mid-eighteenth century. A rise in price of agricultural products resulted in rising gross incomes for the tenants, but with unexpired leases attached to customary tenure in some places, and with rack rents also on unexpired leases in others, and with mixtures of the two even in the same place, the incomes to landlords, that is, their rents, remained stable. Therefore, the Ricardian surpluses which were accruing through the price change were not being shared. In such situations the tenure – either sort of tenure – was based on an economic reality which had passed. Through its clauses and its parliamentary imprimatur, enclosure allowed the renegotiation and conversion of customary tenures to modern forms, and it also allowed existing rack rents to be declared null and void and subject to renegotiation. By this means landlords could catch up on lost Ricardian rent surpluses.[3] The process of changing customary tenures to modern forms was already under way in the Midlands,[4] the particular advantage of enclosures was its attack on unexpired leases.

Enclosure was certainly followed by rent increases, but allowing for this in the rent index has not proved possible; indeed, it is probably impossible to identify the effects of enclosure on rents except by a narrow range of examples in which parish-based studies of rent can be precisely linked to the incidence of enclosure. Apart from examples in the contemporary literature we would point to Purdum's study of five Nottinghamshire manors enclosed between 1787 and 1796. He estimated a large variation in the rate of return on enclosure measured as the adjustment of post-enclosure rents relative to what those rents might have been if the manors had remained unenclosed. The lowest rate of return on investing in enclosure on the five manors was 6.5 per cent and the highest was nearly 32 per cent. Relative to the

[3] R. C. Allen, 'The efficiency and distributional consequences of eighteenth-century enclosures', *Economic Journal*, 92 (1982), 937–53; G. R. Boyer, 'England's two agricultural revolutions', *Journal of Economic History*, 53 (1993), 915–23.
[4] Allen, *Yeoman*, with the whole issue of the conversion of copyholds and other ancient tenures summarised on pp. 96–101.

competing rate of return of between 3 and 5 per cent on investing in the funds, enclosure was declared a profitable venture.[5] We have not looked for, and therefore have not added any additional examples to this, or any other crude measure of landlord efficiency gain.

Fourth, rents should fluctuate according to labour productivity since, in the absence of food imports, it is rising labour productivity, rather than the productivity of land alone, that is a necessary pre-condition for any expansion in the proportion of the nation's workforce employed in the industrial and tertiary sectors of the economy. E. A. Wrigley has inferred a doubling of labour productivity between the early seventeenth and early nineteenth centuries.[6] G. Clark, working from changes in real wage rates, considers the rise in agricultural labour productivity to have begun earlier and to have amounted to a quadrupling in the period from c. 1300 to c. 1850. In his view, by the early nineteenth century the output per farm worker was much higher in England than either in the medieval period, or in contemporary eastern Europe, and this was due to 'more intense labour'.[7] He suggests that the majority of these gains in productivity preceded the agricultural revolution and were complete by about 1770. By contrast, M. Overton has used three different types of measure to suggest that output grew by more than 100 per cent between 1700 and 1850, with the greatest emphasis after 1750. According to his estimates it grew with approximately equal contributions from land and labour productivity.[8]

The trend in labour productivity highlighted by Wrigley and Clark is roughly the same: the importance of Overton's estimates is that labour productivity continues to improve beyond the late eighteenth and early nineteenth centuries and does not slow down. Clark's view is that labour productivity rose as a result of more efficient, better motivated, better fed, and harder working, labourers. Wrigley has added the suggestion that labour productivity would also have been substantially raised by increasing the number of animals employed on the land, thereby substituting animal power for human labour, and that a comparison with France suggests that

---

[5] J. J. Purdum, 'Profitability and timing of parliamentary land enclosures', *Explorations in Economic History*, 15 (1978), 313–26, esp. 318.

[6] E. A. Wrigley, 'Energy availability and agricultural productivity', in B. M. S. Campbell and M. Overton (eds.), *Land, Labour and Livestock: Historical Studies in European Agricultural Productivity* (Manchester, 1991), 323–39.

[7] G. Clark, 'Productivity growth without technical change: European agriculture before 1850', *Journal of Economic History*, 47 (1987), 419–33; G. Clark, 'Yields per acre in English agriculture 1266–1860: evidence from labour inputs', *EcHR*, 44 (1991), 445–60; G. Clark, 'Labour productivity in English agriculture 1300–1860', in Campbell and Overton (eds.), *Land, Labour and Livestock*, 211–35.

[8] M. Overton, 'Re-establishing the English agricultural revolution', *AgHR*, 44 (1996), 1–18, particularly table 1. Our thanks to Professor Overton for the chance to consult this paper before it was published.

this was achieved.[9] Overton summarises a 'string of untested hypotheses as to why labour productivity took place', including: changes in labour practices; increases in the energy available in farm work; increases in farm size; and changes in employment practices.[10] Work patterns were clearly one factor, but what of economies of scale? How far, for example, was labour productivity affected by alterations in farm sizes? The advantage of large farms was generally held to be lower costs, particularly lower unit labour costs. Yet searching questions have been asked about the efficiency of large farms. Arthur Young and James Caird were two of the most passionate advocates of large farms, but they were almost certainly not representative of wider opinion during their times. The majority of commentators called for a suitable mix of sizes, and projected the idea of a farming ladder at work.[11] During the late-nineteenth-century agricultural depression demands for a return to peasant proprietorship pointed to concerns of this nature, and Allen has recently argued that peasant agriculture is frequently efficient and capable of modernisation.[12]

Although labour productivity was rising from at least the sixteenth century it was not until the eighteenth that it was matched by rising land productivity and expanding total output, and it was only at the end of the eighteenth century that the strong positive relationship which had existed from the Middle Ages between the rate of growth in population and the rate of growth in food prices, was finally broken. This reflected the gradual bringing together of effective technology and appropriate farm structures, which enabled farmers to respond to rising demand through increased productivity of land but without sacrificing the productivity of labour. The process may have been enhanced by the gradual elimination of the smallest holdings, although this process was slow and needs to be kept in perspective. Coupled with a slow trend in the direction of large farms and the replacement of open-field by enclosed farms, the result was a long-term increase in labour productivity. Unfortunately the relationship between these changes in structures, and rises in productivity, are still easier to posit than to measure.[13]

Fifth, institutional changes were linked to market opportunities, which were also changing through our period. Urban growth, both absolutely and

---

[9] Wrigley, 'Energy availability'.   [10] Overton, 'Re-establishing'.

[11] J. V. Beckett, 'The debate over farm sizes in eighteenth and nineteenth-century England', *Agricultural History*, 57 (1983), 308–25.

[12] R. C. Allen, 'The two English agricultural revolutions, 1450–1850', in Campbell and Overton, *Land, Labour and Livestock*, 252.

[13] Though see Overton, 'Re-establishing', table 1, for a useful summary of the competing likely estimates of output and productivity change from the seventeenth to the mid-eighteenth centuries.

relatively, had obvious knock-on implications for demand, both in total requirement and foodstuff demands. As the commercial opportunities offered by expanding urban populations increased, so also the opportunities for agricultural producers altered. In some cases these factors transformed the economics of agricultural production, and increased the possibility of regional specialisation. M. Overton and B. Campbell suggest that in the early modern period the idea of a pastoral west and arable east was less meaningful than it was later to become: 'it was in the supposedly arable east that pastoral husbandry assumed its most dynamic and developed forms, often in conjunction with equally developed mixed-farming systems'.[14] By the eighteenth century there may have been a clearer crystallisation of 'pastoral' and 'arable' regions, by which there was a sharper spatial differentiation between regions which bred and reared young animals (the pastoral) and those which fattened, milked, and worked them, or simply specialised in crop production (the arable). A county like Norfolk came into the latter category. However, one problem with the trend towards specialisation is whether Norfolk (or anywhere) could have sensibly specialised in cereals before the advent of artificial fertilisers. Where (in the absence of animals) did the farmer acquire his manure? Why do animal numbers seem to have increased in the 1850s and 1860s, not decreased, when artificials came on stream? Other regions began to specialise in the rearing of replacement stock, ultimately resulting in the fuller articulation of pastoral production on national, regional and local lines. These changes were in part a result of the widening and deepening of market demand for pastoral products. Specialisation led to a clearer differentiation between breeding, fattening and dairying as separate agricultural enterprises. Hence the rise of intensive dairying in north Shropshire and Herefordshire or the decline of dairying and the rise of fattening in Norfolk. However, we need to be careful about the timing of these changes because in Suffolk the specialisation in dairying which had developed in the eighteenth century was upset during the high prices of the French wars when there was a reversion to corn farming.[15]

Many of these questions will be confronted in the remainder of this chapter and also in chapter 11. The trends in English agriculture are well established, but the rent index enables us to revise a number of long-held views about the course of agricultural change. In what follows we will stand back from the detail and place the rent index into a long-term overview of the

[14] B. M. S. Campbell and M. Overton, 'Norfolk livestock farming 1250–1740: a comparative study of manorial accounts and probate inventories', *Journal of Historical Geography*, 18 (1992), esp. 394. See also B. M. S. Campbell and M. Overton, 'A new perspective on medieval and early modern agriculture: six centuries of Norfolk farming, *c.* 1250–*c.* 1850', *Past and Present*, 141 (1993), 38–105.
[15] J. Thirsk and J. Imray, *Suffolk Farming in the Nineteenth Century* (Ipswich, 1958), pp. 18–22.

period 1690–1914 (the remainder of this chapter). We will then paint in much of the detail by placing our findings into the context of the well-understood sub-periods and watersheds of English agricultural history (chapter 11). Where possible we shall try to link the index to both quantitative and qualitative data. Quantitatively, findings can be related to agricultural prices, land prices, and the rate of interest, as well as – less satisfactorily – to changes in wages. Used carefully these should give us an idea of the extent to which the rent index moved in line with, or deviated from, other indexes, and in this way we should be able to draw conclusions about trends in agriculture and their impact on the economy more generally. The index also offers a base for studying the national economy. Although the business of setting a rent was complex and not simply a question of year to year increments or of directly following or copying price trends – and therefore a rent index may not be perfectly sensitive in reflecting the trends in the economy at large – it should provide a firm indication of longer-term trends.

The rent index and incomes

Land is a factor of production which yields a number of incomes. The produce from the land provides a gross income to the farmers. The size of that gross income was a combination of product yields and market prices. There were a number of calls on farmers' gross incomes, principally the rent for the landlords, and the wages for the labour employed on the farm. In the simplest of terms this captures the traditional view of the countryside as a tripartite division of first the landlords, secondly their tenants, and thirdly their labourers. The focus of attention so far has been on rent representing the landlords' income, but this may be related to what is revealed in other data about the separate incomes of the farmers and their labourers. In the case of the farmers these will be proxy data through the course of general agricultural prices, but in the case of the labourers there is an indication of the most important element of unit labour earnings through a wage index. In addition, the ownership of land by landlords can be considered as an investment, and the question can be asked, were there better places for landlords to invest their funds? The returns on government stock may be a way to investigate this question.

Rent was the price paid by one group in society, the farmers, to another group, the landlords, for the utility of the soil. At first glance the rent index seems to follow fairly closely the general ups and downs of any student's appreciation of price trends over the long period. On closer inspection this was not quite the case.

The rent a tenant paid to his landlord was probably the most important

Table 10.1. *Agricultural output and rents, 1700–1900*

	Output £m in 1815 prices	Price index 1815 = base 100	Current output £m	Current output index	Rent shillings/ acre	Rent index
	1	2	3	4	5	6
1700	40	47.2	18.9	69.1	3.0	38.8
1750	59	46.3	27.3	100.0	7.9	100.0
1800	88	98.4	86.6	317.0	12.1	154.3
1850	135	67.3	90.9	332.6	21.1	269.1
1900	—	—	120.9	442.5	19.9	253.8

Sources: See text for construction, but data taken from R. C. Allen, 'Agriculture during the industrial revolution', chapter 5 in R. Floud and D. N. McCloskey (eds.), *The Economic History of Britain Since 1700*, 2nd edition, I: *1700–1860* (Cambridge, 1994), p. 102; P. K. O'Brien, 'Agriculture and the home market for English industry, 1660–1820', *English Historical Review*, C, no. 397 (1985), 773–800; B. R. Mitchell and P. Deane, *Abstract of British Historical Statistics* (Cambridge, 1962), pp. 471–3; M. E. Turner, 'Agricultural output, income and productivity', chapter 2 in E. J. T. Collins (ed.), *The Agrarian History of England and Wales*, VII (Cambridge, forthcoming).

cost which he faced. Ideally, therefore, the best comparison would be between the trend of this cost and the trend of the tenant's income. Not enough is known about long-term national farm output for this to be possible, but there are some cross-sectional estimates which may serve a similar purpose. Table 10.1 compares a recently constructed summary of agricultural output with the rent index. Column 1 is Allen's estimates of agricultural output in England and Wales in real volume terms at 1815 prices for four cross-sections in time. Column 2 is a reconstruction of an appropriate agricultural price index for the same four cross-sections.[16] Column 3 is the agricultural output, and column 4 the index of that output in current price terms which arise from deflating Allen's real volume by the agricultural price index. Column 4 can now be compared directly with columns 5 and 6 which are the estimates of unit acre rents and the resulting index of rents based on ten-year averages for the cross-sectional years concerned. The final row in the table is an estimate of output for England and Wales for the year 1900 which is compared across the table with the rent index.[17]

[16] This is achieved by employing a combination of O'Brien's agricultural price index for 1700, 1750, and 1850 and Rousseaux's price index for 1800 but taking ten-year averages to avoid the distorting affects of aberrant years. P. K. O'Brien, 'Agriculture and the home market for English industry, 1660–1820', *English Historical Review*, C, no. 397 (1985), 787–90; Rousseaux's index from B. R. Mitchell and P. Deane (eds.), *Abstract of British Historical Statistics* (Cambridge, 1962), pp. 471–3.

[17] Output based on M. E. Turner, 'Agricultural output, income and productivity', in E. J. T. Collins (ed.), *The Agrarian History of England and Wales*, VII, *1850–1914* (Cambridge, forthcoming).

The trends in table 10.1 have been indexed on the year 1750. The table shows that the trend of rents gained on the trend of agricultural output in the first half of the eighteenth century. On the contemporary principle that the land yielded three rents, one of which accrued to the landlord, the trend we have identified here suggests a transfer of income to the landlords from the tenants. In the second half of the eighteenth century, when the data are more secure, rents increased by over 50 per cent, but total output increased threefold. This graphically reflects both our appreciation of late eighteenth-century price inflation and the concerns of landlords that the Ricardian rent surpluses were leaking away in declining real rents, while they were hampered by long-term leases. The remarkable thing is that Arthur Young and his contemporaries seemed to miss this point. In the first half of the nineteenth century there was a reversal of the trend. Annual leases were introduced, and rents were bid up in a relatively spectacular fashion. However much rent fell after 1815, in the light of their experiences of the eighteenth century, the landlords still retained enough of the Ricardian surpluses to suggest they had made real gains in the proportion of income derived from the land. However, in the second half of the nineteenth century, almost certainly with a concentration during the decades of the agricultural depression, it was the turn of the tenants to retain a large proportion of the income from the land and successfully to pass on a share, and perhaps the largest share, of the financial impact of the depression to their landlords. The contemporary inquiries of the 1890s suggest that when tenants defaulted on their rents the landlords were unable to take much action against them since they could anticipate problems in attracting replacements. We know also that landlords, or at least the substantial ones, continued to invest heavily in their land.[18] They were very often faced with tenants who, at the current prices available for their products, were just as likely to bail out of agriculture as to struggle on through the depression. Consequently they were ready to accommodate their tenants' problems simply in order to keep their farms in occupation. Too few potential tenants were being chased by too many landlords with too many available farms.

We must not place too much weight on either the output estimates or the appropriateness of these cross-sections, but at first glance these are plausible assessments of both the long-term trends of output and rent and the relative distributions of income from the land to the two main recipients of that income. It is partially, but not precisely corroborated in Ó Gráda's analysis of income distributions. He argued that the share of agricultural incomes which accrued to landlords increased from 22 per cent in 1862 to 24 per cent

---

[18] For which see table 1.1 above.

in 1878 and to 27 per cent in 1896, before falling to 19 per cent in 1905. The comparable share accruing to 'farmers' fell from 43 per cent to 39 and 35 per cent before rising to 44 per cent over the same years.[19] The discontinuities in this story in identifying the precise turning points in income shares may result from the problem of comparing cross-sections with annual estimates, but the overall story is reasonably congruent. In addition, while the number of landed proprietors hardly changed, the number of farmers actually declined from about 312,000 in 1861 to 280,000 in 1911. Thus the average incomes of farmers rose by 26 per cent from the early 1860s to the eve of the First World War while the average income of the landed interest fell by about 30 per cent from the early 1880s to the early Edwardian years.[20]

The calculation of the monetary value of output comes about through multiplying the volume of output by its unit price. Unfortunately we do not have annual, or even regular, output estimates, other than those we have summarised above, but there are good quantities of price material available. Figure 10.1a presents a fuller, and in some ways comparable history to table 10.1, but based on an agricultural price index. This has been constructed by splicing together Patrick O'Brien's price index for the period 1690–1819 and the Rousseaux agricultural price index from 1820 to 1913, but which is available for the longer period from 1800 to 1913.[21]

Figure 10.1a shows the same catching up process in the trend of rents to about 1750, which was a feature of table 10.1. From 1750 until about 1810 the trend of prices and rents moved together but with a lag of exactly 15 years (as in figure 10.1b). That is, the prices moved ahead of rents. Once again this feature is borne out by the mounting trend for adjusting tenures, for shorter leases, and for the emphasis on parliamentary enclosure in this period. Whatever the farming merits of leases so persistently advocated by Arthur Young, the evidence from comparing trends in rents and prices, as well as

[19] C. Ó Gráda, 'British agriculture, 1860–1914', in R. Floud and D. McCloskey (eds.), *The Economic History of Britain Since 1700*: II, *1860–1914* (Cambridge, 1994, 2nd edn), p. 146.
[20] *Ibid.*, pp. 147–8.
[21] For that short period from 1800 to 1820 when these two price indexes overlap they are not always in agreement with one another. There are some spectacular divergencies in trend and magnitude, but there are also far more occasions or years when the two indexes more or less coincide. With a base of 100 in 1810 the O'Brien and Rousseaux indexes trend as follows;

	O'Brien	Rousseaux
1800	101.0	98.9
1805	88.8	92.1
1810	100.0	100.0
1815	79.3	86.3
1820	74.2	75.3

O'Brien, 'Agriculture and the home market', 787–90; Mitchell and Deane, *Abstract*, pp. 471–3.

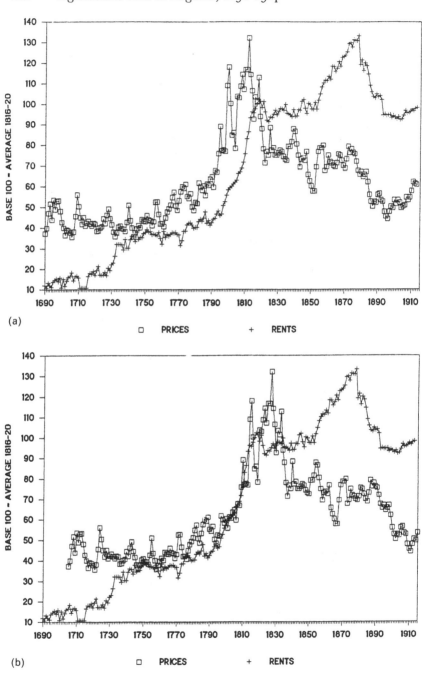

Fig. 10.1 The trend of agricultural prices and unit-acre rents: (b) 15-year lag

from other directions, now makes it clear that from a landlord's point of view the basic economics were not beneficial. When prices declined in the twenty years after the French wars, rents levelled out, but during the period of High Farming, when at best prices simply stabilised, rents took off in just about as spectacular a fashion as they had done during the French wars. In this period, however, investment by both landlords and tenants, which improved the volume of output, enabled them both to enjoy a relatively equitable distribution of the spoils.[22] Even with stable prices, therefore, tenants could enjoy rising incomes, but they could also pay rising rents. During the final period, the depression, the downturn in both prices and rents is evident, and without lags. In the slow recovery from the early 1890s prices recovered more quickly and immediately than rents and almost certainly this feature is picked up in table 10.1.

In its simplest terms, land yields three incomes – one to the landlord, one to the tenant, and one to the labourers – but the last of these is missing thus far from this appraisal of income distribution. A substantial body of wage data from the eighteenth and much of the nineteenth century is not available, but for the half century or so after 1860 it has been estimated that as a group they accrued from 35 per cent of agricultural income in 1862 rising to a peak of 38 per cent in 1896 and then falling rather steeply to 33 per cent in 1913. In 1896, at the bottom of the agricultural depression, they actually accrued a larger share of the total agricultural income than the farmers. Their numbers declined from 1.4 million in 1861 to around one million in 1911 (a decline of almost 30 per cent), which was far greater than the equivalent decline in the number of farmers (about 10 per cent).[23] Thus not only did the share of total income which accrued to the labour force at least remain level, but with a much-reduced labour force the income per labourer, relative to the other calls on total agricultural income, increased. That is not the same as saying that the labourers enjoyed higher wages because at the same time the total agricultural output, in nominal current price terms, fell from about 1870 to the 1890s. In other words, the total agricultural output cake shrank, but the labourers appeared to retain a growing share of it.[24] As it turned out average weekly wages peaked in the mid-1870s and then at best stayed at a plateau level until the 1890s before

---

[22] See C. H. Feinstein, 'Agriculture', in C. H. Feinstein and S. Pollard (eds.), *Studies in Capital Formation in the United Kingdom 1750–1920* (Cambridge, 1988), p. 269, which shows fixed capital formation in farm buildings and works rising through the years of High Farming. We are hesitant about citing this as supporting evidence since in order to make these estimates a prior estimate of rents was required. In other words, in these very calculations the estimates of rent and capital formation are not entirely independent.   [23] Ó Gráda, 'British agriculture', 146, 148.

[24] See M. E. Turner, 'Output and prices in UK agriculture, 1867–1914, and the Great Agricultural Depression reconsidered', *AgHR*, 40 (1992), 38–51, esp. 48 and 50 and associated graphs, which are couched in terms of the UK, not simply of England and Wales.

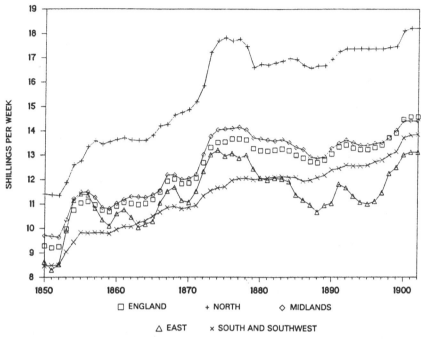

Fig. 10.2 Regional trends in agricultural labourers' wages 1850–1902

resuming their pre-1870 increase. At best, northern agricultural wages, buoyed up by competing demands from industry, fell dramatically in the late 1870s, but then rose modestly, even through the agricultural depression. In contrast, agricultural wages of the eastern arable counties fell continuously from the mid-1870s to the 1890s. In further contrast, the agricultural wages in the pastoral west rose continuously from 1850 to the early twentieth century, as if there was no depression to contend with. Figure 10.2 illustrates the regional breakdown and shows that trends were one thing, but comparative absolute wages levels another.[25]

When we review the longer-run trend in the average earnings of agricultural labourers in comparison with the trend of unit acre agricultural rents we can discern the changing fortunes of labour against those of landlords, but the unifying element is that they were both a cost to the farmers. Figure 10.3 extends that comparison back into the eighteenth century.[26] The rate of growth of average earnings from about 1785 to the end

---

[25] A Wilson Fox, 'Agricultural wages in England and Wales during the last half century', *JRSS*, 66 (1903), 273–348, reprinted in W. E. Minchinton (ed.), *Essays in Agrarian History* II (Newton Abbot, 1968), pp. 121–98, esp. 181–2.

[26] The unit earnings are taken from Bowley and Wood, and Bowley as reproduced in Mitchell and Deane, *Abstract*, pp. 348–50.

of the French wars in 1815 was at least as great as the rise of unit acre rents. Thus, these parallel costs incurred by the farmer increased roughly in tandem. There is a proviso attached to this finding and its interpretation. If average farm size grew in the eighteenth and for much of the nineteenth centuries this would have led to adjustments in the ratio of labourers to farms: it may have meant more labourers per farm, but with fewer farms it may also have meant a lower ratio of labourers per unit acre. The reverse may have been the case in the late nineteenth century when one result of the agricultural depression was the splitting of large farms into smaller farms. The sum of rents and labourers' wages constituted the greater part of the farmers' costs, so that while average earnings grew, the total wage bill may not have grown to the same extent.

Both average labour earnings and unit acre rents declined in the wake of the French wars such that from about 1820 to the early 1850s they remained roughly level and then rose more or less together. But in the late nineteenth century they dramatically diverged, as we have already discovered through the distribution of factor shares. The refinements in the agricultural census in the nineteenth century allow a more or less accurate calculation of the agricultural labour force to be made. In the eighteenth century, however, ideas about the size of the labour force are derived from informed observations from contemporaries, and back-of-the-envelope calculations by historians. The latest summary suggests that the number of men, women, and boys employed in agriculture in England and Wales declined from 1.553 million in 1700 to 1.405 million in 1800, and then rose to 1.524 million in 1851, a see-saw motion of about 9 per cent.[27] These estimates include the labour of the farmer himself, but they are dominated by his hired labour. In other words, if the impression of the trend in unit earnings is correct, and with a relatively constant labour force, the trend in unit earnings is also the trend in the total wage bill. Similarly, since the total supply of land was relatively fixed – though some land certainly fell out of use, or was underused, or was taken 'in-hand' by landlords – the trend in the rent index was also the trend in the rent bill faced by the farmers. Though this argument ignores changes in land use it does put into perspective the principal financial outgoings of the farmers. As already observed, it really did look as though the tenants were able to pass on the excesses of the late-nineteenth-century depression to their landlords, but only in so far as their labour bill allowed them to do so. In addition, in order to attract labourers the landlords sometimes had to build cottages, and this was another call on their estate costs and another way in which their already pinched incomes were further diminished. In general, the labour bill was

[27] R. C. Allen, 'Agriculture during the industrial revolution', in Floud and McCloskey (eds.), *The Economic History*: I, *1700–1860*, p. 107.

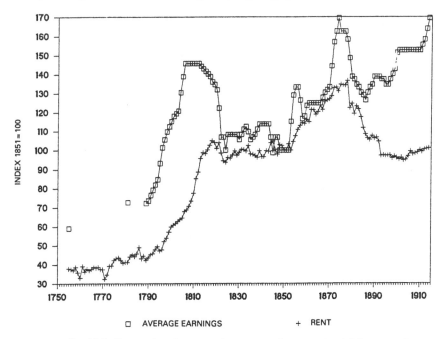

Fig. 10.3 Comparison between the course of rents and unit labour earnings

probably forced upwards by shortages of good labourers during the depression, but even so, the contemporary accounts show agricultural wages well below industrial wages (and see also the regional trend in wages in figure 10.2). Therefore, while farmers' surpluses must also have been limited, perhaps they did better than their landlords. The retreat to smaller (family) farms, which was evident in this period, suggests a joint bid by farmers and landlords alike to improve their incomes, the farmers by reducing their wages bill and other costs (seeds, etc.), and the landlords to take advantage of historically higher unit rents on smaller farm units (see chapter 3 and associated illustrations).

The rent index and investment

After the Restoration, whenever it was felt that Britain was generally free from the threat of invasion, or free from the threat of constitutional crisis and revolution, land was regarded as a safe investment for idle funds. On a substantial scale, however, land was not traded. Whole estates only came onto the market infrequently. More usually the land market operated at a relatively low level: small quantities of land were traded, often by the existing larger landowners wishing to add to their existing holdings, which with the trend in the eighteenth century for consolidation meant that land which was adjacent to or close to principal family seats formed a large but immeasurable portion of the market. In addition owners who acquired land through inheritance or other means, but at locations remote from their main existing holdings, may have taken early opportunities to sell such land as long as it was not encumbered in any way. Inheritance, the provision of marriage portions, and other methods of land exchange which generally circulated amongst the larger landowners also entered into the equation. Nevertheless, to the extent that there is certainty about anything, the total stock of land which constituted the actual land market was limited, and therefore resulted in limited adjustments in the economic and social ownership of land in general. Once acquired, the bulk of land was not easily parted from its owners. Much of it was encumbered by restrictions such as settlements, which further disallowed a large market from emerging and developing. In other words, though idle funds might not find a safer haven than in the land, they could certainly find many more alternative outlets to which to gravitate, and more liquid forms of capital.

For our purposes the questions which arise are, why did owners choose to hold land but not farm it themselves, and why did they choose to hold land rather than other forms of more liquid assets? These are purely economic questions involving a consideration as to whether the ownership of land was an investment which provided income. Numerically, for most landlords it was probably the principal source of income. Did landlords maximise their income and hence their contribution to the national accounts, or could they have done better through alternative investments? These alternatives included a lively commercial world which ranged from banking and attendant financial services, to industry and international trade and investment. In many cases landlords indulged in these enterprises as well as pursuing and further developing their interest in the land. With so much choice available for investing otherwise idle funds surely there was competition for those funds. Equally certainly it should be possible to judge whether landlords were wise to remain in land and not to move into alternative enterprises. One method of judging the good sense in holding and investing in land with its attendant income from rents is to compare those returns with the supposedly equivalent returns from holding or owning other competitive investments.

Within the choices available there was at least one which was also regarded as safe, as safe as land itself, at least after the fiasco of the South Sea Company in 1720, and that was to invest in government funds. Investment in land and in government debts therefore constituted the principal long-term investments of the eighteenth century. Therefore the two forms of investment and their corresponding incomes may bear some comparison. The most appropriate long-term interest rate which can be equated with land in investment terms is reckoned to be the yield on consols.[28] In our comparison this involves a splice of the yield on Old 3 per cent Annuities for 1727–52, with the yield from 3 per cent Consols for 1753–1888, 2.75 per cent Consols for 1889–1902 and 2.5 per cent Consols from 1903.[29] The rate of return on the yield from consols is the return for investing in, for example, £100 worth of government funds at a fixed interest of 3 per cent. Ordinarily this is what the 3 per cent consols returned against the par price at which they were bought. Demonstrably, since there was a non-constant trend in the yield on Consols, there were times when other than the par price was the actual buying price and other than 3 per cent was the return on the investment. What the measurement of the yield on the investment does is to measure that return when the par price was not, as in our example, £100. In 1756 the average buying price of consols for that year was 89 per cent of par. Thus the 3 per cent yield on 100 when the buying price was 89 was 3.37 per cent, (3 per cent of 100/89). When the price was below par the yield exceeded 3 per cent and when it was above par it was less than 3 per cent.

It is at this moment that the analogy with rent as the return on investing in land breaks down, unless of course there was a par price for buying land from which the actual buying price deviated. In other words it supposes that the buying price per unit of land had a tendency to remain unchanged. There was of course no such thing as a par price on land. However, there is a rather different way of gauging the return on investing in land. The buying price of land was calculated on the basis of the current return on land, that is, on the rent, but multiplied by a factor known as the number of years' purchase – literally the number of years' purchase at current rents. But even this is not quite as straightforward as it seems since contemporaries debated the position of taxes and repairs, and other outgoings, when calculating years' purchase. Historically, from empirical observations of the eighteenth century, the years' purchase was set at something between 20 and 30 years.[30] In the seventeenth century it was less than 20 years' purchase, but by the end of the eighteenth century it was very close to 30 years' purchase. Throughout the nineteenth century, if the evidence from the auction sales conducted by Norton, Trist, and Gilbert are representative, the number of years' purchase fluctuated a good deal from year to year both on rising and

[28] A. Offer, 'Farm tenure and land values in England, c. 1750–1950', EcHR, 46 (1991), 2–4.
[29] From Sidney Homer, A History of Interest Rates (New Brunswick, 1963), pp. 161–2, 195–7, 409.
[30] See esp. C. Clay, 'The price of freehold land in the later seventeenth and eighteenth centuries', EcHR, 27 (1974), esp. 174–5.

falling curves. Thus in the French wars it was on or above 30 years but in the post-war depression it fell below 30 years, and in the period of High Farming it rose above 30 years again in selected years.[31] From the fluctuations in the number of years' purchase we can determine the rate of return on buying land. It is the reciprocal of that measure.[32] Thus 20 years' purchase represented a rate of return of 5 per cent, but at 40 years' purchase the rate of return became 2.5 per cent.

Thus the simple rate of return on investing in the funds and on investing in land can be compared in this physical way, but also it seems they can be compared in a complementary way, as follows. It was Nicholas Barbon in 1690 who said that 'Interest is the Rent of Stock, and is the same as the Rent of Land', in which 'The first is the Rent of the Wrought or Artificial Stock; the Latter, of the Unwrought, or natural Stock'.[33] Furthermore, interest

> is the measure of the Rent of Land; it sets the Price in Buying and Selling of Land: For, by adding three Years Interest more than is in the Principle, Makes the usual Value of the Land of the Country; The difference of three Year is allowed; Because Land is more certain than Mony or Stock. Thus in Holland where Mony is at three per. Cent. by reckoning how many times three is in a Hundred Pounds, which is Thirty Three; and Adding three Years more; makes Thirty Six Years Purchase; the Value of the Land in Holland: And by the same Rule, interest being at six per Cent. in England, Land is worth but Twenty Years Purchase; and in Ireland, but Thirteen; Interest being there at Ten per Cent.: so that according to the Rate of Interest, is that Value of the Land in the Country.[34]

Thus the returns on stock and on land will, according to Barbon, trend in a synchronised way the one to the other. This seems to have been the case in the seventeenth century, but did it remain so by the nineteenth?

Figure 10.4 plots the yield on Consols with the yield on land based on the reciprocal of the number of years' purchase. For the latter Clay's observations from the eighteenth century are spliced to the Norton, Trist, and Gilbert estimates from the 1780s. It will be noticed that the annual series on years' purchase is only available from the early 1780s; before that date there are only overlapping ten-year averages available (but since they overlap this effectively provides an observation every five years). The data from the 1780s

[31] Letter of Norton, Trist, and Gilbert to *The Times*, 20 April 1889, p. 11, and reprinted as 'A century of land values: England and Wales', *JRSS*, 54 (1891), 128–31.
[32] In its simplest form the rate of return on an investment is the basic return as a percentage of the original outlay. In the case of land this is the rent as a percentage of the purchase price. Arithmetically this is the rent as numerator and the number of years' purchase times the current rent as the denominator. Rent is represented as both the numerator and denominator, which cancel each other out, leaving the rate of return as the reciprocal of the number of years' purchase.   [33] Nicholas Barbon, *A Discourse of Trade* (London, 1690), p. 20.
[34] *Ibid.*, pp. 20–1.

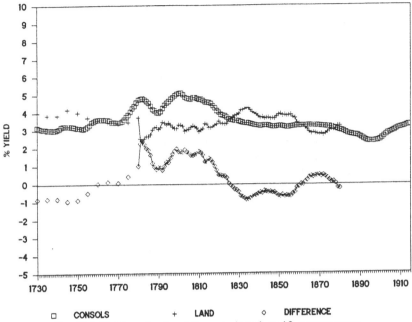

□ CONSOLS   + LAND   ◇ DIFFERENCE

Fig. 10.4 Yields on land and Consols, based on 10-year averages

have been simplified to ten-year averages. The difference between the two
trends indicates the magnitude of the difference in yields between the two
different investments. This was pretty well never greater than plus 2 per cent
or minus 1 per cent. But with a top yield of around 5 per cent these are
significant differences. When the difference was negative, as it was until the
1770s, and then from about 1825 to 1865, it indicates that land yielded a
greater return than the funds. The most significant difference occurred
during the French Revolutionary and Napoleonic Wars during much of
which time, even though the yield on land was rising and the yield on the
funds was falling, the yield on the funds was still up to 2 per cent greater than
the yield on land.

All this may indicate that investment in the funds was mostly more
rewarding than investment in land, and therefore it begs the question, why
did investors persist in their investment in land? The probable answer will
almost certainly involve issues regarding the social advantages of owning
land. For example, while investment in land may have endowed a pecuniary
disadvantage to owners of land relative to another long-term investment, it
was a disadvantage which may have been matched by the non-pecuniary
status and social advantage or positional premium which landownership
brought with it. In addition, few if any landowners are likely to have sold

land to buy higher yielding assets, although, conversely, there might have been cases in which the differential yields influenced the purchasing behaviour of estate owners. Newcomers buying into land were most unlikely to worry about the difference between rental income and the rate of interest, and it was probably only among the lesser landowners that the extra income available from paper assets was an important consideration.[35]

Investments in the funds could be bought and sold fairly easily, at quotable prices, and the market could be augmented by additional issues by the government. To this extent there was a growing supply of such investments. In contrast, the absolute total supply of land was always fixed at the same level, but the actual traded supply was also relatively limited. Funds could be, and almost certainly were seen by some investors as opportunities for financial speculation – buying and selling at capital gain or loss – and by others as a means of raising an income, but usually as a secondary supplement to a primary income. Land in contrast was surely not seen as a speculative investment with the possibility of a quick gain (or indeed quick loss). Rather it was seen as an investment of a different sort, a social investment with economic ramifications, where the element of economic investment was seen as a means of providing long-term primary income, with that income to be enjoyed because of the social advantages of landownership. In this sense the social and economic ownerships were essential complements, such as did not exist in holding funds. To this extent land and the funds were not, after all, long-term investments which offered the same choices for idle funds.

Both forms of investment were in long-term securities, but they were made in an uneasy world of wars and economic booms and slumps. These traumas can certainly be picked out of the data, especially interest-rate adjustments during wartime, and the booms and slumps which show up in the course of rents. To this extent the analysis picks up variations in annual yield, but this is a short-term view of what was a long-term investment. To gauge how the investments were faring in the long term we require a measure which takes into account capital gains and losses. This comparison is made in figure 10.5. The annual capital gains and losses on the funds are easily calculated through the annual average par values. Thus the realised rate of return R on the funds in any year is the product of the nominal yield – which on 3 per cent consols is 3 per cent, otherwise known as the coupon (akin to a dividend) – plus or minus the capital gain or loss on holding the asset from the previous time period. This latter is shown up through the annual average values or prices of the funds:

[35] H. J. Habakkuk, *Marriage, Debt, and the Estates System: English Landownership 1650–1950* (Oxford, 1994), pp. 394, 408.

$R = Coupon\ yield\ (i.e.\ 3\%) + [Value(t+1) - Value(t)] * 100\ /\ Value(t)$.

The equivalent realised rate of return on an investment in land is again the nominal yield, plus or minus the capital gain or loss on the value of holding the asset. The value of the asset is signalled by the earnings derived from it, that is, from the trend in rents as shown up by the rent series. The nominal yield can be taken as a function of the years' purchase – a larger number of years' purchase implies a lower yield, and a smaller number implies a larger yield. A review of the estimates of Clay and of Norton, Trist, and Gilbert indicates that the reciprocal of the years' purchase fluctuated fairly narrowly between 3 and 4 per cent, or close to 25 to 30 years' purchase. By the 1870s they had dipped under 3 per cent. In a comparison with the rate of return on Consuls a nominal rent yield of 4 per cent has been taken and the rent index can be used to judge the year-on-year capital gains and losses. If the annual value of land (V) is the product of the rent times the number of years purchase ($R.YP$), then the capital gain or loss from year to year is

$$[R(t+1).YP - R(t).YP]\ /\ [R(t).YP]$$

which simplifies to

$$[R(t+1) - R(t)]\ /\ R(t)$$

which is the change in rent as a proportion of the base rent. Annually therefore it is the proportional change in rent from year to year. The realised rate of return (R) is

$R = Nominal\ yield\ (4\%) + [Rent(t+1) - Rent(t)] * 100\ /\ Rent(t)$.

The relative steadiness of the realised rate of return on land perhaps signals why its possession was considered the safest of investments, in contrast to the funds, for which except for the period after the French wars the return was both erratic and rarely significantly an obviously better investment. However, this comparison is loaded in favour of land because it is based on an upper bound nominal yield. Adopting the lower bound of 3 per cent as the nominal yield certainly brings the two rates of return on the two types of investment together, and this is what is implied from Nicholas Barbon's observations of the late seventeenth century. The comparison may also be loaded in favour of the investment in land because the rent is measured as gross and not net of administrative and maintenance costs.[36] Perhaps two other important observations might be made from figure 10.5. The first is that once Britain had ceased to be a warmonger, with otherwise a secure Empire, the actual return on long-term investment in government

[36] In his similar calculation Offer made an allowance of 25 per cent for such charges, 'Farm tenure', 14.

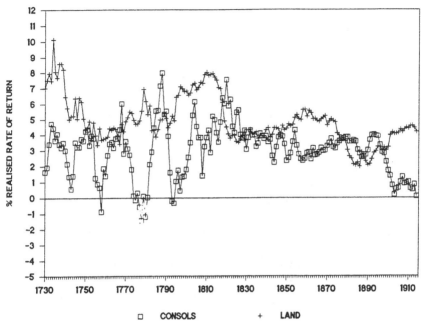

Fig. 10.5 Realised rates of return on land and Consols, based on 10-year averages

stock tended to move to its nominal return of 3 per cent, though taking ten-year averages makes this appear as a smoother process than was actually the case. Secondly, while the return on investment in stock levelled off, the return on land seemed to trend downwards from something close to 6 per cent in the mid-eighteenth century to something nearer to 3 or 4 per cent by Edwardian times.

Having equated the investment in the funds with the investment in land in terms of their intrinsic safety as investments, in reality it was likely that the choice by investors to hold one rather than the other was probably made independently of the choice to invest in the alternative. That is, landholders also held government stock and in general to hold one did not imply a rejection of the other. Sir James Lowther of the Cumbrian gentry was one of the most important non-London or home-counties-based investors in the 1740s. He invested in everything partly because his landed interests were locationally specific and remote in the north-west – though he did purchase the manor of Laleham in Middlesex in 1745 – and he preferred to keep excess money in other forms of investment. His annuity and consol holdings in 1755 amounted to £48,450 out of a personal estate, excluding his land and industrial interests, of £375,996. The income on his annuities amounted to

£1,529 out of a total income from his personal estate of £12,495, which must be compared with his gross property rental of £4,580.[37] Earl Temple of Stowe in Buckinghamshire kept money in the funds until land was available as an investment. He was anxious to avoid having idle funds, and therefore certainly invested in securities, but it appears that his most coveted asset was land.[38] Apart from their fame amongst the peerage and in their role at the centre of Norfolk agricultural improvements, the Earls of Leicester at Holkham were also substantial financial investors, though by the time this became a major interest – from the mid-nineteenth century onwards – British government stock was not nearly so attractive compared with various British and overseas railways, and other investments. These included New South Wales 3.5 per cent stock, Argentine 5 per cent stock and Canadian 4 per cent stock.[39] The second earl had no obvious need to sell one investment, such as land, to finance non-land investments. On the contrary, the rent roll remained buoyant enough to finance these investments in good times, and the investments in turn allowed the earl to sustain a large level of agricultural rent arrears at other times, such as in the late nineteenth-century agricultural depression. By 1894 the value of the second earl's portfolio of investments was half a million pounds.[40]

Apart from some obvious exceptions, most landowners had neither the talent nor the desire to become involved in the choice between land and other investments, and by the second half of the eighteenth century, if not earlier, they generally lacked the spare capital. Indeed the level of landed debt suggested that real investment choices were not available. For example, when Lord Temple agreed to purchase the Northamptonshire estate of Lord Ferrers the transaction included a commitment to pay certain encumbrances on the estate. In the event the encumbrances exceeded the purchase price.[41] Debt, especially inherited debt, was disabling. The 3rd Duke of Sutherland actually sold off half his existing government stock between 1833 and 1850 in order to reduce the debts accumulated by his forebears.[42] But by the late nineteenth century, essentially during the 1880s,

[37] J. V. Beckett, *Coal and Tobacco: The Economic Development of West Cumberland 1660–1760* (Cambridge, 1981), pp. 35–6, 211–19.

[38] J. V. Beckett, 'Aristocratic financial troubles and the operation of the land market: the sale of Astwell and Falcutt in 1774–8', *Northamptonshire Past and Present*, 8, no. 5 (1993–4), 378–82, esp. 381, in which we learn that Earl Temple complained to Lord Ferrers over the delays in the sale of Lord Ferrers' land. Temple bemoaned the fact that he had to withdraw money from the stocks to buy the land, and yet there were delays in the transaction. At the time land was a better investment than the funds, but in the circumstances Temple's point was that his money was idle, neither in the funds nor in the land. This was his argument, but in truth he did not withdraw from the funds until he really had to.   [39] Wade Martins, *Holkham*, pp. 267–9.

[40] D. Spring, 'Land and politics in Edwardian England', *Agricultural History*, 58 (1984), 23.

[41] J. V. Beckett, *The Aristocracy in England 1660–1914* (Oxford, 1989 edn), p. 311.

[42] *Ibid.*, pp. 303–4, and in general on the mounting indebtedness pp. 295–321.

land had become something of a luxury investment and unequivocally more could have been made in the funds, or probably more lucratively from overseas investments. Certainly the estimates in figure 10.5 seem to bear this out for the years from the late 1870s to about 1900.[43] But of course there were exceptions within the ranks of landed society of men who did understand the advantages of capital investment, and who could use it to subsidise otherwise loss-making agricultural estates where the positional premium remained important. There were also plenty of men of business who 'sorted out' some landowners as the agricultural depression began to bite in the late nineteenth century.

Yet others were both landed gentlemen and men of commerce. For example, Lord Overstone was born into and then built upon a fortune made in banking. This was greatly augmented by agricultural rents, and once he retired from banking at what appears to have been a relatively young age he still had his income from his rents, but also the income from judicious investments in the National Debt, followed by his heavy investments in British railways and joint-stock companies. His investment in the National Debt was largely inherited from his banking forebears and by c. 1881 it represented 0.1 per cent of the total funded National Debt. As the nineteenth century proceeded, indebted aristocrats were selling off land, often to holders of their mortgages such as Overstone. He had a 'firm belief that agricultural land was a secure and remunerative investment preferable to any other'.[44] The damage of the late-nineteenth-century agricultural depression however, was a severe blow to those landowners in eastern England who had slavishly followed this kind of advice, and increasingly as the nineteenth century went on numbers of them came to realise the good sense of a diversified portfolio. However late they may have responded to the choices available for investing otherwise idle funds, one of those choices was the stock market which 'provided a prop to the sagging finances of great agricultural landowners'. Some of them, such as the Duke of Bedford came very late to such investments, but it proved better to travel and eventually arrive than never to travel at all.[45] In most cases it seems that these investments were only modestly financed by selling off the ducal acres.[46]

Landowners did not necessarily compare relative pecuniary values, but rather they assessed need, and their needs were partly based on social considerations. Developing an estate along with dabbling in industrialisa-

[43] See also Wade Martins's reading of the evidence presented on Norfolk in general to the 1890s Royal Commission, though this is loaded evidence given the severe collapse in east of England agricultural rents, Wade Martins, *Holkham*, p. 36.

[44] R. C. Michie, 'Income, expenditure and investment of a Victorian millionaire: Lord Overstone, 1823–83', *Bulletin of the Institute of Historical Research*, 58 (1985), 59–77, esp. 67.

[45] Spring, 'Land and politics', 23–4.   [46] *Ibid.*, 26–7.

tion carried a higher social profile than the relatively hidden world of fund speculation. If the relative rates of return on the two investments which we have calculated are anything to go by the continued involvement of landowners in land seemed sensible, especially so in the period of High Farming during the third quarter of the nineteenth century. But the evidence for this period suggests that landowners extended their investment in land, not necessarily on new acquisitions, but on improving their existing farms to such a degree that when the crunch came in the last quarter of the nineteenth century the non-pecuniary advantages of social position were increasingly compromised by landed debt and insecure landed incomes. The realised rate of return on the funds, for the first time for a protracted period, quite eclipsed the social ownership of land.

The rent index is a history of the income from new investment in land or of old investment encumbered by debt and inherited perceptions of the social as well as economic status of holding land. By the late nineteenth century, in many places, the investment had almost certainly outlived its usefulness. In this chapter we have placed this income in the context of the other incomes which derived from agriculture, putatively the farmer's income, mainly through price movements for agricultural products, and through agricultural wages. We have also analysed the trend in rentals as an income flow from investment in land in comparison with an alternative possible income flow from a different investment. We now proceed finally in chapter 11 to place the rent index back wholly into an agricultural setting by looking more closely at the short-term periodic rhythms and trends.

CHAPTER II

The rent index and agricultural history II: the short term

Most historians would agree that between the seventeenth and the nineteenth centuries considerable changes took place in English agriculture. Critically, a major increase in output and productivity ensured that although some food had to be imported, for most of the period a growing and increasingly urbanised and industrialised population was fed from home production. Until about 1760 Britain was essentially a net exporter of grain, but the trend gradually moved in the opposite direction until the normal position that was assumed – and has been the case until very recent times – was that Britain became a net importer of grain. Even so, by 1850 an estimated 6.5 million extra mouths were being fed from home production compared with 1750. By 1868 perhaps still as much as 80 per cent of UK food was home produced.[1] By 1914, however, perhaps only one-half was home produced.[2] For the purpose of further discussion, and to place the rent index within the context of the changes that took place in agriculture, we have divided the period 1690–1914 into convenient time frames, largely reflecting accepted movements in the pattern of farming through the whole period.

1690–1750: agricultural depression or no agricultural depression?

The survival of rent material only comes on stream to any significant extent after 1690, and then as chapter 8 has shown it begins rather slowly. But as we parachute into this last decade of the seventeenth century what understanding of agricultural rents do we bring with us? From the completed researches of individual landed families we can say that in the two decades since the Restoration in 1660 there had been a severe decline in rents, subsequently

---

[1] Chambers and Mingay, p. 208.
[2] C. Ó Gráda, 'British agriculture, 1860–1914', in R. Floud and D. McCloskey (eds.), *The Economic History of Britain Since 1700*: II, *1860–1914* (Cambridge, 1994, 2nd edn), p. 171.

followed by some indications of a recovery. In the years 1640 to 1663, Peter Bowden has located comparative prosperity, but from 1664 until 1691 agricultural prices declined and with them rents. Margaret Gay Davies, using evidence from eight substantial estates in Buckinghamshire, Oxfordshire, Northamptonshire, and Warwickshire, has shown that seven of her sample suffered a fall in rents in the 1660s, and four or five in the 1670s. Contemporary evidence suggests that these estates were not alone. Also suffering were farmers in the Kentish marshland grazing districts, together with farmers in Norfolk, Yorkshire, and Somerset. In 1669 the House of Lords set up a committee to investigate 'the decay of rents and trade', and the following year Parliament passed an Act 'for Improvement of Tillage and the Breed of Cattle' which was designed to counter the problems experienced by farmers.[3]

Conditions did not improve until the 1690s. But was it a short-lived improvement? It has become well established in the literature that in the period 1660–1750 agriculture suffered a long-term decline in prosperity. This was caused in part by falling demand, particularly for cereal crops, as a result of stagnation in the growth of population, or at best only a modest rise and at worst even a fall in one decade (1720s). The compound annual growth rate of English population was at best rising at 0.3 per cent per annum in the 1700s and 1710s compared with the immediately preceding decades, and it did not rise appreciably until the 1730s (a growth of 0.6 per cent per annum after the decline which had been experienced in the 1720s).[4] Agricultural output almost certainly increased as farmers sought to offset stagnant or declining incomes. The most obvious pressure was on arable farmers, and also on mixed farmers on poorer quality soils such as clay. Some small relief was afforded to these producers as a result of favourable corn laws which promoted the export of grain. The Corn Bounty Act of 1688 subsidised corn exports to keep them above 48 shillings a quarter, and thereby protected the farming community from the full implications of falling prices, stagnant population, and good weather. The bounties were suspended in years of dearth when exports were prohibited, but between 1697 and 1801 43 million quarters of wheat were exported, of which 55 per cent (24 million quarters) went abroad in the years 1732 to 1766, and nearly 400,000 quarters a year during the 1740s. Exports, together with government efforts to promote the use of grain for malt, in beer and in spirits, helped to protect the farming

[3] P. J. Bowden 'Agricultural prices, wages, farm profits, and rents', in Thirsk, *AgHist* (1985), pp. 62–79; M. G. Davies, 'Country gentry and falling rents in the 1660s and 1670s', *Midland History*, 4 (1977), 86–96. The Act was 22 Car.II, ch.13.
[4] Based on E. A. Wrigley and R. S. Schofield, *The Population History of England 1541–1871. A Reconstruction* (London, 1981), table A3.1, pp. 528–9.

community from the full impact of overproduction. Without these initiatives prices would have fallen further than they did.[5]

This general history helps to explain the slow pace at which rents recovered from the late seventeenth century. There is enough evidence during the 1730s and 1740s to indicate that agriculture in some locations was indeed suffering from the depression which the historiography has traditionally identified. Real corn prices fell by more than 15 to 20 per cent in the 1730s and 1740s relative to the prices prevailing in the 1720s.[6] But on the basis of the profile of the rent index and the history of arrears, we call into question the depth of the depression. G. E. Mingay, the chief proponent of the depression argument, has written that:

> Landlords complained of unpaid rents and bankrupt tenants from areas so diverse as Denbighshire, Cheshire and Gloucestershire in the west, Yorkshire, East Anglia and Lincolnshire in the north and east, down through Derbyshire, Nottinghamshire, Rutland, Staffordshire, Buckinghamshire, Middlesex and Essex, and as far south as Kent, Sussex and Hampshire.[7]

This is an impressive list, displaying a wide geography of distress, and history written from examples can certainly be very impressive. However, our analysis of arrears in chapter 9 did not support the view that there was a sustained period of difficulty sufficient to be defined as a depression. In some isolated years in the first half of the eighteenth century rental arrears represented up to 5 per cent of agreed rents, but in truth those were isolated years and certainly not long runs of persistent arrears. We have, though, also pointed out that the inheritance of unpaid arrears over many years is highlighted in the early eighteenth century rentals. An uncritical examination of these arrears can easily give a false impression of a period of depression. Even though the price of wheat per quarter fell from 34 shillings in the 1720s to 29 shillings in the 1730s and to just below 29 shillings in the 1740s, we agree with Bowden that 'it would be wrong to rule out the possibility of rising land values and enhanced rents [simply] on this account'.[8] Indeed this clearly was the case. To the extent that there was concern over depressed prices it was felt mostly if not exclusively by arable farmers. Consumers, having switched from barley to wheat bread, now began to purchase alternative foodstuffs, particularly meat and dairy

[5] D. Ormrod, *English Grain Exports and the Structure of Agrarian Capitalism 1700–1760* (Hull, 1985); T. S. Ashton, *An Economic History of England: The Eighteenth Century* (London, 1972); Thirsk, *AgHist* (1985), pp. 887–8.
[6] R. A. Ippolito, 'The effect of the "agricultural depression" on industrial demand in England, 1730–1750', *Economica*, 42 (1975), 298.
[7] Chambers and Mingay, p. 41; G. E. Mingay, 'The agricultural depression 1730–1750', *EcHR*, 8 (1956), 323–38; G. E. Mingay, *English Landed Society in the Eighteenth Century* (London, 1963), pp. 54–6.
[8] Bowden, 'Agricultural prices', 64.

Table 11.1. *Price indices of crops and animal products, 1640–1749 (1640–1749 = 100)*

Decade	Grains	Livestock	Ratio of livestock: grain prices	Animal products	Average of all agricultural products
1640–9	122	85	70	109	104
1650–9	106	93	88	102	101
1660–9	101	93	92	105	97
1670–9	99	94	95	95	95
1680–9	92	98	107	95	97
1690–9	110	109	99	107	108
1700–9	91	108	119	99	99
1710–19	99	107	108	102	104
1720–9	101	105	104	99	101
1730–9	89	107	120	93	98
1740–9	88	108	123	98	100

Source: Thirsk, *AgHist* (1985), pp. 827–56.

products. Consequently the price of livestock moved upwards in almost direct proportion to the fall in grain prices through the period 1640–1749 (table 11.1) and while the prices of animal products in general declined they did so rather less markedly than the prices of grain. As a result, between the 1650s and the 1740s the price of agricultural goods was relatively steady – with an exceptional fluctuation only in the 1690s due to poor harvests – but there was a marked change within the overall trend in which grain prices declined and livestock prices rose.[9] We would expect these trends to be reflected in the experience of farmers in different agricultural regions. Pasture rents rose relative to arable rents, down to and through the 1730s (see figure 9.7 based on Caird's regional division).

Chambers and Mingay assumed for this period that with the exception of a slight rise in the 1720s rents stayed more or less the same throughout the period to 1750. The rent index suggests that rents began from a lower base than they believed, and rose proportionately faster. The profile of the index of agreed rents appears almost as a straight line, rising from a little over 2 shillings per acre in the 1690s to a little under 8 shillings by the 1770s (see figure 9.2). When we include the profile of rent received we can identify some problem years for agriculture, but not an extended problem period.

Since the rent index is based on a relatively small database for this period, disaggregating it to demonstrate regional trends is fraught with difficulties; nevertheless, increasingly there is evidence to counter the claim for depression. Wordie found few symptoms on the Leveson-Gower estates in

[9] For details both of the harvests of the 1690s and their effects on grain prices, see W. G. Hoskins, 'Harvest fluctuations and English economic history, 1620–1759', *AgHR*, 16 (1968), 15–31.

Shropshire and Staffordshire:[10] Brassley showed for Northumberland and Durham that the long-term trend in demand for corn was such that prices remained stable and rents increased;[11] and Beckett has shown that the course of agricultural rents in Cumbria does not support the view of depression in these decades since rents followed a perceptible upward course between about 1720 and 1740 with difficulties only arising briefly in the mid-1740s.[12] Further west, rents moved generally upwards in Pembrokeshire during the first six or seven decades of the eighteenth century, and a temporary levelling-off in some areas of Glamorgan during the 1730s and 1740s failed to disguise a movement equivalent to a rise of about 7 per cent per decade.[13] This evidence is reflected in the rent index. It already includes the data from the Leveson-Gower estates, but added to it is the rent profile from Castle Howard in North Yorkshire which at worst shows a levelling-off in the upward march of unit acre rents in the 1730s and 1740s. At Brandesburton in East Yorkshire the unit acre rent profile is actually flat during these decades. The rents on the Badminton estate in Gloucestershire were unequivocally rising during these decades – apart from occasional years – as were the rents from the Beighton and Holme Pierrepont collections on the Manvers estates of the East Midlands. Those on the Lilford estates in Northamptonshire were generally, if only slightly on the rise. The picture either as a whole or in its constituent parts does not support the idea of a depression.

Are these findings for the period 1690–1750 intrinsically likely to apply more widely, given the small sample? Grain prices fell consistently from the 1640s until the 1740s, with only occasional reverses of this pattern in decades when agricultural conditions were particularly bad (table 11.1).[14] The prices of all grains declined in this period, with wheat and rye showing the most rapid downward movement. Farmers naturally sought ways of bolstering their financial position, and they did so by increasing output. The best estimates available suggest that between 1695 and 1750 the acreage under cereals in England and Wales increased from 5.375 million to 5.732 million,[15]

[10] J. R. Wordie, 'A great landed estate in the eighteenth century: aspects of management on the Leveson-Gower properties, 1691–1833' (University of Reading, PhD thesis, 1967), p. 325.
[11] P. Brassley, *The Agricultural Economy of Northumberland and Durham in the Period 1640–1750* (London, 1985), pp. 69, 171, although his price evidence is not supported by Bowden's figures, 'Agricultural prices', 862.
[12] J. V. Beckett, 'Regional variation and the agricultural depression, 1730–50', *EcHR*, 35 (1982), 35–51.
[13] D. W. Howell, 'The economy of the landed estates of Pembrokeshire, c. 1680–1830', *The Welsh History Review*, 3 (1966–7), 265–86; J. O. Martin, 'The landed estate: Glamorgan, c. 1660–1760' (University of Cambridge, PhD thesis 1978), pp. 49, 80.
[14] Hoskins, 'Harvest fluctuations', graph facing 15.
[15] J. A. Chartres, 'The marketing of agricultural produce', in Thirsk, *AgHist* (1985), p. 444.

so that by 1750 the acreage under crops or fallows was between 9.5 and 10.5 million acres.[16] With more land under the plough output was likely to rise, even if much of the newly cultivated area was of inferior quality soil. However, some farmers were also innovating which allowed them to acquire a more acute sense of comparative advantage: between 1695 and 1750 it is estimated that the gross output of cereals grew by 19 per cent[17] although the area of land sown probably increased by less than 7 per cent. The most substantial increase was in wheat production, which may have increased by 50 per cent over the period, mainly at the expense of rye and to some extent barley. Inventory evidence points to a rapid increase in output brought about by innovation. In Norfolk and Suffolk wheat yields may have increased by 25 to 40 per cent from about 8 bushels an acre in the 1580s to around 14 by the early eighteenth century. Nationally yields touched about 15 to 16 bushels per acre in 1750. Recent estimates point to a phase of strong growth in agricultural output to about 1740, with a growth rate of 0.6 per cent per annum over the period 1700–60 as a whole. It was accompanied by a growth in labour productivity at least to the 1770s.[18]

Innovations in this period took several forms. Considerable emphasis has been placed on the introduction of roots and legumes into otherwise corn-dominated crop rotations. These were undoubtedly important, particularly in East Anglia and other light soiled areas. However, in Hertfordshire output per acre seems to have increased in the later seventeenth and early eighteenth centuries partly through increases in farm sizes, and partly through a shift away from lower-yielding and lower-value crops like rye, towards higher-yielding grains like barley. Systematic ground and seed-bed preparation seems to have been the key to improving yields in the county, and the introduction of fodder crops was not a necessary condition for sustained improvements.[19] Rapid productivity increases were probably achieved in regions where innovations were significant such as East Anglia, but not on the Midland clays.

[16] B. A. Holderness, 'Prices, productivity, and output', chapter 2 in Mingay, *AgHist*, p. 128.

[17] Chartres, 'The marketing of agricultural produce', 444.

[18] E. L. Jones, *Agriculture and the Industrial Revolution* (Oxford, 1974); M. Overton, 'Estimating yields from probate inventories: an example from East Anglia, 1585–1735', *Journal of Economic History*, 39 (1979), 363–78; M. E. Turner, 'Agricultural productivity in England in the eighteenth century: evidence from crop yields', *EcHR*, 35 (1982), 489–510; R. V. Jackson, 'Growth and deceleration in English agriculture', *EcHR*, 38 (1985), 333–51; N. F. R. Crafts, *British Economic Growth during the Industrial Revolution* (Oxford, 1985), esp. chapter 2; G. Clark, 'Yields per acre in English agriculture 1266–1860: evidence from labour inputs', *EcHR*, 44 (1991), 445–60; G. Clark, 'Labour productivity in English agriculture 1300–1860', in B. M. S. Campbell and M. Overton (eds.), *Land, Labour and Livestock: Historical Studies in European Agricultural Productivity* (Manchester, 1991), pp. 211–35.

[19] P. Glennie. 'Continuity and change in Hertfordshire agriculture 1550–1700', *AgHR*, 36 (1988), in two parts, 55–76, 145–61.

Perhaps the most obvious physical evidence of farmers' and landowners' responses to the changing economic environment in which they lived in the 1730s and 1740s was in mixed farming areas. This included the voluntary enclosure to lay land down to grass, particularly on intractable clay soils. Although the Parliamentary phase beyond 1750 is the best-known part of the enclosure movement, it was only the final stage of a much longer process which was particularly significant on the heavy claylands of the Midlands. The impact of falling grain prices after 1650 was felt most severely in these areas where the innovations appropriate to light soils had little effect. Piecemeal enclosure followed, involving landowners offsetting their losses by converting open-field arable to grass. Between 1660 and 1760 the Leicestershire landscape was steadily transformed as village after village turned its arable land into pasture. At least 73 villages were enclosed over the period and more than half the county was enclosed by 1730.[20] A similar tale can be told for parts of Buckinghamshire, Northamptonshire, Warwickshire, and Nottinghamshire. Nor is it any surprise to find the Parliamentary enclosure movement heavily concentrated into these areas during its earliest phases, because it was here that a hunger for convertible land emerged.[21] The effect of the early enclosures on agricultural output and incomes still remains something of a mystery, in spite of a resurgence of interest in the subject in recent years, but rent increases almost certainly occurred. At Compton in Hampshire in 1738 enclosed arable land (with certain rights of pasture) rented at around 10s per acre whereas open-field land, with more generous common rights, fetched only 7s an acre. When the fields were reorganised and partially enclosed at Laxton in Nottinghamshire between 1726 and 1733 the rents were raised by about 11 per cent, partly because of a shift towards sheep, but the downside was that arrears were recorded in every year during the 1730s.[22]

Price indices, and the movement from mixed farming to pasture, all point to the direction in which agriculture was inevitably being pushed. The overall movement in the terms of trade towards livestock production is clear at a national level (see table 11.1), but the trends show no obvious regional pattern.[23] The situation is marginally clearer from rental data (figures 9.6–9.9).

[20] J. Thirsk, 'Agrarian History 1540–1950', in Victoria County History, *Leicestershire*, II (Oxford, 1954), pp. 199–264.

[21] M. E. Turner, *English Parliamentary Enclosure: Its Historical Geography and Economic History* (Folkestone, 1980), chapter 6. See also J. Broad, 'Alternate husbandry and permanent pasture in the Midlands, 1650–1800', *AgHR*, 28 (1980), 77–89.

[22] P. J. Bowden, 'Agricultural prices, wages, farm profits, rents', in Thirsk, *AgHist* (1985), p. 69; J. V. Beckett, *A History of Laxton: England's Last Open-Field Village* (Oxford, 1989), p. 114.

[23] P. J. Bowden, 'Statistics', in Thirsk, *AgHist* (1985), p. 862.

Bowden, writing of the whole period 1640–1750, concluded that 'the task of tracing the movement of rent during the period of our study assumes formidable proportions'. However, he took the view that sufficient empirical evidence and theoretical pointers existed to conclude with some degree of confidence that 'the average level of farm rents in 1740–9 was somewhat higher than in 1640–9, in spite of the generally lower level of agricultural prices obtaining in the later years'. In his view 'the more effective utilization of land – whether achieved through the application of improved agricultural techniques, a better geographical deployment of crops, or otherwise – must considerably have enhanced not only the volume, but also the value, of output on many farm undertakings'. In addition, 'Changes in the system of land tenure, by introducing a greater degree of flexibility into tenurial relationships, undoubtedly served to reinforce these various tendencies making for higher levels of farm rent.' However, 'in so far as farm rents generally tend to move in sympathy with changes in the value of farm output, we should expect the movement of rent in the late seventeenth and early eighteenth centuries to have progressed in a somewhat irregular fashion, at times reversing itself, in line with the ebb and flow of agricultural prices'.[24] Bowden suggested that since from 1713 to the late 1740s the trend of agricultural prices was slightly downward, 'we would expect a reversal, or at least a moderation, in the upward course of farm rents', though his views are hedged with various provisos.[25] He accepted Mingay's analysis for the 1730s and 1740s 'whereby the trend of rents is depicted as being slightly downward and arable farmers are perceived as being especially in need of relief'.[26] By the late 1740s things had begun to pick up.[27] His thoughts are born out in Wales: 'Clearly, rents were unlikely to move up quickly in the first half of the eighteenth century. Yet there was an upward tendency. In one instance improved methods of husbandry were seen as the reason for increases in rents.'[28]

The different pieces of evidence collated here suggest that we would anticipate a rise in assessed rents through the period 1690–1750, but with the linked evidence of some arrears in the 1730s and 1740s, particularly in areas of mixed farming on relatively poor soils like the clays. If this was, as many historians maintain, a period of rising output and productivity (including labour productivity) then we would expect farmers to be in a position to pay more rent, and for the trends located in our index to be real ones.

[24] Bowden, 'Agricultural prices', 73–4.   [25] *Ibid.*, 79.   [26] *Ibid.*, 81.   [27] *Ibid.*, 82.

[28] D. W. Howell, 'Landlords and estate management in Wales', in Thirsk, *AgHist* (1985), p. 289.

1750–1815: prosperity for tenants and landlords alike

The position after 1750 becomes markedly clearer. The growth of population in the second half of the eighteenth century, especially in the closing decades of the century, put pressure back onto home resources which had been relieved for much of the previous century. While the country still managed to export a grain surplus at certain times of the year, there were other times, and increasingly whole years, when that surplus disappeared. By the 1760s the net grain balance had been reversed and Britain became a net importer of grain.[29] The net annual excess of wheat and wheat flour exports from 1697 to 1766 was 210,231 quarters. This was transformed into a net annual deficit of 91,825 quarters from 1767 to 1784, which thereafter rose to over one million quarters in 1799 to 1800. A similar pattern occurred with respect to barley and oats. The crisis of self-sufficiency became so acute that relief from shortages was not only sought in imports of traditional grains but also in the importation of rice and Indian corn.[30] The situation did not improve as the French wars carried into the nineteenth century. At its worst, the estimated shortfall of the home grain crop was equivalent to about nine weeks consumption,[31] though the standard of consumption against which this estimate should be judged is not very clear. The general shortages which arose during the wars, the influence of a series of poor, if not disastrous, harvests in the 1790s, and the resulting grain riots, and the effects of the continental blockade have been well chronicled.[32] E. L. Jones has suggested that in 1800 about 90 per cent of the British population was fed by domestic agricultural production, though a century earlier it had been nearer to 101 per cent.[33]

The net effect was a steady rise in agricultural prices from the mid-eighteenth century, which on a scale of magnitude and persistence was the first such rise for a century or more. From a fairly sedate rise in the 1750s and 1760s the price of grain rose to inflationary proportions during the French wars. Enclosure proceeded apace, but until the inflationary pressures took

---

[29] See the graph of the same in Turner, *English Parliamentary Enclosure*, p. 130.

[30] 'Second Report by the Lords Committee ... [on] ... the Dearth of Provisions, 1800', reprinted in S. Lambert (ed.), *House of Commons Sessional Papers of the Eighteenth Century*, CXXXI (Wilmington, 1975), pp. 448–50.

[31] Chambers and Mingay, pp. 115–16; M. Olson, *The Economics of the Wartime Shortage* (Durham, N.C., 1963), p. 65.

[32] From a large bibliography see M. E. Turner, 'Corn crises in the age of Malthus', in M. E. Turner (ed.), *Malthus and his Time* (London, 1986), pp. 112–28. for a summary; R. Wells, *Wretched Faces: Famine in Wartime England 1793–1803* (Gloucester, 1988), for a detailed account; and J. Bohstedt, *Riots and Community Politics in England and Wales, 1790–1810* (London, 1983) for a detailed account which takes a lot of evidence from Devon.

[33] E. L. Jones, 'Agriculture 1700–80', in R. Floud and D. McCloskey, *The Economic History of Britain since 1700*. I, *1700–1860* (Cambridge, 1981), p. 68.

hold during the last decade of the century, this enclosure was essentially an extension of the types of land which were enclosed before 1750, that is, it was relatively concentrated on the Midland clays and accompanied by further extensions of pastoral farming at the expense of arable. Seemingly this must have contributed to the overall shortfall in home grain supplies from *c.* 1770, but the build-up of agricultural advances from earlier periods, combined with improvements in living standards and the greater variety of diets, and lubricated by the efficiency gains from enclosure, meant that the country could withstand the initial minor crises of self-sufficiency which rising grain imports signalled. But when the crisis increased and was exacerbated by the bad harvests of the 1790s and the supply problems generated by the French wars, a second great wave of enclosures occurred. This time the land was not converted into pasture; it remained in arable production. There was also the enclosure of otherwise underused lands and wastes, land which saw the plough or other forms of regulated agriculture for the first time.[34]

Against this background of rising aggregate demand, exacerbated at times by supply problems, and resulting in several decades of rising agricultural prices, must be set a rise in farming incomes, because the prices the farmers received for their products advanced ahead of any rises in their farm costs. The major costs they faced were their rents and the wages for their labour. We have identified something close to a 15-year lag in the ability of the general rent trend to catch up with the agricultural price trend through the eighteenth century (figure 10.1). This lag of rents behind prices adds support to Allen's theory that enclosures were a device for landlords to recoup or share in the Ricardian surpluses which otherwise their tenants enjoyed alone. The general belief is that rents doubled at enclosure.[35] In addition, the moves which were under way throughout the eighteenth century to convert beneficial leases and other antiquated tenures probably accelerated once it was realised that the price inflation was not a temporary phenomenon. Those estates which were let on 21-year leases were also subject to closer scrutiny by their owners who similarly could see that their clients, the farmers, had gained an advantage in rising prices through a rise in their income while they, the landlords, had to be satisfied with fixed incomes for the duration of the leases. Thus the accelerated chronology of enclosure after 1790 came about through a complex combination of national need during the emergency supply conditions of the French wars –

---

[34] For a summary of this well-known history and chronology see M. E. Turner, *Enclosures in Britain 1750–1830* (London, 1984).

[35] Chambers and Mingay, p. 85; R. C. Allen, 'Agriculture during the industrial revolution', in R. Floud and D. McCloskey, *The Economic History: Vol.* I, *1700–1860* (Cambridge, 1994), p. 118.

especially the enclosure of the commons and wastes – and the desire of landlords who wished to share in the windfall Ricardian surpluses generated by inflation. It was facilitated to a degree by an accommodating Parliament which eased some of the administrative costs through the General Enclosure Act which was introduced in 1801.

External economic factors, coupled with devices such as enclosures which allowed tenures to be re-established on different terms, led to moves towards tenancy at will which allowed the landlords to keep abreast of the changing economic climate through regular reviews of their rent. This is a history of land tenure which yet lacks the large empirical research base it deserves and therefore defies quantification, but apart from some well-known locations where the tenantry resisted the erosion of customary practices,[36] the moves we have described here were certainly under way.

One outcome of these changes was the rise in average grain yields from 15 or 16 bushels per acre in the mid-eighteenth century (with one estimate at 18 bushels) to 20 or 21 bushels by the end of the century. But taking the century as a whole the main impact of agricultural change was probably concentrated before rather than after 1760 or 1770.[37] This is still open to some debate because we are not sure to what extent the yield estimates include the relatively marginal, inferior soils which were taken into cultivation during the war period, the inclusion of which necessarily underplays the advances which might have taken place on the soils in regular cultivation.[38] Nevertheless, if it was the case that output and productivity growth was greatest in the earlier decades of the eighteenth century, then it took landlords a long time to wake up to the benefits they were missing, but they were aroused from their slumbers when price changes affected their own consumption budgets seriously towards the end of the century, and they then reacted decisively and rack rented with some gusto.

No fewer than 14 of the 22 grain harvests between 1793 and 1814 were deficient in varying degrees, with particularly disastrous harvests in 1795–6 and 1799–1800. Coming as they did at a time of rapid population growth, these bad seasons led to prices reaching record levels by 1810. In an effort to increase output, waste land and lands of marginal quality were enclosed. As a result, in the early years of the nineteenth century growth rates advanced

---

[36] C. E. Searle, 'Custom, class conflict and agrarian capitalism: the Cumbrian customary economy in the eighteenth century', *Past and Present*, 110 (1986), 106–33; Searle, 'Customary tenants and the enclosure of the Cumbrian commons', *Northern History*, 29 (1993), 126–53.
[37] M. E. Turner, 'Agricultural productivity in England in the eighteenth century: evidence from crop yields', *EcHR*, 35 (1982), 489–510; M. E. Turner, 'Agricultural productivity in eighteenth-century England: further strains of speculation', *EcHR*, 37 (1984), 252–7; M. Overton, 'Agricultural productivity in eighteenth-century England: some further speculations', *EcHR*, 37 (1984), 244–51; B. A. Holderness, 'Prices, productivity, and output', chapter 2 in Mingay, *AgHist*, esp. pp. 134–42.   [38] Turner, 'Agricultural productivity in England', esp. 505.

and began to exceed those of the pre-1760 period.[39] Crafts has estimated agricultural growth at 0.75 per cent per annum between 1780 and 1801, and 1.18 per cent between 1801 and 1831, although these estimates are not very sensitive to differing land quality.[40]

In 1750 there were perhaps from 9.5 to 10.5 million acres under crops or fallow, rising to 12 million by the end of the Napoleonic Wars. But much of this increase would have been poorer quality land which was brought into cultivation during the food emergency, and just as quickly much of it went out of cultivation again in the years following the wars. In addition, land which was not ordinarily well suited to grain production was nevertheless converted to grain as a result of the prevailing high prices.[41] The effect of including such land in the arithmetic measurement of unit productivity is to level out rather than enhance that productivity, even if total output of grain rose. Nevertheless, wheat yields rose from c. 15–16 bushels per acre in 1750 to around 19–21 bushels at the turn of the century, 24 bushels by the 1830s and maybe 33–4 in the 1840s and 1850s,[42] although it is easy to speculate on a different trend. Thus Holderness suggests 18 bushels between c. 1750 and 1770 rising to 21.5 between c. 1795 and 1800, 23 in c. 1810 and 28 bushels in c. 1850.[43] These two different trends, if not the magnitudes of the various stages within them, are similar, though Kain's estimate for the mid-1830s of just 22 bushels stands very uneasily alongside them,[44] and the Healy/Jones estimates of the 1830s to 1850s look rather high, not only in comparison with Holderness but also in comparison with the contemporary estimates of the third quarter of the nineteenth century produced by Caird and Craigie, amongst others.[45] Overton's indexes of wheat and weighted cereal yields, which are based on four east of England counties and Hampshire (and move more in line with the Holderness summary), along with his national estimates of cereal yields, together put the emphasis of change after rather than before the 1830s.[46]

The rent index can be mapped onto this history. Rents did rise more or less in tune with the general rise of agricultural prices, but with the lag which

[39] Jackson, 'Growth and deceleration'.
[40] Crafts, British Economic Growth, p. 42; see also Allen, 'Agriculture during the industrial revolution', 111; M. Overton, 'Re-establishing the English agricultural revolution', AgHR, 44 (1996), 1–18.
[41] Holderness, 'Prices, productivity, and output', 138.
[42] Turner, 'Agricultural productivity in England', 501, 504, the later estimates based on M. J. R. Healy and E. L. Jones, 'Wheat yields in England, 1815–59', JRSS, 125 (1962), 574–9.
[43] Holderness, 'Prices, productivity, and output', 140.
[44] R. J. P. Kain, An Atlas and Index of the Tithe Files of Mid-Nineteenth-Century England and Wales (Cambridge, 1986), p. 460. Kain's presentation of the tithe data may underestimate output: J. V. Beckett and J. E. Heath, Derbyshire Tithe Files 1836–50 (Derbyshire Record Society, 22, Chesterfield, 1995), pp. xxxii–xxxiii.
[45] Healy and Jones, 'Wheat yields'; Caird, esp. 474; P. G. Craigie, 'Statistics of Agricultural Production', JRSS, 46 (1883), 1–58, esp. 40–2.   [46] Overton, 'Re-establishing', tables 1 and 4.

Table 11.2. *English wheat yields c. 1750–1850/9*

	Wheat Yields[a] bushels/acre	Wheat yields[b] bushels/acre	Arable rents[c] shillings/acre	Arable rents[d] shillings/acre
c. 1750	15.0	18.0	7.4	8.1
c. 1800	19.5	21.5	10.5	13.9
c. 1810	—	23.0	15.0	19.2
1815–29	21.7	—	19.5	23.2
1830–9	23.8	—	19.0	22.4
1840–9	33.5	—	19.7	22.7
1850–9	34.7	28.0	20.9	23.0
Index numbers				
c. 1750	76.9	83.7	70.5	58.3
c. 1800	100.0	100.0 (100)	100.0	100.0
c. 1810	—	107.0	142.9	138.1
1815–29	111.3	—	185.7	166.9
1830–9	122.1	—	181.0	161.2
1840–9	171.8	—	187.6	163.3
1850–9	177.9	130.2 (132)	199.0	165.5

[a] M. E. Turner, 'Agricultural productivity in England in the eighteenth century: evidence from crop yields', *EcHR*, 35, 1982, 504.
[b] B. A. Holderness, 'Prices, productivity, and output', in Mingay, *AgHist*, p. 140; and in brackets, M. Overton, 'Re-establishing the English agricultural revolution' *AgHR*, 44, 1996, table 1.
[c] Based on Caird's division of England (see chapter 9).
[d] Based on Thirsk's division of England (see chapter 9).

we have established. Indeed the rise in rents from 1750 to 1790 was quite modest; in fact it was almost static until it gathered momentum in the 1780s. But then during the twenty-year duration of the French wars rents increased nearly threefold (figure 9.2). This is appreciably greater than the rise in rents adduced by Chambers and Mingay over the same period, which they reckoned to be nearer 90 per cent.[47] However, one of the authorities whom they quoted, but who they reckoned exaggerated the rise in rents, was Thomas Tooke. Tooke believed that war rents rose threefold above their pre-war level, an order of magnitude now confirmed in the new index.[48] Table 11.2 compares plausible estimates of the rise of land productivity (for wheat alone) and the course of agricultural rents for the period 1750–1850. The arable rents are based on the division of the country according to Caird's twofold division and Thirsk's threefold division of England. The comparison of the broad general movement in the trend in wheat yields compared with the trend in arable rents suggests that landlords successfully kept ahead of changes in land productivity for most of this period, and it was

[47] Chambers and Mingay, p. 118.   [48] *Ibid.*, pp. 117–18.

not until the second quarter of the nineteenth century that the trend in land productivity began to catch up with the trend in land rents. The insufficiency of, and lack of confidence in, the eighteenth-century grain yield measurements and observations temper our enthusiasm to press these conclusions too far.

1815–1846: Agriculture in crisis

The crisis of food self-sufficiency which occurred in the 1790s was ever present for the remainder of the French wars, and when the wars ended it continued to act as a reminder of British vulnerability. Thus an important conflict of interest faced the government of the day. On the one hand there was the self-interest of an agricultural class which dominated Parliament and which had enjoyed a period of high prices for their products and high and rising rents, and on the other there were genuine concerns about the vulnerability of food supplies during times of international crisis. On both counts it was in the power of the agricultural class, through its parliamentary majority, to tackle both issues. The members of the landed interest were correct to feel personally vulnerable because they as landlords had enjoyed unprecedentedly high incomes during the war years. But with the close of hostilities and the resulting greater international security in the movement of produce, there was less pressure on insurance charges and freight rates. The cumulative effect of more certain supplies and the relief on transfer charges meant that agricultural prices fell.

The mercantilist state was not born out of the French wars; it already existed before the 1790s. Revisions to the existing corn law in 1791 fixed an upper limit of 54 shillings per quarter, at which price or above there were no limits on the importation of wheat. Below 54 shillings there was a sliding scale of duties down to 50 shillings per quarter, and once prices fell below 50 shillings imports were prohibited. In 1814 the old export bounty which persisted in much of the eighteenth century was abolished. This was a recognition of the vulnerability of supply and the virtues of self-sufficiency because it was intended to discourage exports, but not to prohibit them. In 1815 a new corn law was passed. This abolished the old sliding scale, and replaced it with an absolute prohibition on imports until, in the case of wheat, prices had reached 80 shillings per quarter. Importation was duty free above that price. However, in the circumstances of the post-war years, when prices fell, this offered a far too generous income protection to agriculture and, relative to what might have been achieved with the free importation of cheap overseas grain, it maintained higher than necessary basic food prices. In turn, this encouraged a high-wage economy, at a time when there was a reduction in war-induced demand and the beginnings of a post-war depression. Coincidentally, there was the demobilisation of a large military force, and this led to high levels of unemployment. In combination, these factors and events put pressure on the poor rates and other local services. The 1815 corn law was revised in 1822 when a sliding scale was reintroduced, this time at 80 shillings. In 1828 this was revised to allow protection until wheat prices reached 52 shillings, at which price a sliding scale applied until prices reached 71 shillings, above which level a fixed nominal duty of one shilling per quarter was applied.

These adjustments in the corn laws took place at a time when prices fell quite dramatically. At the wartime height the price of wheat stood at 126 shillings per quarter (rounded) in 1812 falling to 65 shillings in 1815 and 44 shillings in 1822. By 1828 the price had recovered to 60 shillings, but in the period 1815 to 1846 inclusive, the year the corn laws were repealed, the annual average price of wheat was below 60 shillings in 16 of those years and below 70 shillings in 28 years. At the lowest point the price of wheat stood at 39 shillings in 1835, a level which in general had not been seen since the early 1760s.[49] Thus British farmers, even though bolstered by protective duties, experienced a fall in basic product prices which at times were no more than they received before the war, yet now they were paying rents which were three times what they paid before the war. In turn they supported a proportion of the investment costs which the high wartime prices had encouraged. Their landlords, although now enjoying inflated incomes, did so by investment in expensive enclosures and by other means, an investment which they incurred at high wartime nominal interest rates but which in real terms rose during the period of declining prices which followed 1815. This was a feature which affected large and small alike: 'that is where the great evil has been; farmers having some capital, and looking forward to high prices, have purchased estates, and borrowing the greater part of the money, and now they have to pay the same rate of interest as when their produce was making double what it now makes'.[50] In some cases the investment, in enclosure for example, was conceived during the high prices of the war but put into operation during the post-war depression. This occurred at Helpston in Northamptonshire where the enclosure of the

---

[49] B. R. Mitchell and P. Deane (eds.), *Abstract of British Historical Statistics* (Cambridge, 1962), pp. 487–8.

[50] *First Report from the Select Committee on the State of Agriculture; with Minutes of Evidence and Appendix, BPP* [79], VIII, part 1 (1836), Q. 1268. See also D. C. Moore, 'The corn laws and high farming', *EcHR*, 18 (1965), 546–7.

parish was conceived during the war but paid for after the war when prices were depressed and when there were poor credit facilities.[51] The Select Committee of 1836 is retrospective evidence of the difficult times which agriculture faced after 1815.

The 1830s saw the culmination of introspection about the general state of agriculture with the mounting of three government inquiries, from which we can derive evidence of rent arrears, abatements, rent adjustments, and general rural distress on a scale not previously recorded.[52] Landlords often abated rather than reduced rents,[53] but the failure to reduce rents had more general knock-on effects when tenants found they could not pay the tradesmen who serviced them. This was the message from one witness, Mr Umbers of Leamington Spa, and others also commented that farmers endeavoured to pay their rent rather than their bills. In the words of William Thurnall of Duxford, Cambridgeshire, if farmers paid their rents on time it was 'generally by leaving their creditors unpaid', and some farmers said: 'I must pay my landlord, but my other creditors must wait for a considerable time.'[54] The failure to pay bills while rents remained unchanged became a commonplace complaint.[55] Agricultural distress therefore spread its tentacles widely through society.

Some landlords recognised the problem. John Brickwell of Leckhamstead near Buckingham in Buckinghamshire suggested that rent had increased by more than one-quarter compared with before the war 'but now it is lower; quite as low as it was forty years ago'.[56] At Chipping Norton he reported that rents had been reduced by 25 per cent since 1822 following a fall of 15 per cent from 1813, 'in consequence of the complaints made by the tenants they were considerably in arrear of rents, and could not pay until the rent was reduced; it was reduced 25 per cent. under my advice to the landlord, and now the rent is paid up'.[57]

[51] John Barrell, *The Idea of Landscape and the Sense of Place 1730–1840: An Approach to the Poetry of John Clare* (Cambridge, 1972), pp. 207–8.

[52] *Report from the Select Committee Appointed to Inquire into the Present State of Agriculture*, BPP, [612], v (1833); *First Second and Third Reports from the Select Committee on the State of Agriculture; with Minutes of Evidence and Appendix*, BPP [79], VIII, part 1 (1836), BPP [189], VIII, part 1 (1836), BPP [465], VIII, part 2 (1836); *Report from the Select Committee of the House of Lords on the State of Agriculture in England and Wales*, BPP [464], v (1837); these three reports had been preceded by similar inquiries in the early 1820s: *Report from the Select Committee on Petitions Complaining of Agricultural Distress*, BPP [255], II (1820); *Report from the Select Committee to Whom the Several Petitions Complaining of the Depressed State of the Agriculture of the United Kingdom were Referred*, BPP [668], IX (1821); *First and Second Reports from the Select Committee Appointed to Inquire into the Allegations of the Several Petitions Complaining of the Distressed State of the Agriculture of the United Kingdom*, BPP [165], v (1822), BPP [346], v (1822).

[53] For example see *First Report* (1836), Qs. 320, 322, 679, 1653, 1656, 3680.

[54] *Second Report* (1836), Qs. 8630–1, 8604, *Third Report* (1836), 11714, *First Report* (1836), Qs. 699, 2372.

[55] For example, by way of illustration in Buckden, Huntingdonshire, *First Report* (1836), Qs. 3503–6; and in Kent, *Third Report* (1836), Q. 9450.   [56] *First Report* (1836), Q. 657.

[57] *Ibid.*, Qs. 320, 322.

An important theme to emerge from the Inquiries was the need to adjust (i.e. to reduce) rents according to the prevailing price of wheat. The popularity of corn rents – that is, rents which were adjusted according to the annual average movement in grain prices, the most common of which were based on seven or 21-year moving averages – gained converts during this time of declining prices when otherwise fixed rents prevailed.[58] A corn rent was tried on the Trentham estate in Staffordshire from 1822, and it was introduced for a brief period on the Holkham estate in Norfolk in the 1850s. On the Ingestre estate in Staffordshire a half corn rent was introduced in the mid-nineteenth century whereby half the rent fluctuated with the price of corn.[59]

Some witnesses complained that the landlords reacted too slowly to the evidence which was before their eyes. They should have reduced rents earlier, and a consequence of not doing so in Essex was that farmers impoverished the soil in order to pay their rents and yet still also make a living; 'it has been by persisting in the high rents that the farms have been worked out of condition, and then no person would take them except at a very low rent'. Around Thetford in Norfolk the equivalent of this was a complaint of overcropping, and the more general complaint that many farmers 'are farming under war rents, while they are selling their corn at peace prices'.[60]

Abatements of rent and the toleration of arrears by landlords were practical short-term remedies in the 1820s to alleviate financial distress, but inevitably these gave way to real rent reductions. It was a serious business for a landlord to reduce rent because to all practical purposes, on the basis of land values, it was tantamount to saying that the asset was losing value. Abatements and remissions of rent, however, could be dressed up as temporary expedients to help out tenants during times of distress and would also convey the correct image of a landed hierarchy acting with local responsibility. One historian has characterised the toleration of arrears by landowners as their 'acting as a stablizing factor, by, in effect, becoming the farmers' bankers'.[61] On some Norfolk estates rent reductions were regarded as a last and delayed resort, not only during the difficult times of the 1820s

---

[58] *Third Report* (1836), Qs. 15078–81.
[59] R. W. Sturgess, 'The response of agriculture in Staffordshire to the price changes of the nineteenth century' (University of Manchester, PhD thesis, 1965), pp. 497, 502; Wade Martins, *Holkham*, p. 86.
[60] *Third Report* (1836), Qs. 12407–9, 12664, and 12649. References to similar overcropping or impoverishment of the soil can be found in 1833, *Report from the Select Committee* (1833), for example Qs. 8601–7, 9241–5, and also in 1837, *Report from the Select Committee* (1837), Qs. 2749–51. See also P. Roe, 'Norfolk agriculture 1815–1914' (University of East Anglia, MPhil thesis, 1976), p. 21, for evidence of complaints about war rents at peace prices.
[61] Roe, 'Norfolk agriculture', p. 11.

and 1830s but throughout the century.[62] On the Lilleshall estate of the Marquess of Stafford in the early 1830s James Loch announced that abatements would be a mutually beneficial bargain in which tenants would be expected to introduce farm improvements.[63]

Undoubtedly, according to these official inquiries, rents had fallen considerably since the end of the French wars, and yet they were also often reckoned to be still too high. Adam Murray, a land agent, surveyor, and one-time practical farmer argued before the 1833 committee that rents were too high by about 25 per cent relative to product prices, and this was a commonly quoted multiplier.[64] The evidence of witnesses to all three major inquiries in the 1830s conveys an unambiguous picture of declining rents and an impoverished agricultural sector.[65] But where landlords would not or could not reduce or abate rents the tenants were obliged to exhaust their working capital, and sometimes the tenants left the land altogether, which presented the landlord with the problem of finding new tenants. Farms frequently lay idle for considerable periods. At Aylesbury in 1831 it was said, though surely with some exaggeration, that every farm was untenanted and in the hands of the landlords.[66] In general, finding new tenants was not easy, and neither was selling the land, but when tenants left and landlords sold it disrupted what otherwise had been a continuity in land occupancy. There were reports that farmers of long-standing in a neighbourhood were no longer as thick on the ground as traditionally had been the case, indicating an increase in tenant turnover.[67] If a proportion of land which was taken 'in hand' continued in cultivation it became effectively owner-occupied, but the remainder went into permament or semi-permanent disuse. This is a feature which can be identified but it cannot be readily quantified. At best it can be said there was an incalculable, but probably negligible portion of Britain which was left untenanted, and that which remained in occupation did so with remarkably unstable rents.

At times farmers paid their rents not out of the returns from their produce but out of their capital, and this was certainly the case on the heavy clay lands.[68] Charles Howard reported from Holderness in East Yorkshire that

[62] Ibid., pp. 11, 106–7, 243–6.
[63] E. Richards, 'James Loch and the House of Sutherland, 1821–1855' (University of Nottingham, PhD thesis, 1967), p. 174.   [64] Report from the Select Committee (1833), Qs. 322–6.
[65] Readers should note that all three inquiries are very well indexed.
[66] M. E. Turner, 'Economic protest in rural society: opposition to parliamentary enclosure in Buckinghamshire', Southern History, 10 (1988), 112.   [67] Ibid., 122–3.
[68] Evidence of John Houghton, a farmer and receiver of rents in eight different counties of eastern and southern England, First Report (1836), Q. 699. See also, Report from the Select Committee (1837), for examples from Kent in Qs. 119, 1442–4, 2748, Berkshire in Q. 800, Staffordshire in Q. 1372, Middlesex in Q. 3132, Hertfordshire in Q. 3870, Somerset in Qs. 5143–4, E. Yorkshire in Q. 2130, Glamorgan in Q. 2435, and by inference in Somerset, Surrey, Essex, and Hertfordshire in Qs.

they paid about 30 shillings per acre twenty years earlier, but 'If they are paying 20 shillings [now] they are paying part of the rent out of capital.'[69] There was also a more general complaint about the diminution of tenants' capital and therefore a necessary neglect of cultivation for the want of resources. The problem was exacerbated by the over-high level of rents that prevailed because the farmer was unable to make enough from his produce to enable him to expend future capital.[70] William Jacob, the Head of the Corn Department at the Board of Trade, complained of capital flight out of British agriculture and into the trade of her overseas competitors.[71] Finally, farmers also complained about the poor rates and other local charges which against a backcloth of agricultural depression, were high and rising.[72] This was of course in the last years of the Old Poor Law and before the adjustments in the burdens of cost which accompanied the New Poor Law of 1834 could be fully appreciated.

Distress was not evident in every part of the country. Reports from Liverpool, Shropshire, near Evesham in Worcestershire, and from a grazier in Kent suggest little problem in paying rents, and practically every witness from Scotland spoke enthusiastically about the local improvements in agriculture which in places actually led to enhanced rents.[73] However, these are a selection of the relatively few examples which seem to prove the rule: elsewhere in the 1830s Inquiries, and on a very large scale, the tale from the 1830s was indeed one of rent reductions of anything up to 50 per cent. Moreover, this downward pressure on rents seemed to touch practically every corner of England. However, to what extent is this sorry message of distress, depression, and rural dislocation, also reflected in the rent index? In the years immediately after the war there was a reduction in unit acre agreed rent, which fell from about 22 shillings per acre in 1814–15 to 19 shillings in

1573–9. This was also the case on the lighter north Norfolk soils of the Holkham estate, but then these were prosperous farmers anyway, Wade Martins, *Holkham*, p. 92. In contrast, the tenants on the Marquess of Stafford's Lilleshall estate in 1821 were in some distress and certainly encroached on their capital in order to pay their rents, Richards, 'James Loch and the House of Sutherland', p. 172.   [69] *Second Report* (1836), Qs. 5376–7.

[70] This was such a pervasive problem that it seems appropriate to underscore it by weight of reference. Thus see *Report from the Select Committee* (1833), Qs. 168, 482, 747, 873, 918, 989–93, 1100–1, 1192, 1196, 1256, 1904–5, 2506–8, 2632, 2877, 3032, 3807, 4934, 4858, 5063, 5203, 5843, 6010, 6031, 6445, 8650, 9241–5, 9256–68, 9810, 10620–3, 11219, 11534–8, 11925. See also *Report from the Select Committee* (1837), Qs. 162, 190, 608–10, 1203–4, 1227, 3162, 4635.

[71] *Report from the Select Committee* (1833), Qs. 44–9.

[72] *Ibid.*, Qs. 1758, 1760, 1762–3, 7407, 11688, 11839–42. *First Report* (1836), Qs. 3444–7.

[73] *Second Report* (1836), Q. 7028; *Third Report* (1836), Qs. 9410, 13024–6, 13552–9, 13990–4, 14519. This was also reported in 1833, *Report from the Select Committee* (1833), Qs. 452, 462–3 in Shropshire, Q. 1052 by implication in Wiltshire, Q. 1870 in Worcestershire, Qs. 3377 and 3382 in Cornwall, Qs. 3593–9 in Lancashire, though definitely not in Qs. 6093–4 in Cheshire. Such reports continued in 1837, *Report from the Select Committee* (1837), regarding the hop growers in Kent, in Qs. 1461–4, and also in Dorset in Q. 3272.

the mid 1830s, and to a low of 18 shillings in 1850. However, the overall reduction was quite moderate compared with the reductions reported in the 1836 Select Committee. The upward march of the received rents also peaked in about 1814–15 at about 22 shillings per acre, and then dropped to 20 shillings within five years, but thereafter they rose modestly to something between 21 and 22 shillings in the next 20 years. Arguably this shows the landlords making sensible downward adjustments in rents to a level at which their tenants could make equally sensible decisions about paying those rents and maybe even paying off some arrears. The rents agreed and received have been drawn from two overlapping but marginally different samples. The two rent profiles when drawn from a common sample show rents reducing from 21 shillings per acre at the close of the war to 20 shillings per acre within ten years and thereafter stabilising to 19 to 20 shillings. In other words, after a clear but modest fall, rents more or less stabilised.[74]

Whichever rent sample is viewed, however, the history to be interpreted from the rent index does not match the equivalent history from the parliamentary record. Why is this? The Select Committee was commissioned to look into the state of agriculture generally, prompted by complaints from the countryside. In due course it found a depression, because there was a depression. But it was not a national depression, and this is where the rent index offers agricultural history more objectivity than the government inquiries. In the 20 years from Waterloo to the mid-1830s rents per acre fell by between 10 and 20 per cent at Castle Howard, Badminton, Tavistock, Thorndon, Chevening, Ashburnham, Guy's in Hereford, on the Cornwallis estate, on the Manvers estate at Holme Pierrepont, on both the Ancaster estates in Rutland and Lincoln, at Cholmondeley and on the Greenwich Hospital estate in Northumberland and Cumberland, and by between 20 and 30 per cent on three other Manvers estates at Beighton, Crowle, and Thoresby. By way of moderation, the fall in rent on each of the Woburn, Milton, and Holkham estates was negligible. But more dramatically elsewhere, received rents per acre actually rose, and sometimes by very large margins of up to and greater than 30 per cent – on the Emanuel Hospital estate at Brandesburton, at Lilleshall, Trentham, Higham Ferrers, Bolton Abbey, Knowsley, Petworth, Barking Hall, Leconfield, and on Guy's estates in Lincolnshire and Essex. The rent index is partly the result of chance survival but also partly the subsequent efforts we have made to present a geographically representative sample of experiences. In contrast, perhaps the complaints made to the government were not so representative of agriculture as a whole. The varied locations of

---

[74] Calculated as three-year averages centred on 1814 and 1835 and based on the rents assessed and rents received according to the incidence of survival.

the individual estate material listed above does not suggest a hard-and-fast geographical division in the location of the depression. Without further research it is not possible to say too categorically that the east of England arable farmers were the most severely hit, and the pasture areas the least, but to the extent that the regional rent indexes presented in chapter 9 give a clue to the severity of the depression, they do point in this direction. The rise in rents in the pasture areas taken together was not dramatic, but it was perceptible (figures 9.6 to 9.9). The rent index, its regional components, and its individual estate trends, invite a closer inspection of estate management during relative crisis.

1846–1914: agriculture cast to its fate

The depression of the 1830s was mingled with a series of reforms – the Reform Act itself, the introduction of a New Poor Law, and a wide debate about political representation in general, through the reform of the Municipal Corporations in 1835 and thereafter the activities of the Chartists. The Chartists were aided and abetted in a political sense by the willingness of manufacturers to agitate for a repeal of the corn laws. Never before had the landed interest been under such attack, both from within and without. Though they easily maintained political power it was a power which was eroding, and which gave way to the repealers. The uncomfortable events in Ireland in the mid-1840s also suggested that an agricultural industry protected from overseas trade was no longer tenable. What the landed interest feared was a flood of cheap foreign grain waiting to enter the British market when the corn laws were repealed. Such fears were only partially well founded. The initial reaction to the repeal of the corn laws was for imports of wheat to double or even treble their early 1840s level, but prices only stabilised. The annual average import of wheat into the UK in the first half of the 1840s was a little under half a million tons which rose to a little over half a million tons in the second half of the decade, then to 0.8 million tons on average through the 1850s.[75] D. C. Moore suggests that such levels of importation were marginal, and remained so until long after repeal.[76] It was not until the 1860s that the annual import of grain reached significant proportions, and even then total grain imports represented no more than one-fifth of total grain consumption. However, when wheat imports stood at 1.5 million tons during this decade they represented about one-third of wheat consumption.[77] Fairlie's revisions of wheat output indicate a slightly greater emphasis on imports after repeal. On the eve of

[75] Adapted from Mitchell and Deane, *Abstract*, p. 98.   [76] Moore, 'The corn laws', 545.
[77] Chambers and Mingay, p. 148.

repeal wheat imports represented about 7 or 8 per cent of total English and Welsh wheat consumption. This rose to one-fifth immediately upon repeal, and to one-quarter in the 1850s, before becoming truly significant at 40 per cent in the 1860s.[78] Thereafter wheat flooded the British market. There was a similar though less pronounced upward trend in imports of the other principal grains.

The effect on prices was certainly for stabilisation. While wheat prices fluctuated between about 45 to 55 shillings, and on occasion reached 60 shillings per quarter, there was no tendency for a fall in prices. With an open-door policy, however, we must allow for the fact that internal prices were at least partly, if not mainly, determined by international circumstances such as the state of the harvest overseas as well as the condition of the home harvest.[79] The eventual disastrous fall in wheat and other grain prices did not occur until the 1880s and 1890s with the flood of north American grain, which could not have been predicted from the trend before 1880.[80] In general oats and barley prices increased by about 20 per cent from the late 1840s to the 1870s and prices for animal products rose even more, by anything from 30 to 45 per cent.

The third quarter of the nineteenth century has been dubbed a golden age of high farming. Imports may have doubled, trebled, or even quadrupled from the second to the third quarter of the century, but there was a buoyant demand from a rapidly rising population and from greater integration of the arable and animal sectors. The aphorism of the day was that cattle were machines to make manure, meaning that when animal prices were low they were still kept in production to make manure for grain, but when the terms of trade favoured animals the grains were still valuable as animal fodder. Agriculturalists were exhorted to 'refocus their hopes of prosperity upon high production instead of high prices', upon progress through agricultural technology.[81] Mixed farming came into its own, and the label High Farming came to mean high capital inputs. This was the age of underdrainage, though this failed to bring about a revolution on the heavy soils,[82] but it was also the age of increased agricultural investment generally, and the greater application of natural manures and especially imported artificial fertilisers. There have been strong historiographical

[78] S. Fairlie, 'The corn laws and British wheat production 1829–76', *EcHR*, 22 (1969), 88–116, esp. 103.   [79] *Ibid.*, 104–5.
[80] Mitchell and Deane, *Abstract*, for imports and prices, pp. 98–9, 488–9; Chambers and Mingay, p. 158, say the average price of wheat was 53 shillings in the first thirty years after repeal; according to Fairlie the annual average of wheat was just over 53 shillings per quarter in the 1840s and 51 shillings in the 1870s, 'The corn laws', 105.   [81] Moore, 'The corn laws', 546.
[82] A. D. M. Phillips, *The Underdrainage of Farmland in England During the Nineteenth Century* (Cambridge, 1989), pp. 156–7.

pressures to build the wider period from the 1830s into nothing short of a
second agricultural revolution.[83] Whilst profit margins for farmers may not
have expanded greatly, if at all, they were prepared to innovate and to
become more cost conscious than had been the case with earlier generations. In addition, it was during this period that a mechanical revolution
began on the farm.

Did the intensive nature of farming pay off by significantly improving
output and productivity? E. J. T. Collins has suggested that the golden age
was not so golden, and High Farming not so high. Grain yields levelled off
from the late 1850s, and the yields of fodder crops tailed off by the 1880s. In
addition the livestock sector underperformed. The notable exception was
unit milk output which increased by about one-third. A natural protection
of distance was offered for perishable products like live animals or dead
meat, and for dairy products, as well as for fruit and vegetables. This at least
helped to keep up agricultural incomes, but Collins contends that by the late
1860s there was a meat famine. The animal sector was partly bolstered by
the Cattle Diseases Prevention and Contagious Diseases Acts of the 1860s,
responses to the cattle plague and generally to the virulence of animal
diseases. In 1865 and 1866 combinations of rinderpest (cattle plague) and
pleuro-pneumonia raged through the cattle industry. This occurred during
a period not simply of the free import of live animals, essentially without
medical controls, but during an increase in this trade which was facilitated
by the greater use of railways and steamships and therefore the more rapid
transmission of disease once it was introduced. By the spring of 1866 the
government was increasingly under pressure from agricultural societies and
the veterinary profession to do something about it.[84] The Contagious
Diseases (Animals) Act of 1869 resulted, essentially as a device to take
advantage of the moat which surrounded the British Isles and to protect the
home breeding stock from animal diseases. This was achieved by checks on
the livestock trade, compulsory slaughter of diseased animals, and by
disallowing live animals to enter the British market (except from Ireland).
However, the success of these measures in holding diseases in check is open
to doubt.[85] Nevertheless, to a degree the livestock producer was afforded
some protection from international competition, and this remained the case
until refrigeration and the tin-can industry allowed moderately fresh meat to
hit the market from overseas later in the nineteenth century. The main
competition for perishable items came from the rising Danish dairy product
industry – which eventually leapt ahead of its Irish counterpart – and the

---

[83] F. M. L. Thompson, 'The second agricultural revolution, 1815–1880', *EcHR*, 31 (1968), 62–77.
[84] C. S. Orwin and E. H. Whetham, *History of British Agriculture 1846–1914* (Newton Abbot, 1964),
p. 138.   [85] R. Perren, *The Meat Trade in Britain 1840–1914* (London, 1978), pp. 84–5, 108–13.

Danish pork industry.[86] In sum, the rate of growth of the agricultural sector was running at about 0.8 per cent per annum, which was much lower than the growth of the previous quarter century and not much higher than the growth rates in the Great Depression which followed.[87]

The rent index partly reflects this idea of a mildly expansive, certainly not over-cosy, but nevertheless stable period for agriculture. The average received rents rose from 22 shillings per acre around 1850 to 28 shillings per acre in the 1870s. This was a rise of *c.* 27 per cent, and though it did not match the great rise in rents which had occurred during the French wars earlier in the century, nevertheless, after 20 years of stagnating rents it was a welcome boost indicating a recovery in prosperity for tenants and landlords alike, with, as we have seen in chapter 10, a reasonable share passing to the general agricultural labour force. It showed a reasonable return on investment. In a greater competitive world in which Britain maintained an open-door policy with respect to trade, it could be said that under the circumstances the agricultural sector was holding its own.

This period of High Farming, however, was short lived. The initial boost which the repeal of the corn laws gave to grain imports settled at a plateau level until the 1860s, after which time the annual average import of grain rose from 1.5 million tons in the 1860s to 2 or 2.5 million tons in the 1870s, to nearly 3 million tons in the 1880s, to 4 million tons by Edwardian times, and finally to an annual average of 5.2 million tons for the five years leading up to the First World War. The greatest inroads were made by wheat imports from the USA. They represented less than 10 per cent of UK wheat imports in the 1840s, rising to 30 per cent or more during the 1860s (reaching a peak in the early part of the Civil War before tailing off), 39 and 51 per cent for the two halves of the 1870s, 60 and 40 per cent in the 1880s, and 48 per cent in the early 1890s, before diminishing to 20 per cent in the decade leading to the First World War. The dominance of USA imports was challenged by Russian wheat in the 1880s, and Russian, Argentinian, Indian, and Australian wheat in the early twentieth century.[88] By then the damage to the home industry had been done; indeed even when home yields were poor which, under the simplest economic laws of supply and demand, would suggest that prices should have risen, they did so but only marginally. The price of wheat was now determined by international supplies. The average home price of wheat had risen to 57 or 58 shillings per quarter in the early

---

[86] See C. Ó Gráda, 'The beginnings of the Irish creamery system, 1880–1914', *EcHR*, 30 (1977), 284–305; E. Jensen, *Danish Agriculture: Its Economic Development* (Copenhagen, 1937), pp. 373–82; M. E. Turner, *After the Famine: Irish Agriculture 1850–1914* (Cambridge, 1996), pp. 155–60.

[87] E. J. T. Collins, 'Did mid-Victorian Britain fail? Output, productivity and technological change in nineteenth-century farming', *REFRESH*, 21 (1995), 1–4, esp. 2.

[88] Mitchell and Deane, *Abstract*, pp. 98–102.

Table 11.3. *Animal product price movements,*
1845/9–1905/9

Annual averages for five year period (1865–9 = 100)	
Date	Prices
1845–9	81
1855–9	98
1865–9	100
1875–9	100
1885–9	77
1895–9	68
1905–9	77

Source: Reconstructed from the Rousseaux index in B. R. Mitchell
and P. Deane, *Abstract of British Historical Statistics* (Cambridge,
1962), p. 471.

1870s. It then fell to 45 shillings by the late 1870s and early 1880s, and
continued to fall to the lowest annual average price for more than a century
at a little under 23 shillings per quarter in 1894. By the outbreak of the First
World War wheat prices had only recovered to 32 shillings per acre or
thereabouts.[89] By this time the high point of the mid-century wheat acreage
had long since passed, and in general the fall in agricultural prices had
pervaded all of British agriculture. Table 11.3 is a reworking of the
Rousseaux animal product price index to illustrate this fact for the animal
sector.

The onset of the late-nineteenth-century agricultural depression does
not so much mark a watershed in British agriculture, but rather the ill-
conceived direction in which agriculture had been allowed to meander.
Around 1870 Britain still imported only about a quarter of its cereal
requirements, and only 14 per cent of its meat.[90] But this can also be put in
quite a pessimistic light. The indulgence of capital expenditure at relatively
low rates of return on the capital, in order to offer succour to corn
production, probably meant that the wheat acreage in particular was far
too high. 'A more economic form of behaviour by landowners ... would
have mitigated the scale of the agricultural disaster after 1878, by ensuring
an earlier and more gradual contraction of corn acreages.'[91] While it may
not be the case that the repeal of the Corn Laws sacrificed agriculture on
the altar of free trade, their lack of cutting edge also blinded agricultural-

[89] Prices from *ibid.*, p. 489.
[90] R. Perren, *Agriculture in Depression, 1870–1914* (London, 1995), p. 3.
[91] F. M. L. Thompson, 'An anatomy of English agriculture, 1870–1914', in B. A. Holderness and M.
E. Turner (eds.), *Land, Labour and Agriculture, 1700–1820* (London, 1991), pp. 255–6.

ists to the possibilities of fruitful agricultural change, as was embraced by those in Ireland, though in the wake of quite different circumstances.[92] What may have been more important in Britain, and particularly in England, was that the contribution of the agricultural sector to the national economy had been declining throughout the century, and understandably so given the rise of the industrial state. By 1871, agriculture (with forestry and fishing) employed 15 per cent of the British labour force, but in 1911 only 8 per cent. It contributed 14 per cent to the national product in 1871 and well under 10 per cent from 1900.[93] In astronomical terms, the period of High Farming was the exaggerated brightness of a dying star before it exploded in the last quarter of the nineteenth century.

The series of bad harvests and wet seasons in the second half of the 1870s partially protected cereal farmers from overseas competitors with their relatively high burden of transport costs. But the wettest of all seasons in 1879, which continued into the early 1880s, damaged the prospects of crops and animals alike when it induced sheep rot. The traditional compensation for poor harvests was bolstered prices, but this now disappeared. Prices did not simply fall, they nose-dived.[94] The picture is one of deepening depression and decline in incomes for cereal producers, relative stability for livestock producers, with odd years of disquiet but surely never again any extended bumper periods. It may be trite to repeat the oft-quoted idea that this was a period of change as much as it was of decline; nevertheless this is true, and those who were able to change managed to survive. Those changes included conversion from cereal production into fresh meat and other livestock products, and the development of horticulture.

The relative collapse of agriculture has always been clear from the Royal Commission of the 1890s, but not so clear when historians have cast their objective lens on the period.[95] The depression seems unequivocally to be mirrored in the rent index. The high point of rent, and the highest point until after the Second World War, was in 1878 when the national average of received rent was 28.4 shillings per acre. It fell to 20/21 shillings per acre during the years when the Royal Commission listened to the evidence. This was a real fall in rents when measured against the most optimistic gloss on

[92] Turner, *After the Famine.*
[93] S. Pollard and D. W. Crossley, *The Wealth of Britain 1085–1966* (London, 1968), p. 223.
[94] Summarised by Perren, *Agriculture*, pp. 7–9.
[95] For estimates and discussions about agricultural output see M. E. Turner, 'Output and prices in UK agriculture, 1867–1914, and the Great Agricultural Depression reconsidered', *AgHR*, 40 (1992), 38–51. For a general résumé see Perren, *Agriculture*, chapter 2; P. J. Perry, 'Editor's introduction', in P. J. Perry (ed.), *British Agriculture 1875–1914* (London, 1973), pp. xi–xliv. For caution against exaggerated language see Thompson, 'An anatomy of English agriculture'.

the course of late-nineteenth-century agricultural prices.[96] But the ultimate tragedy was when rents continued to fall as prices began to recover, albeit gradually and then rents positively stagnated when prices unambiguously recovered. Rents fell below 20 shillings per acre in every year, except one, from 1898–1904 inclusive (a fall of 29 per cent from the high point of the late 1870s), and only recovered to a bare 20 shillings on the outbreak of the First World War. Of the three depressions we have met over the period, on this occasion the rent index seems fully to support the traditional historiography.

Perversely, in fact, it may even be possible to suggest that the witnesses to the Royal Commission underplayed its significance. If we separate the printed evidence in the Royal Commission from the new estate evidence and the few existing histories which are in print we discover, on average, that the assessed rents in the Royal Commission had fallen by 11 per cent from the three-year average before the depression began (1876–8) to the three-year average when the Royal Commission was at its most active (1892–4). In comparison, the assessed rents from the predominantly new evidence fell over the same period by nearly 20 per cent. This is based on the putative level of rents which the land would bear (assessed rents or rents due). If at any time tenants could not pay their bills it was during depressions; therefore, as we have emphasised several times, a more meaningful measure of rent is one which measures what the tenants are able to pay, or the received rents. This suggests an even worse situation. While the average unit received rents recorded in the Royal Commission fell by almost 20 per cent, the equivalent rents from the new evidence fell by over 40 per cent. This difference is exaggerated because the extremely large drop in rents on the expansive estates of the Duke of Bedford and the Earl of Ancaster, for example, have been counted as new evidence – the former through the estate history, the latter through the archives – even though both landowners also contributed to the Royal Commission. If we take this into account, as we did in table 6.1, we notice that the decline in rents assessed was of the order of 18 per cent, and of rents received 25 per cent.

On average, rents continued to decline throughout the 1890s and into the first few years of Edwardian times. The recovery when it came was hardly a recovery; the general level of rents received remained at about the level of the early 1890s. A few estates in the index did indeed recover, and even came close to, but not quite up to the level of unit rents which existed in the late 1870s (Castle Howard, Emanuel Hospital, Chevening, Thorndon), but others continued to decline or at best levelled out.

Even though there were geographical extremes in this depression, and

---

[96] See Thompson, 'An anatomy of English agriculture', on money illusion, and Turner, 'Output and prices in UK agriculture', for price indexes.

extremes depending on broadly arable and broadly pastoral considerations (figures 9.6 to 9.9), the underlying message is of a depression which was widespread, resulting in a level of rent arrears which was almost unremitting for 20 years. These arrears stood at a level which was at least the equivalent of 5 per cent of the assessed rent, the longest continuous period of distress for at least 200 years (figure 9.4).

Conclusion

Every year millions of pounds passed from English tenant farmers to their landlords in the form of rent, but perhaps because it was a financial transaction it took place in some secrecy. The result was that contemporaries were not particularly well informed about rent levels, hence the problems encountered by the Board of Agriculture reporters when, set to produce information on rents, they either failed altogether or ended up with mainly meaningless comments which are of little value to a quantitative study. As a consequence, information on rents only started to become available on a significant scale in the course of the nineteenth century in conjunction with inquiries into the state of agriculture, and more fully and finally only in the twentieth century as estate records have become available to research scrutiny. Arthur Young, James Caird, and other contemporaries who took a close interest in the subject, would be astonished at just how much more we know today about rents paid by their contemporaries than they themselves understood.

Ironically, the flood of information which has become available has, in some ways, complicated rather than simplified the task. Until now historians have sought, in one form or another, to provide rough guides to the course of rents (chapter 3). To produce a definitive index it was necessary to go further: the pitfalls of generalising from the particular to the general – given that English agricultural land has so much variety in its nature and use – had to be avoided. As we showed in chapter 4, it was necessary to assess very carefully the parameters of a rent index, and in particular to avoid falling into the trap of uncritically repeating contemporary information which might itself be inaccurate. Perhaps most important of all, given the range of data available in the 1890s Royal Commission, we quickly became aware that since government inquiries into depression were looking for a depression, they were likely to find it in the light of their choice of witness and method of inquiry, and therefore we needed to compensate accordingly. It was those landlords who felt the full force of the depression who were most likely to respond to government surveys; and when it came to private inquiry and estate autobiography there was also the suspicion of selectivity. Thus the partial nature of the Duke of Bedford's research into his own estate – leaving out of consideration the profitable Tavistock estate – was a good example of the pitfalls we had to avoid. In the end, we believe that our methodology ensures that we have collected the best data available, and that the way we have proceeded should have reduced the margin of error to a minimum. We accept that the problems of beneficial leasing, and the deficiency of surviving records for the period before 1750, have affected the scope of our work. However, we believe it is unlikely that our results can, or will, easily be improved upon.

Essentially what we have done is to create a database consisting of material collected from three sources: our own work on 40 archives across the country selected on the basis of the guidelines set out in chapter 4; evidence collected in the late nineteenth century by the 1890s Royal Commission and in a number of related studies; and some additional material from other estate biographies. From the database we have created a rent index which gives us a clear pattern for the period 1690–1914. We have argued that while the curve on our graphs (figs. 8.1 and 8.2) may not come as a particular surprise, we have provided an accurately constructed trend devoid of either the guesstimates which characterised the work of Chambers and Mingay, or the regional specificity of the work of more recent scholars such as Allen. We also show that there were clear differences for some periods from what has been until now the generally accepted trend. We now have a definitive rent index for English agricultural land throughout the period of the agricultural and industrial revolutions.

In addition, there are other important lessons to be learned. Historians have long been aware that rent arrears offer important clues to times of feast and famine for the farming community, but we show just how critical it is to appreciate contemporary accounting procedures in their own right in order to distinguish between accumulated arrears and annual arrears. Failure to do so can lead us to paint a picture in which arrears loom far larger as a share of rent than was the case in reality, because we may be including in the equation sums of money which were never (in reality) going to be paid. By allowing for this we are able to give a much more accurate view both of the course of arrears and of their significance for our understanding of agricultural history.

Similarly we have long been aware that there was no such thing as a national average rent, or at least that any figure purporting to represent this would be a fiction. From Arthur Young and his contemporaries, and particularly from the work of James Caird, regional differences in rental patterns have been well understood, but the extent of these differences has not been as clear. Consequently we attempted to disaggregate the index to test the assumption that by the mid-nineteenth century the pastoral districts had much higher pro rata rents than the corn-growing areas. First, we tested our material on the basis of Caird's own division of the country into the grazing west and the corn-growing east. Our figures showed a rather less clear-cut division in rents than Caird had envisaged, with rents in western England going ahead of those in the east only in the late nineteenth century. To refine the picture further we adopted a much simplified reconstruction of Thirsk's agricultural maps in order to test the hypothesis. This showed the trend more clearly with rents in the three main agricultural areas which she has distinguished all going upwards in the mid-nineteenth century, but with the dominance of pastoral rents becoming clear only towards the end of the nineteenth century. In other words the difference between the rent of arable and pasture land was not as pronounced as was sometimes thought, at least not until the ravages of the agricultural depression produced a serious differential in the closing decades of the nineteenth century. Although there is little doubt that it was arable farmers who caught the most serious colds in periods of agricultural 'famine', the *general* impact on rents in the eighteenth century and after the French wars was nothing like as serious as the well-rehearsed individual comparisons have suggested. In this respect we have substantially refined widely accepted views on the course of rents during the famous agricultural depressions of the eighteenth and nineteenth centuries.

The clarity of our findings is such that we have considerable faith in them. They lead directly to our discussion of the fortunes of agriculture over the period 1690–1914, in which we re-examine a number of issues in the light of the rent index. Rents, of course, do not move in a vacuum. Levels were determined by all sorts of considerations including demand for farms, prices for agricultural products, changes in output and productivity, social considerations, and changes in marketing and commercial opportunities. In assessing the level of rents it is not always easy to make adequate allowance for these influences. A good example is enclosure, which was undoubtedly followed by a rise in rents, but quite how this is measured, or allowed for, in an index, is almost impossible to establish. Rather than trying to weight the index by making allowances for non-quantifiable influences, we have preferred to test the results in relation to prices, wages, and the rate of interest. It is possible, as a result, to fit the pattern of rent movement into these long-run series. We showed in figure 10.1 a correlation with prices, albeit with a 15-year time lag reflecting the difficulties of adjusting rents to prices, particularly in generations which favoured long leases. We also found a rough correlation between rent levels and labour costs (fig. 10.3) at least until the late-nineteenth-century agricultural depression. The two series together help us to explain why, in the 1880s and 1890s, farmers sought out small farms. In terms of the prevailing rate of interest as a proxy of commercial investment, relative to changing rent levels, plausible estimates of the rate of return on the two kinds of investment suggest that it was only in the late nineteenth century that investment in land had clearly outlived its usefulness.

In each of these areas the rent index enables us to draw much firmer conclusions than in the past about trends in the national economy. Once we disaggregate the index into different periods we are also able to firm up our understanding of the course of agricultural prosperity from the seventeenth to the early twentieth century. We can be reasonably sure that in the period *c.* 1690–*c.* 1750 there was a slow but significant rise in assessed rents, and that the depression of the 1730s and 1740s was regionally specific, and probably limited to areas of mixed farming on relatively poor soils, like the clays, where it was not easy to adapt to changed economic circumstances. Between the mid-eighteenth century and about 1815 the farming community enjoyed a period of considerable prosperity as grain surpluses turned into grain shortages against a background of rising population. The benefits accrued primarily to tenants. Landlords tried to claw some of them back through enclosure, the conversion of beneficial leases to rack rents and, from the 1790s, the conversion of long leases into tenancies at will. These were sensible economic responses to price trends, and the rent index demonstrates quite clearly the logic that was at work.

The period from 1815 to 1914 embraced three cycles. Farmers and landlords alike struggled initially to adjust to the post-war reversal in the agricultural terms of trade. Tenants complained loudly that their landlords acted too slowly to adjust rents to suit the new conditions. Yet the introspection of the 1830s Parliamentary commissions, with their evidence of falling prices and struggling tenants, can be partially offset by the rent index. The depression and dislocation of the post-1815 period is clear from the index, but not to the degree which the 1830s inquiries suggested. It was an *arable* problem, and it was farmers from the *arable* areas who were most vociferous in their complaints, but the trends in rent from the individual estates do not point clearly to such a sharp division. The index offers a better national picture of the economic impact on farming of the post-war depression, but it also extends an invitation to look closely at individual estate management. Some estates were located in areas and possibly on soils which – if the historiography is correct – should have experienced a more severe depression than actually was the case. Again the rent index shows the prosperity of the middle decades of the nineteenth century, the so-called golden age, as rents rose by about a quarter as a consequence of good farming conditions. Finally, the index reflects the severe problems for both landlords and tenants which set in at the end of the 1870s and which had not really been resolved by 1914. Although the Royal Commission of the 1890s inevitably drew much of its evidence from arable farmers, the index, together with the evidence of rent arrears, suggests that this really was a national crisis on a scale not matched for 200 years.

We now know what happened to the agricultural sector of the English economy between the late seventeenth and the twentieth centuries. While there may still be room for dispute as to the timing and nature of the 'agricultural revolution', the basic trends in terms of rent, prices and labour costs, land prices and the rate of interest, are clearly established.

Sources of the rent index

This appendix sets out the sources from which the rent index was compiled, and establishes for the three source provenances the relative proportions of the materials involved. Part I lists the archival sources from which the data was collected; part II lists material which was originally published in the Minutes of Evidence attached to the *Royal Commission on Agriculture*, 1894–6, and has now been extracted for inclusion in the index; part III lists material collected and collated by other historians in books, articles, and unpublished theses, which have been used in the index; and part IV shows the relative proportion of data from these three sources which make up the index.

The material is named and then listed alphabetically, but the manner of choosing an appropriate name is not regular. In part I the institutional estates – Emanuel and Greenwich hospitals – are listed under their institutional names, but the remainder are listed in the same manner as they have been accessioned in the archives. Usually this means the names registered and by which the individual estates are known, or by which the different collections of large, widely scattered estates, are known. Thus the largest and most famous of the private estates such as Badminton (Duke of Beaufort), Chatsworth (Duke of Devonshire), Holkham (Earl of Leicester), and Tavistock (Duke of Bedford), have been listed alphabetically under those well-known names. They also indicate broad geographical location.

The material collected by the Royal Commission on Agriculture in the 1890s has been collated in part II under two separate lists. The first includes estates which defy a logical method of ordering, including an anonymous estate located in the Andover district of Hampshire, six separate estates under the ownership of the Crown Estates, the widely scattered estate of the Ecclesiastical Commissioners, and the collected material from 69 widely scattered farms. In contrast, in the second part of part II the material from the estates collected and collated by the Royal Commission through its questionnaire survey, as distinct from the evidence provided by individual witnesses, can be ordered more or less in the same way as most of parts I and III have been arranged. They appear alphabetically according to the principal name under which those estates are known, which also indicates geographical location – thus Tavistock, Thorney, and Woburn for the three estates of the Duke of Bedford, Chatsworth for the Duke of Devonshire's principal estate, and others – interleaved with estates located purely by geographical means. A few, however, were described rather imprecisely by county and landowners' names, and in these cases they have been listed under the names of the owners. The exception to this method of ordering in the second part of part II attaches to those estates whose owners chose to remain anonymous when they returned their questionnaires to the Royal Commission. These are collected together at the beginning of the list under the title 'Anon'.

In part III – the listing of estates which have been collated from printed sources – the same general rules have been employed: institutional names for institutionally owned estates, and names indicating how estates are usually known or are usually geographically recognised for the remainder. In the case of most of the institutions there is hardly a more sensible method of listing them since the lands of the Ecclesiastical Commissioners, the Oxford colleges, and St John's College, Cambridge, were spread so widely throughout the English counties as to defy a geographical location. In addition there is a small and relatively unimportant group of mainly anonymous estates which we have simply listed as 'Miscellaneous'.

Bare details of location by county or counties are also included. These are followed by details of the kind of ownership of the different estates – whether private or institutional – and the actual ownership by name of individual, family name, or name of institution. In the case of the Anonymous estates in part II, where possible we have made a reasonable estimate of the likely ownership by cross-referencing with John Bateman, *The Great Landowners of Great Britain and Ireland* (Leicester University Press edn, 1971), and entries in *The Complete Peerage*, 12 volumes (London, 1910–59). The origin of the material for each separate estate is also given, whether in county record offices, private muniments, or printed in published and unpublished sources, with an indication of where other versions of the material, or related material, may be found.

Next we give the precise dates for which the rents assessed and rents received have been extracted and used in the index. Finally we summarise those assessed and received rents (to the nearest £) and the acreages of the individual estates using up to five-year averages around the years indicated. *Note very carefully* however, these are not nominal rents and acreages, but averages. For long runs we have taken these summaries at 40-year intervals, but we have taken them more frequently where it is necessary to demonstrate the inflation of rents during the French wars and the decline in rents thereafter. Because the late-nineteenth-century depression is so important in British agricultural history we have summarised the data at more frequent intervals, at times every ten years.

Part I   Estate records

Adwick

LOCATION   Yorkshire, West Riding

OWNER   Private, the Pierrepont family, Earls and Dukes of Kingston (to 1773) and Earls Manvers (from 1806), Thoresby Park, Ollerton, Nottinghamshire

SOURCE   Nottingham University Manuscripts Department – hereafter NUMD–MaS178, MaS179, MaS182, M4537, M4547

DATES
Assessed   1733–89, 1808–9
Received   1733–89, 1808–9

FACTS	1740	1780
Rent assessed (£s)	523	523
Rent received (£s)	491	523
Acreage	1,001	1,001

Ancaster

LOCATION   Lincolnshire

OWNER   Private, the Bertie family, Earls of Ancaster, Grimsthorpe Castle, near Bourne, Lincolnshire, and Normanton Park, Rutland

SOURCE   Lincolnshire AO – 3/ANC 4/10–12, 15 and 3/ANC 6/27, 40–88, 242–91

CROSS-REFERENCE   See also Ancaster in part II

DATES
Assessed   1793–94, 1802–7, 1810–23, 1825–42, 1844–96
Received   1818–24, 1827–30, 1832–43, 1845–66, 1868, 1871–3, 1875–97

FACTS	1800	1820	1860	1880	1890
Rent assessed (£s)	17,773	24,487	24,258	27,876	22,657
Rent received (£s)	—	23,480	23,947	26,177	21,162
Acreage	18,112	18,480	16,662	16,662	16,662

Ancaster

LOCATION   Rutland

OWNER   Earls of Ancaster

SOURCE   Lincolnshire AO – 3/ANC 4/10–12, 15 and 3/ANC 6/27, 40–88, 242–307

CROSS REFERENCE   See also Ancaster in part II

DATES
Assessed   1814–23, 1825–42, 1844–1905
Received   1817–22, 1826–30, 1832–6, 1837–42, 1844–67, 1870–2,
              1874–1904

FACTS	1820	1860	1880	1900
Rent assessed (£s)	11,952	18,507	20,001	15,270
Rent received (£s)	11,233	18,517	18,544	11,950
Acreage	12,059	13,048	12,920	12,920

Ashburnham

LOCATION   East Sussex

OWNER   Private, the Ashburnham family, Earls of Ashburnham, Ashburnham Place, Battle, East Sussex

SOURCE   East Sussex RO – ASH 1640–1792, 1193–1202, 1170–3

DATES
Assessed   1769–1836, 1838–72, 1874–5, 1878–91, 1893–1914
Received   1769–1836, 1838–91, 1893–1914

FACTS	1780	1820	1860	1880	1900	1910
Rent assessed (£s)	3,705	7,235	8,625	10,363	8,619	9,221
Rent received (£s)	2,880	6,479	8,375	9,329	8,828	9,248
Acreage	8,019	8,516	8,778	10,016	10,016	10,016

Badminton

LOCATION   Gloucestershire

OWNER   Private, the Somerset family, Dukes of Beaufort, Badminton
House, near Chippenham, Wiltshire

SOURCE   Gloucestershire RO and Badminton House – D2700,
QB3/1/1–3; PB 3/13

DATES
Assessed   1724–1914
Received   1724–1914

FACTS	1740	1780	1820	1860	1880
Rent assessed (£s)	1,655	3,403	14,162	15,649	17,053
Rent received (£s)	1,467	3,320	12,768	16,205	16,653
Acreage	12,000	12,000	12,000	12,000	12,000

	1900	1910
	12,381	14,937
	12,960	14,794
	12,000	12,000

Barking Hall

LOCATION   Suffolk

OWNER   Earls of Ashburnham

SOURCE   Suffolk RO, Ipswich – HA1/HB2/2–193

DATES
Assessed   1790–6, 1798–9, 1801–25, 1828–32, 1834–74,
                1878–1908, 1910–12
Received   1790–6, 1798–9, 1801–19, 1821–5, 1828–32, 1834–74,
                1879-1908, 1910–12

FACTS	1800	1820	1860	1880	1900	1910
Rent assessed (£s)	2,397	3,545	4,586	5,349	3,407	2,433
Rent received (£s)	2,379	3,154	4,199	4,784	2,983	2,671
Acreage	3,117	3,256	3,422	3,429	3,424	3,423

Beighton

LOCATION   Yorkshire, West Riding, and Derbyshire

OWNER   Earl Manvers

SOURCE   NUMD – Ma 4538 and all even numbers to 4618, 4623, 4625, 4627, 4637, 4638, Ma/6a unnumbered volumes

CROSS-REFERENCE   G. E. Mingay, 'Landownership and agrarian trends in the eighteenth century' (University of Nottingham, PhD thesis, 1958)

DATES
Assessed   1733–6, 1741–70, 1773–80, 1789–1911
Received   1733–5, 1741–70, 1773–9, 1789–1911

FACTS	1740	1780	1820	1860	1880	1900	1910
Rent assessed (£s)	2,925	2,053	6,980	5,996	6,848	5,388	5,680
Rent received (£s)	2,919	1,948	6,971	6,007	6,617	5,418	5,672
Acreage	4,248	4,248	4,248	4,248	4,248	4,248	4,248

Bolton Abbey

LOCATION   Yorkshire, West Riding

OWNER   Private, the Cavendish family, Dukes of Devonshire, of Chatsworth House, Bakewell, Derbyshire

SOURCE   Chatsworth House – BAS 7/1–4, 8/1–14, 22/1–18, 25/1–5, 26/1–5, 27/1–2, 28/1–4, 29/1–4, 30/1–3, 49/1–5, 50/1–5, 51/1–6, 52/1–6, 61/1–10, 62/1–10, 63/1–13, 64/1–14, 70/1–4

CROSS-REFERENCE   See also Bolton Abbey in part II

DATES
Assessed   1759–1914
Received   1759–1868, 1871–9, 1881–1914

FACTS	1760	1780	1820	1860	1880	1900	1910
Rent assessed (£s)	2,066	3,015	4,859	7,853	12,124	9,530	9,874
Rent received (£s)	2,043	2,993	4,864	7,837	11,966	9,459	9,871
Acreage	10,382	10,515	11,010	11,570	14,303	14,212	14,628

Bradford

LOCATION   Wiltshire

OWNER   Earl Manvers

SOURCE   NUMD – Ma2D35/4/3, MaR214–220, MaR227, MaR Wilts 1852, 1862, 1872

DATES
Assessed   1827–72
Received   1827–72

FACTS	1840	1860	1870
Rent assessed (£s)	1,730	1,580	1,734
Rent received (£s)	1,730	1,580	1,734
Acreage	1,306	1,306	1,306

Broadlands

LOCATION   Hampshire

OWNER   Private, the Mount-Temple family, Lord Mount-Temple, Broadlands, Romsey, Hampshire

SOURCE   Southampton University Library – BR1–5, 106, 108, 120

DATES
Assessed   1757, 1760–1, 1764–6, 1776–81, 1783–1801, 1803–6,
             1813, 1816–18, 1831, 1833, 1835, 1856, 1859, 1865,
             1872, 1877–82, 1884, 1886–98, 1904–5, 1907–14
Received   1746, 1749–50, 1760–2, 1764–6, 1771–81, 1783–5,
             1787–1804, 1819–22, 1831, 1833, 1835, 1856, 1859,
             1865, 1872, 1875, 1877–98, 1902, 1904–5, 1907–14

FACTS

	1760	1780	1820	1860	1880	1900	1910
Rent assessed (£s)	1,018	962	2,429	4,372	5,858	4,436	4,436
Rent received (£s)	989	944	2,283	3,477	5,271	4,381	4,553
Acreage	2,500	2,500	2,800	2,800	4,500	4,500	4,500

Brocklesby

LOCATION   Lincolnshire

OWNER   Private, the Anderson-Pelham family, Earls of Yarborough, Brocklesby Park, Ulceby, Lincolnshire

SOURCE   Lincolnshire AO – YARB 5/2/1/7–8, 5/2/2/1–37, 5/2/4/1, 5/2/8/1–5

DATES
Assessed   1851–1914
Received   1856–8, 1862–3, 1865–9, 1871–3, 1875–9, 1881–1900

FACTS	1860	1880	1900	1910
Rent assessed (£s)	66,335	73,391	47,801	47,511
Rent received (£s)	65,947	65,563	52,083	43,930
Acreage	50,277	50,277	43,514	43,514

Castle Howard

LOCATION   Yorkshire, North and East Ridings

OWNER   Private, the Howard family, Earls of Carlisle, Castle Howard, Malton, Yorkshire

SOURCE   Castle Howard House – CHA F4/6/1–96, F4/8/1–18, F4/9/1–60, F5/5/45–68, F8/34/1–15

DATES
Assessed   1690–7, 1699, 1701–10, 1716–19, 1721–2, 1724–40,
                1743–7, 1750–8, 1770–94, 1796–1809, 1811–68,
                1870–88, 1891–1914
Received   1690–7, 1699, 1701–10, 1716–19, 1721–2, 1724–40,
                1743–6, 1750–7, 1770–2, 1774–94, 1796–1809, 1811–68,
                1870–88, 1891–1914

FACTS

	1700	1740	1780	1820	1860
Rent assessed (£s)	1,012	2,625	5,921	11,567	12,828
Rent received (£s)	1,120	2,625	5,824	11,375	12,166
Acreage	6,562	6,562	11,389	11,169	13,709

FACTS	1880	1900	1910
Rent assessed (£s)	12,266	10,301	11,129
Rent received (£s)	11,055	11,003	10,161
Acreage	13,709	13,709	13,709

Chatsworth

LOCATION   Derbyshire

OWNER   Duke of Devonshire

SOURCE   Chatsworth House – Accounts accessioned by year

CROSS-REFERENCE   See Chatsworth in part II

DATES
Assessed   1820, 1823, 1828–1914
Received   1820, 1823, 1828–1914

FACTS	1820	1860	1880	1900	1910
Rent assessed (£s)	7,819	11,230	14,326	12,410	12,082
Rent received (£s)	7,414	11,593	14,138	12,380	12,077
Acreage	14,027	14,027	14,027	14,027	14,027

Chevening

LOCATION   Kent and Surrey

OWNER   Private, the Stanhope family, Earls Stanhope, Chevening, Sevenoaks, Kent

SOURCE   Centre for Kentish Studies, Maidstone – U 1590 A1/1, E8/1–71, E10/1–2

DATES
Assessed   1724–35, 1754, 1778–1815, 1817–51, 1855–74, 1876–1914
Received   1746–61, 1764, 1778–1815, 1817–51, 1855–74, 1876–1914

FACTS	1730	1760	1780	1820	1860
Rent assessed (£s)	1,199	—	1,342	2,237	2,614
Rent received (£s)	—	674	632	933	2,590
Acreage	3,500	3,500	3,500	3,500	3,700

FACTS	1880	1900	1910
Rent assessed (£s)	3,471	3,865	4,501
Rent received (£s)	3,455	3,976	4,449
Acreage	3,902	4,311	4,311

Cholmondeley

LOCATION   Cheshire

OWNER   Private, the Cholmondeley family, Marquesses of Cholmondeley, Cholmondeley Castle, Nantwich, Cheshire

SOURCE   Cheshire RO – DCH QQ/2/1–4, QQ/7/1–33, QQ/3/15,41–63

CROSS-REFERENCE   See also Anon (? Cholmondeley) in part II

DATES
Assessed   1791–7, 1800–13, 1815–92, 1894–1900
Received   1854–92, 1894–1900

FACTS	1800	1820	1860	1880	1900
Rent assessed (£s)	9,180	15,636	23,782	29,527	26,028
Rent received (£s)	—	—	22,950	28,571	26,361
Acreage	12,603	12,603	12,603	12,603	12,603

Cockermouth

LOCATION   Cumberland

OWNER   Private, the Wyndham family, Lords Leconfield, Petworth House, Sussex

SOURCE   Petworth House – PHA 4296–4337

DATES
Assessed   1860–1901
Received   1860–1901

FACTS	1860	1880	1890	1900
Rent assessed (£s)	1,426	2,665	2,275	1,891
Rent received (£s)	1,375	2,625	2,313	1,631
Acreage	1,391	4,017	4,092	1,955

Cornwallis

LOCATION   Kent and Sussex

OWNER   Private, the Mann-Cornwallis family, Linton Park, Kent

SOURCE   Centre for Kentish Studies, Maidstone – U24 A2/1–43, A4/1–5

DATES
Assessed   1815–44, 1846–50, 1884–92, 1894–1902, 1904–14
Received   1815–21, 1823–5, 1827–43, 1846–50, 1885–92,
              1894–1902, 1904–14

FACTS	1820	1840	1890	1900	1910
Rent assessed (£s)	8,386	6,576	16,190	12,788	11,877
Rent received (£s)	9,218	6,633	16,808	12,541	12,001
Acreage	10,248	9,469	12,030	10,377	9,524

Dalemain

LOCATION   Cumberland and Westmorland

OWNER   Private, the Hasell family, Dalemain, Penrith, Cumberland

SOURCE   Dalemain House – unnumbered volumes

DATES
Assessed   1825–94
Received   —

FACTS	1840	1860	1870	1880	1890
Rent assessed (£s)	1,319	1,430	1,528	1,671	1,460
Rent received (£s)	—	—	—	—	—
Acreage	2,540	2,540	2,540	2,540	2,540

Dytchley

LOCATION   Oxfordshire

OWNER   Private, the Lee-Dillon family, Viscounts Dillon, Dytchley Park,
Charlbury, Oxfordshire

SOURCE   Oxfordshire RO – DIL I/1/3, 5, 9a–n, 35–75, 99a–e

DATES
Assessed   1861–1914
Received   1861–1914

FACTS	1860	1880	1890	1900	1910
Rent assessed (£s)	4,713	4,310	2,330	2,237	2,451
Rent received (£s)	4,779	4,068	2,280	2,258	2,545
Acreage	3,913	4,071	4,110	4,110	4,110

Emanuel Hospital

LOCATION   Yorkshire, East Riding

OWNER   Institutional, Emanuel Hospital, London, re. Brandesburton

SOURCE   Corporation of London RO – EH 115F – Cash Books, Ledgers, Agent's Accounts; EH Box 3.8, 3.10, 7.1–4,

DATES
Assessed   —
Received   1695–1914

FACTS	1700	1740	1780	1820	1860
Rent assessed (£s)	—	—	—	—	—
Rent received (£s)	371	360	1,023	3,063	2,916
Acreage	3,170	3,170	3,170	3,170	3,170

	1880	1900	1910
	—	—	—
	3,287	2,713	2,913
	3,170	3,170	3,170

Greenwich Hospital

LOCATION   Northumberland and Cumberland

OWNER   Institutional, Greenwich Hospital, London

SOURCE   Public RO, Kew – ADM79 3–9

CROSS-REFERENCE   W. M. Hughes, 'Lead, land and coal as sources of landlords' income in Northumberland between 1700–1850' (University of Newcastle, PhD thesis, 1963)

DATES
Assessed   1735–1863
Received   —

FACTS	1740	1780	1820	1860
Rent assessed (£s)	5,877	12,344	36,024	29,916
Rent received (£s)	—	—	—	—
Acreage	33,007	35,212	41,110	38,177

Hackwood

LOCATION   Hampshire

OWNER   Private, the Orde-Powlett family, Lord Bolton, Hackwood House, Basingstoke, Hampshire

SOURCE   Hampshire RO – 11M49 70/1–7

DATES
Assessed   —
Received   1860–1905, 1907–8

FACTS	1860	1880	1890	1900
Rent assessed (£s)	—	—	—	—
Rent received (£s)	7,621	6,895	5,211	5,644
Acreage	8,040	8,040	8,040	8,040

Higham Ferrers

LOCATION   Northamptonshire

OWNER   Private, the Wentworth-Fitzwilliam family, Earls Fitzwilliam, Milton Park, Peterborough, Northamptonshire

SOURCE   Northamptonshire RO – F(WW) 74–142 and unnumbered

DATES
Assessed   1750–61, 1763–79, 1781–97, 1799–1828, 1830–45,
                  1847–72, 1874–1903
Received   1750–61, 1763–79, 1781–97, 1799–1828, 1830–45,
                  1847–72, 1874–1903

FACTS	1760	1780	1820	1860	1880	1890	1900
Rent assessed (£s)	3,016	3,435	5,719	8,247	7,711	6,222	4,305
Rent received (£s)	2,660	2,326	5,736	7,698	6,482	5,874	4,126
Acreage	4,500	4,500	4,500	4,500	4,500	4,500	4,500

Holker

LOCATION Lancashire

OWNER Duke of Devonshire

SOURCE Lancashire RO – DDCa 1/145–325

DATES
Assessed   1836–75, 1877, 1879–81, 1883, 1885, 1887–1907
Received   1846–75, 1877, 1879–81, 1883, 1885, 1887–1907

FACTS	1840	1860	1880	1890	1900
Rent assessed (£s)	2,775	3,557	5,274	4,826	4,965
Rent received (£s)	—	3,514	5,274	5,075	4,961
Acreage	4,920	4,920	5,920	4,920	5,920

Holkham

LOCATION Norfolk

OWNER Private, the Coke family, Earls of Leicester, Holkham Park, Wells, Norfolk

SOURCE Bodleian Library – microfilm 686–91

CROSS-REFERENCE See also R. A. C. Parker, *Coke of Norfolk: A Financial and Agricultural Study 1707–1842* (Oxford, 1975); S. Wade Martins, *A Great Estate at Work: The Holkham Estate and its Inhabitants in the Nineteenth Century* (Cambridge, 1980); P. Roe, 'Norfolk agriculture 1815–1914' (University of East Anglia, MPhil thesis, 1976)

DATES
Assessed   1775–1900
Received   1775–1900

FACTS	1780	1820	1860	1880	1900
Rent assessed (£s)	13,608	31,738	50,190	57,054	32,052
Rent received (£s)	13,319	31,479	50,241	57,817	32,343
Acreage	23,000	23,000	37,000	37,000	37,000

Holme Pierrepont

LOCATION   Nottinghamshire

OWNER   Earl Manvers

SOURCE   NUMD – as for Beighton above

CROSS-REFERENCE   Mingay, 'Landownership and agrarian trends'

DATES
Assessed   1733–70, 1773–80, 1789–1860, 1901–11
Received   1733–70, 1773–9, 1789–1860, 1901–11

FACTS	1740	1780	1820	1860	1900	1910
Rent assessed (£s)	5,557	6,277	18,323	18,373	16,358	16,025
Rent received (£s)	5,564	6,057	18,323	18,374	16,245	16,372
Acreage	10,443	10,443	10,443	10,443	10,443	10,443

Knowsley

LOCATION   Lancashire and Cheshire

OWNER   Private, the Smith-Stanley family, Earls of Derby, Knowsley
Park, Prescot, Lancashire

SOURCE   Lancashire RO – DDK 2020/1–56

DATES
Assessed   1803–36
Received   1787–93, 1795–7, 1799–1837

FACTS	1800	1820
Rent assessed (£s)	—	18,215
Rent received (£s)	6,816	17,285
Acreage	20,150	20,150

Leconfield

LOCATION   Yorkshire, East Riding

OWNER   Lord Leconfield

SOURCE   Petworth House – PHA 4105–259

DATES
Assessed   1797–1846, 1848–52, 1855–69, 1871–1914
Received   1797–1846, 1848–52, 1855–69, 1871–1914

FACTS	1800	1820	1860	1880	1890	1900	1910
Rent assessed (£s)	17,966	31,374	31,564	37,189	29,993	27,436	29,289
Rent received (£s)	17,956	31,423	31,564	36,767	30,179	27,463	29,241
Acreage	24,377	25,607	25,269	25,805	25,849	25,809	25,789

Lilford

LOCATION   Northamptonshire

OWNER   Private, the Powys family, Lilford Hall, Oundle,
Northamptonshire

SOURCE   Northamptonshire RO – POW3-6

DATES
Assessed   1741–81
Received   1741–65, 1767–81

FACTS	1740	1780
Rent assessed (£s)	993	2,382
Rent received (£s)	879	2,323
Acreage	1,772	3,032

Lincolnshire, Crowle, and Basingthorpe

LOCATION   Lincolnshire and Yorkshire, East Riding

OWNER   Earl Manvers

SOURCE   NUMD – as for Beighton above, and MaA119/120–37

CROSS-REFERENCE   Mingay, 'Landownership and agrarian trends'

DATES
Assessed   1733–70, 1773–80, 1783–1875, 1877, 1879–83,
                  1885–1911
Received   1733–70, 1773–80, 1783–1875, 1877, 1879–83,
                  1885–1911

FACTS	1740	1780	1820	1860	1880
Rent assessed (£s)	2,695	1,627	5,584	5,399	6,339
Rent received (£s)	2,991	1,627	6,085	5,385	6,301
Acreage	6,291	3,969	4,530	4,530	4,530

	1890	1900	1910
	4,616	4,237	4,331
	4,721	4,331	4,521
	4,530	4,530	4,530

Longleat

LOCATION   Wiltshire and Somerset

OWNER   Private, the Thynne family, Marquesses of Bath, Longleat House, Warminster, Wiltshire

SOURCE   Longleat House – 10G, 11G, 12A, 14D

CROSS-REFERENCE   D. P. Gunstone, 'Stewardship and landed society: a study of the stewards of the Longleat estate, 1779–1895' (University of Exeter, MA thesis, 1972)

DATES
Assessed   1864–1914
Received   1839–44, 1846–1914

FACTS	1840	1860	1880	1900	1910
Rent assessed (£s)	—	—	40,486	39,647	41,824
Rent received (£s)	15,605	24,934	38,918	39,374	41,615
Acreage	15,463	19,651	24,493	27,775	28,933

Maxstoke

LOCATION   Warwickshire and Staffordshire

OWNER   Private, the Fetherston-Dilke family, Maxstoke Castle, Warwickshire

SOURCE   Maxstoke Castle – unnumbered volumes

DATES
Assessed   1787–1807, 1809–42, 1853–72
Received   1787–1807, 1809–20, 1822–72

FACTS	1800	1820	1860
Rent assessed (£s)	2,017	3,055	4,187
Rent received (£s)	1,781	2,535	4,389
Acreage	3,004	3,004	3,004

Milton

LOCATION   Northamptonshire and Huntingdonshire

OWNER   Earl Fitzwilliam

SOURCE   Northamptonshire RO – F(M) Milton Estate Rentals
1791–1906

DATES
Assessed   1792, 1796–1817, 1822, 1827, 1829–46, 1848–56,
                1860–73, 1875–1907
Received   1796–1816, 1829–46, 1848–56, 1860–73, 1875–1907

FACTS	1800	1820	1860	1880	1900
Rent assessed (£s)	8,111	14,912	24,849	24,754	15,251
Rent received (£s)	7,998	—	23,623	21,203	14,354
Acreage	10,500	10,500	10,333	10,500	10,500

Petworth

LOCATION   Sussex

OWNER   Lord Leconfield

SOURCE   Petworth House – PHA 4105–259

DATES
Assessed   1801–68, 1879–1900, 1902–14
Received   1789–1900, 1902–14

FACTS	1800	1820	1860	1880	1900	1910
Rent assessed (£s)	8,576	13,808	21,170	27,984	19,376	21,020
Rent received (£s)	8,129	12,321	19,216	25,421	19,248	21,298
Acreage	29,720	29,720	29,720	29,720	27,099	28,342

Rushmore

LOCATION   Dorset and Wiltshire

OWNER   Private, the Pitt-Rivers family, Rushmore Lodge, Salisbury, Wiltshire

SOURCE   Dorset RO – D/PIT/E135–7, 189–205, 208–10, 212–26

DATES
Assessed   1850–60, 1862–3, 1868–9, 1871–2, 1877–8, 1881–1900
Received   1850–60, 1862–3, 1868–9, 1871–2, 1881–1900

FACTS	1860	1880	1890	1900
Rent assessed (£s)	25,906	29,829	24,216	26,410
Rent received (£s)	23,327	27,037	28,073	22,296
Acreage	18,979	22,626	22,626	22,626

Tavistock

LOCATION   Devon and Cornwall

OWNER   Private, the Russell family, Dukes of Bedford, Woburn Abbey, Bedfordshire

SOURCE   Devon RO – T1258 M/ER 1–127

CROSS-REFERENCE   See also Tavistock in part II

DATES
Assessed   1786–1841, 1844–1911
Received   1786–1841, 1844–1911

FACTS	1800	1820	1860	1880	1900	1910
Rent assessed (£s)	4,240	8,138	10,269	16,863	14,569	14,449
Rent received (£s)	3,934	8,056	10,295	14,288	14,641	14,538
Acreage	6,168	7,395	9,781	13,060	12,779	12,728

Thoresby

LOCATION   Nottinghamshire

OWNER   Earl Manvers

SOURCE   NUMD – as for Beighton above

CROSS-REFERENCE   Mingay, 'Landownership and agrarian trends'

DATES
Assessed   1733–6, 1741–59, 1761–70, 1773–80, 1789–99, 1901–11
Received   1733–5, 1741–58, 1761–70, 1773–9, 1789–99, 1901–11

FACTS	1740	1780	1820	1860	1880	1900	1910
Rent assessed (£s)	3,911	4,214	13,729	12,082	15,004	10,919	10,824
Rent received (£s)	4,128	4,076	13,777	12,014	14,392	11,721	11,124
Acreage	11,720	11,720	11,720	11,720	11,720	11,720	11,720

Thorndon

LOCATION   Essex

OWNER   Private, the Petre family, Lord Petre, Thorndon Hall,
Brentwood, Essex

SOURCE   Essex RO – D/DP M1595, A68, 90, 91, 127, 148–9, 249–61,
303 and all odd numbers to 325, 340–3, 381, 383, 390, 392, 394, 395 and
all odd numbers to 425, 462–8

DATES
Assessed   1791–1830, 1832–44, 1846–82, 1885–1905, 1907,
                  1909–14
Received   1791–1830, 1832–44, 1846–83, 1886–1905, 1907,
                  1909–14

FACTS	1800	1820	1860	1880	1900	1910
Rent assessed (£s)	8,613	18,105	13,754	16,670	14,543	15,875
Rent received (£s)	8,641	16,752	13,280	14,870	13,994	15,266
Acreage	15,000	15,000	15,000	15,000	15,000	15,000

Trewithen

LOCATION   Cornwall

OWNER   Private, the Hawkins family, Trewithen, Probus, Cornwall

SOURCE   Cornwall RO – DD J 589–94, 596–602, 607–72, 676–7

DATES
Assessed   1841–1905, 1907–8
Received   1841–1908

FACTS	1840	1860	1880	1900	1910
Rent assessed (£s)	4,227	6,625	8,523	8,639	7,001
Rent received (£s)	3,968	6,557	8,092	9,182	7,989
Acreage	5,292	7,399	8,693	8,970	7,684

Wallop

LOCATION   Hampshire

OWNER   Private, the Orde-Powlett family, Lord Bolton, Hackwood Park, Basingstoke, Hampshire

SOURCE   Hampshire RO – 11M49 70/1–7

DATES
Assessed   —
Received   1860–1905, 1907–11

FACTS	1860	1880	1890	1900	1910
Rent assessed (£s)	—	—	—	—	—
Rent received (£s)	1,623	1,511	831	603	1,393
Acreage	3,142	3,142	3,142	3,142	3,142

Wilton

LOCATION   Wiltshire

OWNER   Private, the Herbert Family, Earls of Pembroke, Wilton House, Salisbury, Wiltshire

SOURCE   Wiltshire RO – A1 2057/A1/69–104

CROSS-REFERENCE   See also F. M. L. Thompson, 'Agriculture since 1870', in Victoria County History, *Wiltshire*, IV (London, 1959)

DATES
Assessed   1850–88
Received   1850–88

FACTS	1860	1870	1880	1890
Rent assessed (£s)	40,772	44,044	38,368	24,659
Rent received (£s)	35,018	37,712	31,661	23,490
Acreage	37,772	37,854	34,087	33,169

Part II The Royal Commission on Agriculture 1894–6

The following have been extracted from the Royal Commission on Agriculture, 'First Report of her Majesty's Commissioners appointed to Inquire into the Subject of Agricultural Depression. Minutes of Evidence with Appendices', *BPP*, C. 7400–1, XVI, parts I to III (1894).

Andover

LOCATION   Hampshire

OWNER   Anonymous owners of an estate in the Andover District of Hampshire

SOURCE   Royal Commission, Appendix G

DATES
Assessed   —
Received   1866–1893

FACTS	1870	1880	1890
Rent assessed (£s)	—	—	—
Rent received (£s)	7,769	6,875	5,020
Acreage	7,640	7,640	7,584

Crown Estate – Six estates as follows

SOURCE   Royal Commission, Appendix A, Table III

Crown Estate I

LOCATION   Bedfordshire, Stagsden estate

DATES
Assessed   1888–91
Received   1888–93

FACTS	1890
Rent assessed (£s)	2,176
Rent received (£s)	2,498
Acreage	3,363

Crown Estate II

LOCATION   Essex, Hainault and Stapleford Abbots estates

DATES
Assessed   1888–91
Received   1888–93

FACTS   1890
Rent assessed (£s) 5,543
Rent received (£s) 5,751
Acreage   4,014

Crown Estate III

LOCATION   Lincolnshire, Billingborough estate

DATES
Assessed   1888–91
Received   1888–93

FACTS   1890
Rent assessed (£s) 5,428
Rent received (£s) 5,596
Acreage   4,017

Crown Estate IV

LOCATION   Wiltshire, Bishops Cannings and Bromham estates

DATES
Assessed   1888–91
Received   1888–93

FACTS   1890
Rent assessed (£s) 5,999
Rent received (£s) 6,502
Acreage   8,915

Crown Estate V

LOCATION   Yorkshire, East Riding, Sunk Island estate

DATES
Assessed   1888–91
Received   1888–93

FACTS   1890
Rent assessed (£s) 9,680
Rent received (£s) 9,993
Acreage   6,600

Crown Estate VI

LOCATION   Yorkshire, West Riding, Boroughbridge estate

DATES
Assessed   1888–91
Received   1888–93

FACTS   1890
Rent assessed (£s) 4,575
Rent received (£s) 4,533
Acreage   3,345

Ecclesiastical Commissioners

LOCATION   Most English counties

OWNER   Ecclesiastical Commissioners of England, Whitehall Place, London

SOURCE   Royal Commission, Appendix A, table VII

CROSS-REFERENCE   See also Ecclesiastical Commissioners in part III

DATES
Assessed   1880–92
Received   1880–92

FACTS	1880	1890
Rent assessed (£s)	326,965	309,937
Rent received (£s)	290,916	290,701
Acreage	226,533	275,152

'Farms'

LOCATION   14 counties throughout England

OWNER   Private owners of 69 tenant farms

SOURCE   Royal Commission, C. 8541, XV (1897), Appendix III, Table II

DATES
Assessed   —
Received   1875–94

FACTS   1880   1890
Rent assessed (£s) —   —
Rent received (£s) 7,056   23,785
Acreage   5,587   24,338

All of the following are private estates and can be found in the Royal Commission on Agriculture, 'Particulars of the Expenditures and Outgoings on Certain Estates in Great Britain and Farm Accounts Reprinted from the Reports of the Assistant Commissioners', C. 8125, XVI (1896).

Anon

LOCATION   Cheshire

OWNER   Probably the Marquess of Cholmondeley

CROSS-REFERENCE   See also Cholmondeley in part 1

DATES
Assessed   1872–92
Received   1872–92

FACTS   1870   1880   1890
Rent assessed (£s) 30,920   34,779   32,575
Rent received (£s) 30,688   34,417   32,122
Acreage   15,922   15,922   15,922

Anon

LOCATION   Norfolk

OWNER   Probably the Earl of Leicester

CROSS-REFERENCE   See also Holkham in part 1

DATES
Assessed   —
Received   1842, 1852, 1862, 1872–92

FACTS	1860	1870	1880	1890
Rent assessed (£s)	—	—	—	—
Rent received (£s)	52,640	57,376	55,091	45,082
Acreage	43,571	44,058	44,953	45,192

Anon

LOCATION   Northumberland

OWNER   Probably either the Duke of Portland, or Sir Matthew Ridley, Blagdon, Morpeth

DATES
Assessed   1872–92
Received   1872–92

FACTS	1870	1880	1890
Rent assessed (£s)	8,874	9,195	8,484
Rent received (£s)	8,758	8,599	8,066
Acreage	11,510	10,722	11,153

Anon

LOCATION   Nottingham, Derby, Lincoln, and Worcester

OWNER   Probably the Cavendish-Bentinck family, Dukes of Portland, Welbeck Abbey, Worksop, Nottinghamshire

DATES
Assessed   1881–92
Received   1881–92

FACTS	1880	1890
Rent assessed (£s)	39,985	34,033
Rent received (£s)	33,247	28,943
Acreage	44,886	45,803

Anon

LOCATION   Suffolk

OWNER   Because of the small size of this estate it is impossible to make any kind of guess at its identity from Bateman

DATES
Assessed   1872–92
Received   1872–92

FACTS	1870	1880	1890
Rent assessed (£s)	3,878	4,083	2,913
Rent received (£s)	3,878	4,083	2,891
Acreage	2,712	2,712	2,712

Anon

LOCATION   Suffolk

OWNER   Probably either the Hervey family, Marquesses of Bristol, Ickworth Park, Bury St Edmunds, or the Vanneck family, Lords Huntingfield, Heveningham Hall, Yoxford

DATES
Assessed   1872–92
Received   1872–92

FACTS	1870	1880	1890
Rent assessed (£s)	20,208	20,755	14,786
Rent received (£s)	20,149	20,428	12,460
Acreage	15,002	15,277	11,696

Anon

LOCATION   Suffolk

OWNER   Because there are too many Suffolk estates of about this size listed in Bateman it is impossible to make any kind of guess at the identity

DATES
Assessed   1872–92
Received   1872–92

FACTS	1870	1880	1890
Rent assessed (£s)	9,253	8,438	5,559
Rent received (£s)	9,850	8,512	5,964
Acreage	6,146	6,146	5,546

Anon

LOCATION   Yorkshire (? North and West Riding)

OWNER   Probably the Lascelles family, Earls of Harewood, Harewood House, near Leeds

DATES
Assessed   1872–92
Received   1872–92

FACTS	1870	1880	1890
Rent assessed (£s)	37,315	37,187	31,706
Rent received (£s)	37,245	34,553	31,369
Acreage	28,221	28,062	28,158

Ancaster

LOCATION   Lincolnshire and Rutland

OWNER   Earl of Ancaster

CROSS-REFERENCE   See also Ancaster in part I

DATES
Assessed   1852, 1862, 1872–92
Received   1852, 1862, 1872–92

FACTS	1860	1870	1880	1890
Rent assessed (£s)	44,654	86,684	83,579	66,538
Rent received (£s)	44,707	86,327	76,095	60,462
Acreage	28,643	53,258	51,779	46,218

From the manuscript source listed in part I it was possible to separate the Lincolnshire portion of the estate from the Rutland portion, and therefore it is the manuscript source which has been employed in the rent index

Bective

LOCATION   Westmorland

OWNER   The Taylour family, Earls of Bective (Irish peerage), Underley Hall, Kirkby Lonsdale

DATES
Assessed   1872–92
Received   1872–92

FACTS	1870	1880	1890
Rent assessed (£s)	16,497	23,652	21,642
Rent received (£s)	16,496	23,722	21,614
Acreage	15,810	20,635	22,398

Bolton Abbey

LOCATION   Yorkshire, West Riding

OWNER   Duke of Devonshire

CROSS-REFERENCE   See also Bolton Abbey in part 1

DATES
Assessed   1880–92
Received   1880–92

FACTS	1880	1890
Rent assessed (£s)	12,220	9,947
Rent received (£s)	11,702	9,277
Acreage	14,315	13,848

Because the material listed in part 1 includes a long run of rents it has been preferred in the rent index

Chatsworth

LOCATION   Derbyshire

OWNER   Duke of Devonshire

CROSS-REFERENCE   See also Chatsworth in part 1

DATES
Assessed   1880–92
Received   1880–92

FACTS	1880	1890
Rent assessed (£s)	13,323	12,522
Rent received (£s)	13,111	11,803
Acreage	12,313	12,176

Because the material listed in part 1 includes a long run of rents it has been preferred in the rent index

Eaton

LOCATION   Cheshire

OWNER   The Grosvenor family, Dukes of Westminster, Eaton Hall, near
Chester

DATES
Assessed   —
Received   1883–92

FACTS	1890
Rent assessed (£s)	—
Rent received (£s)	26,462
Acreage	14,316

Fitzhardinge I

LOCATION   Gloucestershire

OWNER   The Berkeley family, Lords Fitzhardinge, Berkeley Castle,
Gloucestershire

DATES
Assessed   1842, 1852, 1862, 1872–92
Received   1842, 1852, 1862, 1872–92

FACTS	1840	1860	1880	1890
Rent assessed (£s)	30,102	34,554	37,615	35,984
Rent received (£s)	28,921	34,412	34,001	31,681
Acreage	17,209	17,209	17,245	17,624

Fitzhardinge II

LOCATION   Middlesex

OWNER   Lord Fitzhardinge

DATES
Assessed   1872–92
Received   1872–92

FACTS	1870	1880	1890
Rent assessed (£s)	1,360	1,376	1,481
Rent received (£s)	1,360	1,355	1,439
Acreage	588	588	588

For reasons stated in chapter 8 this small estate is not included in the rent index

Goodwood

LOCATION   Sussex

OWNER   The Gordon-Lennox family, Dukes of Richmond and Gordon, Goodwood Park, near Chichester, Sussex

DATES
Assessed   1873–92
Received   1873–92

FACTS	1880	1890
Rent assessed (£s)	18,550	17,800
Rent received (£s)	17,070	13,448
Acreage	14,111	13,004

Haklyn

LOCATION   Flintshire

OWNER   Duke of Westminster

DATES
Assessed   1883–92
Received   1883–92

FACTS	1890
Rent assessed (£s)	2,969
Rent received (£s)	2,459
Acreage	2,408

Hardwick

LOCATION   Derbyshire

OWNER   Duke of Devonshire

DATES
Assessed   1881–92
Received   1881–92

FACTS	1880	1890
Rent assessed (£s)	11,304	9,797
Rent received (£s)	10,191	9,396
Acreage	7,202	7,168

Jervaulx Abbey

LOCATION Yorkshire, North Riding

OWNER The Lister family, Lords Masham, Swinton, Masham, Yorkshire

DATES
Assessed   —
Received   1889–92

FACTS	1890
Rent assessed (£s)	10,010
Rent received (£s)	9,885
Acreage	8,126

Meux

LOCATION Wiltshire

OWNER Sir Henry B. Meux, Theobalds, Cheshunt, Hertfordshire

DATES
Assessed   1878–92
Received   1878–92

FACTS	1880	1890
Rent assessed (£s)	26,885	18,986
Rent received (£s)	24,076	19,033
Acreage	19,273	19,273

Poynder I

LOCATION Wiltshire, Hillmarton estate

OWNER Sir J. Dickson Poynder, Hillmarton Manor, Calne, Wiltshire

DATES
Assessed   1878, 1880–92
Received   1878–92

FACTS   1880   1890
Rent assessed (£s) 4,925   4,130
Rent received (£s) 4,324   3,740
Acreage   3,486   3,521

Poynder II

LOCATION   Wiltshire, Hartham estate

OWNER   Sir J. Dickson Poynder

DATES
Assessed   1878, 1880–92
Received   1878–92

FACTS   1880   1890
Rent assessed (£s) 3,047   2,359
Rent received (£s) 2,373   2,137
Acreage   2,125   3,029

Rolle I

LOCATION   Devon, East Devon estate

OWNER   The Hon. Mark G. K. Rolle, Stephenstone, Torrington, Devon

DATES
Assessed   1872–92
Received   1872–92

FACTS   1870   1880   1890
Rent assessed (£s) 23,960   25,113   22,418
Rent received (£s) 23,712   24,690   22,160
Acreage   15,520   15,520   15,520

Rolle II

LOCATION   Devon, North Devon estate

OWNER   The Hon. Mark G. K. Rolle

DATES
Assessed   1876–92
Received   1876–92

FACTS   1880   1890
Rent assessed (£s)   21,158   19,531
Rent received (£s)   20,912   19,409
Acreage   23,431   22,846

Shottle and Pentrich

LOCATION   Derbyshire

OWNER   Duke of Devonshire

DATES
Assessed   1880–92
Received   1880–92

FACTS   1880   1890
Rent assessed (£s)   7,707   7,000
Rent received (£s)   7,092   6,725
Acreage   5,281   5,110

Staveley and Chesterfield

LOCATION   Derbyshire

OWNER   Duke of Devonshire

DATES
Assessed   1881–92
Received   1881–92

FACTS   1880   1890
Rent assessed (£s)   14,838   12,393
Rent received (£s)   13,472   11,543
Acreage   10,262   10,032

Tavistock

LOCATION   Devon, Cornwall and Dorset

OWNER   Duke of Bedford

CROSS-REFERENCE   See also Tavistock in part 1

DATES
Assessed   —
Received   1842, 1852, 1862, 1872–92

FACTS	1840	1860	1870	1880	1890
Rent assessed (£s)	15,192	24,597	33,187	36,619	37,701
Rent received (£s)	15,527	25,797	35,560	33,241	35,927
Acreage	18,138	20,572	23,847	24,442	24,738

Because the material listed in part 1 includes a long run of rents it has been preferred in the rent index

Thorney

LOCATION   Cambridgeshire, Huntingdonshire, and Northamptonshire

OWNER   Duke of Bedford

CROSS-REFERENCE   See also Thorney in part III

DATES
Assessed   1842, 1852, 1862, 1872–92
Received   1842, 1852, 1862, 1872–92

FACTS	1840	1860	1880	1890
Rent assessed (£s)	30,748	39,969	43,464	39,419
Rent received (£s)	31,267	39,826	33,347	33,042
Acreage	21,645	22,377	23,178	22,943

Because the material listed in part III includes a long run of rents it has been preferred in the rent index

Thurlow Hundon and Great Wratting

LOCATION   Suffolk

OWNER   The Hon. W. F. D. Smith

DATES
Assessed   1878–92
Received   1878–92

FACTS	1880	1890
Rent assessed (£s)	7,600	6,937
Rent received (£s)	6,684	4,157
Acreage	4,837	3,086

Woburn

LOCATION   Bedfordshire and Buckinghamshire

OWNER   Duke of Bedford

CROSS-REFERENCE   See also Woburn in part III

DATES
Assessed   1842, 1852, 1862, 1872–92
Received   1842, 1852, 1862, 1872–92

FACTS	1840	1860	1880	1900
Rent assessed (£s)	34,422	42,680	49,933	35,859
Rent received (£s)	34,890	42,655	40,944	31,414
Acreage	28,485	29,325	29,878	24,053

Because the material listed in part III includes a long run of rents it has been preferred in the rent index

Part III: Printed sources

Audley End

LOCATION   Essex

OWNER   Private, the Griffin family, Lords Howard de Walden and Lords Braybrooke, Audley End, Saffron Walden, Essex

SOURCE   J. D. Williams, 'A study of an eighteenth-century nobleman, his house, household and estate: Sir John Griffin, 4th Lord Howard de Walden, 1st Lord Braybrooke, of Audley End, Essex, 1719–1797' (University of London, PhD thesis, 1974)

DATES
Assessed   —
Received   1754–91

FACTS	1760	1780
Rent assessed (£s)	—	—
Rent received (£s)	1,314	1,735
Acreage	3,355	3,703

Ecclesiastical Commissioners

LOCATION   Most English counties

OWNER   Institutional, the Ecclesiastical Commissioners

SOURCE   Royal Commission on Tithe Rentcharge, Minutes of Evidence (HMSO, London, 1934)

CROSS-REFERENCE   See Ecclesiastical Commissioners in part II; see also H. A. Rhee, *The Rent of Agricultural Land in England and Wales* (London, 1946)

DATES	
Assessed	—
Received	1901–14

FACTS	1900	1910
Rent assessed (£s)	—	—
Rent received (£s)	297,250	302,470
Acreage	290,000	290,000

Guy's estate I

LOCATION   Essex

OWNER   Institutional, Guy's Hospital, London

SOURCE   Royal Commission on Agriculture, 'First Report of her Majesty's Commissioners appointed to inquire into the subject of Agricultural Depression. Minutes of Evidence with Appendices', *BPP*, C. 7400–1, XVI, parts I to III, 1894, Appendix A, Table IX

CROSS-REFERENCE   B. E. S. Trueman, 'The management of the estates of Guy's Hospital 1726–1900' (University of Nottingham, PhD thesis, 1975)

DATES
Assessed   1801–93
Received   1801–93

FACTS	1800	1820	1860	1880	1890
Rent assessed (£s)	5,651	7,783	10,038	11,638	6,385
Rent received (£s)	5,651	7,783	9,977	11,380	6,454
Acreage	7,968	7,867	8,077	8,784	8,790

Guy's estate II

LOCATION   Herefordshire

OWNER   Institutional, Guy's Hospital, London

SOURCE   Royal Commission

CROSS-REFERENCE   Hereford and Worcester RO (C99); Trueman, 'The Management of the estates of Guy's Hospital'

DATES
Assessed   1801–93
Received   1802–93

FACTS	1800	1820	1860	1880	1890
Rent assessed (£s)	5,971	8,526	11,360	11,957	10,086
Rent received (£s)	6,057	8,262	11,360	11,881	10,051
Acreage	9,220	9,220	9,010	8,564	8,551

Guy's estate III

LOCATION   Lincolnshire

OWNER   Institutional, Guy's Hospital, London

SOURCE   Royal Commission

CROSS-REFERENCE   Trueman, 'The management of the estates of Guy's Hospital'

DATES
Assessed   1801–8, 1810–93
Received   1801–8, 1810–93

FACTS	1800	1820	1860	1880	1890
Rent assessed (£s)	4,602	6,379	10,813	15,261	10,713
Rent received (£s)	4,602	5,896	10,813	14,035	10,742
Acreage	4,967	5,262	5,821	6,329	6,316

Lichfield

LOCATION   Staffordshire

OWNER   Five assorted estates in and around Lichfield

SOURCE   R. W. Sturgess, 'The response of agriculture in Staffordshire to the price changes of the nineteenth century' (University of Manchester, PhD thesis, 1965)

DATES
Assessed   —
Received   1818–21, 1826, 1828–9, 1834, 1843–5, 1850, 1852, 1855, 1857, 1859–60, 1863–4, 1866, 1869–71, 1877, 1879–80, 1882, 1884, 1887

FACTS	1820	1860	1880
Rent assessed (£s)	—	—	—
Rent received (£s)	12,848	4,042	8,138
Acreage	7,454	2,386	3,837

Lilleshall

LOCATION   Shropshire

FAMILY   Private, the Leveson-Gower, later Sutherland-Leveson-Gower family, Earls of Gower, Marquesses of Stafford, Dukes of Sutherland, Dunrobin Castle, Sutherland and Trentham Hall, Staffordshire

SOURCE   J. R. Wordie, 'Rent movements and the English tenant farmer, 1700–1839', *Research in Economic History*, 6 (1981); E. Richards, 'James Loch and the House of Sutherland, 1821–1855' (University of Nottingham, PhD thesis, 1967); Sturgess, 'The response of agriculture in Staffordshire'; R. Perren, 'The effects of agricultural depression on the English estates of the dukes of Sutherland, 1870–1900' (University of Nottingham, PhD thesis, 1967)

DATES
Assessed   1700–1, 1704–5, 1707–9, 1712, 1714, 1716–32, 1754–98,
                  1804–33, 1839, 1870–1900
Received   1718–32, 1754–89, 1792–3, 1804–39, 1870–1900

FACTS	1720	1780	1820	1880	1900
Rent assessed (£s)	3,012	5,894	19,877	22,831	19,911
Rent received (£s)	2,894	5,894	18,741	22,529	19,914
Acreage	15,000	15,379	16,628	13,953	13,953

Miscellaneous

LOCATION   Five estates in Oxfordshire/Berkshire, Cambridgeshire (x2), Devon and Yorkshire

OWNER   Institutional (Oriel College, Oxford), and four private but miscellaneous estates

SOURCE   H. A. Rhee, *The Rent of Agricultural Land in England and Wales* (London, 1946)

CROSS-REFERENCE   For Oriel College see also L. L. Price, 'The recent depression in agriculture as shown in the accounts of an Oxford college, 1876–90', *JRSS*, 55 (1892)

DATES
Assessed   —
Received   Oriel College 1876–1914; Cambridge(1) 1877–1914;
                  Cambridge(2) 1870–1914; Devon 1912–14; York
                  1913–14

FACTS	Oriel	1880	1890	1900	1910	
Rent assessed (£s)		—	—	—	—	
Rent received (£s)		7,650	5,658	4,920	4,991	
Acreage		5,300	5,300	5,300	5,300	

FACTS	Cambridge 1	1880	1890	1900	1910	
Rent assessed (£s)		—	—	—	—	
Rent received (£s)		4,109	3,071	2,692	3,165	
Acreage		2,500	2,500	2,500	2,500	

FACTS	Cambridge 2	1870	1880	1890	1900	1910
Rent assessed (£s)		—	—	—	—	
Rent received (£s)			6,722	6,800	5,137	4,433	4,975
Acreage			5,000	5,000	5,000	5,000	5,000

FACTS	Devon	1912/14
Rent assessed (£s)		—
Rent received (£s)		5,005
Acreage		4,400

FACTS	Yorkshire	1913/14
Rent assessed (£s)		—
Rent received (£s)		1,720
Acreage		1,600

Northumberland

LOCATION   Northumberland

OWNER   Private, the Percy family, Dukes of Northumberland, Alnwick Castle, Alnwick, Northumberland

SOURCE   F. M. L. Thompson, 'The economic and social background of the English landed interest, 1840–70, with particular reference to the estates of the dukes of Northumberland' (University of Oxford, DPhil thesis, 1956)

CROSS-REFERENCE   Hughes, 'Northumberland'

DATES
Assessed	1850–70
Received	1850–70

FACTS	1860	1870
Rent assessed (£s)	107,050	116,325
Rent received (£s)	103,679	112,417
Acreage	164,000	164,000

For reasons explained in chapter 8, the rents from this estate were not employed in the construction of the rent index

Oxford colleges

LOCATION   Most English counties

OWNER   Institutional, the Oxford colleges, Oxford University

SOURCE   L. L. Price, 'The recent depression in agriculture as shown in the accounts of an Oxford college, 1876–90', *JRSS*, 55 (1892); L. L.

Price, 'The colleges of Oxford and agricultural depression', *JRSS*, 58 (1895); L. L. Price, 'The accounts of the colleges of Oxford, 1893–1903; with special reference to their agricultural revenues', *JRSS*, 67 (1904); L. L. Price, 'The estates of the colleges of Oxford and their management', *Transactions of the Surveyors' Institution*, 45, paper no. 399 (1912–13); L. L. Price, 'The estates of the colleges of Oxford and their management', *JRSS*, 76 (1913)

DATES
Assessed   —
Received   1871, 1883–1903, 1911

FACTS	1870	1890	1900	1910
Rent assessed (£s)	—	—	—	—
Rent received (£s)	27,402	69,744	120,623	137,022
Acreage	22,744	78,866	134,177	140,600

St John's College, Cambridge

LOCATION   Many counties

OWNER   Institutional, St John's College, Cambridge

SOURCE   H. F. Howard, *The Finances of St John's College Cambridge 1511–1926* (Cambridge, 1935)

DATES
Assessed   —
Received   1882–1914

FACTS	1880	1890	1900	1910
Rent assessed (£s)	—	—	—	—
Rent received (£s)	24,773	19,124	15,383	15,051
Acreage	15,902	15,941	15,550	15,424

Sledmere

LOCATION   Yorkshire, East Riding

OWNER   Private, Sir Tatton Sykes, Sledmere House, Malton, Yorkshire, East Riding

SOURCE   B. English, 'On the eve of the Great Depression: the economy of the Sledmere estate 1869–1878', *Business History*, 24 (1982)

CROSS-REFERENCE   M. G. Adams, 'Agricultural change in the East
Riding of Yorkshire, 1850–1880: an economic and social history'
(University of Hull, PhD thesis, 1977)

DATES
Assessed   —
Received   1869–78, 1882–92

FACTS	1870	1880	1890
Rent assessed (£s)	—	—	—
Rent received (£s)	33,816	42,124	31,559
Acreage	30,000	30,000	30,000

Stittenham

LOCATION   Yorkshire, West Riding

FAMILY   Duke of Sutherland

SOURCE   Perren, 'The effects of agricultural depression'

DATES
Assessed   —
Received   1870–1900

FACTS	1870	1880	1890	1900
Rent assessed (£s)	—	—	—	—
Rent received (£s)	2,201	2,388	2,010	1,730
Acreage	2,500	2,500	2,500	2,500

Thorney

LOCATION   Cambridgeshire, Huntingdonshire, and Northamptonshire

OWNER   Duke of Bedford

SOURCE   Duke of Bedford, *The Story of a Great Agricultural Estate*
(London, 1897)

CROSS-REFERENCE   See also Thorney in part II

DATES
Assessed   —
Received   1816–95

FACTS	1820	1860	1880	1890
Rent assessed (£s)	—	—	—	—
Rent received (£s)	20,669	34,682	28,154	28,150
Acreage	18,904	19,101	19,311	19,320

Trentham

LOCATION   Staffordshire

FAMILY   Duke of Sutherland

SOURCE   Wordie, 'Rent movements'; Richards, 'James Loch'; Sturgess, 'The response of agriculture'; Perren, 'The effects of agricultural depression'

DATES
Assessed	1700–1, 1703–5, 1707–10, 1712, 1714, 1716–1839, 1870–1900
Received	1703, 1717–1839, 1870–1900

1700	1740	1780	1820
806	1,366	3,306	12,261
852	1,687	3,300	11,959
5,000	5,019	6,404	7,718

1880	1900
13,140	10,568
12,574	10,683
6,534	6,534

Woburn

LOCATION   Bedfordshire and Buckinghamshire

OWNER   Duke of Bedford

SOURCE   Duke of Bedford, *A Great Agricultural Estate*

CROSS-REFERENCE   See also Woburn in part II

DATES
Assessed	—
Received	1816–95

FACTS	1820	1860	1880	1890
Rent assessed (£s)	—	—	—	—
Rent received (£s)	30,968	41,831	40,622	30,476
Acreage	24,704	30,333	31,685	26,294

Wolverhampton

LOCATION   Staffordshire

FAMILY   Leveson-Gower (later Duke of Sutherland)

SOURCE   Wordie, 'Rent movements'

DATES
Assessed	1730–55
Received	1730–55

FACTS	1740
Rent assessed (£s)	996
Rent received (£s)	1,029
Acreage	3,000

Part IV Acreage

Table A1.1 sets out on an annual basis the proportion of the acreage included in the rent index and drawn from the three collections summarised in parts I–III. Thus column 2 gives the total acreage included in the rent index on an annual basis, and columns 3–5 show what proportion originated from the archival sources outlined in part I, the material from the Royal Commission on Agriculture outlined in part II, or the other sources set out in part III. The table highlights the extent to which the rent index is based on newly collected material, with the proportion only significantly dropping below half for an extended period during the most agriculturally depressed years of the 1880s when the Royal Commission was busy collecting material, and in the years from 1901 when the material from the Ecclesiastical Commissioners dominates.

Table A1.1. *Archival origins of the rent index (percentages – subject to rounding errors)*

Year	Acreage	New archives	Royal Commission	Printed archives
1690	6,562	100	—	—
1691	6,562	100	—	—
1692	6,562	100	—	—
1693	6,562	100	—	—
1694	6,562	100	—	—
1695	9,732	100	—	—
1696	9,732	100	—	—
1697	9,732	100	—	—
1698	3,170	100	—	—
1699	9,732	100	—	—
1700	3,170	100	—	—
1701	9,732	100	—	—
1702	9,732	100	—	—
1703	14,732	66	—	34
1704	9,732	100	—	—
1705	9,732	100	—	—
1706	9,732	100	—	—
1707	9,732	100	—	—
1708	9,732	100	—	—
1709	9,732	100	—	—
1710	9,732	100	—	—
1711	3,170	100	—	—
1712	3,170	100	—	—
1713	3,170	100	—	—
1714	3,170	100	—	—
1715	3,170	100	—	—
1716	9,732	100	—	—
1717	14,751	66	—	34
1718	29,751	33	—	67
1719	29,751	33	—	67
1720	23,189	14	—	86
1721	29,751	33	—	67
1722	29,751	33	—	67
1723	23,189	14	—	86
1724	41,751	52	—	48
1725	41,751	52	—	48
1726	41,751	52	—	48
1727	41,751	52	—	48
1728	41,751	52	—	48
1729	41,751	52	—	48
1730	44,751	49	—	51
1731	44,751	49	—	51
1732	44,751	49	—	51
1733	63,454	87	—	13
1734	63,454	87	—	13
1735	63,454	87	—	13
1736	47,486	83	—	17
1737	47,486	83	—	17
1738	47,486	83	—	17
1739	47,486	83	—	17

Table A1.1. *Continued*

Year	Acreage	New archives	Royal Commission	Printed archives
1740	47,486	83	—	17
1741	58,664	86	—	14
1742	58,664	86	—	14
1743	69,708	88	—	12
1744	69,708	88	—	12
1745	69,708	88	—	12
1746	76,084	89	—	11
1747	62,540	87	—	13
1748	62,736	87	—	13
1749	65,236	88	—	12
1750	80,780	90	—	10
1751	78,280	90	—	10
1752	78,280	90	—	10
1753	78,280	90	—	10
1754	96,916	72	—	28
1755	96,932	72	—	28
1756	93,948	75	—	25
1757	93,965	75	—	25
1758	82,937	71	—	29
1759	81,615	71	—	29
1760	84,132	72	—	28
1761	95,868	75	—	25
1762	85,385	72	—	28
1763	90,381	74	—	26
1764	96,398	75	—	25
1765	93,111	74	—	26
1766	90,108	74	—	26
1767	90,405	74	—	26
1768	90,476	74	—	26
1769	98,502	76	—	24
1770	109,869	78	—	22
1771	77,184	69	—	31
1772	77,202	69	—	31
1773	97,341	75	—	25
1774	109,882	78	—	22
1775	133,066	82	—	18
1776	135,825	82	—	18
1777	137,553	82	—	18
1778	141,071	82	—	18
1779	135,736	81	—	19
1780	108,286	76	—	24
1781	108,275	76	—	24
1782	101,840	75	—	25
1783	106,119	76	—	24
1784	106,138	76	—	24
1785	106,156	76	—	24
1786	108,738	76	—	24
1787	134,411	81	—	19
1788	134,430	81	—	19
1789	195,666	87	—	13

Table A1.1. *Continued*

Year	Acreage	New archives	Royal Commission	Printed archives
1790	182,405	94	—	6
1791	197,408	95	—	5
1792	208,861	90	—	10
1793	208,845	90	—	10
1794	173,300	96	—	4
1795	182,045	96	—	4
1796	203,918	97	—	3
1797	226,268	97	—	3
1798	204,718	97	—	3
1799	229,352	97	—	3
1800	226,220	97	—	3
1801	240,494	92	—	8
1802	250,206	89	—	11
1803	250,190	89	—	11
1804	266,802	83	—	17
1805	264,286	83	—	17
1806	264,440	82	—	18
1807	265,935	82	—	18
1808	265,136	82	—	18
1809	263,006	84	—	16
1810	255,982	82	—	18
1811	267,678	83	—	17
1812	268,021	83	—	17
1813	268,522	83	—	17
1814	268,506	83	—	17
1815	278,837	83	—	17
1816	318,575	72	—	28
1817	323,819	72	—	28
1818	345,111	74	—	26
1819	357,977	75	—	25
1820	366,094	75	—	25
1821	348,703	74	—	26
1822	335,788	73		27
1823	344,451	74	—	26
1824	330,572	73	—	27
1825	316,260	71	—	29
1826	312,030	71	—	29
1827	340,544	73	—	27
1828	371,348	75	—	25
1829	370,407	75	—	25
1830	371,021	75	—	25
1831	330,758	72	—	28
1832	372,474	75	—	25
1833	372,170	75	—	25
1834	387,611	76	—	24
1835	375,379	75	—	25
1836	384,621	76	—	24
1837	362,521	75	—	25
1838	364,493	75	—	25
1839	379,554	76	—	24

Table A1.1. *Continued*

Year	Acreage	New archives	Royal Commission	Printed archives
1840	355,777	81	—	19
1841	361,590	81	—	19
1842	373,594	76	5	19
1843	345,722	79	—	21
1844	347,924	80	—	20
1845	328,291	79	—	21
1846	366,604	81	—	19
1847	335,006	79	—	21
1848	373,004	81	—	19
1849	372,924	81	—	19
1850	443,588	84	—	16
1851	421,574	83	—	17
1852	436,619	80	4	16
1853	391,733	82	—	18
1854	404,772	82	—	18
1855	437,737	84	—	16
1856	487,673	85	—	15
1857	483,284	85	—	15
1858	477,484	85	—	15
1859	432,666	83	—	17
1860	455,744	84	—	16
1861	429,795	83	—	17
1862	516,687	83	3	14
1863	502,309	86	—	14
1864	434,511	83	—	17
1865	486,174	85	—	15
1866	495,049	84	2	15
1867	474,373	83	2	15
1868	502,655	84	2	15
1869	491,669	78	2	21
1870	452,125	69	2	29
1871	602,104	73	1	26
1872	709,404	62	19	19
1873	677,831	58	22	20
1874	621,887	54	24	21
1875	702,880	59	22	19
1876	722,211	56	25	19
1877	745,530	57	24	19
1878	750,490	54	27	19
1879	743,557	57	28	15
1880	898,350	40	47	12
1881	1,065,226	42	48	10
1882	1,110,230	40	47	14
1883	1,199,251	37	46	17
1884	1,187,433	36	47	17
1885	1,204,520	36	47	17
1886	1,212,744	36	47	17
1887	1,237,355	37	46	16
1888	1,279,531	35	48	17
1889	1,252,895	32	50	18

Table A1.1. *Continued*

Year	Acreage	New archives	Royal Commission	Printed archives
1890	1,258,545	32	50	18
1891	1,274,966	33	49	18
1892	1,277,346	32	49	19
1893	672,904	58	10	32
1894	620,529	67	2	31
1895	608,865	68	—	32
1896	558,535	74	—	26
1897	571,246	72	—	28
1898	579,950	68	—	32
1899	573,603	68	—	32
1900	563,876	67	—	33
1901	710,528	36	—	64
1902	741,297	39	—	61
1903	726,441	38	—	62
1904	600,614	47	—	53
1905	587,501	46	—	54
1906	557,018	43	—	57
1907	587,862	46	—	54
1908	557,691	43	—	57
1909	552,672	42	—	58
1910	556,299	43	—	57
1911	697,148	34	—	66
1912	514,269	37	—	63
1913	513,207	37	—	63
1914	513,322	37	—	63

Statistical summary

The following tables set out the raw data from which figures 8.1, 8.2, 9.1, and 9.2 were compiled. Tables A2.1 and A2.2 summarise annually and respectively the total rents received and assessed, including also the number of sources from which the material was drawn, the total acreage involved and the rent per acre (in shillings rounded to the first decimal place). Table A2.3 gives a similar summary but using only those sources where both rents received and assessed occurred in the same year.

Table A2.1. *Summary of rents received*

Year	Total rent received (£s)	Number of sources	Total number of acres	Rent/acre (shillings)
1690	831	1	6,562	2.5
1691	748	1	6,562	2.3
1692	914	1	6,562	2.8
1693	837	1	6,562	2.6
1694	782	1	6,562	2.4
1695	1,505	2	9,732	2.9
1696	1,509	2	9,732	3.1
1697	1,581	2	9,732	3.3
1698	470	1	3,170	3.0
1699	1,625	2	9,732	3.3
1700	366	1	3,170	2.3
1701	1,546	2	9,732	3.2
1702	1,206	2	9,732	2.5
1703	2,231	3	14,732	3.0
1704	1,639	2	9,732	3.4
1705	1,689	2	9,732	3.5
1706	1,892	2	9,732	3.9
1707	1,490	2	9,732	3.1
1708	1,689	2	9,732	3.5
1709	1,724	2	9,732	3.5
1710	1,623	2	9,732	3.3
1711	360	1	3,170	2.3
1712	360	1	3,170	2.3
1713	360	1	3,170	2.3
1714	360	1	3,170	2.3
1715	360	1	3,170	2.3
1716	1,700	2	9,732	3.5
1717	2,819	3	14,751	3.8
1718	5,574	4	29,751	3.7
1719	5,973	4	29,751	4.0
1720	4,177	3	23,189	3.6
1721	6,088	4	29,751	4.1
1722	6,713	4	29,751	4.5
1723	4,214	3	23,189	3.6
1724	7,528	5	41,751	3.6
1725	7,612	5	41,751	3.6
1726	8,226	5	41,751	3.9
1727	7,446	5	41,751	3.6
1728	9,086	5	41,751	4.1
1729	8,600	5	41,751	4.1
1730	10,523	6	44,751	4.7
1731	10,931	6	44,751	4.9
1732	12,539	6	44,751	5.6
1733	21,590	10	63,454	6.8
1734	21,616	10	63,454	6.8
1735	21,622	10	63,454	6.8
1736	16,086	8	47,486	6.8
1737	14,828	8	47,486	6.2
1738	17,383	8	47,486	7.3
1739	15,231	8	47,486	6.4

Table A2.1. *Continued*

Year	Total rent received (£s)	Number of sources	Total number of acres	Rent/acre (shillings)
1740	15,263	8	47,486	6.4
1741	21,399	10	58,664	7.3
1742	22,398	10	58,664	7.6
1743	26,457	11	69,708	7.6
1744	24,788	11	69,708	7.1
1745	27,974	11	69,708	8.0
1746	27,895	13	76,084	7.3
1747	23,514	11	62,540	7.5
1748	23,461	11	62,736	7.5
1749	25,832	12	65,236	7.9
1750	32,448	14	80,780	8.0
1751	32,594	13	78,280	8.3
1752	31,681	13	78,280	8.1
1753	31,909	13	78,280	8.2
1754	37,943	15	96,916	7.8
1755	38,127	15	96,932	7.9
1756	36,625	14	93,948	7.8
1757	36,086	14	93,965	7.7
1758	33,325	13	82,937	8.0
1759	30,338	13	81,615	7.4
1760	28,806	14	84,132	6.8
1761	39,004	15	95,868	8.1
1762	32,130	12	85,385	7.5
1763	35,470	13	90,381	7.8
1764	36,970	15	96,398	7.7
1765	36,434	14	93,111	7.8
1766	36,128	13	90,108	8.0
1767	35,996	13	90,405	8.0
1768	36,343	13	90,476	8.0
1769	38,547	14	98,502	7.8
1770	42,801	15	109,869	7.8
1771	25,893	11	77,184	6.7
1772	27,788	11	77,202	7.2
1773	39,634	14	97,341	8.1
1774	44,929	15	109,882	8.2
1775	58,425	16	133,066	8.8
1776	60,970	17	135,825	9.0
1777	62,269	17	137,553	9.1
1778	61,972	18	141,071	8.8
1779	57,466	18	135,736	8.5
1780	46,345	14	108,286	8.6
1781	46,278	14	108,275	8.5
1782	46,566	12	101,840	9.1
1783	49,819	14	106,119	9.4
1784	48,815	14	106,138	9.2
1785	59,471	14	106,156	9.5
1786	55,299	14	108,738	10.2
1787	60,017	17	134,411	8.9
1788	62,402	17	134,430	9.3
1789	86,077	21	195,666	8.8

Table A2.1. *Continued*

Year	Total rent received (£s)	Number of sources	Total number of acres	Rent/acre (shillings)
1790	82,558	20	182,405	9.1
1791	92,822	21	197,408	9.4
1792	99,191	21	208,861	9.5
1793	103,726	21	208,845	9.9
1794	88,882	19	173,300	10.3
1795	89,092	19	182,045	9.8
1796	101,244	21	203,918	9.9
1797	122,227	21	226,268	10.8
1798	114,427	20	204,718	11.2
1799	136,140	22	229,352	11.9
1800	140,562	21	226,220	12.4
1801	151,735	24	240,494	12.6
1802	159,867	25	250,206	12.8
1803	163,661	25	250,190	13.1
1804	175,877	26	266,802	13.2
1805	176,996	25	264,286	13.4
1806	186,067	25	264,440	14.1
1807	190,068	25	265,935	14.3
1808	194.346	25	265,136	14.7
1809	200,691	25	263,006	15.3
1810	206,122	24	255,982	16.1
1811	236,303	25	267,678	17.7
1812	246,116	25	268,021	18.4
1813	266,170	25	268,522	19.8
1814	274,220	25	268,506	20.4
1815	284,242	26	278,837	20.4
1816	330,855	27	318,575	20.8
1817	343,510	28	323,819	21.2
1818	375,014	30	345,111	21.7
1819	385,217	31	357,977	21.5
1820	382,674	31	366,094	20.9
1821	375,561	30	348,703	21.5
1822	342,517	29	335,788	20.4
1823	336,800	29	344,451	19.6
1824	321,376	28	330,572	19.4
1825	314,813	28	316,260	19.9
1826	310,641	26	312,030	19.9
1827	344,447	29	340,544	20.2
1828	383,383	32	371,348	20.6
1829	373,217	32	370,407	20.2
1830	379,890	32	371,021	20.5
1831	344,234	30	330,758	20.8
1832	386,869	32	372,474	20.8
1833	383,836	32	372,170	20.6
1834	411,168	33	387,611	21.2
1835	381,549	33	375,379	20.3
1836	390,174	32	384,621	20.3
1837	365,432	30	362,521	20.2
1838	364,918	31	364,493	20.0
1839	394,120	32	379,554	20.8

Table A2.1. *Continued*

Year	Total rent received (£s)	Number of sources	Total number of acres	Rent/acre (shillings)
1840	357,276	30	355,777	20.1
1841	363,089	31	361,590	20.1
1842	387,482	31	373,594	20.7
1843	357,051	30	345,722	20.7
1844	375,550	30	347,924	20.6
1845	357,285	29	328,291	21.8
1846	382,596	31	366,604	20.9
1847	341,100	30	335,006	20.4
1848	398,452	32	373,004	21.4
1849	396,520	32	372,924	21.3
1850	461,345	35	443,588	20.8
1851	437,650	33	421,574	20.8
1852	467,731	34	436,619	21.4
1853	406,489	31	391,733	20.8
1854	439,087	32	404,772	21.7
1855	488,908	35	437,737	22.3
1856	561,867	36	487,673	23.0
1857	567,226	35	483,284	23.5
1858	567,521	34	477,484	23.8
1859	512,789	35	432,666	23.7
1860	550,503	38	455,744	24.2
1861	513,404	36	429,795	23.9
1862	651,600	39	516,687	25.2
1863	632,929	39	502,309	25.2
1864	536,550	37	434,511	24.7
1865	607,853	38	486,174	25.0
1866	635,629	39	495,049	25.7
1867	598,517	37	474,373	25.2
1868	657,001	38	502,655	26.1
1869	644,997	37	491,669	26.2
1870	596,306	40	452,125	26.4
1871	803,928	46	602,104	26.7
1872	978,257	54	709,404	27.6
1873	936,096	49	677,831	27.6
1874	846,121	48	621,887	27.2
1875	981,559	51	702,880	27.9
1876	1,006,580	51	722,211	27.9
1877	1,038,059	56	745,530	27.8
1878	1,063,966	55	750,490	28.4
1879	944,063	58	743,557	25.4
1880	1,161,415	58	898,350	25.9
1881	1,319,339	65	1,065,226	24.8
1882	1,419,264	67	1,110,230	25.6
1883	1,515,084	70	1,199,251	25.3
1884	1,448,014	68	1,187,433	24.4
1885	1,398,631	70	1,204,520	23.2
1886	1,365,882	70	1,212,744	22.5
1887	1,365,508	72	1,237,355	22.1
1888	1,401,268	77	1,279,531	21.9
1889	1,399,194	76	1,252,895	22.3

Table A2.1. *Continued*

Year	Total rent received (£s)	Number of sources	Total number of acres	Rent/acre (shillings)
1890	1,387,767	76	1,258,545	22.1
1891	1,412,658	77	1,274,966	22.2
1892	1,387,350	76	1,277,346	21.7
1893	677,796	51	672,904	20.1
1894	627,130	43	620,529	20.2
1895	613,072	42	608,865	20.1
1896	563,366	40	558,535	20.2
1897	576,452	40	571,246	20.2
1898	575,797	39	579,950	19.9
1899	575,895	38	573,603	20.1
1900	561,554	37	563,876	19.9
1901	701,305	32	710,528	19.7
1902	739,332	33	741,297	19.9
1903	713,753	31	726,441	19.7
1904	592,307	31	600,614	19.7
1905	590,395	30	587,501	20.1
1906	574,457	26	557,018	20.6
1907	597,634	30	587,862	20.3
1908	568,821	27	557,691	20.4
1909	566,497	25	552,672	20.5
1910	577,362	26	556,299	20.8
1911	717,198	27	697,148	20.6
1912	535,564	21	514,269	20.8
1913	536,588	21	513,207	20.9
1914	538,157	21	513,322	21.0

Table A2.2. *Summary of rents assessed*

Year	Total rent assessed (£s)	Number of sources	Total number of acres	Rent/acre (shillings)
1690	822	1	6,562	2.5
1691	764	1	6,562	2.3
1692	1,013	1	6,562	3.1
1693	789	1	6,562	2.4
1694	789	1	6,562	2.4
1695	962	1	6,562	2.8
1696	1,035	1	6,562	3.2
1697	1,001	1	6,562	3.1
1698	—	—	—	—
1699	1,001	1	6,562	3.0
1700	2,622	2	20,000	2.6
1701	3,697	3	26,562	2.8
1702	1,023	1	6,562	3.1
1703	2,029	2	11,562	3.5
1704	4,210	3	26,562	3.2
1705	4,334	3	26,562	3.3
1706	1,487	1	6,562	4.5
1707	4,567	3	26,562	3.4
1708	4,426	3	26,562	3.3
1709	4,593	3	26,562	3.5
1710	2,351	2	11,562	4.1
1711	—	—	—	—
1712	3,666	2	20,000	3.7
1713	—	—	—	—
1714	3,830	2	20,019	3.8
1715	—	—	—	—
1716	5,122	3	26,581	3.9
1717	5,246	3	26,581	3.9
1718	5,497	3	26,581	4.1
1719	5,700	3	26,581	4.3
1720	4,367	2	20,019	4.4
1721	6,138	3	26,581	4.6
1722	6,293	3	26,581	4.7
1723	4,487	2	20,019	4.5
1724	8,376	5	42,081	4.0
1725	8,742	5	42,081	4.2
1726	8,789	5	42,081	4.2
1727	8,985	5	42,081	4.3
1728	9,516	5	42,081	4.5
1729	10,097	5	42,081	4.8
1730	11,714	6	45,081	5.2
1731	11,842	6	45,081	5.3
1732	11,908	6	45,081	5.3
1733	21,128	10	63,784	6.6
1734	22,782	10	63,784	7.1
1735	28,025	11	96,791	5.8
1736	26,809	10	93,291	5.7
1737	20,554	8	77,323	5.3
1738	21,326	8	77,323	5.5
1739	21,478	8	77,323	5.6

Table A2.2. *Continued*

Year	Total rent assessed (£s)	Number of sources	Total number of acres	Rent/acre (shillings)
1740	21,465	8	77,323	5.6
1741	26,739	10	88,501	6.0
1742	27,375	10	88,501	6.2
1743	32,431	11	99,545	6.5
1744	32,115	11	99,545	6.5
1745	32,232	11	99,545	6.5
1746	31,863	11	99,921	6.4
1747	33,145	11	99,921	6.6
1748	28,697	10	89,073	6.4
1749	28,808	10	89,073	6.5
1750	36,339	12	104,617	6.9
1751	37,739	12	104,617	7.2
1752	36,556	12	104,617	7.0
1753	36,792	12	104,617	7.0
1754	42,995	14	123,496	7.0
1755	41,763	13	119,996	7.0
1756	40,571	12	116,996	6.9
1757	42,385	13	119,496	7.1
1758	42,109	12	116,996	7.2
1759	42,002	12	117,914	7.1
1760	39,096	12	108,694	7.2
1761	43,446	13	120,414	7.2
1762	39,576	11	113,414	7.0
1763	42,988	12	118,393	7.3
1764	44,095	13	120,893	7.3
1765	44,371	13	121,090	7.3
1766	44,634	13	121,090	7.4
1767	43,687	12	118,349	7.4
1768	44,198	12	118,403	7.5
1769	46,965	13	126,411	7.4
1770	51,670	14	137,761	7.5
1771	35,281	10	105,059	6.7
1772	36,298	10	105,059	6.9
1773	54,301	14	136,570	8.0
1774	53,880	14	137,704	7.8
1775	66,810	15	160,870	8.3
1776	69,292	16	163,611	8.5
1777	70,270	16	165,321	8.5
1778	71,995	17	168,821	8.5
1779	69,980	17	163,468	8.6
1780	71,559	16	163,452	8.8
1781	61,968	13	137,011	9.0
1782	59,426	11	130,558	9.1
1783	61,671	13	134,819	9.1
1784	61,577	13	134,819	9.1
1785	63,886	13	134,819	9.5
1786	67,932	14	139,882	9.7
1787	68,735	15	142,886	9.6
1788	71,791	15	142,886	10.0
1789	89,877	18	174,383	10.3

Table A2.2. *Continued*

Year	Total rent assessed (£s)	Number of sources	Total number of acres	Rent/acre (shillings)
1790	195,022	18	176,481	10.8
1791	111,172	20	202,052	11.0
1792	120,275	21	212,536	11.3
1793	129,351	21	220,132	11.8
1794	131,584	21	220,116	12.0
1795	110,208	19	190,599	11.6
1796	125,590	21	212,472	11.8
1797	139,835	21	234,822	11.9
1798	133,832	20	222,835	12.0
1799	140,863	20	211,940	13.3
1800	148,874	20	221,411	13.4
1801	178,326	25	274,625	13.0
1802	199,264	25	290,729	13.7
1803	209,503	27	313,363	13.4
1804	225,777	28	329,975	13.7
1805	231,693	28	329,959	14.0
1806	240,051	28	330,113	14.5
1807	250,882	27	334,590	15.0
1808	235,872	26	315,679	14.9
1809	239,823	26	313,549	15.3
1810	274,276	26	327,080	16.9
1811	306,824	27	336,776	18.2
1812	318,041	27	337,119	18.9
1813	346,870	28	340,420	20.4
1814	355,407	27	337,060	21.1
1815	381,967	29	359,994	21.2
1816	378,375	29	359,431	21.1
1817	389,614	30	363,065	21.5
1818	370,007	29	352,549	21.0
1819	370,749	28	349,734	21.2
1820	382,254	29	364,045	21.0
1821	373,608	28	350,281	21.3
1822	376,967	29	360,111	20.9
1823	349,043	29	363,163	19.2
1824	308,063	26	318,938	19.3
1825	344,826	29	351,787	19.6
1826	359,734	28	348,734	20.6
1827	376,214	30	360,578	20.9
1828	371,920	31	368,595	20.2
1829	390,381	31	375,400	20.8
1830	392,893	32	379,886	20.7
1831	384,981	32	370,620	20.8
1832	393,034	32	380,080	20.7
1833	394,181	32	379,300	20.8
1834	363,950	31	361,318	20.1
1835	364,379	32	364,240	20.0
1836	360,010	32	378,097	19.0
1837	330,846	30	349,194	18.9
1838	338,225	31	358,558	18.9
1839	364,371	32	375,556	19.4
1840	330,281	30	351,158	18.8

Table A2.2. *Continued*

Year	Total rent assessed (£s)	Number of sources	Total number of acres	Rent/acre (shillings)
1841	340,330	31	356,753	19.1
1842	365,697	31	364,845	20.0
1843	300,369	27	313,403	19.2
1844	350,858	30	354,029	19.8
1845	332,509	28	329,918	20.2
1846	348,130	29	350,686	19.9
1847	304,561	28	318,802	19.1
1848	360,794	30	356,049	20.3
1849	362,362	30	356,057	20.4
1850	414,032	32	415,319	19.9
1851	468,316	32	452,750	20.7
1852	496,809	32	465,247	21.4
1853	443,330	31	424,929	20.9
1854	452,880	31	426,469	21.2
1855	506,387	33	456,802	22.2
1856	516,366	34	460,281	22.4
1857	503,653	32	445,334	22.6
1858	510,438	32	447,418	22.8
1859	517,572	33	451,470	22.9
1860	545,436	34	459,174	23.8
1861	505,983	33	432,316	23.4
1862	582,581	35	471,022	24.7
1863	555,644	34	453,758	24.5
1864	528,965	33	419,561	25.2
1865	537,813	34	424,399	25.3
1866	545,190	33	421,102	25.9
1867	552,257	33	421,574	26.2
1868	595,458	34	446,073	26.7
1869	582,200	33	432,618	26.9
1870	548,914	33	391,318	28.1
1871	620,512	35	439,068	28.3
1872	818,919	45	572,555	28.6
1873	785,582	40	543,763	28.9
1874	781,253	41	550,393	28.4
1875	811,019	41	562,218	28.9
1876	812,684	39	565,093	28.8
1877	868,320	43	602,172	28.8
1878	912,055	47	630,083	29.0
1879	1,030,624	48	714,083	28.9
1880	1,224,851	51	869,752	28.2
1881	1,319,006	55	973,149	27.1
1882	1,335,397	54	971,462	27.5
1883	1,303,746	54	972,796	26.8
1884	1,267,233	54	984,509	25.7
1885	1,268,444	56	1,006,403	25.2
1886	1,235,458	56	1,005,130	24.6
1887	1,223,966	57	1,012,268	24.2
1888	1,222,397	63	1,050,118	23.3
1889	1,192,429	62	1,012,391	23.6
1890	1,190,088	62	1,015,733	23.4
1891	1,200,070	63	1,031,882	23.3

Table A2.2. *Continued*

Year	Total rent assessed (£s)	Number of sources	Total number of acres	Rent/acre (shillings)
1892	1,238,264	57	1,058,753	23.4
1893	556,069	34	489,934	22.7
1894	491,467	32	424,720	23.1
1895	483,247	31	422,718	22.9
1896	472,292	31	420,031	22.5
1897	435,693	30	403,590	21.6
1898	429,927	30	401,594	21.4
1899	422,249	29	395,679	21.3
1900	415,245	28	385,952	21.5
1901	302,070	24	288,618	20.9
1902	329,766	24	314,937	20.9
1903	315,742	23	304,581	20.7
1904	328,170	24	312,931	21.0
1905	327,565	24	312,738	20.9
1906	286,952	20	272,833	21.0
1907	314,442	23	300,179	22.0
1908	280,111	20	270,008	20.7
1909	286,010	19	273,029	21.0
1910	288,254	20	276,656	20.8
1911	292,257	20	276,905	21.1
1912	240,162	15	233,368	20.6
1913	238,491	14	230,706	20.7
1914	242,233	14	230,821	21.0

Table A2.3. *Summary of rents received and rents assessed where they both coincide*

Year	Rents received (£s)	Rents assessed (£s)	Common acres	Number of sources	Rent received (shillings/acre)	Rent assessed (shillings/acre)
1690	831	822	6,562	1	2.5	2.5
1691	748	764	6,562	1	2.3	2.3
1692	914	1,013	6,562	1	2.8	3.1
1693	837	789	6,562	1	2.6	2.4
1694	782	789	6,562	1	2.4	2.4
1695	927	926	6,562	1	2.8	2.8
1696	1,039	1,035	6,562	1	3.2	3.2
1697	1,112	1,001	6,562	1	3.4	3.1
1698	—	—	—	—	—	—
1699	1,155	1,001	6,562	1	3.5	3.0
1700	—	—	—	—	—	—
1701	1,181	1,011	6,562	1	3.6	3.1
1702	1,023	1,023	6,562	1	3.1	3.1
1703	1,691	2,029	11,562	2	2.9	3.5
1704	1,279	1,320	6,562	1	3.9	4.0
1705	1,328	1,334	6,562	1	4.0	4.1
1706	1,532	1,487	6,562	1	4.7	4.5
1707	1,310	1,360	6,562	1	4.0	4.1
1708	1,149	1,236	6,562	1	3.5	3.8
1709	1,364	1,221	6,562	1	4.2	3.7
1710	1,263	1,223	6,562	1	3.8	3.7
1711	—	—	—	—	—	—
1712	—	—	—	—	—	—
1713	—	—	—	—	—	—
1714	—	—	—	—	—	—
1715	—	—	—	—	—	—
1716	1,340	1,340	6,562	1	4.1	4.1
1717	2,459	2,542	11,581	2	4.2	4.4
1718	5,214	5,497	26,581	3	3.9	4.1
1719	5,613	5,700	26,581	3	4.2	4.3
1720	3,817	4,367	20,019	2	3.8	4.4
1721	5,728	6,138	26,581	3	4.3	4.6
1722	6,353	6,293	26,581	3	4.8	4.7
1723	4,034	4,487	20,019	2	4.0	4.5
1724	6,988	7,311	38,581	4	3.6	3.8
1725	7,252	7,638	38,581	4	3.8	4.0
1726	7,866	7,682	38,581	4	4.1	4.0
1727	7,086	7,861	38,581	4	3.7	4.1
1728	8,726	8,441	38,581	4	4.5	4.4
1729	8,240	8,958	38,581	4	4.3	4.6
1730	10,163	10,571	41,581	5	4.9	5.1
1731	10,571	10,550	41,581	5	5.1	5.1
1732	12,179	10,563	41,581	5	5.9	5.1
1733	21,230	19,885	60,284	9	7.0	6.6
1734	21,256	21,541	60,284	9	7.1	7.1
1735	21,262	21,600	60,284	9	7.1	7.2
1736	15,726	15,013	44,316	7	7.1	6.8
1737	14,468	15,262	44,316	7	6.5	6.9
1738	17,023	15,441	44,316	7	7.7	7.0
1739	14,871	15,607	44,316	7	6.7	7.0

Table A2.3. *Continued*

Year	Rents received (£s)	Rents assessed (£s)	Common acres	Number of sources	Rent received (shillings/acre)	Rent assessed (shillings/acre)
1740	14,903	15,590	44,316	7	6.7	7.0
1741	21,039	20,864	55,494	9	7.6	7.5
1742	22,038	21,496	55,494	9	7.9	7.7
1743	26,097	26,553	66,538	10	7.8	8.0
1744	24,328	26,229	66,538	10	7.3	7.9
1745	27,674	26,357	66,538	10	8.3	7.9
1746	25,437	25,976	66,914	10	7.6	7.8
1747	22,130	22,613	55,870	9	7.9	8.1
1748	22,252	22,811	56,066	9	7.9	8.1
1749	23,509	22,917	56,066	9	8.4	8.2
1750	30,034	30,447	71,610	11	8.4	8.5
1751	31,367	31,847	71,610	11	8.8	8.9
1752	30,311	30,664	71,610	11	8.5	8.6
1753	30,645	30,793	71,610	11	8.6	8.6
1754	36,102	36,823	90,489	13	8.0	8.1
1755	35,510	35,559	86,989	12	8.2	8.2
1756	33,947	34,346	83,989	11	8.1	8.2
1757	33,451	35,086	83,989	11	8.0	8.4
1758	30,639	30,664	72,945	10	8.4	8.4
1759	27,998	71,759	71,607	10	7.8	8.0
1760	26,266	29,956	74,107	11	7.1	8.1
1761	36,647	34,307	85,827	12	8.5	8.0
1762	30,291	30,509	78,827	10	7.7	7.7
1763	33,554	33,926	83,806	11	8.0	8.1
1764	34,582	35,033	86,306	12	8.0	8.1
1765	34,538	35,282	86,503	12	8.0	8.2
1766	34,234	33,734	83,483	11	8.2	8.1
1767	34,082	34,551	83,762	11	8.1	8.2
1768	34,407	35,056	83,816	11	8.2	8.4
1769	36,601	37,823	91,824	12	8.0	8.2
1770	40,636	42,489	103,174	13	7.9	8.2
1771	23,690	26,059	70,472	9	6.7	7.4
1772	25,597	27,006	70,472	9	7.3	7.7
1773	37,898	39,758	90,594	12	8.4	8.8
1774	42,886	44,367	103,117	13	8.3	8.6
1775	55,771	57,308	126,283	14	8.8	9.1
1776	57,914	59,769	129,024	15	9.0	9.3
1777	59,276	60,535	130,734	15	9.1	9.3
1778	59,193	62,300	134,234	16	8.8	9.3
1779	54,719	60,215	128,881	16	8.5	9.3
1780	43,642	46,969	105,661	13	8.3	8.9
1781	43,479	47,887	101,383	12	8.6	9.4
1782	43,802	45,348	94,930	10	9.2	9.6
1783	47,003	47,380	99,191	12	9.5	9.6
1784	45,958	47,571	99,191	12	9.3	9.6
1785	48,130	49,944	99,191	12	9.7	10.1
1786	51,520	52,058	101,754	12	10.1	10.2
1787	53,343	53,993	107,258	14	9.9	10.1
1788	55,512	56,769	107,258	14	10.4	10.6
1789	72,096	74,871	138,755	17	10.4	10.8

Table A2.3. *Continued*

Year	Rents received (£s)	Rents assessed (£s)	Common acres	Number of sources	Rent received (shillings/acre)	Rent assessed (shillings/acre)
1790	68,567	72,664	125,474	16	10.9	11.6
1791	78,253	82,650	140,458	17	11.1	11.8
1792	87,249	91,596	155,821	18	11.2	11.8
1793	91,257	92,709	155,805	18	11.7	11.9
1794	81,107	86,882	140,410	17	11.6	12.4
1795	76,322	80,393	129,005	16	11.8	12.5
1796	87,593	94,329	150,878	18	11.6	12.5
1797	107,309	108,572	173,228	18	12.4	12.5
1798	105,003	108,743	171,828	18	12.2	12.7
1799	120,721	124,521	176,312	19	13.7	14.1
1800	125,147	123,052	173,180	18	14.5	14.2
1801	143,390	144,601	217,174	22	13.2	13.3
1802	149,907	153,766	224,386	22	13.4	13.7
1803	162,463	165,289	247,020	24	13.2	13.4
1804	174,676	178,412	263,632	25	13.3	13.5
1805	175,786	179,738	261,116	24	13.5	13.8
1806	184,927	187,840	261,270	24	14.2	14.4
1807	188,378	193,981	262,765	24	14.3	14.8
1808	192,513	196,816	261,966	24	14.7	15.0
1809	198,707	202,416	259,836	24	15.3	15.6
1810	203,909	210,569	252,812	23	16.1	16.7
1811	234,090	240,548	264,508	24	17.7	18.2
1812	244,051	250,612	264,851	24	18.4	18.9
1813	264,661	271,613	265,352	24	19.9	20.5
1814	272,995	280,930	265,336	24	20.6	21.2
1815	282,912	294,176	275,667	25	20.5	21.3
1816	279,153	287,444	272,304	24	20.5	21.1
1817	286,646	288,917	277,497	25	20.7	20.8
1818	313,793	316,485	296,036	26	21.2	21.4
1819	305,275	320,042	296,021	26	20.6	21.6
1820	312,343	328,169	307,016	26	20.3	21.4
1821	308,274	318,188	293,564	25	21.0	21.7
1822	287,272	303,511	285,929	25	20.1	21.2
1823	286,716	291,567	297,391	26	19.3	19.6
1824	251,711	261,505	265,225	24	19.0	19.7
1825	257,951	264,726	265,296	24	19.4	20.0
1826	262,812	269,690	264,833	23	19.8	20.4
1827	296,309	303,693	293,324	26	20.2	20.7
1828	310,679	315,294	312,342	28	19.9	20.2
1829	313,958	333,844	319,147	28	19.7	20.9
1830	327,364	336,137	323,633	29	20.2	20.8
1831	291,188	294,685	283,140	27	20.6	20.8
1832	332,622	337,102	324,856	29	20.5	20.8
1833	330,763	338,428	324,076	29	20.4	20.9
1834	308,611	313,065	307,392	28	20.1	20.4
1835	307,078	314,954	310,314	29	19.8	20.3
1836	314,739	311,829	319,551	28	19.7	19.5
1837	270,577	272,693	277,600	25	19.5	19.6
1838	291,358	291,773	299,712	27	19.4	19.5
1839	324,856	317,665	316,710	28	20.5	20.1

Table A2.3. *Continued*

Year	Rents received (£s)	Rents assessed (£s)	Common acres	Number of sources	Rent received (shillings/acre)	Rent assessed (shillings/acre)
1840	283,766	283,989	292,312	26	19.4	19.4
1841	290,893	293,317	297,907	27	19.5	19.7
1842	309,913	318,260	305,999	27	20.3	20.8
1843	247,295	253,008	254,557	23	19.4	19.9
1844	272,704	274,419	267,535	24	20.4	20.5
1845	281,694	284,950	270,972	24	20.8	21.0
1846	298,840	302,244	296,760	26	20.1	20.4
1847	255,758	258,372	264,876	25	19.3	19.5
1848	311,303	314,432	302,123	27	20.6	20.8
1849	308,012	315,683	302,131	27	20.4	20.9
1850	354,155	367,187	361,393	29	19.6	20.3
1851	352,375	356,513	350,082	28	20.1	20.4
1852	378,099	384,523	362,579	28	20.9	21.2
1853	322,197	331,820	322,261	27	20.0	20.6
1854	353,680	362,514	334,869	28	21.1	21.7
1855	395,569	409,738	365,202	30	21.7	22.4
1856	467,155	489,145	418,958	32	22.3	23.4
1857	449,948	473,532	404,011	30	22.3	23.4
1858	463,645	479,479	406,095	30	22.8	23.6
1859	405,981	417,898	359,870	30	22.6	23.2
1860	434,068	448,855	368,953	31	23.5	24.3
1861	398,436	414,217	345,944	30	23.0	23.9
1862	536,055	551,541	432,730	33	24.8	25.5
1863	510,305	524,457	415,466	32	24.6	25.2
1864	442,450	458,140	366,744	31	24.1	25.0
1865	520,400	535,998	421,859	33	24.7	25.4
1866	529,825	544,036	418,562	32	25.3	26.0
1867	499,742	523,131	402,372	31	24.8	26.0
1868	553,878	572,897	430,613	32	25.7	26.6
1869	506,205	522,477	387,016	29	26.2	27.0
1870	421,418	432,850	308,359	29	27.3	28.1
1871	601,908	619,050	436,528	34	27.6	28.4
1872	806,055	817,389	570,015	44	28.3	28.7
1873	750,910	763,135	528,303	38	28.4	28.9
1874	667,254	677,141	480,914	38	27.7	28.2
1875	798,232	809,433	559,678	40	28.5	28.9
1876	803,452	810,980	562,553	38	28.6	28.8
1877	816,124	835,144	578,342	41	28.2	28.9
1878	853,750	867,384	597,981	42	28.6	29.0
1879	837,627	915,929	645,356	46	26.0	28.4
1880	1,039,859	1,129,803	798,532	46	26.0	28.3
1881	1,214,564	1,317,190	970,609	54	25.0	27.1
1882	1,224,918	1,333,674	968,922	53	25.3	27.5
1883	1,223,325	1,302,078	970,256	53	25.4	26.8
1884	1,177,382	1,254,135	969,832	52	24.3	25.9
1885	1,167,873	1,252,507	988,863	54	23.6	25.3
1886	1,126,778	1,233,623	1,002,590	55	22.5	24.6
1887	1,126,137	1,221,890	1,009,728	56	22.3	24.2
1888	1,155,851	1,220,414	1,047,578	62	22.1	23.3
1889	1,130,583	1,190,776	1,009,851	61	22.4	23.6

Table A2.3. *Continued*

Year	Rents received (£s)	Rents assessed (£s)	Common acres	Number of sources	Rent received (shillings/acre)	Rent assessed (shillings/acre)
1890	1,130,197	1,188,638	1,013,193	61	22.3	23.5
1891	1,153,379	1,198,614	1,029,342	62	22.4	23.3
1892	1,124,012	1,190,983	1,018,654	61	22.1	23.4
1893	465,333	506,439	440,500	37	21.1	23.0
1894	452,666	490,089	422,180	31	21.4	23.2
1895	451,082	483,247	422,718	31	21.3	22.9
1896	446,110	472,292	420,031	31	21.2	22.5
1897	428,280	435,693	403,590	30	21.2	21.6
1898	420,972	429,927	401,594	30	21.0	21.4
1899	416,785	422,249	395,679	29	21.1	21.3
1900	400,693	415,245	385,952	28	20.8	21.5
1901	244,565	254,280	243,725	23	20.1	20.9
1902	281,839	281,833	270,044	23	20.9	20.9
1903	258,953	267,970	259,688	22	19.9	20.6
1904	270,935	280,349	268,038	23	20.2	20.9
1905	261,899	264,903	254,925	22	20.5	20.8
1906	237,844	239,383	227,940	19	20.9	21.0
1907	262,612	267,050	255,286	22	20.6	20.9
1908	233,117	232,673	225,115	19	20.7	20.7
1909	232,357	238,517	228,136	18	20.4	20.9
1910	242,750	240,846	231,763	19	20.9	20.8
1911	246,291	244,700	232,012	19	21.2	21.1
1912	193,384	192,505	188,475	14	20.5	20.4
1913	189,614	190,654	185,812	13	20.4	20.5
1914	191,505	193,962	185,929	13	20.6	20.9

Bibliography

Manuscript sources

Badminton House
   Badminton estate archives
Bodleian Library
   Holkham microfilms
Castle Howard House
   Castle Howard estate archives
Centre for Kentish Studies, formerly Kent RO
   Chevening MSS
   Cornwallis MSS ˙
Chatsworth House, Archives of the Trustees of the Chatsworth Settlement
   Bolton Abbey estate archives
   Chatsworth estate archives
Cheshire RO
   Cholmondeley MSS
Cornwall AO
   Hawkins MSS: Trewithen estate
Corporation of London RO
   Emanuel Hospital MSS
Dalemain House, Cumberland
   Dalemain private archives
Devon RO
   Bedford MSS: Tavistock estate
Dorset RO
   Pitt-Rivers MSS: Rushmore estate
East Sussex RO
   Ashburnham MSS
Essex RO
   Petre MSS: Thorndon estate
Gloucestershire RO
   Badminton estate MSS

Hampshire RO
  Bolton MSS: Hackwood estate; Wallop estate
Hatfield House, Hertfordshire
  Hatfield estate accounts
Hereford and Worcester RO
  Guy's Hospital archives
Huntington Library, San Marino, California
  STG Correspondence
Lancashire RO
  Holker MSS
  Knowsley estate MSS
Lincolnshire AO
  Ancaster MSS
  Yarborough MSS
Longleat House
  Longleat estate MSS
Magdalen College archives
  Miscellaneous
Maxstoke Castle
  Fetherston-Dilke estate MSS
Northamptonshire RO
  Fitzwilliam MSS: Higham Ferrers estate; Milton estate
  Powys MSS: Lilford estate
Nottingham University Manuscripts Division
  Manvers MSS
Petworth House, Sussex
  Cockermouth MSS
  Leconfield MSS
  Petworth MSS
Public RO
  Admiralty Papers – Greenwich Hospital
Sheffield AO
  Wentworth Woodhouse MSS
Southampton University Library
  Broadlands MSS
Suffolk RO
  Barking Hall MSS
William L. Clements Library, Ann Arbor, Michigan
  Sheffield papers
Wiltshire RO
  Pembroke MSS: Wilton estate

Parliamentary papers (*BPP*) and other 'official' sources (in date order)

Second Report by the Lords Committees ... [on] ... the Dearth of Provisions, 1800, reprinted in S. Lambert (ed.), *House of Commons Sessional Papers of the Eighteenth Century*, CXXXI (Wilmington, Delaware, 1975)

Account of the Net Receipts of the Permanent, Annual, and War Taxes for the Years ending the 10th October 1811 and 1812; Accounts Relating to the Property Tax', VII (1812–13)

Reports of the Charity Commissioners (in 32 volumes, 1819–40)

Report from the Select Committee on Petitions Complaining of Agricultural Distress [255], II (1820)

Report from the Select Committee to Whom the Several Petitions Complaining of the Depressed State of the Agriculture of the United Kingdom were Referred [668], IX (1821)

First Report from the Select Committee Appointed to Inquire into the Allegations of the Several Petitions Complaining of the Distressed State of the Agriculture of the United Kingdom [165], V (1822)

Second Report from the Select Committee Appointed to Inquire into the Allegations of the Several Petitions Complaining of the Distressed State of the Agriculture of the United Kingdom [346], V (1822)

Report from the Select Committee Appointed to Inquire into the Present State of Agriculture [612], V (1833)

First Report from the Select Committee on the State of Agriculture: with Minutes of Evidence and Appendix [79], VIII, part 1 (1836)

Second Report from the Select Committee on the State of Agriculture [189], VIII, part 1 (1836)

Third Report from the Select Committee on the State of Agriculture: with Minutes of Evidence and Appendix [465], VIII, part 2 (1836)

Report from the Select Committee of the House of Lords on the State of Agriculture in England and Wales [464], V (1837)

Report of the Commissioners appointed to inquire into the property and income of the Universities of Oxford and Cambridge, and of the colleges and halls therein, 'Volume I. Report including Abstracts and Synoptical Tables, and Appendix', C. 856, XXXVII (1873), part 1

Report of the Commissioners appointed to inquire into the property and income of the Universities of Oxford and Cambridge, and of the colleges and halls therein, 'Volume II. Returns from the University of Oxford and from the Colleges and Halls therein', C. 856-I, XXXVII (1873), part 2

Report of the Commissioners appointed to inquire into the property and income of the Universities of Oxford and Cambridge, and of the colleges and halls therein, 'Volume III. Returns from the University of Cambridge and from the Colleges and Halls therein', C. 856-II, XXXVII (1873), part 3

Return of Owners of Land 1872–3, LXXII (1874)

Royal Commission on Agriculture, 'First Report of Her Majesty's Commissioners Appointed to Inquire into the Subject of Agricultural Depression: Minutes of Evidence with Appendices', C. 7400, XVI, parts 1–3 (1894)

Royal Commission on Agriculture, 'Garstang and Glendale: Reports by Assistant Commissioner Mr Wilson-Fox', C. 7334, XVI, part 1 (1894)

Royal Commission on Agriculture, 'North Devon: Report by Assistant Commissioner Mr R. Henry Rew', C. 7728, XVI (1895)

Royal Commission on Agriculture, 'Lincolnshire: Report by Assistant Commissioner Mr Wilson Fox', C. 7671, XVI (1895)

Royal Commission on Agriculture, 'Second Report of Her Majesty's Commissioners Appointed to Inquire into the Subject of Agricultural Depression', C. 7981, XVI (1896), 'Minutes of Evidence', C. 8021, XVII (1896)

Royal Commission on Agriculture, 'Final Report of Her Majesty's Commissioners Appointed to Inquire into the Subject of Agricultural Depression', C. 8540, XV (1897), 'Appendix', C. 8541, XV (1897)

Royal Commission on Agriculture, 'Particulars of the Expenditures and Outgoings on Certain Estates in Great Britain and Farm Accounts', C. 8125, XVI (1896)

Royal Commission on Tithe Rentcharge: Minutes of Evidence (London, 1934)

Contemporary printed sources – pre 1914

Adkin, B. W. *Copyhold and other Tenures of England* (London, 1907)

Barbon, N. *A Discourse of Trade* (London, 1690)

Batchelor, T. *General View of the Agriculture of the County of Bedford* (London, 1813)

Bateman, J. *The Great Landowners of Great Britain and Ireland* (Leicester University Press edn., 1971, a reprint of the fourth and last edn of 1883)

Bedford, Duke of. *The Story of a Great Agricultural Estate* (London, 1897)

Boys, J. *General View of the Agriculture of the County of Kent* (London, 1796)

Buckland, G. 'On the farming of Kent', *JRASE*, 6 (1845), 251–302

Caird, J. *English Agriculture 1850–1* (London, 1852)

Colbeck, T. L. 'On the agriculture of Northumberland', *JRASE*, 8 (1847), 422–37

Corringham, R. W. 'Agriculture of Nottinghamshire', *JRASE*, 6 (1845), 1–43

Craigie, P. G. 'Statistics of agricultural production', *JRSS*, 46 (1883), 1–58

Eden, F. M. *The State of the Poor* (London, 1928 edn edited and abridged by A. G. L. Rogers)

Gentleman's Magazine, 7, (1737), 104–6

Grey, J. 'A view of the past and present state of agriculture in Northumberland', *JRASE*, 2 (1841), 151–92

Historical Manuscripts Commission. *The Le Fleming MSS* (London, 1890)

Jonas, S. 'On the farming of Cambridgeshire', *JRASE*, 7 (1846), 35–72

Kent, N. *Hints to Gentlemen of Landed Property* (London, 1775)

Laurence, E. *The Duty of a Steward to his Lord* (London, 1727)

Legard, G. 'Farming of the East Riding of Yorkshire', *JRASE*, 9 (1848), 85–136

Low, D. *Observations on the Present State of Landed Property, and on the Prospects of the Landholder and the Farmer* (Edinburgh, 1823)

   Landed Property and the Economy of Estates (London, 1844)

McCulloch, J. R. *A Statistical Account of the British Empire*, I (London, 1837)

Marshall, M. *On the Landed Property of England* (London, 1804)
   Review and Abstract of the County Reports to the Board of Agriculture (5 vols, York, 1818)
Norton, Trist and Gilbert. 'A century of land values: England and Wales', *JRSS*, 54 (1891), 128–31, originally published in *The Times*, 20 April 1889, p. 11
Pitt, W. *General View of the Agriculture of the County of Leicester* (London, 1809)
   General View of the Agriculture of the County of Northampton (London, 1813)
Price, L. L. 'The recent depression in agriculture as shown in the accounts of an Oxford college, 1876–90', *JRSS*, 55 (1892), 2–36.
   'The colleges of Oxford and agricultural depression', *JRSS*, 58 (1895), 36–74
   'The accounts of the colleges of Oxford, 1893–1903; with special reference to their agricultural revenues', *JRSS*, 67 (1904), 585–660.
   'The estates of the colleges of Oxford and their management', *Transactions of the Surveyors' Institution*, 45, paper no. 399 (1912–13), 542–603
   'The estates of the colleges of Oxford and their management', *JRSS*, 76 (1913), 787–90
Pusey, P. 'Some introductory remarks on the present state of the science of agriculture in England', *JRASE*, 1 (1840), 1–21
   'On the agricultural improvement of Lincolnshire', *JRASE*, 4 (1843), 287–315
Raynbird, H. 'On the farming of Suffolk', *JRASE*, 8 (1847), 261–329.
Read, C. S. 'Report on the farming of Buckinghamshire', *JRASE*, 16 (1855), 269–322
   'Recent improvements in Norfolk farming', *JRASE*, 19 (1858), 265–310
Ricardo, D. *The Principles of Political Economy* (London, 1973 Everyman edn with introduction by Donald Winch)
Rider Haggard, H. *Rural England*, II (2 vols, London, 1906 edn)
   A Farmer's Year (London, Cresset Press, 1987 edn)
Robertson, T. *Outline of the General Report upon the Size of Farms and upon the Persons who Cultivate Farms* (Edinburgh, 1796)
Rowley, J. J. 'The farming of Derbyshire', *JRASE*, 14 (1853), 17–66
Smith, A. *An Inquiry into the Nature and Causes of the Wealth of Nations* (London, 1900 edn)
Squarey, E. P. 'Farm capital', *JRASE*, 2nd series, 14 (1878), 425–44
Steele, J. C. 'The agricultural depression and its effects on a leading London hospital', *JRSS*, 55 (1892), 37–48
Stephenson, W. 'England', in D. Brewster (ed.), *Edinburgh Encylopaedia*, VIII (Edinburgh, 1830)
Tanner, H. 'The farming of Devonshire', *JRASE*, 9 (1848), 451–95
Thompson, R. J. 'An inquiry into the rent of agricultural land in England and Wales during the nineteenth century', *JRSS*, 70 (1907), 587–625, and reprinted in Minchinton (ed.), *Essays in Agrarian History*, II (1968), pp. 56–88
Tuckett, P. D. 'On land valuing', *JRASE*, 24 (1863), 1–7
Wilson Fox, A. 'Agricultural wages in England and Wales during the last half century', *JRSS*, 66 (1903), 273–348, reprinted in Minchinton (ed.), *Essays in Agrarian History*, II (1968), pp. 121–98
Young, A. *A Six Weeks' Tour through the Southern Counties of England and Wales* (London, 1768)

The Farmer's Tour through the East of England, I (London, 1771)
A Six Months' Tour Through the North of England (London, 1771)
General View of the Agriculture of the County of Hertfordshire (London, 1804)
General View of the Agriculture of the County of Norfolk (London, 1813)
General View of the Agriculture of the County of Oxfordshire (London, 1813)
General View of the Agriculture of the County of Suffolk (London, 1813)
General View of the Agriculture of the County of Lincolnshire (London, 1813)

Books and articles

Allen, R. C. 'The efficiency and distributional consequences of eighteenth-century enclosures', *Economic Journal*, 92 (1982), 937–53
'The price of freehold land and the rate of interest in the seventeenth and eighteenth centuries', *EcHR*, 41 (1988), 33–50
'The two English agricultural revolutions, 1450–1850', in Campbell and Overton, *Land, Labour and Livestock* (1991), 236–54
Enclosure and the Yeoman: The Agricultural Development of the South Midlands 1450–1850 (Oxford, 1992)
'Agriculture during the industrial revolution', in Floud and McCloskey (eds.), *The Economic History of Britain*, I (1994), pp. 96–122
Anderson, J. S. *Lawyers and the Making of English Land Law 1832–1940* (Oxford, 1992)
Ashton, T. S. *An Economic History of England: The Eighteenth Century* (London, 1972)
Barber, W. J. *A History of Economic Thought* (London, 1967)
Barrell, J. *The Idea of Landscape and the Sense of Place 1730–1840: An Approach to the Poetry of John Clare* (Cambridge, 1972)
Beckett, J. V. 'Local custom and the "New Taxation" in the seventeenth and eighteenth centuries: the example of Cumberland', *Northern History*, 12 (1976), 105–26
'Westmorland's "Book of Rates"', *Transactions of the Cumberland and Westmorland Antiquarian and Archaeological Society*, 77 (1977), 127–37
Coal and Tobacco: The Lowthers and the Economic Development of West Cumberland 1660–1760 (Cambridge, 1981)
'Regional variation and the agricultural depression, 1730–50', *EcHR*, 35 (1982), 35–51
'The debate over farm sizes in eighteenth and nineteenth-century England', *Agricultural History*, 57 (1983), 308–25
'Land tax or excise: the levying of taxation in eighteenth-century England', *English Historical Review*, 100 (1985), 285–308
'Land tax administration at the local level 1693–1798', in Turner and Mills, *Land and Property* (1986), pp. 161–79
The Aristocracy in England 1660–1914 (Oxford, 1989 edn)
A History of Laxton: England's Last Open-Field Village (Oxford, 1989)
'Landownership and estate management', in Mingay, *Agrarian History of England and Wales*, VI (1989), pp. 545–640
'Estate management in eighteenth-century England: the Lowther-Spedding

relationship in Cumberland', in Chartres and Hey (eds.), *English Rural Society 1500–1800* (1990), pp. 55–72

'The Stowe papers', *Archives*, 20 (1993), 187–99

'The land market in nineteenth-century England: the sale of Burton Dassett, 1826–36', *Warwickshire History*, 9 (1993), 2–11

'Aristocratic financial troubles and the operation of the land market: the sale of Astwell and Falcutt in 1774–8', *Northamptonshire Past and Present*, 8, no. 5 (1993–4), 378–82

The Rise and Fall of the Grenvilles (Manchester, 1994)

Beckett, J. V. and Heath, M. E. *Derbyshire Tithe Files 1836–50* (Derbyshire Record Society, 22, Chesterfield, 1995)

Beckett, J. V. and Turner, M. E. 'Taxation and economic growth in eighteenth-century England', *EcHR*, 43 (1990), 377–403

Bellerby, J. R. 'Distribution of farm income in the United Kingdom 1867–1938', *Proceedings of the Journal of the Agricultural Economics Society*, 10, no. 2 (1953), 127–44

'Gross and net farm income in the United Kingdom', *Proceedings of the Journal of the Agricultural Economics Society*, 10, no. 4 (1954), 356–62

Bohstedt, J. *Riots and Community Politics in England and Wales, 1790–1810* (London, 1983)

Bowden, P. J. 'Agricultural prices, wages, farm profits, and rents', in Thirsk, *Agrarian History of England and Wales*, V, II (1985), pp. 1–118

'Statistics', in Thirsk, *Agrarian History of England and Wales*, V, II (1985), pp. 815–402

Boyer, G. R. 'England's two agricultural revolutions', *Journal of Economic History*, 53 (1993), 915–23

Brassley, P. *The Agricultural Economy of Northumberland and Durham in the Period 1640–1750* (London, 1985)

Broad, J. 'Alternate husbandry and permanent pasture in the Midlands, 1650–1800', *AgHR*, 28 (1980), 77–89

Campbell B. M. S. and Overton, M. 'Norfolk livestock farming 1250–1740: a comparative study of manorial accounts and probate inventories', *Journal of Historical Geography*, 18 (1992), 377–96

'A new perspective on medieval and early modern agriculture: six centuries of Norfolk farming, c. 1250–c. 1850', *Past and Present*, 141 (1993), 38–105

Campbell, B. M. S. and Overton, M. (eds.), *Land, Labour and Livestock: Historical Studies in European Agricultural Productivity* (Manchester, 1991)

Cannadine, D. *The Decline and Fall of the British Aristocracy* (New Haven, Conn., 1990)

Chambers, J. D. and Mingay, G. E. *The Agricultural Revolution, 1750–1880* (London, 1966)

Chartres, J. A. 'The marketing of agricultural produce', in Thirsk, *Agrarian History of England and Wales*, V, II (1985), pp. 406–502

Chartres, J. A. and Hey, D. (eds.). *English Rural Society 1500–1800* (Cambridge, 1990)

Clark, G. 'Productivity growth without technical change: European agriculture before 1850', *Journal of Economic History*, 47 (1987), 419–33

'Yields per acre in English agriculture 1266–1860: evidence from labour inputs', *EcHR*, 44 (1991), 445–60

'Labour productivity in English agriculture 1300–1860', in Campbell and Overton (eds.), *Land, Labour and Livestock* (1991), pp. 211–35

'Agriculture and the industrial revolution: 1700–1850', in Mokyr (ed.), *The British Industrial Revolution* (1993), pp. 227–66

Clay, C. 'The price of freehold land in the later seventeenth and eighteenth centuries', *EcHR*, 27 (1974), 173–89

'Lifeleasehold in the western counties of England, 1650–1750', *AgHR*, 29 (1981), 83–96

'Landlords and estate management in England', in Thirsk, *Agrarian History of England and Wales*, V, II (1985), pp. 119–251

Coleman, D. C. *The Economy of England 1450–1750* (Oxford, 1977)

Collins, E. J. T. 'Did mid-Victorian Britain fail? Output, productivity and technological change in nineteenth-century farming', *REFRESH*, 21 (1995), 1–4

Collins, E. J. T. (ed.). *The Cambridge Agrarian History of England and Wales, Vol.* VII *1850–1914* (Cambridge, forthcoming)

Crafts, N. F. R. *British Economic Growth during the Industrial Revolution* (Oxford, 1985)

Cronne, H. A., Moody, T. W. and Quinn, D. B. (eds.). *Essays in British and Irish History in Honour of James Eddie Todd* (London, 1949)

Currie, J. M. *The Economic Theory of Agricultural Land Tenure* (Cambridge, 1981)

Davies, M. G. 'Country gentry and falling rents in the 1660s and 1670s', *Midland History*, 4 (1977), 86–96

Deane, P. and Cole, W. A. *British Economic Growth 1688–1959* (Cambridge, 1969, 2nd edn)

Denham, P. V. 'The Duke of Bedford's Tavistock estate. 1820–1838', *Reports and Transactions of the Devon Association of the Advancement of Science*, 110 (1978), 19–51

Dictionary of National Biography, XII, XVII (Oxford, 1921–2), unnumbered volume for 1931–40 (Oxford, 1949)

Dunbabin, J. P. D. 'Oxford and Cambridge college finances, 1871–1913', *EcHR*, 28 (1975), 631–47

English, B. 'On the eve of the Great Depression: the economy of the Sledmere estate 1869–1878', *Business History*, 24 (1982), 23–47

'Patterns of estate management in East Yorkshire c. 1840–c. 1880', *AgHR*, 32 (1984), 29–48

The Great Landowners of East Yorkshire 1530–1910 (London, 1990)

Fairlie, S. 'The corn laws and British wheat production 1829–76', *EcHR*, 22 (1969), 88–116

Farrant, S. 'John Ellman of Glynde in Sussex', *AgHR*, 26 (1978), 77–88

Feinstein, C. H. 'Agriculture', in Feinstein and Pollard (eds.), *Studies in Capital Formation* (1988), pp. 267–80

Feinstein, C. H. and Pollard, S. (eds.). *Studies in Capital Formation in the United Kingdom 1750–1920* (Cambridge, 1988)

Fisher, J. R. *Clare Sewell Read 1826–1905: A Farmers' Spokesman of the Late Nineteenth Century* (University of Hull Occasional Papers in Economic and Social History, 8, 1975)

Fletcher, T. W. 'The Great Depression of English agriculture, 1873–1896', *EcHR*, 13 (1961), 417–32, reprinted in Minchinton (ed.), *Essays in Agrarian History* II (1968), pp. 239–56

Floud, R. and McCloskey, D. (eds.). *The Economic History of Britain since 1700. Vol. I, 1700–1860* (Cambridge, 1st edn, 1981)
    The Economic History of Britain since 1700: Vol I, 1700–1860; Vol. II 1860–1914 (Cambridge, 2nd edn, 1994)

Gavin, Sir William, *Ninety Years of Family Farming: The Story of Lord Rayleigh's and Strutt and Parker Farms* (London, 1967)

G.E.C. *The Complete Peerage*, 12 vols. (London, 1910–59)

Ginter, D. E. *A Measure of Wealth: The English Land Tax in Historical Analysis* (London, 1992)

Glennie, P. 'Continuity and change in Hertfordshire agriculture 1550–1700', *AgHR*, 36 (1988), in two parts, 55–76, 145–61

Goody, J., Thirsk, J. and Thompson, E. P. (eds.), *Family and Inheritance: Rural Society in Western Europe, 1200–1800* (Cambridge, 1976)

Gregson, N. 'Tawney revisited: custom and the emergence of capitalist class relations in north-east Cumbria, 1600–1830', *EcHR*, 42 (1989), 18–42

Grigg, D. B. 'A note on agricultural rent and expenditure in nineteenth-century England', *Agricultural History*, 39 (1965), 147–54

Habakkuk, H. J. 'English landownership, 1680–1740', *EcHR*, 1st series, 10 (1939–40), 2–17
    Marriage, Debt, and the Estates System: English Landownership 1650–1950 (Oxford, 1994)

Hainsworth, D. R. *Stewards, Lords and People: The Estate Steward and His World in Later Stuart England* (Cambridge, 1992)

Hainsworth, D. R. and Walker, C. (eds.)., *The Correspondence of Lord Fitzwilliam of Milton and Francis Guybon, His Steward 1697–1709* (Northampton, 1990)

Healy, M. J. R. and Jones, E. L. 'Wheat yields in England, 1815–59', *JRSS*, 125 (1962), 574–9

HMSO, *A Century of Agricultural Statistics: Great Britain 1866–1966* (London, 1968)

Holderness, B. A. 'Landlord's capital formation in East Anglia, 1750–1870', *EcHR*, 25 (1972), 434–47
    'The Victorian farmer', in Mingay (ed.), *The Victorian Countryside*, 1 (1981), pp. 227–44
    'Agriculture, 1770–1860', in Feinstein and Pollard (eds.), *Studies in Capital Formation* (1988), pp. 9–34
    'Prices, productivity, and output', in Mingay, *Agrarian History of England and Wales*, VI (1989), pp. 84–189

Holderness, B. A. and Turner, M. E. (eds.). *Land, Labour and Agriculture, 1700–1820* (London, 1991)

Holmes, G. S. 'Gregory King and the social structure of pre-industrial England', *Transactions of the Royal Historical Society*, 27 (1977), 41–68

Homer, S. *A History of Interest Rates* (New Brunswick, 1963)

Hoskins, W. G. 'Harvest fluctuations and English economic history, 1620–1759', *AgHR*, 16 (1968), 15–31

Howard, H. F. *An Account of the Finances of the College of St John the Evangelist in the University of Cambridge 1511–1926* (Cambridge, 1935)

Howell, D. W. 'The economy of the landed estates of Pembrokeshire, c. 1680–1830', *Welsh History Review*, 3 (1966–7), 265–86

    Land and People in Nineteenth Century Wales (London, 1977)

    'Landlords and estate management in Wales', in Thirsk, *Agrarian History of England and Wales*, V, II (1985), pp. 252–97

    Patriarchs and Parasites: The Gentry of South-West Wales in the Eighteenth Century (Cardiff, University of Wales Press, 1986)

Hoyle, R. W. 'Tenure and the land market in early modern England: a late contribution to the Brenner debate', *EcHR*, 43 (1990), 1–20

Hueckel, G. 'English farming profits during the Napoleonic Wars, 1793–1815', *Explorations in Economic History*, 13 (1976), 331–45

Hughes, E. 'The eighteenth-century estate agent', in Cronne, Moody, and Quinn (eds.), *Essays in British and Irish History* (1949), pp. 185–99

Hunt, H. G. 'Agricultural rent in south-east England, 1788–1825', *AgHR*, 6 (1958), 98–108

Ippolito, R. A. 'The effect of the "agricultural depression" on industrial demand in England, 1730–1750', *Economica*, 42 (1975), 298–312

Jackson, R. V. 'Growth and deceleration in English agriculture', *EcHR*, 38 (1985), 333–51

Jensen, E. *Danish Agriculture: Its Economic Development* (Copenhagen, 1937)

Jones, E. L. *Agriculture and the Industrial Revolution* (Oxford, 1974)

    'Agriculture 1700–80', in Floud and McCloskey (eds.), *The Economic History of Britain* (1981)

Jones, E. L. and Mingay, G. E. (eds.). *Land, Labour and Population in the Industrial Revolution* (London, 1967)

Kain, R. J. P. *An Atlas and Index of the Tithe Files of Mid-Nineteenth-Century England and Wales* (Cambridge, 1986)

Kelch, R. A. *Newcastle: A Duke Without Money: Thomas Pelham-Holles 1693–1768* (London, 1974)

Kerridge, E. *The Agricultural Revolution* (London, 1967)

Lennard, R. 'Rural Northamptonshire under the Commonwealth', in Vinogradoff (ed.), *Oxford Studies* (1916)

Lindert, P. H. and Williamson, J. G. 'Revising Britain's social tables, 1688–1913', *Explorations in Economic History*, 19 (1982), 385–408

MacCarthy, R. B. *The Trinity College Estates 1800–1923: Corporate Management in an Age of Reform* (Dublin, 1992)

Mathias, P. 'The social structure in the eighteenth century: a calculation by Joseph Massie', *EcHR*, 10 (1957), 30–45

    The First Industrial Nation: An Economic History of Britain 1700–1914 (London, 1969)

Megarry, R. and Wade, H. W. R. *The Law of Real Property* (London, 1984, 5th edn)

Michie, R. C. 'Income, expenditure and investment of a Victorian millionaire: Lord Overstone, 1823–83', *Bulletin of the Institute of Historical Research*, 58 (1985), 59–77

Milward, A. S. and Saul, S. B. *The Development of the Economies of Continental Europe 1850–1914* (London, 1977)

Minchinton, W. E. (ed.). *Essays in Agrarian History* II (Newton Abbot, 1968)

Mingay, G. E. 'The agricultural depression 1730–1750', *EcHR*, 8 (1956), 323–38

   English Landed Society in the Eighteenth Century (London, 1963)

   'The eighteenth-century land steward', in E. L. Jones and G. E. Mingay (eds.), *Land, Labour and Population in the Industrial Revolution* (London, 1967), pp. 3–27

Mingay, G. E. (ed.). *Arthur Young and His Times* (London, 1975)

   (ed.). *The Victorian Countryside* (2 vols., London, 1981)

   'The East Midlands', in Thirsk, *Agrarian History of England and Wales*, V, I (1984), pp. 89–128

   'The course of rents in the age of Malthus', chapter 6 of M. E. Turner (ed.), *Malthus and His Time* (London, 1986)

   (ed.). *The Cambridge Agrarian History of England and Wales*, VI *1750–1850* (Cambridge, 1989)

Mitchell, B. R. and Deane, P. (eds.). *Abstract of British Historical Statistics* (Cambridge, 1962)

Mitchison, R. 'The Old Board of Agriculture (1793–1822)', *English Historical Review*, 74 (1959), 41–69

Mokyr, J. (ed.). *The British Industrial Revolution: An Economic Perspective* (Oxford, 1993)

Moore, D. C. 'The corn laws and high farming', *EcHR*, 18 (1965), 544–61

Obelkevich, J. *Religion and Rural Society: South Lindsey 1825–1875* (Oxford, 1976)

O'Brien, P. K. 'British incomes and property in the early nineteenth century', *EcHR*, 12 (1959), 255–67

   'Agriculture and the home market for English industry, 1660–1820', *English Historical Review*, C, no. 397 (1985), 773–800

Offer, A. 'Farm tenure and land values in England, *c.* 1750–1950', *EcHR*, 44 (1991), 1–20

Ó Gráda, C. 'The beginnings of the Irish creamery system, 1880–1914', *EcHR*, 30 (1977), 284–305

   'British agriculture, 1860–1914', in Floud and McCloskey (eds.), *The Economic History of Britain*, II (1994), pp. 145–72

Olson, M. *The Economics of the Wartime Shortage* (Durham, N.C., 1963)

Ormrod, D. *English Grain Exports and the Structure of Agrarian Capitalism 1700–1760* (University of Hull Occasional Papers in Economic and Social History, 12, 1985)

Orwin, C. S. and Whetham, E. H. *History of British Agriculture 1846–1914* (Newton Abbot, 1964)

Overton, M. 'Estimating yields from probate inventories: an example from East Anglia, 1585–1735', *Journal of Economic History*, 39 (1979), 363–78

   'Agricultural productivity in eighteenth-century England: some further speculations', *EcHR*, 37 (1984), 244–51

'Re-establishing the English agricultural revolution', *AgHR*, 44 (1996), 1–18

Oxley Parker, J. *The Oxley Parker Papers: From the Letters of an Essex family of Land Agents in the Nineteenth Century* (Colchester, 1964)

Parker, R. A. C. *Coke of Norfolk: A Financial and Agricultural Study 1702–1842* (Oxford, 1975)

Perren, R. *The Meat Trade in Britain 1840–1914* (London, 1978)

Agriculture in Depression, 1870–1914, (London, 1995)

Perry, P. J. (ed.), *British Agriculture 1875–1914* (London, 1973)

Perry, P. J. and Johnston, R. J. 'The temporal and spatial incidence of agricultural depression in Dorset, 1868–1902', *Journal of Interdisciplinary History*, 3 (1972), 297–311

Peters, G. H., Parsons, S. T. and Patchett, D. M. 'A century of land values 1781–1880', *Oxford Agrarian Studies*, 11 (1982), 93–107

Phillips, A. D. M. *The Underdrainage of Farmland in England During the Nineteenth Century* (Cambridge, 1989)

Pollard, S. *The Genesis of Modern Management* (London, 1965)

Pollard, S. and Crossley, D. W. *The Wealth of Britain 1085–1966* (London, 1968)

Pressnell, L. S. *Country Banking in the Industrial Revolution* (Oxford, 1956)

Prince, H. C. 'The changing rural landscape, 1750–1850', in Mingay, *Agrarian History of England and Wales*, VI (1989), pp. 7–83

Purdum, J. J. 'Profitability and timing of parliamentary land enclosures', *Explorations in Economic History*, 15 (1978), 313–26

Rhee, H. A. *The Rent of Agricultural Land in England and Wales* (London, Central Landowners Association, 1946)

Richards, E. *The Leviathan of Wealth* (London, 1973)

'"Leviathan of wealth": west Midland agriculture 1800–50', *AgHR*, 22 (1974), 97–117

'The land agent', in Mingay (ed.), *The Victorian Countryside*, II (1981), pp. 439–56

Robinson, O. 'The London companies as progressive landlords in nineteenth century Ireland', *EcHR*, 15 (1962), 103–18

Roebuck, P. 'Absentee landownership in the late seventeenth and early eighteenth centuries: a neglected factor in English agrarian history', *AgHR*, 21 (1973), 1–17

Yorkshire Baronets 1640–1760: Families, Estates and Fortunes (Oxford, 1980)

Rogers, G. 'Lancashire landowners and the Great Agricultural Depression', *Northern History*, 22 (1986), 250–68

Searle, C. E. 'Custom, class conflict and agrarian capitalism: the Cumbrian customary economy in the eighteenth century', *Past and Present*, 110 (1986), 106–33

'Customary tenants and the enclosure of the Cumbrian commons', *Northern History*, 29 (1993), 126–53

Sharples, M. 'The Fawkes–Turner connection and the art collection at Farnley Hall, Otley, 1792–1937: a great estate enhanced and supported', *Northern History*, 26 (1990), 131–59

Spring, D. 'Land and politics in Edwardian England', *Agricultural History*, 58 (1984),
    17–42
Stamp, Sir Josiah, *British Incomes and Property* (London, 1927 reprint)
Thirsk, J. 'Agrarian history 1540–1950', in Victoria County History, *Leicestershire*, II
    (Oxford, 1954), pp. 199–264
    England's Agricultural Regions and Agrarian History, 1500–1750 (London, 1987)
Thirsk, J. (ed.). *The Cambridge Agrarian History of England and Wales*, IV *1500–1640*
    (Cambridge, 1967)
    The Cambridge Agrarian History of England and Wales, V *1640–1750* I, *Regional Farming
    Systems* (Cambridge, 1984)
    The Cambridge Agrarian History of England and Wales, V *1640–1750* II, *Agrarian Change*
    (Cambridge, 1985)
Thirsk, J. and Imray, J. *Suffolk Farming in the Nineteenth Century* (Ipswich, 1958)
Thompson, E. P. 'The grid of inheritance: a comment', in Goody, Thirsk, and
    Thompson (eds.), *Family and Inheritance* (1976), pp. 328–60
Thompson, F. M. L. 'Agriculture since 1870', in Victoria County History, *Wiltshire*,
    IV (London, 1954), pp. 92–114
    'The land market in the nineteenth century', *Oxford Economic Papers*, 9 (1957),
    285–300, reprinted in Minchinton (ed.), *Essays in Agrarian History* (1968),
    pp. 29–54
    English Landed Society in the Nineteenth Century (London, 1963)
    'The social distribution of landed property in England since the sixteenth
    century', *EcHR*, 19 (1966), 505–17
    'The second agricultural revolution, 1815–1880', *EcHR*, 31 (1968), 62–77
    'An anatomy of English agriculture, 1870–1914', in Holderness and Turner (eds.),
    Land, Labour and Agriculture (1991), pp. 211–40
Trueman, B. E. S. 'Corporate estate management: Guy's Hospital agricultural
    estates, 1726–1815', *AgHR*, 28 (1980), 31–44
Turner, M. E. *English Parliamentary Enclosure: Its Historical Geography and Economic
    History* (Folkestone, 1980)
    'Costs, finance, and parliamentary enclosure', *EcHR*, 34 (1981), 236–48
    'Agricultural productivity in England in the eighteenth century: evidence from
    crop yields', *EcHR*, 35 (1982), 489–510
    Enclosures in Britain 1750–1830 (London, 1984)
    'Agricultural productivity in eighteenth-century England: further strains of
    speculation', *EcHR*, 37 (1984), 252–7
    'Corn crises in the age of Malthus', in Turner (ed.), *Malthus* (1986), pp. 112–28
    (ed.), *Malthus and His Time* (London, 1986)
    'Crop distributions, land productivity and English parliamentary enclosure',
    Journal of Economic History, 46 (1986), 669–92
    'Economic protest in rural society: opposition to parliamentary enclosure in
    Buckinghamshire', *Southern History*, 10 (1988), 94–128
    'Output and prices in UK agriculture, 1867–1914, and the Great Agricultural
    Depression reconsidered', *AgHR*, 40 (1992), 38–51

After the Famine: Irish Agriculture 1850–1914 (Cambridge, 1996)

'Agricultural output, income and productivity', in Collins (ed.), *The Agrarian History* VII (forthcoming)

Turner, M. E., Beckett, J. V. and Afton, B. 'Taking stock: farmers, farm records, and agricultural output in England 1700–1850', *AgHR*, 44 (1996), 21–34

Turner, M. E. and Mills, D. R. (eds.). *Land and Property: The English Land Tax 1692–1832* (Gloucester, 1986)

Vinogradoff, P. (ed.). *Oxford Studies in Social and Legal History*, 5 (Oxford, 1916)

Wade Martins, S. *A Great Estate at Work: The Holkham Estate and its Inhabitants in the Nineteenth Century* (Cambridge, 1980)

Wake, Joan *The Brudenells of Deene* (London, 1953)

Ward, J. T. 'Farm sale prices over a hundred years', *The Estates Gazette, Centenary Supplement*, 3 May 1958, 47–9

'The Earls Fitzwilliam and the Wentworth Woodhouse Estate in the nineteenth century', *Yorkshire Bulletin of Economic and Social Research*, 12 (1960), 19–27

Wells, R. *Wretched Faces: Famine in Wartime England 1793–1803* (Gloucester, 1988)

Wilkes, A. R. 'Adjustments in arable farming after the Napoleonic Wars', *AgHR*, 28 (1980), 90–103

Williams, J. D. 'The finances of an eighteenth-century Essex nobleman', *Essex Archaeology and History*, 9 (1977), 113–27

Wordie, J. R. 'Social change on the Leveson-Gower estates', *EcHR*, 27 (1974), 593–609

'Pilot investigation into the sources available for the study of English landed estates between 1640–1840', *SSRC Final Report*, HR 4510, September 1978

'Rent movements and the English tenant farmer, 1700–1839', *Research in Economic History*, 6 (1986), 193–243

Wrigley, E. A. 'Energy availability and agricultural productivity', in Campbell and Overton (eds.), *Land, Labour and Livestock* (1991), pp. 323–39

Wrigley, E. A. and Schofield, R. S. *The Population History of England 1541–1871. A Reconstruction* (London, 1981)

Unpublished theses

Adams, M. G. 'Agricultural change in the East Riding of Yorkshire, 1850–1880: an economic and social history' (University of Hull, PhD thesis, 1977)

Barnes, P. B. 'The economic history of landed estates in Norfolk since 1880' (University of East Anglia, PhD thesis, 1984)

Beckett, J. V. 'Landownership in Cumbria, 1680–1750' (University of Lancaster, PhD thesis, 1975)

Bettey, J. H. 'Agriculture and society in Dorset, *c.* 1560–1700' (University of Bristol, PhD thesis, 1977)

Chesher, V. M. 'A social and economic study of some west Cornwall landed families, 1690–1760' (University of Oxford, BLitt thesis, 1956)

Davies, O. R. F. 'The dukes of Devonshire, Newcastle, and Rutland, 1688–1714: a study in wealth and political influence' (University of Oxford, DPhil thesis, 1971)

Gunstone, D. P. 'Stewardship and landed society: a study of the stewards of the Longleat estate, 1779–1895' (University of Exeter, MA thesis, 1972)

Hughes, W. M. 'Lead, land and coal as sources of landlords' income in Northumberland between 1700–1850' (University of Newcastle, PhD thesis, 1963)

Martin, J. O. 'The landed estate: Glamorgan, c. 1660–1760' (University of Cambridge, PhD thesis, 1978)

Mingay, G. E. 'Landownership and agrarian trends in the eighteenth century' (University of Nottingham, PhD thesis, 1958)

Nunn, P. 'The management of some south Yorkshire landed estates in the eighteenth and nineteenth centuries, linked with the central economic development of the area (1700–1850)' (University of Sheffield, PhD thesis, 1985)

Perren, R. 'The effects of agricultural depression on the English estates of the dukes of Sutherland, 1870–1900' (University of Nottingham, PhD thesis, 1967)

Raybould, T. J. 'The Dudley estate: its rise and decline between 1774 and 1947' (University of Kent, PhD thesis, 1970)

Richards, E. 'James Loch and the House of Sutherland, 1821–1855' (University of Nottingham, PhD thesis, 1967)

Roake, M. 'The Camer estate, 1716–1852' (University of Kent, MA thesis, 1969)

Roe, P. 'Norfolk agriculture 1815–1914' (University of East Anglia, MPhil thesis, 1976)

Rogers, G. 'Social and economic change on Lancashire landed estates during the nineteenth century with special reference to the Clifton estate, 1832–1916' (University of Lancaster, PhD thesis, 1981)

Searle, C. E. 'The Odd Corner of England: an analysis of a rural social formation in transition, c. 1700–1914' (University of Essex, PhD thesis, 1983)

Shrimpton, C. 'The landed society and the farming community of Essex in the late eighteenth and early nineteenth centuries' (University of Cambridge, PhD thesis, 1965)

Sturgess, R. W. 'The response of agriculture in Staffordshire to the price changes of the nineteenth century' (University of Manchester, PhD thesis, 1965)

Swann, B. A. S. 'A study of some London estates in the eighteenth century' (University of London, PhD thesis, 1964)

Thompson, F. M. L. 'The economic and social background of the English landed interest, 1840–1870, with particular reference to the estates of the Dukes of Northumberland' (University of Oxford, DPhil thesis, 1956)

Trueman, B. E. S. 'The management of the estates of Guy's Hospital 1726–1900' (University of Nottingham, PhD thesis, 1975)

Walton, J. R. 'Aspects of agrarian change in Oxfordshire, 1750–1880' (University of Oxford, DPhil thesis, 1976)

Ward, J. T. 'A study of capital and rental values of agricultural land in England and Wales between 1858 and 1958' (London University, PhD thesis, 1960)

Wilkes, A. R. 'Depression and recovery in English agriculture after the Napoleonic Wars' (University of Reading, PhD thesis, 1975)

Williams, J. D. 'A study of an eighteenth-century nobleman, his house, household and estate: Sir John Griffin, 4th Lord Howard de Walden, 1st Lord Braybrooke, of Audley End, Essex, 1719–1797' (University of London, PhD thesis, 1974)

Wilmot, S. A. H. 'Landownership, farm structure and agrarian change in south-west England, 1800–1900: regional experience and national ideals' (University of Exeter, PhD thesis, 1988)

Wordie, J. R. 'A great landed estate in the eighteenth century: aspects of management on the Leveson-Gower properties, 1691–1833' (University of Reading, PhD thesis, 1967)

Index

abatements, *see* rent
accounting practices 15, 72, 87–8
Acland estate, Devon 89
acreages
    raw data 260–302
Adams, Michael
    on Sledmere 143
Adwick estate, Yorkshire W 82, 158
    arrears 181–2
    estate details 260
agricultural depression 4, 14, 253–4
    early-eighteenth-century 149–50, 179–84,
        226–9
    post-French wars 20, 24, 43, 68, 108–11,
        150, 171, 179–84, 200, 238–45, 255–6
    late-nineteenth-century 24n, 81, 104,
        111–37, 150, 171, 173–4, 179–84, 197,
        200, 208, 211, 213, 223, 213, 249–52,
        257
    see also crisis in agriculture; 'Feast and
        Famine'
Agricultural Distress Committee of 1833
    68
    see also agricultural depression, post-French
        wars; Select Committee, 1836
agricultural output, *see* output
agricultural prices, *see* prices
agricultural productivity 225, 203–4, 235–6
    see also labour productivity
agricultural prosperity 233–8
agricultural regions, *see* Caird; Kerridge;
        Prince; Thirsk
Agrarian History of England and Wales 2, 6, 52
Allen, R.C. 4, 174
    on agricultural output 207
    on enclosure 16, 201, 234
    on long-term rents 52–7
    on rent estimates 163–5
    on rent index 254
    on Ricardian surpluses 67–8
Allgood estates, Northumberland 51
allowances, *see* rent
Ancaster, Earl of 251, 260–1, 285
    see also Ancaster estates
Ancaster estates, Lincolnshire and Rutland
    agricultural depression 114–15, 244
    estate details 260, 285
Anderson-Pelham family, *see* Yarborough,
        Earl of
Andover, Hampshire 258
    estate details 279
animal imports 111–12
animal product prices, *see* prices; livestock
annual tenancies, *see* tenancy at will
annuities, *see* interest rates
arable
    regions 185–98
    rents 38, 41, 45
    rents and other land uses 46, 191–8
archaic rents, *see* beneficial leases; copyhold;
        tenure
archival sources 77–83
Argentina
    bank stock 222
    imports from 111, 248
arrears, *see* rent
Ashburnham, Earls of 261–2
    see also Ashburnham; Barking Hall;
        Petworth
Ashburnham estate, Sussex 89–90, 244
    estate details 261
    industrial rents 93
assessed rent, *see* rent
Audley End estate, Essex 146
    estate details 293
    land acquisitions of 89
Australasia
    imports from 111, 248

Aylesbury, Buckinghamshire
  untenanted farms   242
  see also Vale of Aylesbury

Badminton estate, Gloucestershire   99, 182,
  189, 244, 258
  agricultural depression   229
  estate details   262
  industrial rents   93
Balliol College, Oxford   30
Barbon, Nicholas
  on interest rates   217, 220
Barking Hall estate, Suffolk   244
  estate details   262
  estate surveys   101–2
Basingthorpe estate, Yorkshire E, *see* Crowle
Bassett family, of Tehidy, Cornwall, *see*
  Tehidy
Batchelor, Thomas
  on Bedfordshire rents   40
Bateman, John
  on arrears   184
  The Great Landowners   119n, 129, 158n, 161,
  258
Bath, Marquess of   33, 274
  see also Longleat
Battle Abbey estate, Sussex   89
Beaufort, Duke of   262
  see also Badminton
Beckett, J.V.
  on agricultural depression   229
Bective, Earl of   285
Bective estate, Westmorland   285
Bedfont, Middlesex   46, 109
Bedford, Duke of   4, 137, 251, 254, 276,
  291–3, 300–1
  and agricultural depression   113
  and capital provision   24
  and income   134
  and investment   223
  and R.J. Thompson's rent index   129,
  131–2
  and Royal Commission of 1890s   116
  on inheritance   130–1
  see also Bedford estates; Tavistock;
  Thorney; Woburn
Bedford estates   98, 115, 119, 124
  and R.J. Thompson's rent index   120
  estate surveys   101n
  see also Tavistock; Thorney; Woburn
Bedfordshire   34, 38, 40, 53, 279, 293, 301
  and Caird's agricultural regions   185
  and R.J. Thompson's rent index   125–8,
  166
  beneficial leases   26
  customary tenants   26

density of cover of rent index   162
  see also Bedford, Duke of; Bedford estates;
  Stagsden; Woburn
Beeke, Rev. Henry   52
  rent estimates   164
Beighton estate, Derbyshire and Yorkshire
  182, 244
  agricultural depression   229
  estate details   263
Bellerby, J.R.
  long-run rent series   166, 168, 170
Belvoir
  estates of Duke of Rutland   77
beneficial leases   2–3, 24–32, 73–4, 79, 95–6,
  134n, 136, 234, 256
beneficial rents   100
Bennet, Thomas
  witness to 1836 Select Committee   110
Berkeley family, *see* Fitzhardinge, Lord
Berkshire   41, 45, 110, 297
  and Caird's agricultural regions   185
  and Oriel College, Oxford   135–6
  and the Property Tax   30
  density of cover of rent index   162
Bertie family, *see* Ancaster, Earl of
Bilborough Crown estate, Lincolnshire   280
Bishops Cannings Crown estate, Wiltshire
  with Bromham
  estate details   280
Blandford, Dorset   38
Board of Agriculture   3, 15, 47, 111, 164,
  253
  and farmers   70
  General Views and rents   39–43
  on rents during French wars   66
Bolton Abbey estate, Yorkshire W   102–3,
  244
  estate details   263, 286
  estate surveys   102–3
  free rents   96
  pattern of land acquisition   102–4
Bolton, Lord   270, 278
  see also Hackwood; Wallop
Boroughbridge Crown estate, Yorkshire N
  281
Bowden, Peter
  on prices   226, 232
  on rents   232
Boys, John
  on Kent rents   41
Bradford estate, Wiltshire   82, 158, 264
Brandesburton, Yorkshire E
  agricultural depression   229
  see also Emanuel Hospital
Brasenose College, Oxford
  income   30

Brassley, Paul
  on Northumberland rents   229
Braybrooke, Lord   293
Brickwell, John
  witness to 1836 Select Committee   20, 240
Brigg estate, Lincolnshire   83
  see also Brocklesby; Yarborough
Bristol, Marquess of   284
Broadlands estate, Hampshire
  estate details   264
Brocklesby estate, Lincolnshire   82–3
  estate details   265
Bromham Crown estate, Wiltshire, see
  Bishops Canning
Brudenell family   32
Buckingham, Duke of   78, 185
Buckinghamshire   20, 38, 44–5, 109–10, 222,
    240, 293, 301
  agricultural depression   227
  and the Coke estate   141
  and Oriel College Oxford   135
  and Prize Essay   48
  and R.J. Thompson's rent index   125–9,
    166
  enclosure   231
  seventeenth-century rents   226
  Stowe rents   66
  untenanted farms   242
  see also Woburn
Buckland, George
  Prize Essay on Kent   48
Burton Constable, Yorkshire E   78
  copyholds   31
Burton Dassett, Warwickshire   66

Caird, James   50, 52, 253
  on agricultural production   236
  on agricultural regions   191–4, 185–6, 188,
    198, 237, 255
  on county-wide rents c. 1850   44–5
  on rent estimates   164
  on under-renting   16
Calthrop, Mr
  witness to 1836 Select Committee   108
Cambridge colleges   28–9, 46, 83, 133,
    135–6
  beneficial leases   31n, 95
  see also under names of individual colleges
Cambridgeshire   40, 146, 240, 292, 297,
    300
  and the Ecclesiastical Commissioners
    129
  and the Property Tax   30
  and R.J. Thompson's rent index   125–8,
    166
  Prize Essay on   48

  see also King's College; St John's College;
    Thorney
Camer estate, Kent
  long leases   68
Campbell, B.M.S.
  on regional specialisation   205
Canadian bank stock   222
capital   2, 11
  improvements   11
  investment   246, 249
  provision of   22–3
  return on tenant capital   9–11, 20
capital flight   243
capital formation   211n
Cardiganshire
  land tax   62
Carlisle, Earl of   51, 265
Carrington, Lord
  and R.J. Thompson's rent index   129
Castle Howard estate, Yorkshire N and E
    154, 156, 178, 189, 244
  agricultural depression   229
  arrears   182
  economic recovery   251
  estate details   265
  free rents   96
Cattle Diseases Prevention Act   247
cattle plague   247
Cavendish estates   104–5
  see also Devonshire, Duke of
Cavendish family, see Devonshire, Duke of
Cavendish-Bentinck family, see Portland,
  Duke of
chalklands
  and Thirsk's agricultural regions   187
Chambers, J.D. and Mingay, G.
  long-run rent index   50–3, 57, 148–9, 237,
    254
  on agricultural depression   228
Chandos, Marquess of
  member of 1836 Select Committee   109
charities
  rents from charity lands   76
  see also under individual hospital names
Charity Commissioners   57n, 76
Chatsworth estate, Derbyshire   77, 137n,
    258
  estate details   266, 286
  organisation of rents   99
  see also Devonshire, Duke of
Cheshire   198n, 267, 272, 282, 287
  agricultural depression   227
  and the Ecclesiastical Commissioners   125
  density of cover of rent index   162
  see also Cholmondeley; Eaton; Haklyn;
    Knowsley

Chesterfield estate, Derbyshire, *see* Staveley
Chevening estate, Kent and Surrey   244
  economic recovery   251
  estate details   266
Chichester-Constable family
  Yorkshire farms   75
Chiltern Hills   185
  Prize Essay and rents 1850s   48
Chipping Norton, Gloucestershire   240
Chirk Castle, Denbighshire, *see* Myddleton
Cholmondeley estate, Cheshire   244
  estate details   267
Cholmondeley, Marquess of   267, 282
Chortley estate, Staffordshire   105
Christ Church College, Oxford
  income   30
chronology of cover
  of rent index   154–9
Church of England
  and beneficial leases   25, 95
Civil War (English)   71–2
Civil War (USA)   248
Clark, Gregory
  on labour productivity   203
  on long-term rents   57n
classical economists   7–12
  see also Malthus; Physiocrats; Ricardo;
    Smith, Adam
Clay, Christopher
  on beneficial leases   25
  on years' purchase   217–18, 220
Clifton estate, Lancashire   24
Cobham estate, Kent   66
  long leases   68
Cobham, Viscount
  member of 1890s Royal Commission
    113
Cockermouth estate, Cumberland
  estate details   267
  estate surveys   101
Coke, T.W. of Holkham, Earl of Leicester
  13–14, 66, 141, 271, 282
  and capital provision   22–3
  and income   134
  and investment   222
  and long leases   68
  see also Holkham; Parker, R.A.C.; Wade
    Martins
Colbeck, T.L.
  Prize Essay on Northumberland   48–9,
    189–90
colleges, of Oxford and Cambridge
see under separate names
  see also Oxford Colleges
Collins, E. J. T.
  on High Farming   247

Colquhoun, Patrick
  and national income   59–60
Compton, Hampshire
  enclosure and rents   231
consols, *see* interest rates
Constable, Sir Clifford of Burton Constable,
    Yorkshire E   78
Constable, Sir Marmaduke of Everingham,
    Yorkshire E   33
Contagious Diseases Acts of 1860s   112, 247
copyhold tenure   1, 25–6
  copyhold cottages   73
  Copyhold Enfranchisement Acts   31
corn
  rents   241
  scarcity   19
  trade   225–6
  see also arable; grain, trade
Corn Bounty 1688   226
corn laws   111, 226, 238–9, 245–50
Cornwall   17, 41, 198n, 276–7, 291
  and the Property Tax   92
  mineral rents   92
  tenurial practices   25, 28
  see also Tavistock; Trewithen
Cornwallis estate, Kent and Sussex   98, 244
  estate details   268
corporate bodies, *see* under proper names of
Corringham, R.W.
  Prize Essay on Nottinghamshire   48
cottage rents, *see* rent
Courtenay estate, Devon   89
Crafts, N.F.R.
  on agricultural output   236
  on national income   60
Craigie, Major P.G.
  on agricultural production   236
  witness to 1890s Royal Commission   114
Crawfurd, Thomas, chief accountant to the
  1st Duke of Buckingham   78, 185–6
crisis in agriculture   238–52
  see also agricultural depression; 'Feast and
    Famine'
crop yields, *see* grain, yields
Crowle estate, Lincolnshire   244
  arrears   182
  estate details   273
Crown estates   83, 258
  estate details   279–81
Cumberland   38, 45, 198n, 267–9
  land tax   62
  mineral rents   92–3
  see also Cockermouth; Dalemain
Cumbria   229
  density of cover of rent index   162
  tenurial practices   27

customary practices 1, 3, 25–6, 202
  see also beneficial leases; copyhold tenure
customaryhold 25–6

Dalemain estate, Cumberland and
    Westmorland
  estate details 268
  farm rents 100
Darnley, Lord
  Cobham rents, Kent 66
Davies, Margaret Gay
  on seventeenth-century rents 226
Davies, O.R.F.
  on the Cavendish estates 104–5
Davis, Thomas, steward at Longleat 33
Dean and Chapter, Durham
  archaic leases 29
Deanston, Perthshire 110
Deene estate, Northamptonshire
  rent audit 32
Denbighshire
  agricultural depression 227
  see also Myddleton estate
Denham, Buckinghamshire 109
Denmark
  competition in trade 247–8
density of cover
  of rent index 159–62
depression, see agricultural depression
  see also crisis in agriculture; 'Feast and
    Famine'
Derby, Earl of 272
  Lancashire rents 135n
  see also Knowsley
Derbyshire 40, 45, 49, 119, 263, 266, 283,
    286, 288, 291
  agricultural depression 227
  agricultural regions 189–91
  density of cover of rent index 162
  mineral rents 92
  see also Beighton; Chatsworth; Hardwick;
    Pentrich; Shottle; Staveley
Derwentwater estate, Durham and
    Northumberland, see Greenwich
    Hospital
Devon 17, 40, 89, 146, 276, 290–1, 297
  and the Ecclesiastical Commissioners 125
  density of cover of rent index 162
  long-term rents 58–9, 144
  rents and size of farms in 1894 117–18
  see also Rolle; Tavistock
Devonshire, Duke of 263, 266, 286, 288,
    291
  estates of 77
  industrial rents 93
  mineral rents 92

tenure 73
  see also Bolton Abbey; Cavendish;
    Chatsworth;
Dillon, Viscount 268
  see also Dytchley
Dinton, Buckinghamshire 110
distance decay effects, see London; Property
    Tax; railways; rent
Dorset 38, 40, 276, 291
  and Caird's agricultural regions 185
  and the Coke estate 141n
  copyholds 25n, 27–8
  see also Pitt-Rivers
Duchy of Cornwall
  agricultural depression 114
Duchy of Lancaster
  agricultural depression 114
  tenure 73
Dudley estate, Staffordshire 21, 42n, 140
  cottage rents 80
  tenure 27, 73
dukes, earls, lords, etc., see under individual
    names
Dunstable, Bedfordshire 38
Durham 40, 45, 51, 66
  and Caird's agricultural regions 185
  and the Ecclesiastical Commissioners 129
  archaic leases 29
  density of cover of rent index 162
  see also Greenwich Hospital
Duxford, Cambridgeshire 240
Dytchley estate, Oxfordshire 24, 268

earls, lords, dukes, etc., see under individual
    names
earnings, see wages
East Anglia
  agricultural depression 227
  agricultural output 230
  arrears 184n
  density of cover of rent index 161–2
East Midlands
  density of cover of rent index 162
Eaton estate, Cheshire
  estate details 287
Ecclesiastical Commissioners 83, 125, 137,
    146–7, 156–7, 159, 162, 258, 302
  and R.J. Thompson's rent index 120, 129
  estate details 281, 294
  estate income 121–2
  rents and size of farms 118
economic recovery 251–2
economic rent, see rent
Eden, Sir Frederick Morton
  on data collecting 38
  on rents 42n

Edwardian period   150, 209, 248, 251
Egremont family, *see* Petworth
Ellman, John
    witness to 1836 Select Committee   110
Elmshall, William, of the Deene estate   32
Emanuel Hospital estate, Yorkshire E   154,
        189, 244, 258
    economic recovery   251
    estate details   269
enclosure   233–6, 239
    and agricultural change   231
    and redistribution of income   16
    and rents   75, 201–3
    and tenure   201–2
    and urbanisation   95
enfranchisement, of customary tenure   24–32
English, Barbara
    on Sledmere estate   143, 146
English rent index, *see* rent
entry fines   29, 25
ESRC Data Archive   82n
Essex   20, 109, 144, 277, 280, 293–4
    agricultural depression   227, 241
    and King's College, Cambridge   29
    and Thirsk's agricultural regions   187
    and R.J. Thompson's rent index   125–9,
        166
    density of cover of rent index   161–2
    tenant farms   123
    see also Audley End; Guy's Hospital;
        Hainault; Thorndon
estates
    debts of   222–3
    management of   15
    records of   85–106
    surveys of   79, 100–5
    see also under names of estates
Everingham estate, Yorkshire E
    arrears   33
Eversley, Viscount and Baron, *see*
        Shaw-Lefevre
Evesham, Worcestershire   243
Eyns estate, Cornwall
    beneficial leases   25

Fairlie, S.
    on the corn laws   245
Farley estate, Staffordshire   105
'Farm' estates
    estate details   281
farm rents, *see* rent
farmers   206–9, 211, 214
    and agricultural change   230–1
    and capital   242–3
    and debts   240
    and income   60
    see also tenants
Farmers' Union
    and agricultural depression   114
farming regions, *see* agricultural regions
farms   13, 242
    see also rent; size of farms
Fawkes family of Farnley Hall, Wharfedale
        134
'Feast and Famine'   179–81
fens
    and Thirsk's agricultural regions   187–8
Ferrers, Lord   222
Fetherston-Dilke family   274
    see also Maxstoke
field rents, *see* rent
fines, *see* entry fines; Property Tax
First World War   71, 111, 150, 172, 197, 209,
        248–9, 251
Fitzhardinge, Lord   287–8
Fitzhardinge estate, Gloucestershire   114n,
        119
    estate details   287
Fitzhardinge estate, Middlesex   114n
    estate details   287
Fitzwilliam, Earl   33, 94, 270, 275
Fleming, William, MP
    on the land tax   62
Fletcher, T.W.
    on Lancashire rents   135n
Flintshire   288
    see also Haklyn estate
food supply   225, 238
Fox, Arthur Wilson
    witness to 1890s Royal Commission   114
free rents, *see* rent
French wars   54, 107–8, 205, 212, 238
    and food shortages   233–5
    and interest rates   217–18, 220
    and rents   52n, 66–7, 165, 171, 237
Frewen estate, Sussex   89
Frome, Somerset   42
funds (the), *see* government debt

General Enclosure Act   1801   235
Giffen, Sir Robert
    member of 1890s Royal Commission   113
    witness to 1890s Royal Commission   114
'Giffen good'   113n
Glamorgan   229
    and R.J. Thompson's rent index   129
Gloucestershire   40, 262, 287
    agricultural depression   227
    density of cover of rent index   161
    industrial rents   93
    see also Badminton; Fitzhardinge
Glynde, Sussex   110

Glynde Place estate, Sussex   89
Gooch, Rev. W.
  on Cambridgeshire rents   40
Goodwood estate, Sussex
  estate details   288
Gordon-Lennox family, *see* Richmond and
  Gordon, Duke of
government debt   215–19
government inquiries   4, 109–11, 240–5,
  257–8
  see also Royal Commission of 1890s
Gower, Earl of, *see* Leveson-Gower
Grafton estates, Northamptonshire
  beneficial leases   26
grain
  imports   111–12, 245–9
  prices   228–9, 231
  trade   233–4
  yields   230, 235–7, 247
grass, *see* pasture
Great Chart, Kent   38
Great Depression   249–52
  see also agricultural depression,
  late-nineteenth-century
Great Wratting estate, Suffolk, *see* Thurlow
Greenwich Hospital, Derwentwater estate,
  Durham and Northumberland   97,
  244, 258
  arrears   182
  estate details   269
  industrial rents   93
  mineral rents   92
Grenville family estates
  Burton Dassett, Warwickshire   66
  Stowe, Buckinghamshire   66
  Wotton, Buckinghamshire   66
Griffin, Sir John, *see* Audley End; Howard de
  Walden, Lord
Grigg, David
  on Lincolnshire rents   143
Grimsby estate, Lincolnshire   83
  see also Brocklesby
Grosvenor family, *see* Westminster, Duke of
Guybon, Francis, steward to Lord
  Fitzwilliam   33
Guy's Hospital estate, Essex, Herefordshire
  and Lincolnshire   82–3, 124–5, 132–3,
  144, 244
  agricultural depression   114, 135
  and R. J. Thompson's rent index   120,
  129
  estate details   294–5
  estate surveys   101

Hackwood estate, Hampshire
  agricultural depression   104

estate details   270
Haggard, H. Rider
  on rent audit   32
Hainault Crown estate, Essex
  with Stapleford Abbots   280
Haklyn estate, Flintshire   115
  estate details   288
Hampshire   20, 258, 264, 270, 278–9
  agricultural depression   227
  and the Property Tax   30
  enclosure   231
  grain yields   236
  see also Andover; Broadlands; Hackwood;
  Wallop
Hardwick estate, Derbyshire
  estate details   288
Harewood, Earl of   285
harvest fluctuations   233, 250
Hasell family   268
  see also Dalemain
Hatfield estate, Hertfordshire
  urban rents   95
Hawkins family   277
  see also Trewithen
Healy, M. J. R.
  on grain yields   236
Helpston, Northamptonshire   239–40
Hendon, Middlesex   42
Herbert family, *see* Pembroke, Earl of
Herefordshire   295
  and R.J. Thompson's rent index   125–8,
  166
  see also Guy's Hospital
Hertford
  urban rents   95
Hertfordshire
  agricultural output   230
  and Caird's agricultural regions   185
  density of cover of rent index   162
Hervey family, *see* Bristol, Marquess of
Hesket, Cumberland   38
High Farming   211, 217, 224, 245–9
Higham Ferrers estate, Northamptonshire
  100, 144, 244
  estate details   270
Hillesden, Buckinghamshire
  and the Coke estate   141n
Holderness, B.A.
  on grain yields   236
Holderness, Yorkshire E
  farmers' capital   242–3
Holker estate, Lancashire
  estate details   271
  industrial rents   93
Holkham estate, Norfolk   13, 22–3, 119n,
  158, 222, 258

capital provision   24n
corn rents   241
estate details   271
farmers' capital   243n
land acquisition   88
rents   66, 77, 141–2, 244
see also Coke, T. W.; Parker, R. A. C.;
    Wade Martins
Holme Pierrepont estate, Nottinghamshire
    244
agricultural depression   229
arrears   181–2
estate details   272
see also Manvers estate
Holt, John
on Lancashire rents   43
Home Counties   42
density of cover of rent index   162
hospitals, *see* under names of different
    hospitals
Houghton, John
witness to 1836 Select Committee   110
Houghton Regis, Bedfordshire   38
House of Lords
and seventeenth-century rents   226
Howard, Charles
witness to 1836 Select Committee   242–3
Howard de Walden, Lord   89, 293
see also Audley End
Howard family, *see* Carlisle, Earl of
Hughes, W. M.
on Northumberland   74n, 94n
on determinants of a rent index   90
Hull, Yorkshire E   42
Hundon estate, Suffolk, *see* Thurlow
Huntingdonshire   275, 292, 300
and Caird's agricultural regions   105
and the Ecclesiastical Commissioners   125
long-term rents   42, 53
see also Milton; Thorney
Huntingfield, Lord   284

imports   225, 233–4
income
agricultural   247
and rents   206–14
landlords'   215, 234
distribution of   9, 11–12, 208–9, 211
farm   234
shares   9, 11
Income Tax   3, 52
as proxy for rents   64–8
see also Schedule A
India
grain imports from   248
industrial rents, *see* rents

inflation   67, 107–8, 200, 205, 236, 239
see also French wars
Ingestre estate, Staffordshire
corn rents   241
institutional owners, *see* under names of
    institutions
interest rates   216–24, 256
investment   214–24
Irby estate, Lincolnshire   83
see also Brocklesby
Ireland   250
dairy products from   247–8
in the 1840s   245
Isle of Wight
density of cover of rent index   162

Jacob, William
witness to 1836 Select Committee   243
Jersey, Earl of
and R. J. Thompson's rent index   129
Jervaulx Abbey estate, Yorkshire N
estate details   289
Jonas, Samuel
Prize Essay on Cambridgeshire   48
Jones, E. L.
on agricultural production   233
see also Healy, M. J. R.
Journal of the Royal Agricultural Society of England
    (JRASE)   3, 18, 121
and the *Prize Essays*   47–9, 188

Kain, R. J. P
on grain yields   236
Kelch, Ray
on the Dukes of Newcastle   77–8
Kemp, John, .
witness to 1836 Select Committee   20
Kent   38, 41, 48, 243, 266, 268
agricultural depression   227
and King's College, Cambridge   29
and Oriel College, Oxford   135
and the Coke estate   141n
and the Ecclesiastical Commissioners   129
and the Property Tax   30
long leases   68
rent day   34
seventeenth-century rents   226
see also Chevening; Cornwallis
Kent, Nathaniel   13
on Norfolk   40
on under-renting   15
Kerridge, Eric
on agricultural regions   186–7
King, Gregory   3, 163
on national income   59–60
Kingston, Duke of, *see* Manvers, Earl

King's College, Cambridge
    archaic leases   29
Knowsley estate, Cheshire and Lancashire
    100, 244
    estate details   272

labour productivity   203–4, 230, 232
labourers   211–14
    see also wages
Laleham, Middlesex   221
Lancashire   43, 45, 135n, 271–2
    and the Ecclesiastical Commissioners
    125
    beneficial leases   27
    industrial rents   93
    see also Holker; Knowsley
land
    as a positional asset   172
    market   214–15
    productivity   237–8
    reform   21
    values   112
    see also tenure
landlords   6, 8–10, 14–16, 21–4, 206–8, 211,
    214–15
    and investment   215–24
    and long leases   68
    and tenants   12, 33–4
    income of   12, 112, 237–9, 241
landowners
    and agricultural change   230–1
    income of   60
land tax
    as a proxy for rent   60–4
    county distribution in   1707   63
Langdale estate, Yorkshire East   75
Lascelles family, see Harewood, Earl of
Lawes, Sir John Bennet
    witness to 1890s Royal Commission
    114
Laxton, Nottinghamshire
    enclosure and rents   231
Leamington Spa, Warwickshire   110–11, 240
leases   11–14, 81
    leasehold   25
    long leases   13, 67–8, 234
    see also beneficial leases
Leckhamstead, Buckinghamshire   20, 240
Leconfield, Lord   267, 275
    see also Cockermouth; Leconfield
Leconfield estate, Yorkshire E   98, 244
    estate details   272
    estate surveys   101
Lee-Dillon family, see Dillon, Viscount
Legard, George
    Prize Essay on Yorkshire E   48

Leicester, Earl of, see Coke, T. W. of
    Holkham
Leicestershire   34, 40, 44, 231
    density of cover of rent index   162
Leveson-Gower estate   139–40, 146, 189,
    296, 302
    agricultural depression   228–9
    beneficial leases   26
    industrial rents   94n
    see also Lilleshall; Stittenham:
    Trentham; Wolverhampton
Lewisham, Surrey   42
Lichfield estate, Staffordshire   42
    estate details   296
    lifeleasehold   25
Lilford estate, Northamptonshire   99
    agricultural depression   229
    estate details   273
    estate surveys   100–1
Lilleshall estate, Shropshire   105, 139–40,
    242, 244
    arrears   182
    estate details   296
    farmers' capital   243n
    lifeleasehold   26n
Lincolnshire   17, 39–40, 44n, 45, 108, 110,
    123, 256, 260, 273, 280, 283, 285, 295
    agricultural depression   227
    and Caird's agricultural regions   185
    and King's College, Cambridge   29
    and Oriel College, Oxford   135
    and the Ecclesiastical Commissioners   125,
    129
    and the Royal Commission 1890s   119
    and R. J. Thompson's rent index   125–8,
    166
    density of cover of rent index   162
    see also Ancaster; Bilborough; Brocklesby:
    Crowle; Guy's Hospital
Lindert, Peter
    on national income   60
Lister family, see Masham, Lord
Little, W. C.
    witness to 1890s Royal Commission   114
Liverpool, Lancashire   243
livestock
    prices   228
    production   231
Loch, James, chief agent to the Sutherland
    estate   12–13, 109, 242
    member of 1836 Select Committee   109
London
    and the Coke estate   141n
    and Thirsk's agricultural regions   187
    distance decay effects from   44
    rents   41–3, 45–6, 95

Longleat estate, Somerset and Wiltshire   33,
    98, 158
    estate details   274
    mineral rents   140
Lonsdale, Lord
    on taxes   22
lords, dukes, earls, etc, see under individual
    names
Low, David
    on tenant capital   20
Lowther, Sir James
    and investment   221–2

McCulloch, J.R.
    on rents   43–4, 65–6, 164
Magdalen College, Oxford
    archaic tenures   31
    income   30
Maids Moreton, Buckinghamshire   38
Malthus, Rev. Thomas Robert   12
Mann-Cornwallis family   268
    see also Cornwallis
Manvers, Earl   260, 263–4
Manvers estates, various counties   82, 94–5,
    98, 158, 161, 189, 244
    agricultural depression   229
    arrears   181–2
    see also Adwick; Bradford; Crowle:
    Holme Pierrepont; Thoresby
Marshall, William   185
    on Arthur Young   17, 39–40
    on rent and capital   20–1
    on rent day   33–4
    on setting rents   17–19
    on taxes and rates   21–2
    on the Board of Agriculture   40–1
Masham, Lord   289
Massie, Joseph
    on national income   59–60
Mavor, William
    on Berkshire rents   41
Maxstoke estate, Warwickshire and
    Staffordshire
    estate details   274
Meapham estate, Kent
    long leases   68
Merton College, Oxford
    income   30
Meux estate, Wiltshire
    estate details   289
Middlesex   44, 46, 109–10, 221, 287
    agricultural depression   227
    and Caird's agricultural regions   185
    and R.J. Thompson's rent index   129
    density of cover of rent index   162
    land tax   62

    see also Fitzhardinge
Midlands   45, 119, 123–4, 185, 201
    agricultural regions   189, 191
    density of cover of rent index   161–2
    enclosure   231, 234
    rents   52–7, 163–5
    and Thirsk's agricultural regions   187
Milton estate, Northamptonshire and
    Huntingdonshire   244
    estate details   275
Ministry of Agriculture
    R. J. Thompson as Assistant Secretary   7
mineral rents, see rents
Mingay, G. E.
    on agricultural depression   227
    on eighteenth-century rents   232
    on rent arrears   182
    see also Chambers, J.D.
'Miscellaneous' estates, various counties
    estate details   297
Monmouthshire   42
Monson, Lord
    arrears on Lancashire estate   182
Moore, D.C.
    on the corn laws   245
Morton, Henry
    witness to 1836 Select Committee   109
Mount-Temple, Lord   264
Mulhall, George
    on rents   44
Municipal Corporations
    reform of   245
Murray, Adam
    witness to 1833 Select Committee   242
Myddleton estate, Denbighshire
    arrears   182

National Debt   223
New Poor Law   243, 245
New South Wales stock   222
New World
    food imports from   111
Newcastle, Duke of
    and R.J. Thompson's rent index   129
    estates of   77–8
non-agricultural rents, see rent
Norfolk   13, 19n, 40, 66, 77, 140–2, 222, 271,
    282
    agricultural depression   24n, 241–2
    agricultural specialisation   205
    and the Audley End estate   89
    and the Property Tax   30
    and Thirsk's agricultural regions   187
    beneficial leases   25
    capital provision   24
    crop yields   230

Norfolk (*cont.*)
  long leases 68
  rent day 33
  seventeenth-century rents 226
  see also Holkham
Norfolk, Duke of
  urban rents 94
North America
  food imports from 112, 246, 248
Northampton, Marquess of
  and R.J. Thompson's rent index 129
Northamptonshire 32, 34–5, 66, 110, 222,
    270, 273, 275, 292, 300
  and Oriel College, Oxford 135
  and R.J. Thompson's rent index 129
  and the Audley End estate 89
  beneficial leases 26–7
  density of cover of rent index 161–2
  enclosure 231, 239–40
  farm rents 54–6
  long-term rents 53, 58–9, 144
  seventeenth-century rents 226
  see also Higham Ferrers; Lilford; Milton;
    Thorney
Northumberland 51–2, 66, 90, 92n, 229,
    269, 283, 298
  agricultural regions 189–90
  and Caird's agricultural regions 185
  beneficial leases 27
  density of cover of rent index 162
  farm rents 74n
  industrial rents 93
  long-term rents 58–9
  mineral rents 92
  Prize Essay on 49
  see also Greenwich Hospital;
    Northumberland estates
Northumberland, Duke of 298
Northumberland estates 150–1, 156
  estate details 298
Northumbria
  density of cover of rent index 162
North Wales
  and R.J. Thompson's rent index 125–8,
    166
Norton, Trist, and Gilbert, estate agents
  land sales 216–18
  long-run rent series 113, 170–3
  on years' purchase 220
Nottingham
  urban rents 94–5
Nottingham University Archives 77
Nottinghamshire 40, 202–3, 272, 276, 283
  agricultural depression 227
  and R.J. Thompson's rent index 129
  and the Ecclesiastical Commissioners 125

beneficial leases 27
density of cover of rent index 161–2
enclosure 231
Prize Essay on 48
see also Holme Pierrepont; Manvers estate;
  Thoresby

O'Brien, Patrick
  on income tax 65, 68–9
  on price indexes 207n, 209
Ó Gráda, C.
  on income distribution 208–9
Old Poor Law 243
Onslow, Earl of
  and R.J. Thompson's rent index 129
Orde-Powlett family, *see* Bolton, Lord
Oriel College, Oxford 135–6, 297
  agricultural depression 113
Orpington, Kent 42
output
  agricultural output 225–6, 230–2
  and rents 200–2, 207–9
Overstone, Lord
  and investment 223
Overton, Mark
  on agricultural productivity 203–4
  on grain yields 236
  on regional specialisation 205
Oxford colleges 46, 83, 133, 135–6, 146, 157,
    159, 162, 258
  beneficial leases 95
  estate details 298
  income 30
Oxford and Cambridge Colleges
  archaic leases 28–9
  beneficial leases 25
  Elizabethan statutes and tenure 26
Oxfordshire 268, 297
  and R.J. Thompson's rent index 129
  and the Coke estate 141n
  and the Property Tax 226
  farm rents 54–6
  long-term rents 53
  seventeenth-century rents 226
  and R.J. Thompson's rent index 129
  see also Dytchley; Oriel College; Oxford
    colleges

Parker, Christopher Comyns
  witness to 1836 Select Committee 109, 114
Parker, R. A. C.
  on Holkham 141
Parkinson, Richard
  on Huntingdonshire rents 42
pasture
  regions 185–98

rents   38, 41–3, 45–6, 191–8
Peel, Sir Robert
    member of 1836 Select Committee   109
Pell, Albert
    witness to 1890s Royal Commission   114
Pembroke, Earl of   278
    see also Wilton
Pembrokeshire   229
Pennines
    and Thirsk's agricultural regions   187
Pentrich estate, Derbyshire, see Shottle
Percy estate, Cumberland
    mineral rents   93
Percy estate, Northumberland
    beneficial leases   27
Percy family, see Northumberland, Duke of
Perren, Richard
    on Stittenham estate   146
    on Trentham and Lilleshall estates
        139–40
Perthshire   110
Petre, Lord   277
Petty, Sir William   7–8
Petworth estate, Sussex   158, 244
    estate details   275
Phillips, A.D.M.
    on long-run rent series   57–9, 144–5
    on the Northumberland estates   151
Physiocrats   8–9, 11, 13
Pitt, William
    on Leicestershire rents   40
    on rent and credit   34–5
    on Staffordshire rents   41
    on Worcestershire rents   40
    rent estimates   164
Pitt-Rivers estate, Dorset and Wiltshire   276
    estate surveys   102
Plymley, Joseph
    on Shropshire rents   42
Porter, Alfred de Bock, Secretary to the
        Ecclesiastical Commissioners
    witness to 1890s Royal Commission   118n
Portland, Duke of   283
Portland estates, various counties   77, 158
Powys, Earl of   99
    see also Lilford
Powys family   273
    see also Lilford
Poynder estates, Wiltshire
    estate details   289–90
Price, L. L., Treasurer of Oriel College   4,
        113
    witness to 1890s Royal Commission   114
price indexes   207, 228
prices   202, 226–9, 231–4, 236, 238–9, 246,
        248–50

and rents   200, 209–11, 255–6
animal product prices   248–9
high prices   19
late nineteenth-century prices   112
long-run prices   2, 5, 10
stock prices   217–21
Prince, Hugh
    on agricultural regions   186–8
Pringle, R. Hunter
    witness to 1890s Royal Commission   114
Prize Essays, of Royal Agricultural Society
        47–9
    see also JRASE
productivity, see agricultural productivity;
        labour productivity
Property Tax
    and distance decay   45–6
    and fines and manorial profits   29–30
    and rent   43–4
    as proxy for rents   64–8
    county distribution in 1810–11   46, 65
    protection   247
    see also corn laws
proxies for rent, see rent
public schools
    and beneficial leases   95
Purdom, J. J.
    on enclosure and rents   202–3
pure rent, see rent
Pusey, Philip   47–8
putative arrears   181–4

rack rent, see rent
railways
    and distance decay   45–6
rate of return
    on investments   217–24, 249
rates and taxes   8–9, 12, 14, 20–2, 44, 123
    and rents   80, 97, 99
rates of growth   248
rates of interest, see interest rates
Rayleigh, Lord
    and agricultural depression   114
Raynbird, Hugh
    Prize Essay on Suffolk   48
    witness to 1890s Royal Commission   114
Read, C.S.
    Prize Essay on Bucks   48
    witness to 1890s Royal Commission   114
recovery, see economic recovery
Reform Act   245
regions, see agricultural regions
remission of rent, see rent
rent
    abatements   7, 33, 52, 88, 98, 125, 240–2
    agreed, see assessed

rent (*cont.*)
allowances 88, 96–8
and agricultural depression 51, 53, 68,
  179–84
and capital provision 22–3
and distance decay 41–6
and enclosure 53
and farm sizes 54–6
and grain yields 236–7
and interest rates 214–2
and long leases 65
and national income 60
and prices 209–11, 234, 255–6
and size of farms 117–21, 158
and tenurial changes 26–32
and the Board of Agriculture 39–43
arable rents 55–7, 119–20, 124, 129–30,
  161, 191–8, 237, 255
arrears of 33, 51, 88, 96–8, 179–84, 222,
  227, 232, 240–1, 252, 254
assessed rent 88, 96–8, 103, 105, 148–53,
  176–8, 232, 244, 251, 256
assessed rent, data 260–302
assessed rent, indexes 314–23
cottage rents 79–80
county-wide rents *c.* 1800 39–43
county-wide rents *c.* 1810 44
county-wide rents *c.* 1850 44–5, 47
due rent 115–16, 139–41
economic rent 10
English rent index 148–75
estate rents 77–83
farm rents 53–7, 74–6
field rents 76–7
free rents 96
industrial rents 79, 92–4, 140
long-run series 50–9, 191–8
mineral rents 92, 140
non-agricultural rents 79, 86
pasture rents 55–7, 119–20, 191–8, 255
paying the rent 32–5
proxies for rent 59–68
pure 10, 13
rack 2–3, 7–24, 73–4, 79, 95–6, 133–4
received rent 88, 96–8, 115–16, 123,
  139–41, 148–78, 244, 248, 250, 256
received rent, data 260–302
received rent, indexes 309–13, 319–23
regional variations, of rent index 184–98
reductions of 7, 125, 240–2, 251
relative rents 191–8
remissions of 7, 124, 241
rent audit 32
rent by auction 17
rent collection 6–7
setting the rent 37

seventeenth-century 226
short-run movements of 178–84, 225–52
urban rents 92, 94–5
village-based rents 53–7
see also Ricardian rent surpluses; Ricardian
  rent theory
see also under individual estate and county
  names
rent index 148–75, 254
and agricultural depression 243–5, 250–2
and High Farming 248
and the national economy 256–7
chronology of cover of 154–9
rent indexes compared 163–74
definitive index 309–23
density of cover 159–62
determinants of 3–4, 70–84
in the long term 199–224, 255
in the short term 228–52
regional variations 191–8
sources 258–60, 303–7
see also Allen; Bellerby; Chambers; Norton;
  Phillips; Thompson, R. J.; Ward
repairs
  and rents 14, 22–3, 97, 99
Restoration period 72, 214, 225–6
Rew, R. Henry
  witness to 1890s Royal Commission 114
Ricardian rent surpluses 11–12, 20, 67–8,
  201–2, 208, 234–5
Ricardian rent theory 11–12, 18
Ricardo, David,
  on rent theory 7, 10
Richards, E.
  on Trentham and Lilleshall estates
    139–40
Richmond and Gordon, Duke of 288
Ridley, Sir Matthew 283
Ripon, Marquess of
  and R.J. Thompson's rent index 129
Robertson, Thomas
  on under-renting 15
Rolle estates, Devon
  estate details 290
Rousseaux
  price index 207n, 209n, 249
Rowley, John Jephson
  Prize Essay on Derbyshire 48
Royal Agricultural Society 18, 47–9
Royal Commission on Agriculture, 1890s 4,
  23–4, 83, 111–25, 128, 137, 146, 158, 191,
  193, 250–4, 258–9, 302
see also agricultural depression, late
  nineteenth century
see also individual names of members and
  witnesses

Royal Commission on Tithe Rentcharge,
    1834   128, 157
Royal Statistical Society   125
rural distress   240–5
    see also agricultural depression
Rushmore estate, Dorset and Wiltshire
    estate details   276
Russell, Lord John
    member of 1836 Select Committee   109
Russell family, see Bedford, Duke of
Russia
    grain imports from   111, 248
Rutland   53, 261, 285
    agricultural depression   227
    density of cover of rent index   162
    see also Ancaster
Rutland, Dukes of
    estates of   77

St Bartholemew's Hospital   42, 83
St John's College, Cambridge   146, 162, 258
    estate details   299
    revenues   133–4
    tenures   28–9, 134n
St Pancras, Middlesex   42
St Thomas's Hospital   42
Sandwell estate, Staffordshire   105
Schedule A   166–7, 169–70, 198n
Scotland   243
Select Committee, 1836   20, 45–6, 68,
    109–11, 240–5
    see also agricultural depression, post-French
    wars
    see also individual names of members and
    witnesses
self-sufficiency, see food supply
Shaw–Lefevre, Charles, later Viscount
    Eversley
    chairman, 1836 Select Committee   109
Shaw–Lefevre, George John, later Baron
    Eversley
    chairman, Royal Commission 1890s   113
Sheffield, Lord   20
Sheffield, Yorkshire W
    urban rents   94
Sherborn, Francis
    on distance decay   45–6
    witness to 1836 Select Committee   109
Shottle and Pentrich estate, Derbyshire
    estate details   291
Shropshire   42, 66, 243, 296
    archaic tenure   26, 28
    density of cover of rent index   161
    industrial rents   94n
    mineral rents   140
    see also Leveson-Gower; Lilleshall

Sinclair, Sir John, Chairman of Board of
    Agriculture   39
size of farms, see rent
Sledmere estate, Yorkshire E   34, 143, 146,
    158
    estate details   299
Smith, Adam   2–3, 9–10, 13
Smith, Hon. W.F.D.   292
Smith, James
    witness to 1836 Select Committee   110
Smith-Masters family
    long leases at Westdown, Kent   68
Smith-Stanley family, see Derby, Earl of
Sneinton, Nottingham
    and urbanisation   95
Somerset   42, 274
    and Oriel College, Oxford   135–6
    and the Coke estate   141n
    and the Ecclesiastical Commissioners   125,
    129
    and Thirsk's agricultural regions   187
    density of cover of rent index   162
    mineral rents   140
    seventeenth-century rent   226
    see also Longleat
Somerset family, see Beaufort, Duke of
South Africa
    food imports from   111
South America
    food imports from   111
South Sea Company   215
Southdown estate, Sussex   89
Spalding, Lincolnshire   108
Squaery, Elias
    on capital and rent   18
    witness to 1890s Royal Commission   114
Stafford, Lord   12–13
Stafford, Marquess of   26n, 242
    see also Leveson-Gower
Staffordshire   41, 274, 296, 301–2
    and the Coke estate   141n
    and the Property Tax   30
    agricultural depression   227
    beneficial leases   26
    density of cover of rent index   161
    industrial rents   94n
    see also Leveson-Gower; Lichfield:
    Maxstoke; Trentham; Wolverhampton
Stagsden Crown estate, Bedfordshire   279
Staines, Middlesex   46, 109
Stanhope, Earl   266
Stapleford Abbots Crown estate, Essex, see
    Hainault
Stares, R. H.
    witness to 1836 Select Committee   20
statistical summary   309–23

Staveley and Chesterfield estate, Derbyshire
  estate details 291
Steele, J. C., superintendent of Guy's
  Hospital 4, 121, 132
Stephenson, William
  on Surrey rents 41
Stittenham estate, Yorkshire W 146
  estate details 300
Stowe estate, Buckinghamshire 66, 222
Strutt, E. G.
  on estate management 173–4
  witness to 1890s Royal Commission 114
Strutt family, Essex 144
Sturgess, Roy
  on Staffordshire rents 105
  on Trentham and Lilleshall estates
    139–40
Suffolk 40–1, 110, 262, 283–4, 292
  agricultural depression 24n
  agricultural specialisation 205
  and the Audley End estate 89
  and the Coke estate 141n
  and Thirsk's agricultural regions 187
  crop yields 230
  Prize Essay on rents 1840s 48
  see also Barking Hall; Thurlow
Sunk Island Crown estate, Yorkshire E 280
Sunning-Hill, Berkshire 110
Surrey 41, 110, 266
  and R.J. Thompson's rent index 129
  and the Property Tax 30
  density of cover of rent index 162
  see also Chevening
Sussex 89, 110, 261, 268, 275, 288
  agricultural depression 227
  density of cover of rent index 162
  industrial rents 93
  see also Ashburnham estate; Cornwallis:
    Goodwood; Petworth
Sutherland, Duke of 300–1
  and investment 222
  see also Leveson-Gower
Swinburne estate, Northumberland and
    Durham 51
Sykes family, see Sledmere
Sykes, Sir Tatton 299

Tavistock estate, Cornwall and Devon 82,
    89–90, 131–3, 144, 244, 254, 258
  beneficial leases 95–6
  estate details 276, 291
  estate surveys 101
taxes, see rates and taxes
Taylour family, see Bective, Earl of
Tehidy estate, Cornwall
  mineral rents 92

Temple, Earl
  and investment 222
tenancy at will 11, 13, 199–200
tenant right 11, 68
tenants 6, 8, 10, 14–15, 81, 206–8, 211
  and capital 21
  and enclosure 16
  and leases 11
  and rates and taxes 12, 22
  and repairs 22–3
  incomes of 33–4, 112
  see also farmers
tenure 10, 13, 24–32, 73–4, 95, 199–202,
    234–5
  see also beneficial leases; copyhold
terms of trade
  of rents between land uses 192–7, 231–2
Thetford, Norfolk 241
Thirsk, Joan
  on agricultural regions 186–7, 188n, 191,
    193–8, 237, 255
Thomas, Sir Charles Howell, Permanent
    Secretary at Ministry of Agriculture
  and R.J.Thompson's rent index 125–8,
    157
Thompson, F.M.L.
  on rents during French wars 66
  on the land market 71, 174
Thompson, R.J. 4, 7, 44n, 120, 146–7
  and the Ecclesiastical Commissioners
    157
  long-run rent index 113, 125–30, 166–9
Thoresby estate, Nottinghamshire 88, 182,
    244
  estate details 276
  see also Manvers estate
Thorndon estate, Essex 244, 251
  estate details 277
Thorney estate, Cambridgeshire,
    Huntingdonshire
and Northamptonshire 82, 130–3, 146, 258
  estate details 292, 300
  see also Bedford, Duke of
Thurlow, Hundon and Great Wratting
    estate, Suffolk
  estate details 292
Thurnall, William
  witness to 1836 Select Committee 240
Thynne family, see Bath, Marquess of
Tithe Commissioners 119
Tithe Rentcharge, see Royal Commission on
    Tithe Rentcharge
tithes 39, 80, 97, 99, 123
Tooke, Thomas 52, 237
trade 233–4, 245–9
  see also food supply; grain, trade

Trentham estate, Staffordshire   105, 139–40,
    244
    arrears   182
    corn rents   241
    estate details   301
Trewithen estate, Cornwall
    estate details   277
Trinity College, Oxford
    income   30
Trueman, B. E. S.
    on Guy's Hospital   121, 144
Tuckett, Philip
    on land valuing/setting rents   18
Turnbull, R.E.
    witness to 1890s Royal Commission   114
Turner, M.E.
    on enclosure and corn yields   201
Turnor, Christopher   44n
    and R.J. Thompson's rent index   129

Umbers, Mr
    witness to 1836 Select Committee   110–11,
    240
underdrainage   246
under-renting   15–16, 108n
universities, see Cambridge; Oxford
University Commission, 1872   136
untenanted farms   242
urban rents, see rent
USA
    grain imports from   248

Vale of Aylesbury   38
    Prize Essay on rents of 1850s   48
Vancouver, Charles
    on Devon rents   40
Vanneck family, see Huntingfield, Lord
village rents, see rent
Von Thunen effect   42
    see also distance decay

Wade Martins, S.
    on Holkham   88, 141–2
wages   2, 5, 9, 11, 13, 234, 239
    and rents   211–14
Walden, Essex
    and the Audley End estate   89
Wallop estate, Hampshire
    agricultural depression   104
    estate details   278
Ward, J.T.   151–2
    and R.J. Thompson's rent index   168–9
    long-run rent index   172–3
Warwickshire   66, 274
    and R.J. Thompson's rent index   129
    enclosure   231

mineral rents   93
    seventeenth-century rents   226
    see also Maxstoke
Wash, The
    and Thirsk's agricultural regions   187
Weald, The
    and Thirsk's agricultural regions   187
Welbeck estates, Nottinghamshire   77
Welsh border
    and Thirsk's agricultural regions   187
Wentworth Woodhouse estate, Yorkshire W
    urban rents   94
Wentworth-Fitzwilliam family, see Fitzwilliam,
    Earl
West Country   124
    density of cover of rent index   161
Westdown estate, Kent
    long leases   68
Western counties   45
Westminster, Duke of   287–8
Westmorland   22, 44, 198n, 268, 285
    see also Bective; Dalemain
Weston estate, Staffordshire   105
Wharton estate, Cumberland
    mineral rents   92
wheat yields, see grain, yields
Williams, J. D.
    on Audley End   146
    see also Audley End
Williamson, J. G., see Lindert
Wilmot, Sarah
    on life-leasehold   73n
Wilton estate, Wiltshire   158
    estate details   278
Wiltshire   40, 45, 264, 274, 276, 278, 280,
    289–90
    and Caird's agricultural regions   185
    and Oriel College, Oxford   135
    and the Ecclesiastical Commissioners   129
    density of cover of rent index   162
    see also Bishops Cannings; Bradford;
        Longleat; Meux; Pitt-Rivers; Poynder;
        Rushmore; Wilton
Woburn estate, Bedfordshire and
    Buckinghamshire   24, 82, 110, 130–3,
    137n, 146, 158, 244, 258
    estate details   293, 301
    see also Bedford, Duke of
Wolverhampton estate, Staffordshire   146
    estate details   302
Woodham Mortimer, Essex   109
Worcestershire   40, 243, 283
    and the Ecclesiastical Commissioners   129
    density of cover of rent index   162
Wordie, J. R.   85
    on agricultural depression   228–9

Wordie, J. R. (*cont.*)
  on rent arrears 182
  on Trentham and Lilleshall estates
    139–40, 146
Worgan, G. B.
  on Cornwall rents 41
Wotton estate, Buckinghamshire 66
Wrigley, E. A.
  on labour productivity 203–4
Wyndham family, *see* Leconfield, Lord

Yarborough, Earl of 265
Yarborough estates, Lincolnshire 82–3, 158
  see also Brocklesby
years' purchase
  of land 216–20
yields (crop), *see* grain, yields
yields (financial), *see* interest rates
Yorkshire 22, 31, 40, 42, 75, 146, 158, 260,
    262, 265, 269, 273, 280–1, 285–6, 289,
    297, 300
  agricultural depression 227
  and Caird's agricultural regions 185
  and King's College, Cambridge 29
  and Oriel College, Oxford 135

and R. J. Thompson's rent index 129
and the Ecclesiastical Commissioners
    129
and Thirsk's agricultural regions 187
copyholds 27
density of cover of rent index 162
farmer's capital 242–3
Prize Essay, East Riding 48
seventeenth-century rent 226
urban rents 94
see also Adwick; Beighton; Bolton Abbey;
    Boroughbridge: Castle Howard;
    Emanuel Hospital; Jervaulx Abbey:
    Leconfield; Sledmere; Stittenham; Sunk
    Island
Young, Arthur, Secretary of Board of
    Agriculture 3–4, 39, 50, 52, 125, 174,
    253–5
  on data collecting 37–8
  on defining rent 19–20
  on leases 208–10
  on rental estimates 37–8
  on Suffolk rents 40–1
  on under-renting 16
  rent estimates 163–4, 171

Printed in the United States
By Bookmasters